Dear Pitman Publishing Customer

IMPORTANT – Read This Now!

We are delighted to announce a special free service for all of our customers.
Simply complete this form and return it to the address overleaf to receive:
A   Free Customer Newsletter
B   Free Information Service
C   Exclusive Customer Offers – which have included free software, videos and relevant products
D   Opportunity to take part in product development sessions
E   The chance for you to write about your own business experience and become one of our respected authors

Fill this in now and return it to us (no stamp needed in the UK) to join our customer information service.

Name: _____   Position: _____

Company/Organisation: _____

Address (including postcode): _____

_____   Country: _____

Telephone: _____   Fax: _____

Nature of business: _____

Title of book purchased: _____

Comments: _____

------------------------------ | **Fold Here Then Staple** | ------------------------------

We would be very grateful if you could answer these questions to help us with market research.

1   Where/How did you hear of this book?
☐ in a bookshop
☐ in a magazine/newspaper
    (please state which):

☐ information through the post
☐ recommendation from a colleague
☐ other (please state which):

2   Which newspaper(s)/magazine(s) do you read regularly?:

3   When buying a business book which factors influence you most?
(Please rank in order)
☐ recommendation from a colleague
☐ price
☐ content
☐ recommendation in a bookshop
☐ author
☐ publisher
☐ title
☐ other(s):

4   Is this book a
☐ personal purchase?
☐ company purchase?

5   Would you be prepared to spend a few minutes talking to our customer services staff to help with product development?
YES/NO

We occasionally make our customer lists available to companies whose products or services we feel may be of interest.
If you do not want this service write 'exclude from other mailings' on this card. The Customer Information Service is liable to change without notice.

The Business Publisher

Written for managers competing in today's tough business world, our books will help you get the edge on competitors by showing you how to:

- increase quality, efficiency and productivity throughout your organisation
- use both proven and innovative management techniques
- improve the management skills of you and your staff
- implement winning customer strategies

In short they provide concise, practical information that you can use every day to improve the success of your business.

FINANCIAL TIMES
PITMAN PUBLISHING

Free Information Service
Pitman Professional Publishing
FREEPOST
128 Long Acre
LONDON
WC2E 9BR, UK

No stamp necessary in the UK

INVESTING FOR
THE FUTURE

INVESTING FOR THE FUTURE

New Firm Funding in Germany, Japan, the UK and the USA

STEVEN ABBOTT
and
MICHAEL HAY

FINANCIAL TIMES
PITMAN PUBLISHING

PITMAN PUBLISHING
128 Long Acre, London WC2E 9AN

A Division of Longman Group Limited

First published in Great Britain in 1995

© Steven Abbott and Michael Hay 1995

British Library Cataloguing in Publication Data
A CIP catalogue record for this book can be obtained
from the British Library.

ISBN 0 273 60850 9

All rights reserved; no part of this publication may be reproduced, stored
in a retrieval system, or transmitted in any form or by any means, electronic,
mechanical, photocopying, recording, or otherwise without either the prior
written permission of the Publishers or a licence permitting restricted copying
in the United Kingdom issued by the Copyright Licensing Agency Ltd,
90 Tottenham Court Road, London W1P 9HE. This book may not be lent,
resold, hired out or otherwise disposed of by way of trade in any form
of binding or cover other than that in which it is published, without
the prior consent of the Publishers.

1 3 5 7 9 10 8 6 4 2

Typeset by Northern Phototypesetting Co. Ltd, Bolton
Printed and bound in Great Britain by
Biddles Ltd, Guildford and King's Lynn

*The Publishers' policy is to use paper manufactured
from sustainable forests.*

CONTENTS

Preface	ix
Acknowledgements	xi

PART I
OVERVIEW

1 The Global Venture Capital Industry	3
Historical perspective	4
Recent global activity	17
The role of classic venture capital in helping young companies	26
The UK dimension	28
Summary	34
Notes	35

PART II
THE FUNDING ENVIRONMENT IN FOUR KEY COUNTRIES

2 Venture Capital Funding in the USA	39
Market size and growth	40
Breakdown by funding stage	47
Industry sectors attracting investment	49
Investment size	51
Characteristics of investors	52
Funding sources and methods	53
The venture capitalist/entrepreneur relationship	55
Period of investment, exit opportunities and valuation	56
Returns required by the providers of debt and equity	61
Government initiatives	63
The taxation environment	65
Notes	67

3 Venture Capital Funding in Germany — 68
- Market size and growth — 70
- Breakdown by funding stage — 74
- Industry sectors attracting investment — 75
- Investment size — 78
- Characteristics of investors — 80
- Funding sources and methods — 81
- The venture capitalist/entrepreneur relationship — 89
- Period of investment, exit opportunities and valuation — 90
- Returns required by the providers of debt and equity — 93
- Government initiatives — 95
- The taxation environment — 100
- Economic and social returns on investment — 101
- Growth and performance of NTBFs — 102
- Appendices — 106
- Notes — 109

4 Venture Capital Funding in Japan — 111
- Introduction and background — 111
- Market size and growth — 117
- Breakdown by funding stage — 121
- Industry sectors attracting investment — 122
- Investment size — 123
- Characteristics of investors — 123
- Funding sources and methods — 125
- The venture capitalist/entrepreneur relationship — 132
- Period of investment, exit opportunities and valuation — 133
- Returns required by the providers of debt and equity — 136
- Government initiatives — 139
- The taxation environment — 140
- Economic and social returns on investment — 141
- Growth and performance of NTBFs — 141
- Appendices — 144
- Notes — 148

5 Venture Capital Funding in the UK — 149
- Market size and growth — 150
- Breakdown by funding stage — 155
- Industry sectors attracting investment — 158
- Investment size — 161

Characteristics of investors	164
Funding sources and methods	168
The venture capitalist/entrepreneur relationship	175
Period of investment, exit opportunities and valuation	176
Returns required by the providers of debt and equity	182
Government initiatives	184
The taxation environment	188
Economic and social returns on investment	189
Growth and performance of NTBFs	191
Notes	192

PART III
DIMENSIONS OF NATIONAL DIFFERENCE

6 National Differences in the Characteristics and Impact of Venture Capital — 197
Market and investment characteristics	197
Funding sources and methods	203
Period of investment, exit opportunities and valuation	205
Return on investment	210
Notes	212

7 National Differences in the Cost of Capital, Government Initiatives and the Taxation Environment — 214
Cost of capital	214
Government initiatives and the taxation environment	222
Notes	228

PART IV
VENTURE CAPITAL FUNDING: RECOMMENDATIONS FOR THE UK

8 The Case for Additional Taxation-related Incentives for the Creation and Development of NTBFs — 231
Government policy on support	232
Analysis of the distribution of wealth created by NTBFs	233
Expected returns to the Exchequer on support costs	244
The optimal use of 'tax credits'	249
Additional economic justification for incentives	251
Appendices	253
Notes	268

9 UK NTBF Case Studies and Analysis — 269
Comparison of case study data with model inputs — 270
Conclusions — 279
Appendices — 280
Notes — 325

10 Specific Proposals and Recommendations — 326
Outline of NTBF problems — 326
Proposed taxation measures — 330
Estimated impact on UK NTBF case study — 339
Summary — 341
Appendices — 343
Notes — 349

Index — 351

PREFACE

For generations, rich individuals and families have provided risk capital to other individuals for the purpose of starting up, or expanding, business enterprises. In today's terminology this activity would be referred to as 'informal' venture capital investment and the rich individuals as 'business angels'. The modern global venture capital industry (which provides so-called 'formal' venture capital), on the other hand, is a far more recent development and can trace its roots to the United States, shortly after the Second World War. Since then, however, it has spread into most of the developed capitalist nations, with formal venture capital activity in Europe (and the UK in particular) having now grown to a size that is comparable with the US.

Nevertheless, much of the expansion in the industry has occurred since the beginning of the 1980s. In addition, and concurrent with this dramatic expansion in the scale of formal venture capital (VC) investment, there has been a shift in emphasis away from the classic venture capital (CVC) approach of the early US industry, and towards the provision of what has recently been referred to as 'merchant' or 'development' capital (DC).

In this regard, the CVC approach might be characterized by the 'hands-on' provision of relatively small amounts of finance (a few hundred thousand or a million dollars, pounds, etc., of equity capital), business advice and management input to (often) potentially world-scale new technology based firms (NTBFs) in their seed, start-up and early stages of development. In contrast, DC might be best exemplified by much greater emphasis on the essentially 'hands-off' provision of (usually) substantially larger sums of capital (often equity plus mezzanine and/or debt packages) for activities such as management buy-outs and/or buy-ins and later stage financings.

The reasons, economic and otherwise, for the industry's shift away from CVC and towards DC will be dealt with later. Suffice to say at this stage, however, that it is the CVC approach which has historically provided the means either to create or, at the very least, to accelerate dramatically the creation of world-scale multi-billion dollar high technology/high added value industries. Examples of industries whose early development was critically dependent on CVC include semiconductors (Intel), computer hardware

(DEC, Apple, Cray), computer software (Lotus, Microsoft) and biotechnology (Genentech, Celltech, British Bio-technology), among others.

In playing a key role in the creation of these industries, CVC (both formal and informal) has made a significant contribution towards the creation of jobs (both highly skilled and otherwise), national wealth and higher standards of living for those economies in which it has been practised (especially in the US). As such, CVC is perceived as potentially being of such national importance as to warrant the attention of governments in ensuring its continuing long-term well-being and enhanced importance.

It is with the aim of making a significant contribution to the policy debate within the UK that we have sought to analyse the current situation and future anticipated trends with respect to the provision of CVC to NTBFs in the seed, start-up and early phases of their development. In this regard, we have chosen to study venture capital investment in the USA, Germany and Japan, as well as in the UK, in an effort to learn from the broadest possible range of culturally distinct approaches to financing NTBF development. In addition, these three nations are widely considered as being the leaders in the development of technology based industries.

At the same time, we have sought to focus on some of the key financing and economic issues relating to the provision of CVC (both formally and informally) to NTBFs, and to make outline proposals as to how CVC activity can be most cost effectively and efficiently encouraged within the UK. With this goal in mind, we have tried to address not only what the physicist Lord Rutherford might have referred to as the 'stamp collecting' aspects of the venture capital marketplace, that is, the collection of data (relating to market size, growth, internal rates of return, participants, etc.) and analysis of trends therein, but also to address the 'physics' of the venture capital process, the mechanisms, dynamics and economics of the funding and generation of returns from NTBFs.

Michael Hay, London Business School
Steven Abbott, Abbott Consulting

ACKNOWLEDGEMENTS

The authors would like to acknowledge and express their gratitude to Kazuto Adachi and to Simon Gledhill, who made major contributions to the chapters on the Japanese and German venture capital markets, respectively, during their second year London Business School MBA projects.

The authors also wish to acknowledge and express their gratitude to the following people, who freely and generously gave their help, advice and encouragement during the preparation of this work: Rick Armitage (Korda & Co. Ltd), Graham Bannock (Graham Bannock & Partners Ltd), John Bates (Cambridge Management Group), Business Development Group (London Stock Exchange), Professor William Bygrave (Babson College), Anthony Costley-White (formerly of Oxford Seedcorn Capital Ltd), Nicholas Cross, Marcus Darville (NatWest Ventures Ltd), Dr Stephen Davis, Paul Davis (Linx Printing Technologies plc), Rolf Dienst (Wellington Finanz Beratungs GmbH), Mark Firth, Christine Fowles (Coopers & Lybrand Deloitte), Dr Elizabeth Garnsey (Cambridge University Engineering Department), George Grey (Tadpole Technology plc), Bill Hassell (Price Waterhouse), Carolyn Hayman (Korda & Co. Ltd), Andrew Jordan (Coopers & Lybrand Deloitte), Dirk Kanngiesser (Baring Venture Partners Unternehmensberatung GmbH), Dr Alistair Keddie (Department of Trade and Industry), Mike Keeling (Linx Printing Technologies plc), Terry Kelly (Macro 4 plc), Dr Keith McCullagh (British Bio-technology Group plc), Michael Maskall (Price Waterhouse), Graham Minto (Domino Printing Sciences plc), Victoria Mudford (British Venture Capital Association), Martin Nonhebel (Department of Trade and Industry), Kazunori Ozaki (Japan Associated Finance Co. Ltd), Steve Pesenti (Priory Investments Ltd), Dr David Potter (Psion plc), Thomas Schwarz (VCM Venture Capital Management und Beteiligungsgesellschaft mbH), Dr Nicholas Scott-Ram (British Bio-technology Group plc), William Stevens (European Venture Capital Association), Peter Swann (London Business School), Peter Whitelaw (Coopers & Lybrand Deloitte), Howard Whitesmith (Domino Printing Sciences plc), Udo Wupperfeld (Fraunhofer-Institut fur Systemtechnik und Innovationsforschung (ISI)).

Finally, the authors would like to express their particular gratitude to Sir David Cooksey of Advent Limited. As the inspiration behind this book, Sir David's tireless support, enthusiasm and challenging engagement with the work at every stage has been invaluable. We would therefore like to dedicate this book to him.

Part I
OVERVIEW

1

THE GLOBAL VENTURE CAPITAL INDUSTRY

It must have been soon after the concept of 'money' was invented that the idea evolved that one individual could lend money to another individual for some risky – although potentially highly profitable – venture, in return for a share of the profits. The concept of what is now referred to as 'venture capital', therefore, is probably almost as old as money itself. Indeed, all the business enterprises that exist today have involved somebody, somewhere in (possibly) the dim and distant past, risking some amount of money to get those businesses up and running, even though in a number of cases that money may have already belonged to the entrepreneurs themselves.

Against this background of 'informal' venture capital and 'business angels', the modern global venture capital industry and the provision of 'formal' venture capital is a far more recent phenomenon, regarded as originating in the United States shortly after the Second World War.[1] It grew so rapidly that in 1987 $4 billion of formal venture capital was invested in the US,[2] and the total funds under management by the US formal venture capital industry in 1991 had risen to $33 billion.[3]

Nevertheless, that $4 billion peak invested during the bull market of 1987 is still dwarfed by the annual amount of US informal venture capital investment, which has been estimated as being anything up to $30 billion.

At the same time the formal venture capital industry has spread into most of the developed capitalist nations, with formal venture capital activity in Europe (and the UK in particular) having now grown to a size that is comparable to that of the US. While the ratio of informal to formal venture capital investment is believed to be somewhat smaller outside the US, it is nevertheless likely to be substantial (the informal pool in the UK has been estimated at £2–4 billion).

For the purpose of this book, we have had to confine our description, analysis and comments to the formal venture capital industry, except where specifically stated otherwise. Insufficient information exists to be able to say much of any sense (except in limited and specific circumstances) regarding the provision of informal venture capital. The reader should keep in mind, however, the existence of the substantial amount of informal venture capital activity taking place, when considering the material we present here.

HISTORICAL PERSPECTIVE

Before discussing the origin and development of the venture capital industry and the economic and social impact of the industries it has spawned, it is perhaps helpful to consider first a typical life-cycle for a successful new technology based firm, frequently the focus of classic venture capital investment, in order to provide a common frame of reference and a context for subsequent comments. A diagrammatic representation of the 'NTBF life-cycle' for a high-growth NTBF is given in Fig. 1.1, showing the key stages of the financing process (seed, start-up, early growth, rapid expansion/follow-on and harvest).

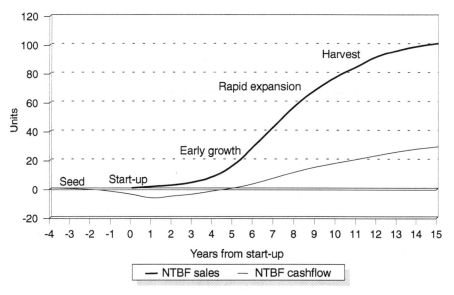

Figure 1.1 Life-cycle of the high-growth NTBF

Although there is some definitional variation between different countries, with respect to the degree of company development associated with the various financing stages, we have reproduced below the financing stage definitions produced by the European Venture Capital Association (EVCA).[5]

Seed Financing provided to research, develop and assess an initial concept before a business has reached the start-up stage.

Start-up Financing provided to companies for product development and initial marketing. Companies may be in the process of being set up or may have been in business for a short time, but have not sold their product commercially.

Other early stage Financing provided to companies that have completed the product development stage and require further funds to initiate commercial manufacturing and sales. They will not yet be generating a profit.

Expansion Financing provided for the growth and expansion of a company which is breaking even or trading profitably. Capital may be used to finance increased production capacity, market or product development and/or to provide working capital.

The missing definition, *Harvest*, is not specifically defined by the EVCA, but it is of course the stage where the venture capital investors, entrepreneurs, etc., realize some or all of their investment via an initial public offering (IPO), an outright sale of the company to a third party, or other means.

ARD and the birth of classic venture capital in the USA

The formal venture capital industry, or at least the CVC part of it, could be considered as having been born in the USA in 1946, with the formation of a company called ARD (American Research & Development).[6] This was the first firm specifically set up to provide a source of risk capital for companies in the seed, start-up and early phases of their development, and resulted in part from concerns over the lack of new company formation in the US following the Second World War. New companies were perceived as being an essential part of fostering continuing economic regeneration and growth.

ARD's founder members, including Ralph Flanders (President of the Federal Reserve Bank of Boston) and General Georges Doriot (a Harvard Business School professor), believed that technology developed at the Massachusetts Institute of Technology (MIT) during the war could be commercialized within the private sector. In order for this to happen, however, finance would have to be made available to those who had developed the technology, and hands-on assistance given to them to help with setting up and growing the resulting NTBFs. Based on this belief, ARD managed to raise $3.5m; by the end of 1947 it had invested in six start-up and two early stage investments. The CVC industry had been born.

As the industry's creator, it is perhaps fitting that probably the most important event in the history of formal venture capital (other than the creation of the industry itself) happened to ARD some eleven years later in 1957, when it invested just under $70,000 for a 77 per cent equity stake in Digital Equipment Corporation (DEC), a Massachusetts minicomputer manufacturer. Over the next fourteen years (up to 1971), the value of ARD's equity stake rose 5000-fold, thus setting alight the imagination of investors and simultaneously providing a benchmark for the sort of returns that could be achieved by CVC investment. A year later ARD was sold to Textron (a large conglomerate) at more than thirty times its initial stock price, which meant that ARD had managed a cumulative rate of return of nearly 15 per cent per annum since its formation (twenty-six years earlier). If one had stripped out the impact of DEC, however, this rate of return would have halved, thus highlighting another characteristic of venture capital investment: the overwhelming dependence of the returns generated upon one (or possibly two) star investments.

The above, somewhat brief, outline of the history of ARD captures the essence of classic venture capital, in that the activity involves the provision of long-term equity investment in expectation of potentially dramatic capital gains, while at the same time requiring the acceptance of the inevitable (and much more numerous) losers and poorly performing investments.

The need for CVC

We have seen that a concern for economic growth in the country as a whole was an important motive in the founding of ARD,[7] and the economic impact of venture capital investment has since been documented in a number of studies. Typical are the results of a US survey by Venture Economics and Coopers & Lybrand, presented at Venture Forum '90.[8] This study showed that the venture capital backed companies responding to the survey (235 out of 1650) had only been trading for an average of just under two years, but had already created 36 000 new jobs, nearly $800 million of exports, had spent over $700 million on R&D, and had paid an aggregate of roughly $170 million in corporate taxes. In addition, the study showed that these venture capital backed firms were far more prolific exporters, per unit of equity invested, than were the much larger 'Fortune 500' companies. Later on it will be seen that this pattern of a high rate of job creation, coupled with a marked export orientation, was also very evident in our UK NTBF case studies.

Two other macroeconomic observations, again relating to the US, are also worth noting at this stage, since they serve to highlight the role of small and new firms in providing the engine for US economic growth, and how necessary they are for economic rejuvenation and renewal. First, a study by David Birch of MIT showed that all areas of the US lose jobs at roughly similar rates, but that the most prosperous areas are the ones which generate new jobs through high rates of innovation.[9] In addition, this rather comprehensive study (of 5.6 million firms, accounting for 82 per cent of all private sector employment) clearly showed that small/new firms are far more prolific job creators than larger firms. Indeed, over the study period (1969 to 1976), firms with twenty or fewer employees created no less than two-thirds of all new jobs. Furthermore, four out of every five jobs were generated by companies which had been in existence for four years or less! While the rate of job loss by small firms is also known to be high, the fact remains that small firms constitute a powerful driving force for economic rejuvenation.

Secondly, in 1990, *Forbes* noted that during the 1980s the companies included in the magazine's 'Forbes Sales 500' lost an aggregate total of some 2.7 million jobs. It would appear to be rather fortunate (to say the least), therefore, that over pretty much the same period companies with fewer than a hundred employees more than made up for this loss, by creating somewhere in the region of 6.5 million jobs (see Fig. 1.2).[10]

Macroeconomic statistics like these certainly highlighted the need for an active new/small company creation process as far as the US was concerned, and indeed, to the extent that it helped to promote this activity, the need for classic venture capital. We shall revisit the question of the economic importance to the UK of new/small company creation, and CVC backing of NTBFs in particular, towards the end of the chapter.

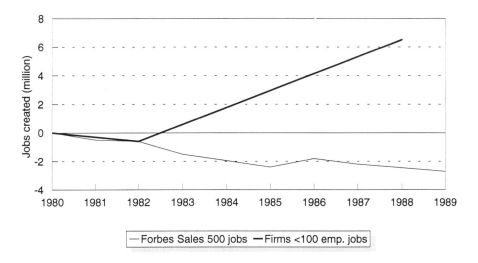

Figure 1.2 Sources of job creation and loss in the US during the 1980s
(*Sources*: *Forbes*: Bygrave and Timmons, *Venture Capital*)

New NTBF industries financed by CVC

Partly driven by the early formation of a formal venture capital investment community (possibly two or three decades before most other nations), and partly driven by a number of other factors which will be discussed later, all the major industries whose growth was either initiated or materially accelerated by CVC activities originated in the USA. (It is no coincidence, as will be seen later, that *all* these industries are technology based and have resulted from the growth of NTBFs.)

We shall now look at the development of these technology based industries (in brief only) and the role played by both formal and informal venture capital in their development. In particular, key developments in three industries will be outlined: the semiconductor industry; the computer industry; the biotechnology industry.[11]

The key events in the semiconductor industry occurred in the following years:

1955 William Shockley founds first (transistor) company in what was to become known as Silicon Valley, financially backed by Arnold Beckman (of Beckman Instruments fame).

1957 Eight of Shockley's employees leave to found Fairchild Semiconductor, also in Silicon Valley, financially backed by Sherman Fairchild of Fairchild Instruments and Camera (FI&C), although venture capitalist Arthur Rock helped to arrange the financing.[12] This was the first company to focus on silicon (rather than germanium) devices. The business was sold to FI&C in 1964, netting $250,000 for each of the eight founders, for their original $500 investment.[13]

1968 Robert Noyce (one of the two co-inventors of the integrated circuit) and Gordon Moore leave Fairchild to launch Intel. Ted Hoff at Intel invents the microprocessor in the following year. Arthur Rock is lead

1967 Between these years, about thirty semiconductor companies were
–72 started with venture capital, including National Semiconductor and Advanced Micro Devices (AMD)

The Global Venture Capital Industry 9

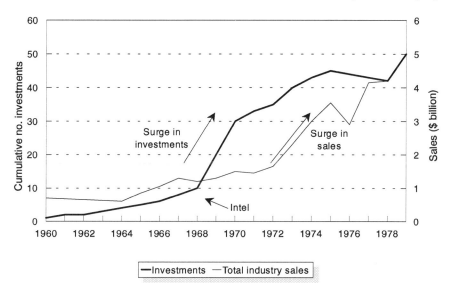

Figure 1.3 Semiconductor industry: VC investments compared with industry sales in the US, 1960–1979
(*Sources*: Venture Economics; Bygrave and Timmons, *Venture Capital*)

Figure 1.3 combines a picture of investments in venture capital backed firms *only*, and the pattern of sales for the semiconductor industry *as a whole*. The relationship between the two lines is interesting: the surge in the number of companies invested in preceded the sales boom by around four years. This is indicative, perhaps, of the time taken for NTBFs to become established and enter their 'rapid expansion' phase.

As is evident from this brief historical outline, venture capital, both 'informal' (such as the Beckman and Fairchild investments) and 'formal' (Arthur Rock), played a decisive role in the development of the semiconductor industry. At the very least, it was responsible for dramatically accelerating the rate of growth of the industry during the first fifteen years or so of its existence.

Two decades after the CVC semiconductor investment surge of 1967–72, the largest of these companies, Intel, now generates no less than $2 billion *per quarter*, and it continues to grow apace. Indeed, its chairman, Andrew Grove, was recently quoted as saying: '*It took us twenty-two years to get to $1 billion a quarter in revenues and, thanks to the explosion in demand for our 486 chip, less than three years to get to $2 billion a quarter.*'[14] A major factor driving this phenomenal and sustained growth was the industry we turn to next, the computer industry.

10 Overview

With the development of the computer industry, we have perhaps an even better example of the impact of CVC availability on the development of NTBFs, since its formation dates from the period immediately following the Second World War, when venture capital was very hard, if not impossible, to find. Once again we summarize the key events in the creation of this industry, and the role played by venture capital (both formal and informal) in its development:

1946 The first working version of a general purpose computer (the forerunner of today's mainframe), ENIAC, is produced at the University of Pennsylvania by J. P. Eckert Jr and J. Maulchy. Soon after, they leave to form the Eckert–Maulchy Corporation, in order to develop and sell their next generation UNIVAC computer, which they begin marketing in 1948 (some six years before IBM entered the fray).[15] Despite a very positive response from potential customers, the business is hampered by lack of adequate financing, and is subsequently sold to American Totalizer, who in due course sells it on to Remington Rand.

1951 –6 Although the first UNIVAC I is delivered in mid-1951, IBM enters the market in 1954 and captures a 70 per cent share over the next two years.

1957 ARD provides $70,000 of equity and $30,000 of debt funding to Ken Olsen and Harlan Anderson from MIT, in order to set up the Digital Equipment Corporation, in return for a 77 per cent stake in the company. In true CVC style, the majority of DEC's board seats are occupied by ARD staff. Two years later, DEC builds the first minicomputer, using semiconductors rather than valves, providing substantial price/performance gains and allowing the user to communicate directly with the computer via a keyboard.

1966 –9 As with the semiconductor industry, after DEC's creation of the minicomputer the surge in minicomputer start-up companies happens nearly a decade later (see Fig. 1.4) and, indeed, is instrumental in causing the explosive growth in semiconductor sales. It should be noted that many of the hundred or so new minicomputer start-up companies entering the fray in the two decades following the creation of the market by DEC were backed by venture capital. In 1992, thirty-three years after launching its first minicomputer, DEC's sales had grown to $14.4 billion and its employee numbers to over 100,000 (although it took roughly the first third of its life to reach the 1,000 employees level).[16]

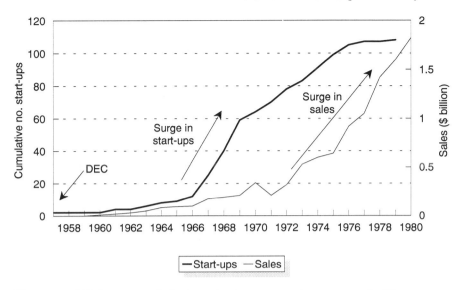

Figure 1.4 Minicomputer industry: start-up companies compared with industry sales in the US, 1957–1980
(*Sources*: Venture Economics; Bygrave and Timmons, *Venture Capital*)

1957 William Norris (formerly of UNIVAC) sets up Control Data Corporation (CDC) to build the fastest computers in existence, supercomputers, designed by Seymour Cray. Cray subsequently leaves CDC to start his own supercomputer company, Cray Research, with venture capital backing. Today, although Cray Research still leads the field (with 1992 sales in the region of $800 million), a number of other venture capital backed US computer companies are competing to build ever faster and more powerful supercomputing machines. This competition is being spurred on by a number of Japanese companies (in particular, Fujitsu, NEC and Hitachi) who are now challenging for market leadership.

1974 With the advent of the Intel 8080A microprocessor, the first microcomputers appear (initially in kit form, such as the Altair 8800). The breakthrough, however, comes in June 1976 with the first sales of the Apple I by Steven Jobs and Stephan Wozniak. Although the first $1,300 of equity is sourced from their own funds, the rate of product take-off is such that a few months later, Jobs and Wozniak require substantial further funds. After an initially difficult time trying to raise the money, a retired (and wealthy) ex-Intel man, Mike Markkula sees the potential of the product, personally invests $91,000 and raises a further $600,000 of venture capital.

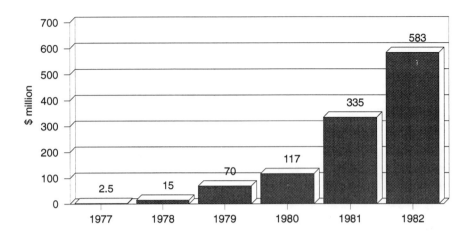

Figure 1.5 Build-up of Apple computer sales, 1977–1982
(*Source*: Bygrave and Timmons, *Venture Capital*)

With the introduction of the first computer spreadsheet in 1978 ('Visicalc' specifically designed for the Apple), Apple's sales take off (see Fig. 1.5) and Apple enters the ranks of the Fortune 500 in 1982.[17]

It is interesting to note that, as a consequence of the almost immediate availability of venture capital, Apple was able to use its five-year lead time over IBM (which responded to Apple's success with the launch of its own 'personal (micro)computer' (PC) in August 1981) to gain a strong and sustainable foothold in the microcomputer market. This situation should be compared with the six years of lead time wasted by UNIVAC in the mainframe market, probably as a direct result of the lack of availability of venture capital to fund its development.

Nevertheless, in 1982 Apple still only accounted for 11 per cent of total PC sales, which amounted to $5.4 billion, with the rest of the market being dominated by the mighty IBM. Conversely, ten years later in 1992, out of estimated annual worldwide sales of personal computers of $46.5 billion, IBM accounted for only 12.4 per cent, while Apple had actually increased its share to 11.9 per cent. Today, Apple's total sales are approaching $2 billion per quarter.[18]

1975 James Treybig starts Tandem Computer, to produce 'fail-safe' or 'fault-tolerant' minicomputers, with very high online reliability. Not only does the venture capitalist Kleiner Perkins ultimately back the start-up venture, but it also provides $50,000 for Treybig to carry out a marketing study in advance of any capital commitment, thus becoming one of the first examples of 'seed capital' investment. Once again, Tandem's revenue has grown rapidly and it is currently around $500 million per quarter, although many other venture capital backed companies in this area never became viable.[19]

1980 Lastly, the venture capital backed Apollo computers brings into being the concept of 'workstations'. Apollo was soon surpassed by Sun Microsystems, however, a venture capital backed 1983 start-up, which is currently generating sales of $1.3 billion per quarter.[20]

The names that have been mentioned above represent only some of the CVC backed companies in the computer hardware business. As can be seen, the provision of venture capital to finance NTBFs in the computer hardware field not only enabled or at least accelerated the growth of the companies financed, but also provoked the industry giant IBM into action. Finally, it is also interesting to note that even IBM depended heavily on venture capital backed companies when entering the PC market, such as Intel for hardware and Microsoft DOS and Lotus 1-2-3 (not discussed here) for software.

Biotechnology has some important differences from the semiconductor and computer industries surveyed so far, although it too has seen rapid growth. Between 1971 and 1987, more than 350 biotechnology firms came into being in the US.[21] The total investment in these companies was estimated to be $1–2 billion, although today that investment has grown to tens of billions of dollars. But compared with the previous two industries, any returns on biotechnology investment will tend to occur much further into the future, due to the very long time taken to develop new products. In this regard, it typically takes a minimum of eight to ten (and more usually twelve) years between the time of discovery and the marketing of a new pharmaceutical. In addition, development costs (and hence up-front investment) are expected to be enormous. Indeed, at the time of launch, the cumulative pretax cost of developing a new pharmaceutical, including 'time' and 'failure' costs, has been estimated to average around $231 million.[22] It stands as a testament to the venture capital industry that it is prepared to finance such very long-term investments.

It is not always the case, however, that biotechnology investment necessitates such heavy up-front costs and far-off returns. In particular, the largest and best known of all of the biotechnology companies, Genentech, was founded in 1976 by Robert Swanson, who had been a partner in the venture capital company Kleiner Perkins (which was to become its first investor). Sixteen months after the initial investment was made, following an early product success, the value of Genentech had risen from $400,000 to $11 million. Furthermore, by the time of the company's IPO in 1980 its implied valuation had risen to $300 million, while ten years later, 60 per cent of the company was sold to Hofmann–La Roche at an implied price of $3.5 billion for the company as a whole. Indeed the story for Genentech has since been repeated, albeit on a much smaller scale to date, by other biotechnology companies, such as Hybritech and Gen-Probe.

Finally, there is yet another instructive difference between the financing of the biotechnology industry and the financing of the semiconductor and computer industries, in that the largest source of capital appears to have come from corporate strategic partners, as shown in Fig. 1.6 for San Diego's biotechnology companies.[23]

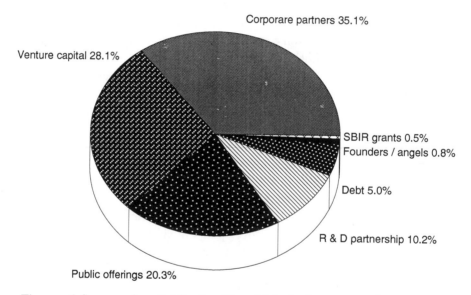

Figure 1.6 Sources of capital for San Diego biotechnology companies
(*Sources*: Mitton, 'Tracking the trends in designer genes'; Bygrave and Timmons, *Venture Capital*)

The advantages of US NTBFs

We have already commented on the fact that, to date, all of the major industries whose growth was either initiated or materially accelerated by CVC activities have originated in the USA. There are a number of factors at work here. In the first place, the US was (and still is) the largest indigenous market in the world for the products of NTBFs, with a large population and high standards of living in terms of per capita income levels. It is also, relatively speaking, a highly uniform market. There is a substantial degree of legal and procedural uniformity among the states, in addition to the presence of a common language and culture.

The climate surrounding the early days of the formal venture capital community was important, too. It was formed immediately after the Second World War, perhaps three decades before it grew to any significant size in any other country. In initially targeting investment towards the commercial exploitation of technology that had been developed at MIT (and, indeed, elsewhere) as part of the war effort, the NTDF investments could benefit from probably billions of dollars of pure and applied technological development 'sunk costs' already incurred by the US government. Furthermore, the US military would prove to be large and wealthy customers for the growing semiconductor and computer industries.

A further factor was the strong and commercially aware science and technology base in and around several US universities, such as MIT, Stanford and the University of California at San Diego (UCSD), which led to the formation of a number of 'technology clusters' (Route 128 for minicomputers, Silicon Valley for semiconductors, San Diego for biotechnology). Indeed, both MIT and Stanford actively and *contractually* encourage academic entrepreneurs.[24]

Last but not least, there was a strong and pervasive entrepreneurial culture and attitude in the US, particularly in the regions around the technology clusters. This entrepreneurial spirit was also constantly being reinforced by a stream of NTBF 'role models' and people who had made their fortunes by founding NTBFs. There were, therefore, examples of 'the American dream' being realized in everyone's neighbourhood, providing a source of continual motivation to the aspiring entrepreneurs in these regions.

There is an obvious question that follows from such a list. Given that these factors materially assisted the formation of NTBFs in the US and the global industries that grew from them, is it possible, and indeed likely, that major technology based industries will grow from NTBFs based in other countries? Although this is, as it were, the '$64,000 question', we will make the following observations in an attempt to provide the answer, in particular from the point of view of an NTBF initiated in the UK.

1   While the US is likely to remain a dominant potential market for the products of most NTBFs (probably in addition to Japan), it is fortunately one of the most open markets to the import of such products, although in the long run it will be necessary to have US production. We are also fortunate to speak the same language as the United States, and our culture and historical relationship are probably closer than, perhaps, any other nation.
2   With regard to the provision of venture capital, the UK now has the second

largest industry in the world (after the United States). The very much smaller proportion of the UK's venture capital funds being applied to the area of CVC investment in NTBFs, however, is perceived as being a major handicap to the development of new technology based industries and will be discussed in detail later.

3 The issue of commercially exploiting the pure and applied technology base which has been, and will continue to be, financed by the UK government, was examined in the recent White Paper, 'Realising our potential: a strategy for science, engineering and technology'.[25] We would concur with the views expressed in the White Paper regarding the need to enhance the country's economic returns from government expenditure in this area (£5.3 billion in 1991-2).[26] In this respect, it would appear that one (although possibly not the only) efficient mechanism for doing so would be to promote the supply of CVC in the UK to NTBF entrepreneurs for seed, start-up and early stage investment. This idea will again be dealt with in detail at a later stage.

4 The presence of technology clusters of NTBFs at or around major universities is already a reality in the UK, one of the country's largest and best-known examples being the Cambridge Science Park. There are also a number of less well-known (internationally), smaller scale or more recent UK science parks in earlier stages of their development.[27] It should be noted that these technology clusters (taken as including the science parks, the universities and NTBF companies formed in the surrounding areas) have spawned a number of notable successes (including some of our case study companies).

5 Finally, what we still lack in the UK is a sufficiently high number of role models, of successful NTBFs and their entrepreneurs originating from these technological clusters, to inspire other NTBF entrepreneurs in the cluster and the country as a whole. There are good indications, however, that these role models are emerging, including some of our case study companies, but as we saw in the US industry examples the process can take decades.

In short, therefore, we would suggest that the answer to the $64,000 question posed earlier is *yes* and, indeed, we also perceive that the UK could be particularly well placed to originate such industries. The process, however, is likely to take a decade or two rather than a year or two. It may also depend on a material acceleration of development by encouraging CVC investment activity in NTBFs.

RECENT GLOBAL ACTIVITY

We have already said that much of the non-US formal venture capital industry was formed during a period of explosive growth, commencing more or less at the beginning of the 1980s. As a result of this growth, by 1992 the European total venture capital pool had risen to around $50 billion (measured according to 1 ECU = $1.29), in comparison with an estimated $35 billion in the US, with the UK alone accounting for roughly $13 billion (£1 = $1.76).[28] It is interesting to note that the UK venture capital pool, expressed in terms of per capita of its population, ranks first in the world, being around twice as large as that of any other country!

Figure 1.7 shows the relative rates of growth in the three largest geographical venture capital regions, the United States, Europe and Japan, over the last few years.[29] The latest figures for the US (1992) and Japan (1991 and 1992) are our estimates. When interpreting the figure, note that exchange rate movements inevitably distort any international comparisons of annual growth rates, although the overall trends are genuine. Note also that the constitution of the 'venture capital' totals varies from region to region, so one is not strictly comparing like with like.

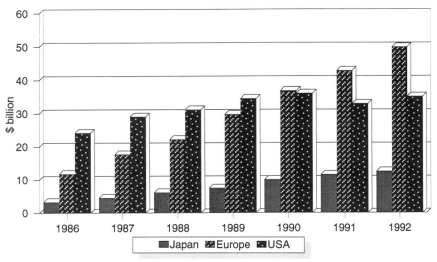

Figure 1.7 **Growth of the venture capital pool in key global regions, 1986–1992**
(*Sources*: Bygrave and Timmons, *Venture Capital*; *Asian VCJ*; EVCA yearbooks; *VCJ*)

It will be seen that the growth in the US pool seems to have more or less plateaued, at least for the time being, although a pick-up in the amount of funds being raised during 1992 tentatively seems to have ended a trend of continuing decline since 1987 (the year of the crash in the securities markets).

18　Overview

The growth in the European venture capital pool, however, seems to have continued unabated, although its progress in some countries is clearly faster than in others. Finally, the Japanese 'venture capital' pool, while still significantly smaller than either the US or European pools, and similar in size to the UK, has also shown marked growth. As we shall see later, however, what the Japanese represent as being venture capital is rather different from its US or European counterparts.

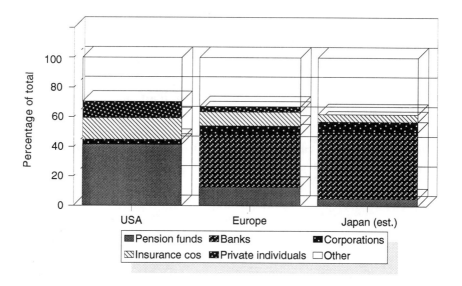

Figure 1.8 Sources of venture capital fund investments in 1991 and 1992 in the USA, Europe and Japan
(*Sources*: *VCJ*; 1993 EVCA yearbook; JAFCO data)

There are very marked differences in the ultimate sources of venture capital fund investment between the three largest venture capital regions.[30] These differences become immediately obvious in Fig. 1.8, based on the most recently available data (see also Chapter 6 for more detail). The first thing to notice is that each region has one dominant source of funds. In the US, pension funds are the prime source of capital, accounting for 42 per cent of the total in 1992, in contrast to 13 per cent for Europe and an estimated 5 per cent in Japan. In Europe, the leading contributors are the banks, at 35 per cent of the total (although in the UK the pension funds dominate as in the US). Under US banking law (Glass–Steagall), banks are prohibited from making significant direct equity investments (over 5 per cent) in companies to which they have lent money. They are allowed to do so indirectly, however, by setting up 'arms-length' and independent subsidiary companies.

Finally, in Japan, banks account for an even greater proportion of venture capital fund investment, an estimated 45 per cent of the total. While an equivalent law to Glass–Steagall prohibits significant shareholdings in banking customers, the banks have set up a number of affiliated venture capital firms through which they invest. Note also that securities houses account for an estimated 35 per cent of the total (included in the 'Other' category).

Industry performance: rates of return

Perhaps one of the most active areas of analysis in the venture capital world at the moment, at least outside the US, is the measurement of rates of return on venture capital funds. In the US, in response to the need for independent and accurate figures on the returns that were being generated by venture capital funds (so that investors could compare the performance of funds more easily), Venture Economics set up a returns database in 1985–6. Prior to this time, a number of studies (including simulations) had tried to measure compound annual rates of return (RORs) on venture capital and had come up with a very wide range of figures between 11 and 27 per cent per annum.[32] The Venture Economics data, however, was able to set these figures in context by demonstrating that measured RORs were critically dependent on a number of key factors, especially: the age of the fund, since the ROR tended to increase with the fund age (as the 'lemons' – bad investments – were much quicker to ripen than the 'plums' – good ones); the calendar years in which the fund was started and in which the ROR measurement was being made; and the average stage of investment that the fund concentrated on, since early stage investments did appear to generate higher average RORs than late stage investments, as perhaps finance theory would predict.

Taking all this into account, and notwithstanding the difficulties in obtaining fund ROR data which had been prepared on a broadly consistent basis, Venture Economics was able to generate US RORs for funds of five or more years of age.[33] What Fig. 1.9 suggests, we believe, is that on average US venture capital investment might generate RORs somewhere in the region of 15–20 per cent in the long run, that is, maybe 3–5 per cent higher than the returns on US equities. This is likely to be compensated for, however, by a greater variability of returns (and hence risk) around this central ROR expectation.

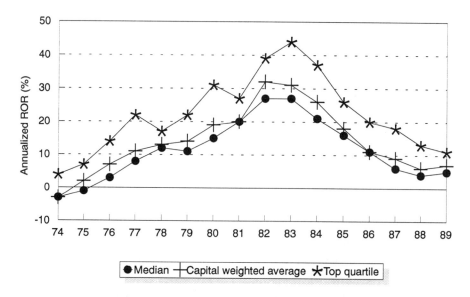

Figure 1.9 US rates of return by mature funds five or more years old
(*Sources*: Bygrave and Timmons, *Venture Capital*; Soja and Reyes, *Investment Benchmarks*)

In contrast to the above, very little work has so far been completed on the industry's returns outside the US, although surveys have been, or are currently being, carried out in the Netherlands, France and the UK.

With regard to the generation of returns over time *within a particular fund*, we have already noted that the losses from poor investments tend to be realized more quickly than the exceptional returns from good investments. In addition, investment outflows in the early years and the subsequent delay before receiving cash returns from the few investments that turn out to be winners mean that a long period may elapse before the fund reaches breakeven in cashflow terms, while the time taken to recover the original investment is even longer. This characteristic of fund cashflows was very well demonstrated by Bygrave and Timmons in *Venture Capital at the Crossroads*, which reported summarized data on 157 US companies backed and owned by the Dutch firm Indivers.[34] This data, relating to the period 1972–82, showed that it took thirty months to reach breakeven cashflow and seventy-five months to recover the initial equity investment.

Having said the above, we noted earlier (in the context of ARD) that the ultimate returns for any particular fund will critically depend on the very small percentage of 'star' investments that it might have managed to make. To further stress this point, analysis by Venture Economics suggests that only one in fifteen US investments returned ten or more times their investment outlay, and that these few investments accounted for roughly half of the final portfolio value.[35]

We shall say more on the subject of returns later on.

The changing emphasis of venture capital funding

While there is still some variation from country to country, most venture capital firms are structured in the form of a 'limited partnership' or similar arrangement. Under this structure, those who invest in the venture capital fund (the pension funds, banks, corporate investors, etc.) are referred to as 'limited partners', while those who manage the fund (the venture capitalists) are designated as the 'general partners'.

In return for investing and managing the limited partners' capital, the venture capitalists receive remuneration in two forms: an annual fee, which might typically be of the order of 2 per cent of the total capital committed; and an entitlement to a percentage, perhaps somewhere in the region of 20 per cent, of the realized capital gains on the fund's investments. Based on this remuneration structure, we can see that the venture capitalists are motivated, in the first place, to raise the largest fund that it is possible for them to manage adequately, since the fee income is invariably independent of the returns generated (although there will, of course, be problems in raising a further fund to manage if returns prove inadequate); and in the second, to generate the maximum possible amount of capital gain from the fund's investments.

Considering the above, the second motivation might be expected to encourage the venture capitalists to invest in earlier stage investments, by virtue of the fact that theoretically and anecdotally such investments would be expected to yield higher capital gains. Unfortunately, the first motivation has proved to be a much stronger influence and has acted to reduce the industry's willingness to invest in seed, start-up and early stage investments. This has led to a change in emphasis in the industry's funding preferences and activities, away from classic venture capital and towards later stage development capital.

To look at the motivation behind this change in emphasis in more detail, we shall assume that the venture capitalist acts in such a way as to maximize its own profits in the long run. This can be done: (1) by maximizing the revenue that it generates for a given cost structure; or (2) by minimizing the cost structure for a given revenue; or (3) by obtaining an optimal trade-off between (1) and (2).

Let us first consider how revenue might be maximised. In order to do this, we posit a base case whereby the returns from CVC-type investments (seed, start-up and early stage) are 8 per cent per annum higher than those from

DC-type investments (later stage development capital, MBOs, restructurings, etc.), which we shall assume to be 15 per cent per annum. (It should be noted that these assumed percentages are not meant to be indicative of the actual returns expected from these investment activities, but are assumed in order to provide a differential in CVC's favour in the base case.) Over a ten-year period, which might be the typical life of a fund, assuming that all the capital can be invested soon after it has been raised, the CVC investments would have returned 7.9 times the original amount invested, while the DC investments would have returned 4.0 times the original amount. If we further assume that the venture capitalist receives 20 per cent of the gain, this amounts to a payment of 1.39 times the amount raised for CVC, versus 0.61 times the amount raised for DC.

In summary, therefore, it would appear that the capital gain, *for a given investment amount*, is maximized by CVC investment. Adding in the annual management fee of (say) 2 per cent, the venture capitalist receives a total *nominal* remuneration of 1.59 times the amount raised for CVC, versus 0.81 times the amount raised for DC (ignoring 'time value' due to the earlier receipt of the fee income and the CVC/DC risk differential). The conclusion, therefore, is similar to the above, that in order to maximize the amount of revenue generated *for a given investment amount*, CVC would be the venture capitalist's choice. (Note, too, that we are assuming that the venture capitalist would be prepared to assume the increased risk associated with CVC in return for the additional reward.)

With regard to costs, let us assume that the costs associated with a CVC investment/transaction (due diligence, transaction and day-to-day management after the investment) are the same as those for DC. In reality, they are likely to be much higher, due to the greater preinvestment due diligence and postinvestment management required to nurture the young firm, but for the moment we shall assume them to be the same. This being the case, the most profitable *transactions* to undertake are those which maximize the total revenue income *per transaction* (since costs are the same).

Let us consider the average size of the two different types of transaction. The data in Table 1.1 is the most recent for the UK, Europe as a whole and the US.[36] As can be seen, on average, the most profitable transactions based on our assumptions would appear to be those of DC in the UK and Europe and CVC in the US (driven by the larger US transaction size). Sensitizing this result to the percentage return premium assumed for CVC investment, would suggest that CVC is more profitable at a 4 per cent return premium in the US, but only at a 13 per cent return premium in either the UK or Europe!

In reality, it is likely that DC transactions are much more profitable, relatively, than suggested above, for three reasons: the differential between the cumulative expected rates of return for CVC and DC is unlikely to be as high as 8 per cent per annum over a ten-year period, based on anecdotal accounts of returns experienced to date; applying discounted cashflow techniques to the revenues from CVC and DC would theoretically narrow the gap between the two investment categories per unit amount invested (after adjusting for risk) to zero; and, as we pointed out above, in reality the due diligence and management costs for CVC investments are much higher per unit amount invested than for DC investments.

Table 1.1 The incentive structure of classic venture capital and development capital in the UK, Europe and the USA, 1992

Average size per transaction (£000s)		Expected revenue per transaction (£000s)
UK		
CVC	370	587
DC	1,066	863
Europe		
CVC	220	349
DC	619	501
USA		
CVC	967	1,533
DC	1,284	1,039

Although the above analysis is, necessarily, crude, the results seem to fit the most recent available data, in that DC investment appears to be much preferred in the UK (83 per cent of transactions) and Europe (85 per cent of transactions). The US, on the other hand, is more favourable for CVC (29 per cent of transactions in the first half of 1992, 34 per cent in 1991), presumably helped by the much larger average CVC deal size. The pie charts in Fig. 1.10, relating to the US (for 1992, first half) and Europe (1992), show the situation in terms of the amount invested. The UK is identical to Europe as a whole.

Finally, it should be noted that the general trend in both the US and Europe has been towards a fall (in both relative and absolute terms) in the amount of money being devoted to CVC-type financings. In particular, Europe has seen a precipitous fall in the CVC share of total disbursements, to only around one third of that in 1986, as can be seen in Fig. 1.11. By any measure, CVC activity has become increasingly unpopular in Europe.

24 Overview

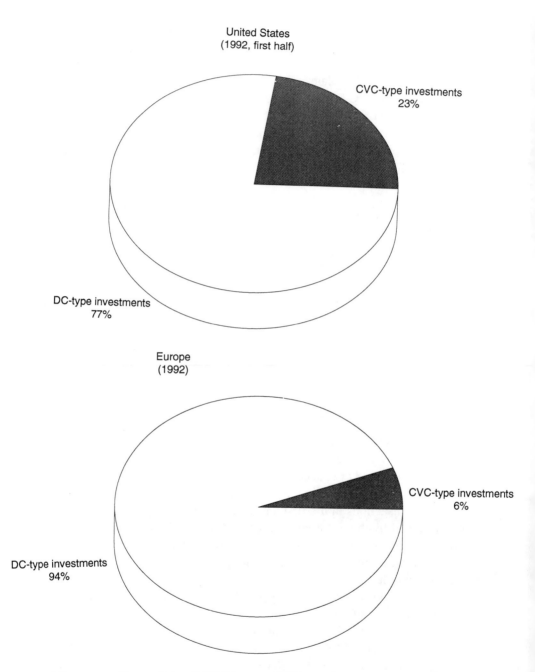

Figure 1.10 Proportions of CVC-type and DC-type investments according to the amount disbursed, United States and Europe
(*Sources*: Venture Economics, Inc./*VCJ*; 1993 EVCA yearbook)

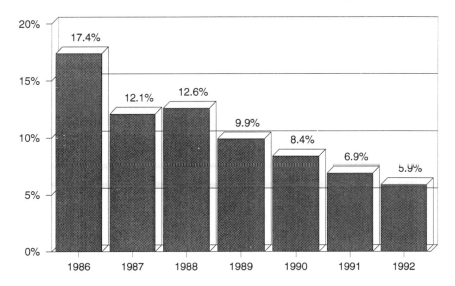

Figure 1.11 Shares of amounts disbursed allocated to CVC-type investments in Europe, 1986–1992
(*Sources*: 1991, 1992, 1993 EVCA yearbooks)

From the analysis and observed trends, it is clear that CVC investment is perceived as being unlikely to be as profitable as DC investment, from the point of view of the venture capitalists' remuneration. Indeed, this has now become conventional wisdom within at least the European venture capital industry (although there are some who would disagree). Of course theoretically, in the long run, the popularity of DC investment would be expected to drive the profitability (to venture capitalists) of DC downwards, while the relative unpopularity of CVC investment would tend to increase profitability to a point at which it becomes attractive. From Fig. 1.11, however, even at the current low levels of CVC activity, it is questionable whether this point has yet been reached. In addition, we shall show later that decreasing CVC activity has a detrimental effect on the economy as a whole, and vice versa.

Harvesting NTBF investments

Of critical importance to the overall venture capital process is the harvesting of the investments made. This is especially true for the small number of companies who generate the vast majority of the venture capital fund's return, as the amount obtained for these one or two companies on exit will determine the overall fund performance. The principal routes for harvesting an investment are via:

1 an initial public offering;
2 an outright, phased or partial sale to a third (corporate) party ('trade sale');
3 a buy-back of the company's equity by its management;
4 liquidation of the company;
5 writing-off the total amount invested;
6 a secondary sale to a third (non-corporate) party.

In brief, route 1 tends to be the preferred route in the US, UK and Japan (among others), but in normal times tends to be more or less the exclusive domain of the most successful companies. Routes 2 and 3, on the other hand, are used by both successful and unsuccessful companies. This is particularly so for successful companies whose investors wish to exit at times when the IPO markets are weak, as in the two to three years following the 1987 market crash, or who are in countries where the IPO markets are poor or non-existent (such as Germany). Of particular note, route 3 appears to be common in Germany when management do not wish to exit but their outside investors do. Finally, routes 4 and 5 are for the corporate failures, with the route chosen being dependent on the extent of the failure, while route 6 tends to be reserved for distressed venture capital funds.

We shall discuss the detailed trends and exit routes for the US, Japanese, German and UK markets in the appropriate country chapter, but we show in Fig. 1.12 the 1992 divestment patterns for the countries in the European Venture Capital Association, according to EVCA data. (It should be noted, however, that this data should be treated with caution, as there could be reporting inconsistencies between the various countries.) As can be seen, during 1992 the dominant exit mechanism for most EVCA countries would appear to be the trade sale, not least because of the poorly functioning equity markets in most countries coupled with the recession, with the latter acting to suppress stock market and hence IPO activity.

THE ROLE OF CLASSIC VENTURE CAPITAL IN HELPING YOUNG COMPANIES

Having seen how the CVC approach played a substantial role in creating major new global scale industries in the USA, it is appropriate to examine briefly the way the venture capitalist can contribute to the growth of young companies, particularly NTBFs. The most obvious contribution is the money that is made available. In addition, the venture capitalist should also be experienced in knowing how to raise capital from other sources. For example, in the UK these might include the banks and any government-backed initiatives such as the loan guarantee scheme, 'business expansion' type schemes and the SMART awards.

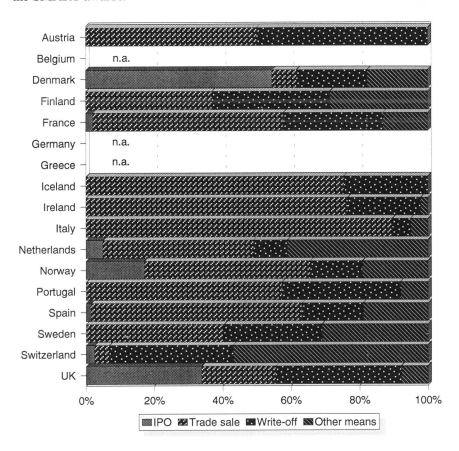

Figure 1.12 Divestment routes in EVCA countries as proportions of total amounts, 1992
(*Source*: 1993 EVCA yearbook)

The money provided by the classic venture capitalist, particularly to very young companies – that is, for seed or start-up expenditure – is usually 'drawn down' in a series of stages, with each draw-down being contingent on certain specified targets being met. In the event that the NTBF's requirement for capital is either large at the outset, or subsequently becomes large after (say) a critical development stage has been passed (for example, with biotechnology start-ups), then the venture capitalist can arrange for syndication of the required investment, often among other firms in the venture capital industry which it knows well. As a final stage, the venture capitalist will be able to advise the NTBF's entrepreneur(s) on the subject of realizing the investment, based on its extensive experience in exiting.

Over and above the supply of money, the venture capitalist should be able to provide more general business advice and consultancy, as part of its 'value added' service. This would include, but not be limited to: specialist industry knowledge, to add to the entrepreneur's understanding of the market to be served, especially in cases where this market does not already exist; help with 'reality checking' of the business plan and the NTBF's assumptions, often by playing the devil's advocate, thus providing a sounding board for the entrepreneurs; help with financial and longer term strategic planning with regard to the development of the business; and moral and psychological support when things go wrong, as on occasion they will do. Most of these are likely to be critical to the success of the NTBF in maximizing the long-term potential of the business, yet they would not be available from passive investors and would have to be procured at great cost from specialist consultants.

More than anything else, it is 'hands-on' management input that distinguishes CVC from other forms of investment management and, indeed, from DC. In this regard, the venture capitalists should be able to help with such matters as: the recruitment of key management team members, by virtue of their contacts in relevant industries and their experience in identifying successful managers of NTBFs; temporarily helping fill gaps in the management teams (especially key financial ones such as the finance director) prior to appointments being made; business development, using their contacts with potential customers, suppliers, etc.; identifying opportunities for and structuring alliances, joint ventures, etc., with major international companies or companies in non-domestic markets.

Most of these involve knowhow, relationships and so on which are usually not present in seed, start-up or early stage NTBFs. In particular, NTBFs more than any other type of company need to be able to gain early access to the international marketplace. It is not often, however, that they know how to achieve this or have the management resources required to learn.

THE UK DIMENSION

While it was suggested earlier that the UK was perhaps particularly well placed to originate and grow new technology based industries over the next ten to twenty years, this view was on the proviso that CVC activity be encouraged, so as to reverse the decline in CVC financing experienced from the latter part of the 1980s to date. In the remaining part of this chapter, we shall review pertinent macroeconomic data in order to underline the need for continued and extensive NTBF driven economic regeneration within the UK.

As a starting point, Fig. 1.13 shows an index of the growth in *real* GDP for the UK over the last twenty-four years; for comparison, we also give the corresponding real GDP indices for our three principal European competitor nations, Germany, France and Italy, in addition to the USA and Japan. It should be noted that the picture would have been very much the same if we had chosen a different period over which to conduct the comparison.

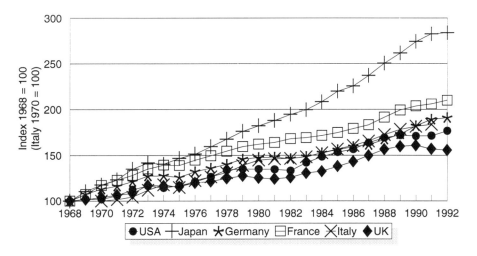

Figure 1.13 Growth in real GDP in key competitor nations, 1968–1992
(*Source*: Datastream)

There are, of course, many factors distorting the comparison of growth in real GDP between the countries – for example the high agricultural produce component of US GDP, which has acted as a drag on the reported US growth rate. Nevertheless, it would appear from the figure that the UK has persistently lagged behind our main competitor nations, having the lowest overall annual compound GDP growth rate of the nations shown. These growth rates are summarized in Table 1.2. Although the growth in the UK's real GDP accelerated somewhat during the 1980s, under the more entrepreneurial environment fostered by the Conservative government, the UK has been hit much harder than any of the other countries during the latest recession. In addition to the problem of slower GDP growth in comparison with our principal competitors, the UK has also been running substantial trade deficits for a number of years and, more recently, a very high and unsustainable public sector borrowing requirement (which now appears unlikely to be resolved by even a substantial bout of economic recovery).[37]

30 Overview

Table 1.2 A comparison of mean compound growth rates, 1968–1992

	Mean compound growth rate (%)
Japan	4.4
France	3.1
Italy	2.9
Germany	2.7
USA	2.4
UK	1.9

Many (including the government) have sought to establish definitive cause-and-effect relationships for the poor UK real GDP growth rate, the trade deficit and the high PSBR. Unfortunately, such is the complexity of domestic and international economic interactions, not to mention the age-old difficulty of trying to get any group of economists to agree about anything, that any (persuasive and intelligent) opinion can usually be subject to (equally persuasive and equally intelligent) counter-opinion. In the light of that, we shall not purport to offer yet another 'definitive' view of 'what's wrong', but shall, instead, restrict our comments to pointing out that it is generally agreed that there is a problem with the rate of GDP growth (since per capita GDP is *the* major influence on the living standards of our citizens), the persistent trade deficit and the unsustainably high PSBR. In a similar vein, we go on to outline the extent of two more generally agreed problem areas, which must at least be related to the above, namely the deterioration of the UK's position with respect to manufactured goods and with respect to the creation of jobs.

Building the manufacturing base

It is clear since the budget of March 1993 that the government now considers it essential to play a more active role in encouraging manufacturing industry. Let us consider, therefore, the recent trends in two key aspects of the UK's manufacturing industry: the UK's share of world trade in manufactured goods and the UK's trade balance in manufactured goods.

Figure 1.14 shows the trend in the UK's share of total world trade in manufactured goods over the last forty two years.[38] Three trends are immediately obvious:

1 the postwar decline in the share of world trade in manufactured goods represented by the UK and the US (although the US looks to have increased its share slightly over the period 1979–92);
2 the dramatic rise in the German and Japanese shares (although the German share appears to have declined slightly over the 1979-92 period);

3 the relatively stable market share of France and, indeed, the 'rest of the world' total.

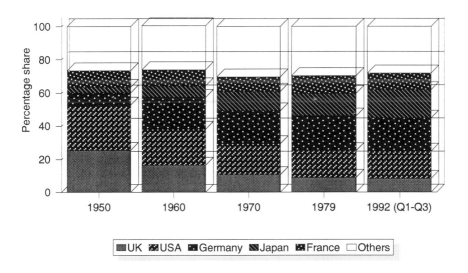

Figure 1.14 UK share of world trade in manufactured goods, 1950–1992
(*Source: Financial Times*)

The apparent shift in manufactured goods production from the UK and US to Germany and Japan was due to a multiplicity of factors. Of particular importance, however, was the multitude of aggressive entrepreneurial engineering and manufacturing 'start-up' companies that, out of necessity, grew in these two countries after the war as they began to rebuild their devastated economies. This legacy survives even today, in that the powerhouse of the German economy remains the *Mittelstand*, that is the small and medium size enterprises (SMEs). The UK, on the other hand, has 40 per cent of the largest 500 European companies (versus 16 per cent for Germany).[39]

Unfortunately, the large US technology based manufacturing industries discussed earlier, whose origination benefited so much from venture capital assistance, have only recently (during the 1980s) grown to such a size as to have a significant impact on the international market shares. Indeed, their impact will only really have become noticeable in the market share data for the first three quarters of 1992 in Fig. 1.14, although they would certainly have contributed to the observed apparent improvement between 1979 and 1992.

Finally, and we only present this as supportive rather than conclusive evidence, it is interesting to note that the two nations that have markedly increased their share of world trade in manufactured goods, Germany and Japan, have a substantial positive trade balance, the two nations that have suffered a marked decrease in their share, the US and the UK, have a substantial negative trade balance, and France, which has more or less maintained its share, has experienced more or less of a balance in its trade. Indeed, the negative trade balance in manufactured goods in the UK (see Fig. 1.15) has accounted for the majority of the UK's visible trade balance deficit throughout the 1980s.[40]

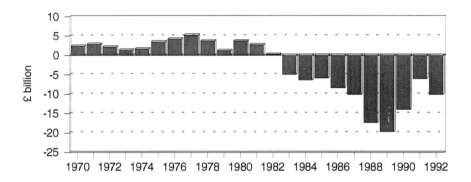

Figure 1.15 **UK trade balance in manufactured goods, 1970–1992**
(*Sources: Financial Times*; Datastream)

Job creation

One of the most pressing problems on the political agenda during the current world recession is the problem of unemployment or, to put it another way, how to encourage the creation of jobs, especially in the private sector. In this regard, let us consider the trends in private sector job creation over the period 1974 to 1991 for North America (including Canada), the European Community and Japan, as shown in Fig. 1.16.[41]

It is evident from the figure that whereas North America (principally the US) has been highly successful in creating private sector jobs, 29.8 million in fact over the period shown, the European Community countries have generated only 3.1 million. Indeed, since 1960, North American employment has nearly doubled while EC employment has risen by only around 10 per cent.

Furthermore, Japan's job creation record is almost as impressive as that of North America, particularly when one considers that its population is only half that of the US (or one-third of the EC total), in addition to the fact that for some time now its unemployment rate has been only 2–3 per cent. Finally, and almost certainly related to the fact that so few jobs have been created, the EC also has a low rate of employment, in that less than 60 per cent of its population of working age are in work, compared to around 70 per cent in the US and over 75 per cent in Japan.[42]

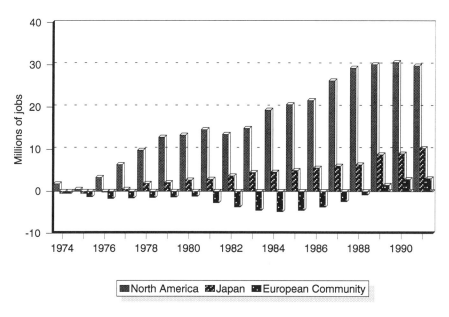

Figure 1.16 International comparison of cumulative private sector employment creation, 1974–1991
(*Sources: Financial Times*; OECD)

Looking a little deeper behind these figures yields two important observations. First, as a broad generalization, many of the US jobs that have been created are in the lowly paid sectors of the economy. This has resulted from a significant fall in real wages at the poorest end of the jobs spectrum, as a consequence of the US's deregulated employment market and its relatively poor unemployment benefits (providing a strong economic motivation to work). Second, a disproportionate number of jobs in Japan have been created in the better paid areas of employment, such as technology based manufacturing. In addition, there is a strong cultural motivation to work, which is reinforced by the relatively poor level of social security benefits. To most EC members, although perhaps rather less so in the UK, encouraging employment through US-style labour market deregulation and substantial unemployment benefit reductions is a politically unpalatable choice. The 'Japanese' solution of increasing the number of 'high quality/pay' jobs in technology and knowledge based areas, on the other hand, is highly desirable, although it is a considerably more difficult option to put into effect than the former one.

Because they are potentially a major contributor to the creation of the required number of 'high quality/pay' jobs, we would suggest that the encouragement of NTBFs should form a key component of any government's strategy. It is clear that US employment has benefited from the millions of jobs created as a result of the development of the semiconductor and computer industries (including the massive amount of quality *indirect* employment gains in information technology, communications, etc.). It is also clear that employment within those countries into which the technology has diffused, especially Japan, has also been a substantial beneficiary. We shall return to this point again later on, drawing on case studies, in order to address and demonstrate the employment creation aspects of the NTBFs formed within the UK.

SUMMARY

In this chapter we have endeavoured to put today's global formal venture capital industry into context, both with respect to the provision of informal (business angel) venture capital and with respect to the formal industry's historic US roots. Since the birth of the industry in the United States, shortly after the Second World War, classic venture capital has played a critical role in the creation and development of some of the world's largest and most technologically advanced industries, which in turn have contributed towards the creation and development of many others. In doing so, CVC has also played a key role in generating national wealth, jobs and taxes. Although the US is perceived as having had many natural advantages assisting the development of these industries, we believe that the UK is also very well placed to create world-scale NTBFs and industries. It appears, however, that this process is being materially handicapped relative to the US, in the UK and throughout Europe, by the dramatic fall-off in funds flowing into NTBF/CVC investments. Central to this increasing CVC aversion, is the economic and remuneration structure of the industry, which appears very much to favour development capital transactions (particularly within Europe).

Despite problems in the CVC segment of the industry, overall venture capital investment continues to grow apace, with the European pool now having passed that of the US, and the Japanese pool showing similar rapid growth. The supply of money to the industry is dominated by pension funds in the US and banks in Europe and Japan. Although earlier expectations of very high rates of return have now been shown to have been far too optimistic, based on the available data, it appears that venture capital investment remains attractive to investors despite these revised (and more realistic) expectations.

Finally, we believe that further measures to promote NTBF/CVC investment in the UK will, in the longer run, make a significant contribution towards solving the problems of slow real GDP growth, the trade deficit, the unsustainable PSBR, the rebuilding of the manufacturing base (in high added-value, technology based areas), job creation of a politically welcome sort and many others. We shall make specific recommendations as to how NTBF/CVC funding activity could most effectively be promoted in the UK in Part IV of this work.

Notes

1. W. D. Bygrave and J. A. Timmons, *Venture Capital at the Crossroads* (Harvard Business School Press, Boston, 1992).
2. Ibid., p.310; Kathleen Devlin, 'A surge in disbursements', *Venture Capital Journal (VCJ)* Dec. 1992, pp.33–7. All 'billion' amounts in this book refer to US billions (1000m).
3. Kathleen Devlin, 'Decade-long rise in VC pool is over', *Venture Capital Journal*, Oct. 1992, pp.38–43.
4. Colin Mason and Richard Harrison, 'The financing of technology based new firms in the UK: the role of informal venture capital', Proceedings of the Anglo-German Seed-Capital Workshop, Oxford Science Park, 30 Sept. 1 Oct. 1992.
5. *Venture Capital in Europe: 1991 EVCA Yearbook* (EVCA, Zaventum, Belgium, 1991).
6. Bygrave and Timmons, *Venture Capital*, p. 16.
7. Ibid., p.17; Patrick Liles, 'Sustaining the venture capital firm', Ph.D. dissertation, Harvard Business School, 1969, p.29.
8. 'The economic impact of venture capital', a joint study by Coopers & Lybrand, Strategic Management Services and Venture Economics, presented by Joseph Schlosser at Venture Forum '90, San Francisco, 25 Oct. 1990.
9. David Birch, *Choosing a Place to Grow: Business Location Decisions in the 1970s*, MIT Program on Neighborhood and Regional Change (MIT, Cambridge, Mass., 1981).
10. 'What I learned in the eighties', *Forbes*, 8 Jan. 1990, p. 100.
11. It should be noted that much of the material in this section draws on Bygrave and Timmons, *Venture Capital at the Crossroads*, and the references it contains. This book offers by far the most accessible account of the development of these industries.
12. Everett M. Rogers and Judith K. Larsen, *Silicon Valley Fever: Growth of High-Technology Culture* (Basic Books, New York, 1984), p. 102.
13. D. Hanson, *The new alchemists: Silicon Valley and the microelectronics revolution* (Little, Brown, Boston, 1982).
14. 'Financial Times survey: computer industry', *Financial Times*, section 4, 26 May 1993.
15. T. M. Doerflinger and J. L. Rivkin, *Risk and Reward: Venture Capital and the Making of America's Great Industries* (Random House, New York, 1987), p. 11.

36   Overview

16. *Financial Times*, 29 July 1993.
17. Glen Rifkin and George Harras, *The Ultimate Entrepreneur* (Contemporary Books, Chicago, 1988), p. 195.
18. 'Financial Times survey: computer industry'; Louise Kehoe, 'Apple share price falls to lowest since October 1990', *Financial Times*, 17 July 1993, p. 12.
19. *Financial Times*, 29 July 1993.
20. Ibid.
21. M. D. Dibner, *Biotechnology Guide – USA* (Stockton Press, New York, 1988).
22. By Professor Henry Grabowski.
23. D. G. Mitton, 'Tracking the trends in designer genes', in *Frontiers of Entrepreneurial Research 1991*, ed. N. Churchill (Center for Entrepreneurial Studies, Babson College, Wellesley, Mass., 1991).
24. Personal communication from Bill Bygrave.
25. 'Realising our potential: a strategy for science, engineering and technology', Cm 2250, HMSO, May 1993.
26. 'Review of allocation, management and use of government expenditure on science and technology', Cabinet Office (OPSS), May 1993.
27. 'Financial Times survey: science and business parks', *Financial Times*, 7 July 1989, pp.35–9; 'Financial Times survey: business parks', *Financial Times*, 11 May 1990, pp.17-20; information also from the UK Science Parks Association.
28. Mason and Harrison, 'The financing of technology based new firms in the UK'; EVCA yearbook for 1993.
29. In addition to the sources cited on Fig. 1.7, we have drawn on Devlin, 'The decade-long rise in the venture capital pool is over'; Bygrave and Timmons, *Venture Capital*, p. 70.
30. EVCA yearbook for 1993; Japan Associated Finance Co. (JAFCO); Jason Huemer, 'Is this the trough?', *Venture Capital Journal*, Mar. 1992, pp. 32–9; Jason Huemer, 'Fund raising bounces back', *Venture Capital Journal*, July 1992, p.17; Michael Vachon,'Venture capital reborn', *Venture Capital Journal*, Jan. 1993, pp. 32–6.
32. See Bygrave and Timmons, *Venture Capital*, p.151.
33. See the discussion in T. A. Soja and J. E. Reyes, *Investment Benchmarks: Venture Capital* (Venture Economics, Inc., Needham, Mass., 1990), p. 118; also Bygrave and Timmons, *Venture Capital*, p. 157.
34. Bygrave and Timmons, *Venture Capital*, p. 5.
35. R. Khoylian, *Venture Capital Performance* (Venture Economics, Inc., Needham, Mass., 1988), p. 6.
36. Devlin, 'A surge in disbursements'; 'Report on investment activity 1992', British Venture Capital Association, 1993, p.9; Kathleen Devlin, 'Disbursements hit ten-year low', *Venture Capital Journal*, June 1992, pp.27–31.
37. *Financial Times*, 21 June 1993, p. 4.
38. Tony Jackson, 'Charm offensive with some value', *Financial Times*, 20 and 21 March 1993.
39. 'Of company size and economic growth', in *3i Analysis*, 1993.
40. *Financial Times*, 21 June 1993, p. 4.
41. See Edward Balls, 'European Commission looks for more jobs', *Financial Times*, 21 June 1993.
42. *Financial Times*, 21 June 1993, p. 3.

Part II

THE FUNDING ENVIRONMENT IN FOUR KEY COUNTRIES

In order to analyse the UK's current competitive position in funding NTBFs, we have chosen to focus our attention on the venture capital markets and related activities that exist within the UK and in three of our key competitor nations, the USA, Germany and Japan. To this end, a preliminary outline of the funding environment and the key features of the systems operating in each of these countries is given in the following four chapters of Part II. A more detailed analysis, including a discussion of the dimensions of national difference, will follow in Part III.

It should be noted that although it was our intention to be as uniform as possible in our description of these markets, the degree of national variation in venture capital activities, coupled with substantial differences in the type of information and data available, was such that this goal proved elusive. Nevertheless, this fact should be looked on as just one of the dimensions of national difference.

2
VENTURE CAPITAL FUNDING IN THE USA

As we have seen, the United States was the first country to develop a formal venture capital industry, widely regarded as having been initiated by the formation of ARD shortly after the Second World War, in 1946.¹ Probably the next key event in the development of the US industry was the formation of the so-called small business investment companies (SBICs), following the 1958 Act of the same name. This Act had come into existence in an effort to encourage the formation and development of new and early stage companies, which often experienced financing difficulties, an activity whose importance to the economy's well-being had now been recognized by the government of the day.

As a result of this Act, privately owned SBICs had access to low-interest government loans equivalent to four times the amount that the SBIC itself invested. Unfortunately, the resulting high gearing of the SBIC's funds usually led to highly leveraged capital structures for the ventures that were financed, in order to match the SBICs' asset structures with their (predominantly debt-based) liabilities. In consequence, investments became concentrated in later stage firms which could manage to generate sufficient cashflow to maintain their highly leveraged capital structures. Thus the whole point of the exercise was somewhat defeated.

Nevertheless, driven by the easy availability of cheap government funding, the number of SBICs grew dramatically to approaching 700 by the mid-1960s. Unfortunately, the type of CVC expertise required to nurture the investee companies grew at nothing like this pace, leading to SBIC failure, incompetence and fraud. Since the SBIC excesses of the early 1960s, however, increased regulation has resulted in a substantial reduction in both the number and significance of SBICs in today's US venture capital marketplace. Having said this, their role in building the current formal US venture capital industry should not be underestimated.

Despite the failure of many of the SBICs, the 1970s saw the advent of a large number of new, privately owned, non-SBIC venture capital firms, spurred on by ARD's investment in Digital Equipment Corporation which had become a highly visible success. Furthermore, these new firms typically took the form of limited partnerships, which remains the dominant legal structure at the present time. The developing US industry suffered another severe setback, however, when the 1974–5 recession devastated its fund raising, investment and harvesting activities. Nevertheless, the real renaissance in US venture capital activity came only three years later, when a number of legislative and taxation measures, enacted over the 1978–81 period, led to a tenfold explosion in the US venture capital pool during the 1980s. Today we estimate that the total US venture capital pool amounts to somewhere in the region of $35 billion and involves over 600 firms, if one also includes the SBICs.[2] The overall modern industry structure has been succinctly described in diagrammatic form by W. D. Bygrave and J. A. Timmons in *Venture Capital at the Crossroads*, see Fig. 2.1.

As we noted, the dominant legal structure in the US industry is that of the limited partnership. Under this arrangement, the general partners (the venture capitalists managing the fund) might typically provide 1 per cent or so of the fund's capital, in return for 15–25 per cent of the realized capital gains of the fund and an annual fee of up to 2–3 per cent of the total capital committed. One other point worthy of note is the increasing role played by 'gatekeepers'. These are firms who principally act to advise investors on the funds in which to invest, often in return for an annual fee of perhaps around 1 per cent. The impact of gatekeepers on the industry structure will be discussed later on.

MARKET SIZE AND GROWTH

After the period of explosive growth in the early 1980s, the rate of increase in the US venture capital pool has slowed down considerably over the last few years, particularly when compared to the continuing rapid growth of the European and Japanese industries. It will be useful to examine the trends underlying and accompanying these changes in the US venture capital pool.[3]

Figure 2.2 shows the most recent trends in total capital under management (excluding specialist buy-out funds). It should be remembered that these figures compare with the much smaller sum of around $3.5 billion under management prior to 1980 and the introduction of the legislative and tax changes of the 1978-81 period.[4] Accompanying the squeeze on the venture capital pool during the recent recession was a dramatic improvement in liquidations during 1991 (driven by the 'red hot' IPO market), which exceeded the amount of new money committed by over $3 billion and caused a net reduction in the total pool. For 1992, despite a sustained high level of liquidations, driven by the continuing strength in the IPO market, fundraising increased substantially.

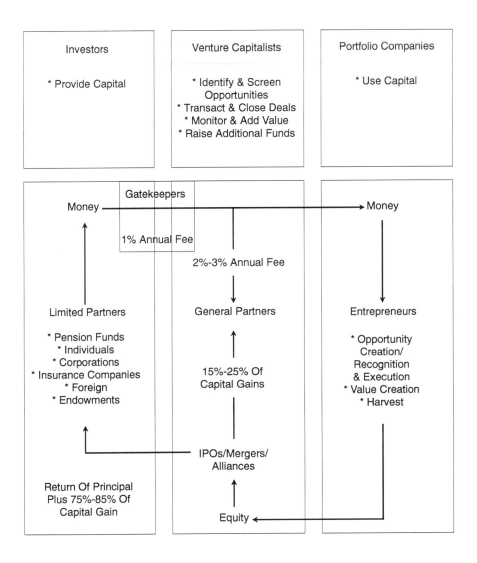

Figure 2.1 The structure of the modern US venture capital industry
(*Source*: Bygrave and Timmons, *Venture Capital*)

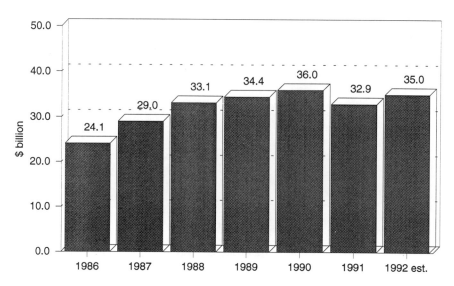

Figure 2.2 Total capital under management, 1986–1992
(*Sources*: *VCJ*; Venture Economics)

It is interesting to note that almost two-thirds of the US venture capital pool is concentrated within only three states. Considering what was said in Chapter 1 regarding the presence of 'technology clusters', it will come as no surprise that two of these states are California and Massachusetts, with New York, as financial centre of the United States, being the other. The geographical distribution of the venture capital pool according to the state in which it is managed, as it stood at the end of 1991, is shown in the pie chart in Fig. 2.3.

The difficulties experienced by many firms in raising funds, on the back of the recent poor returns data, has also had the effect of initiating the long-anticipated industrywide 'shake-out', leading to a slight reduction in the number of venture capital firms. This has been accompanied by an increasing tendency for new money to be allocated to long established firms with solid track records, not least because of the actions of the gatekeepers, who have added an extra layer of risk aversion between investors and funds.

The recent trend in the total number of US venture capital firms (including the SBICs) is shown in Fig. 2.4. It is anticipated that, despite a recent upturn in fundraising, this trend will continue for some time yet, with 1992 believed to have shown a further fall from 1991. This belief is based on the fact that there were only forty-one funds raised during 1992, a marginal improvement on the 1991 ten-year-low of thirty. Firms without a strong track record are experiencing great difficulty in raising funds.

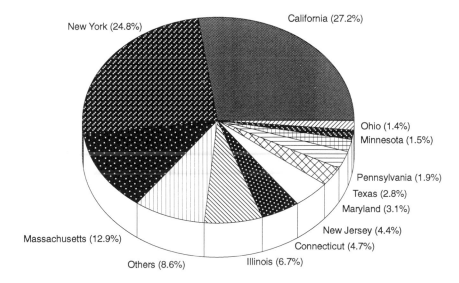

Figure 2.3 Venture capital pool by US state, 1991
(*Sources*: VCJ; Venture Economics)

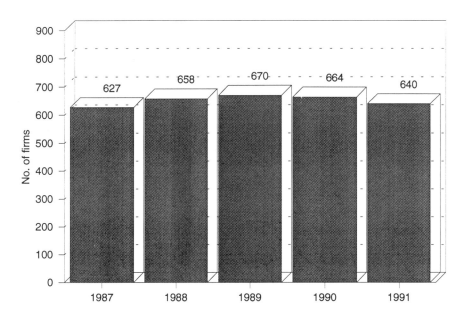

Figure 2.4 Changes in the numbers of venture capital firms, 1987–1991
(*Sources*: VCJ; Venture Economics)

We now turn to the two key elements of venture capital fund management, raising the capital and investing the capital. Over the last few years, roughly four-fifths of the venture capital pool has been accounted for by private independent funds, with the balance being made up of corporate financial (12 per cent) and industrial (8 per cent) groups.[5] To define these groups: *independent private* funds include private and public funds, non-bank SBICs and family groups, and they are currently believed to number around 500 or so; *corporate financial* funds mostly consist of bank subsidiaries and SBICs, and at present number probably only around 60–70 companies; and *corporate industrial* funds are those set up by major corporations such as 3M and Xerox, believed to amount to some 80 funds. The growth and subsequent dominance of venture capital fundraising by the private independents can be seen in Fig. 2.5.[6]

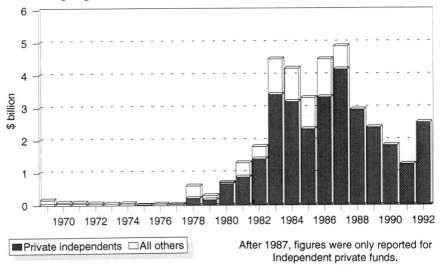

Figure 2.5 Capital commitments and the rise of the private independent funds, 1969–1992
(*Sources*: *VCJ*; Bygrave and Timmons, *Venture Capital*)

Although one of the factors which drove fundraising to previously unheard of amounts in the 1980s was the legislative and taxation measures enacted during the 1978–81 period, there were also two other critical driving forces. First, there was an explosion in capital-hungry investment opportunities in the form of the second leg of the 'computer boom', that is in PCs, workstations and software, and the start of the biotechnology boom. The investors' excitement in these sectors was driven higher by the prospect of backing the next Apple Computer or Genentech, both of which had become highly visible 'mega-successes' by the start of the 1980s. Secondly, driven by the 'super-hot' 1983 US IPO market, the reported US venture capital investment IRRs (internal rates of return) were sufficiently high to wake up even the sleepiest investor to the returns that the industry seemed to be able to deliver.

Unfortunately, the resulting massive inflow of funds during the mid-1980s, in expectation of unrealistic IRRs, led to a substantial fall in returns during the late 1980s. This, coupled with the 1987 securities market crash and deepening recessionary fears, produced a dramatic fall off in commitments, which persisted until 1992.

As one might expect, the trend in the number of new funds formed has tended to follow fairly closely the amount of capital raised, although there has been a tendency towards larger average amounts per fund, which has continued through to the present time. The trend since 1977 is shown in Fig. 2.6.[7] Within these figures, the numbers of new funds raised by financial and industrial corporate firms (including SBICs, as defined earlier) have declined in relative importance, leading to a parallel decline in the proportion of the venture capital pool accounted for by these firms. By way of example, since 1978 SBICs have declined from representing 21 per cent of the pool to just 1 per cent today. Over the same timeframe, the corporate share of the pool has been reduced from 34 per cent to 19 per cent.

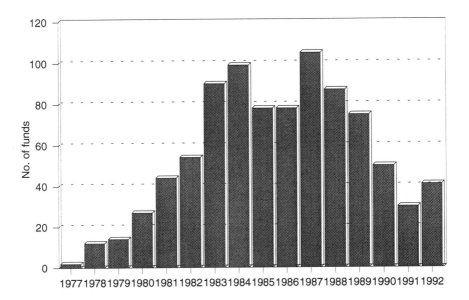

Figure 2.6 Numbers of new funds raised, 1977–1992
(*Sources*: *VCJ*; Bygrave and Timmons, *Venture Capital*)

46 The Funding Environment in Four Key Countries

With regard to the investment of the funds raised – referred to in venture-capital-speak as 'disbursement' – disbursements trailed behind the amount of capital committed to funds during most of the 1980s, although they have exceeded commitments in every year from 1988 onwards. While the largest proportion (maybe 60 per cent or so) of the amount disbursed has invariably been focused on the follow-on financing of existing investments, the split has become much more skewed towards follow-on investments since 1988, see Fig. 2.7.[8]

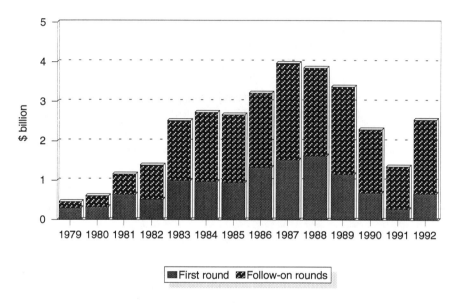

Figure 2.7 Total disbursements by round of financing, 1979–1992
(*Sources*: VCJ; Venture Economics)

Indeed, this change in emphasis towards follow-on investments is even more evident in the data relating to the number of companies financed by round of financing, see Fig. 2.8, although in both cases there appears to have been a reversal in this trend during 1992 (the latest available data), along with a pick-up in the disbursement rate.

Underlying this trend, particularly evident from 1989 onwards, were three factors which acted to reduce fund availability for first round investments: (1) the recession-related deterioration in the trading environment for existing portfolio companies, which probably led to a greater proportion of 'distress financing' than was normal; (2) the unwillingness to commit funds to new firms, given the general state of the economy and the difficulties already being experienced by existing investments; and (3) the poor 1988-90 IPO market, which meant that venture funds had to provide expansion finance in place of the equity market.

Following the commencement of a hot IPO market in 1991, and the subsequent marked improvement in availability of funds (from both fundraising and substantial investment realizations), 1992 may have seen the start of a reversal in this trend.

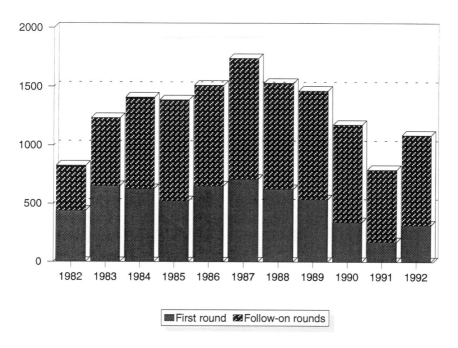

Figure 2.8 Numbers of companies financed, by round of financing, 1982–1992
(*Sources*: *VCJ*; Venture Economics)

BREAKDOWN BY FUNDING STAGE

We noted in the last chapter that US venture capitalists seemed to be more willing than their European counterparts to invest in classic venture capital opportunities, that is, in seed, start-up and early stage companies. Here we shall examine disbursement trends by funding stage of investment during the most recent years.

Figure 2.9 shows the percentage of the total amount disbursed to each funding stage over the period 1985 to 1992.

A number of points are worth noting:

1 investment by acquisition or leveraged buy-out (LBO) has shown a dramatic decline from the 1988 peak, both in monetary terms and as a percentage of all disbursements (although it may be increasing in 1993);
2 by far the largest single funding stage of US venture capital investment is that of expansions and, indeed, this category of investments has more or less maintained its share of total disbursements throughout the period shown;
3 early stage financing has similarly maintained a healthy share of total disbursements, albeit at a rather lower level than expansion financings;
4 both seed and, in particular, start-up financing have accounted for a declining share of the total amount disbursed over the period.

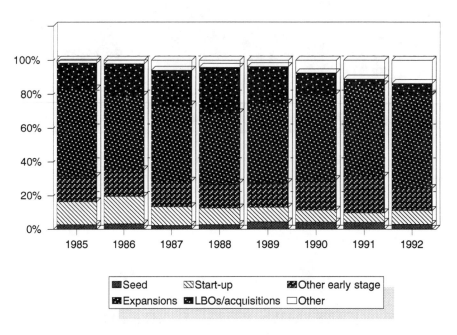

Figure 2.9 Disbursements by funding stage as a proportion of total amount disbursed, 1985–1992
(*Sources*: *VCJ*; Bygrave and Timmons, *Venture Capital*)

These trends are also evident when the situation is looked at in terms of the total number of disbursements made in each year, see Fig. 2.10.

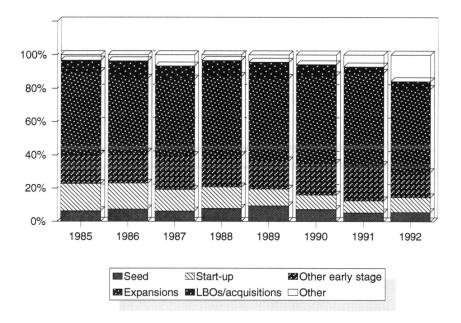

Figure 2.10 Disbursements by funding stage as a proportion of total number of disbursements, 1985–1992
(*Sources*: *VCJ*; Bygrave and Timmons, *Venture Capital*)

The apparent move away from seed and start-up investment since 1989 is likely to be related to the previously noted increase in follow-on financing, although it may also have been caused by a (probably temporary) fall-off in new technology based investment opportunities, which tend to be concentrated in these categories.

INDUSTRY SECTORS ATTRACTING INVESTMENT

As one might predict, the industry sectors which attract venture capital investment change over time. As new industries arise they create large numbers of outstanding investment opportunities, and subsequently become the focus of venture capital disbursements. In mature industries, on the other hand, there tend to be far fewer good opportunities, and they invariably take the form of LBO/acquisitions (although here individual investments can, of course, be of substantial size). Figure 2.11 shows the percentage of the total amount disbursed associated with each industry sector for three periods in time, 1978–80, 1987–9 and 1992. The shares of industry sectors in the total number of investments made display similar patterns.

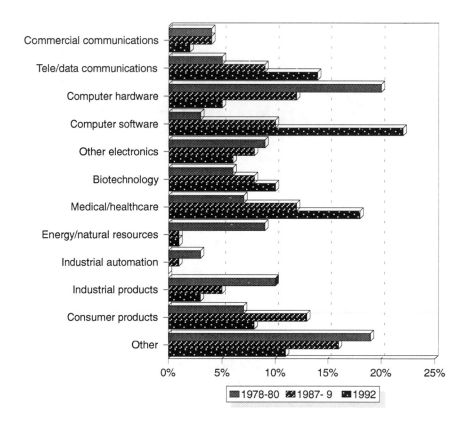

Figure 2.11 Disbursements by industry sector as a proportion of total amount disbursed, 1978–1980, 1987–1989, 1992
(*Sources*: *VCJ*; Bygrave and Timmons, *Venture Capital*)

A number of trends are clearly evident. Key among them are the following.

1 The boom in computer hardware investment is now clearly over, for at least the present time, with many areas of the market that were only just developing in 1978-80 (PCs, failsafe computing, etc.) having become mature. Indeed, to judge by the recent trading statements from IBM, Compaq, Apple, Tandem and many others, the industry faces a very tough time ahead as a result of intense pricing competition, despite substantial volume growth in many areas.

Venture Capital Funding in the USA 51

2 Investment in computer software (and related services), on the other hand, is the current hot area, as the prospects for multimedia, virtual reality, voice activated software and many other innovations have captured the investors' imagination. A related development is the boom in telecommunications and data communications, as the information society of the 1990s and beyond comes into being.

3 The established favourites of biotechnology and healthcare continue to do well, although US healthcare reforms and increasing healthcare pricing pressures in the US and just about every other part of the world might presage a decline in this area of investment over the next few years.

4 Perhaps most importantly, if the first seven categories of Fig. 2.11 are grouped together as 'technology based investments' and the last five as 'non-technology based investments', then there has been a marked shift in the US industry's investment pattern towards the former category. In particular, in the 1978–80 period the technology based categories accounted for 54 per cent of the total amount invested. This share had risen to 63 per cent by 1987–9 and hit 77 per cent just three years later, during 1992.

The last feature, a high and increasing focus on technology based investments, is especially significant. While no long-term trends for Europe as a whole can be established, because of the relative youth of the European venture capital industry, it appears that technology based investment is materially lower and is on a declining trend. For example, in Europe technology based investment accounted for only 26 per cent of funds disbursed during 1988–9 and fell to under 22 per cent in 1992.[9]

INVESTMENT SIZE

To look at the size of investment transactions in the US, the average has remained relatively stable over the last ten years, at between $1.7 and $2.5 million.[10] Variation within this range has tended to correlate closely with the amount of LBO/acquisition activity (seen above), since this form of investment often involves significantly larger deal sizes. Indeed, the precipitous fall-off in LBO/acquisition transactions after 1988, coupled with a worsening fundraising climate, caused a significant fall in the average size of disbursements (see Fig. 2.12). It is interesting to note, however, that 1992 saw a restoration of disbursement size *without* a significant increase in LBO/acquisition activity.

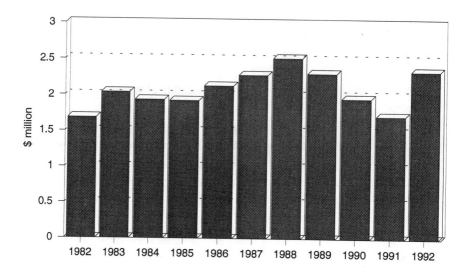

Figure 2.12 Average amount disbursed per investment, 1982–1992
(*Sources*: VCJ; Venture Economics)

CHARACTERISTICS OF INVESTORS

Venture capital fund investors in the US can be classified into one of the following groups: pension funds; endowments and foundations; foreign investors; insurance companies and banks; corporations; and individuals and families. The relative historic importance of each of these categories as a source of funds over the period 1979–92 is indicated in Figs. 2.13 and 2.14.[11] A number of points can be noted. In the first place, the largest single contributing group of investors, the pension funds, has become increasingly important. Secondly, the contributions from endowments and foundations have tended to grow in importance, to such an extent that they now represent the second largest contributing group. Thirdly, both corporations and individuals/families have declined in relative importance. Indeed, it appears that corporate investors may have been particularly badly hit by the recent recession, which looks to have all but wiped out their venture capital new investment activities.

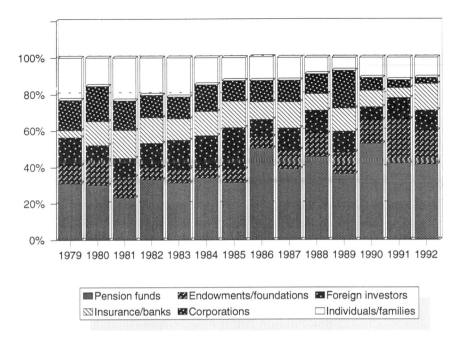

Figure 2.13 Capital commitments by source as a proportion of total commitments (excluding funds-of-funds), 1979–1992
(*Sources*: *VCJ*; Bygrave and Timmons, *Venture Capital*)

The reasons behind the observed trends are, necessarily, complex. Three significant factors influencing the observed trends have been suggested, however: the legislative and taxation moves enacted over the 1978–81 period; the effective rate of capital gains tax (CGT); and the state of the IPO market. An analysis of the influence of these factors on the venture capital market will be given later.

FUNDING SOURCES AND METHODS

We noted earlier that the venture capital pool was dominated by the private independent funds (80 per cent), with the balance being split roughly 60:40 between the corporate financial and corporate industrial funds, respectively. Furthermore, it also appeared that in the most recently available data new capital commitments tended to be more or less in line with this split. It might come as no surprise, therefore, that private independent funds are also the principal source of formal venture capital.[12]

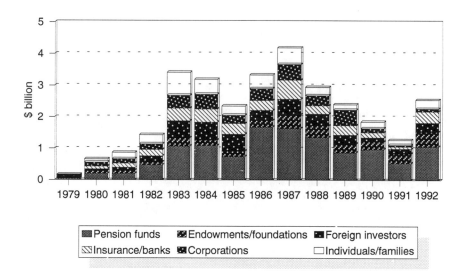

Figure 2.14 Capital commitments by source in value terms (excluding funds-of-funds), 1979–1992
(*Sources: VCJ*; Bygrave and Timmons, *Venture Capital*)

These private independent firms, as a category, invest across the entire spectrum of venture capital activities, from the seed stage through to LBOs (although within the category there are many funds who specialize in particular types of transaction). Usually, the investment is made up either of all or mostly equity, with the equity component tending to decrease with the maturity of the company being financed. A typical investment might be between $250,000 and $2.5 million in size, with larger amounts usually being syndicated with other venture capitalists. It is quite common that, particularly with seed, start-up and other early stage investments, the investment will be made in stages (or in 'rounds'), with each further investment being contingent on certain targets being met (hence the split between first round and follow-on disbursements seen earlier).

By and large, private independent firms tend to focus their investment activities in technology based areas, and are generally 'hands-on' investors. It should be noted that their motivation for investing is the expectation of a profitable exit, typically on a five to seven years' time horizon, or possibly shorter for more mature businesses.

Corporate industrial firms, in contrast to the above, tend to fall into one of two categories: strategic, 'window on technology' types of investors, or 'strictly for profit' types of investors. Unfortunately, the track record of both types of investors is not particularly good, as the activities tend too often to be thought of as a peripheral by the senior corporate executives. In addition, a new chief executive can often lead to a discontinuation of this activity, especially in difficult economic times. Nevertheless, in theory, corporations can offer a great deal to their portfolio companies where the investments have been strategic in nature. In particular, they often have a great deal of skill and expertise in areas where the portfolio company will typically be weak, in manufacturing, marketing, sales, and so on.

Corporate financial firms usually consist of the 'arms length' venture capital subsidiaries of banks, insurance companies, etc. These firms often focus on later stage, larger deals, with investments perhaps in the $1 to $5 million range. Frequently, where the parent is a bank, the activity is looked on as an extension of its lending business. The style of these companies is, perhaps predictably, invariably 'hands-off'.

Finally, contained within the above three categories are the bank and non-bank small business investment companies. As we noted earlier in the chapter, because SBICs generally borrow a portion of their capital from the government, they commonly use debt as well as equity instruments to finance their portfolio companies. Having said that, SBICs are often willing to finance small businesses which have rather less than the 'stellar' growth potentials required by the private independent firms.

THE VENTURE CAPITALIST/ENTREPRENEUR RELATIONSHIP

In outlining the role of classic venture capital in the growth of new technology based firms, we saw that it extended beyond the provision of finance, to business advice and consultancy, and to hands-on management input. In reality, since the majority of US venture capital investment is in technology related areas and tends to be hands-on, this was also a description of the typical entrepreneurial enterprise/venture capitalist relationship in the US. While the worth of hands-on value-added by venture capitalists is the subject of much controversy, with views being split between the high worth and the worthless camps, we believe that two further points are worth making.

First, an extensive field study of entrepreneurs and venture capitalists in the US by Timmons and Sapienza[13] noted the following generalizations:

1. the most intense involvement by the venture capitalist occurs at the early stages of the business's development;
2. a high degree of openness and good personal chemistry between the

entrepreneur and venture backer are critical to the success of the venture;
3 venture capitalists do indeed add value in the manner described earlier, although their strategic and supportive roles were highlighted as being particularly noteworthy;
4 the venture capitalist's key roles become more important as the business grows and develops.

Second, Brook Byers (of the prestigious US venture capitalists Kleiner Perkins Caufield & Byers), whose style is one of 'significant involvement', noted that the approach can also have several drawbacks from the point of view of the venture capitalist.[14] He pointed to:

1 the substantial amount of time required;
2 the initial tendency of some managers to view a significant degree of investor involvement as intrusive;
3 the subsequent tendency of some managers, having been awakened to the benefits of investor involvement, to start to expect their almost unlimited support;
4 attempts by 'quiet' investors to 'piggy-back' on the hard work of the active investors;
5 the pressure on an involved investor to participate in later equity financings in order for that offer to be successful;
6 the danger that an involved investor may cease to be objective about that investment.

PERIOD OF INVESTMENT, EXIT OPPORTUNITIES AND VALUATION

Harvesting venture capital investments is a critical factor influencing the overall investment return to the venture capitalist, and this harvesting process has three dimensions: the time taken between investment and harvest; the method of exit (or, indeed, phased exit); the amount of cash obtained on exit.

At the time of investment, US venture capitalists are usually seeking to exit successful investments in five to seven years, although earlier stage investments will be at the upper end of this scale, while later stage investments will be at the lower end. We shall see that the preferred exit route for successful US investments is the initial public offering. The average age of venture-backed companies prior to IPO is shown in Fig. 2.15.[15]

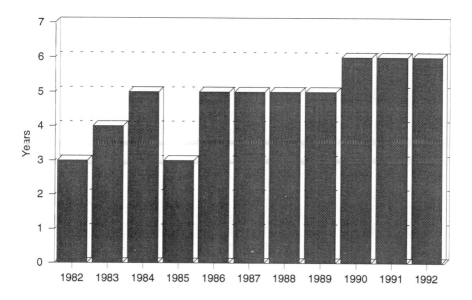

Figure 2.15 Median age of venture-backed companies at IPO, 1982–1992
(*Sources*: VCJ; Venture Economics)

As the figure shows, the median age of the IPO company, which can be looked on as being the same as the period of investment for the company's first venture capital backers, has averaged at just below five years over the period shown. At the same time, venture capitalists often retain some or all of their shareholding following the IPO. Thus the average period of investment in successful companies is probably somewhat longer than five years. It should also be remembered that the average period of investment prior to the IPO is strongly influenced by the strength of the IPO market.

The two principal methods of exiting successful investments in the United States are the IPO and the acquisition or 'trade sale'. The balance between these two exit routes in any one year appears to be very much dependent on the strength of the IPO market in that year, since this is deemed by the industry to be the method of choice, all else being equal. Figure 2.16 shows the number of exits by venture-backed companies taking place via each route since 1982.[16] (It should be noted that the number of acquisitions/trade sales is likely to be understated due to under-reporting of these exits.) The figure also indicates the effect of 'hot' IPO markets on the choice of exit route. Over the period, however, exits have been split almost equally between the two alternative routes.

58 The Funding Environment in Four Key Countries

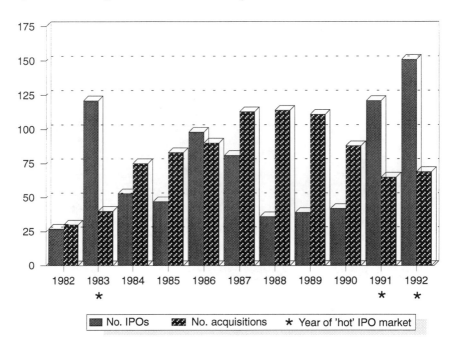

Figure 2.16 Acquisitions versus IPOs for private venture-backed companies, 1982–1992
(*Sources*: *VCJ*; Venture Economics)

Other than IPOs and acquisitions, a significantly smaller number of companies allow the venture capitalist to exit via a 'buy-back' of its equity from them, while in recent times 'secondary sales' of equity have been on the increase. A rather old study of US exits during 1970–82 showed them to be distributed as in Fig. 2.17.[17]

There are a number of possible reasons for the apparent preference by US venture capitalists and entrepreneurs for IPOs over acquisitions as an exit route. From a purely *financial* point of view, the rationale for the IPO might be, first, that it allows the venture capitalists and entrepreneurs to realize only part of their investment in star performers at the time of the IPO, while retaining the balance to attract further gains. Acquisitions/trade sales, on the other hand, usually involve a total exit by both the venture capitalists and the entrepreneurs (although the entrepreneurs may have to work an earn-out period). Second, they might be able to get a higher exit price or valuation via an IPO than through an acquisition. In addition to the possible financial reasons for preferring an IPO, the method also allows the management to retain their independence. Let us examine the possible financial motives in more detail.

Venture Capital Funding in the USA 59

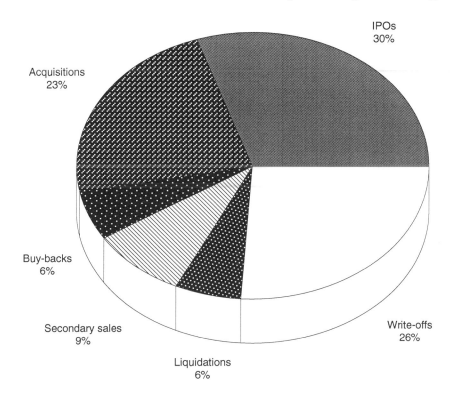

Figure 2.17 Venture capital exits by method, 1970–1982
(*Sources*: Venture Economics; Bygrave and Timmons, *Venture Capital*)

The same 1970–82 study of the distribution of exit routes also estimated the average gains accruing to investors in companies using each method. These are shown in Fig. 2.18. It would be tempting to interpret the figure to mean that the most profitable exit route is demonstrably via IPOs and *therefore* that venture capitalists/entrepreneurs naturally favour this route. Such an explanation, however, contains a serious logical flaw. The source of the flaw is that this interpretation *assumes* that had the companies who chose to exit via an IPO chosen to be acquired instead, then they would have received materially less, and vice versa. While this might be true and, indeed, probably is true in some cases, it is certainly not necessarily the case.

Consider, for example, the case of Genentech. Did its backers decide to go via the IPO route because they would have got a rather lower valuation from a corporate buyer than the $300 million implied market valuation (the second of the rationales above)? Or did they opt for an IPO because they had a vision of the $3.5 billion the company would become worth in the eyes of Hofmann–La Roche only ten years later and, therefore, wanted to hang on to a good portion of their equity (the first of the rationales above)?

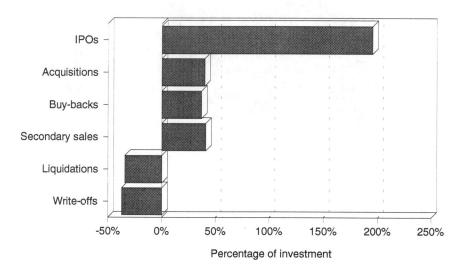

Figure 2.18 Average gain or loss as a percentage of investment in relation to exit method used, 1970–1982
(*Sources*: Venture Economics; Bygrave and Timmons, *Venture Capital*)

We believe that the reality of the situation is that the latter rationale is the motivation which operates most of the time – that it is the better companies which tend to choose to go via the IPO route or, at the very least, that the poorer companies are unable to attract sufficient IPO interest to make the route a viable proposition. Supporting this view is the fact that many of the poorer performing companies seek an acquiring 'big brother' out of necessity, thus depressing the average returns from acquisitions. In addition, all the venture-backed industry 'pace setters' initially took the IPO route, for instance, Intel, Microsoft, Lotus, Apple, Seagate and Conner.[18] If IPO firms are truly 'better', therefore, then this is the source of their superior returns.

Note, however, that there are clearly times when the rationale of the higher exit price becomes the key driving force, such as during periods when the IPO market is 'hot' and even the more marginal IPOs can enjoy inflated market multiples. These hot IPO markets are generally driven to unjustified and unsustainable company valuations, by unsophisticated private investors on the one hand, and by both inexperienced and speculative professional investors on the other. After the party comes the hangover, however, and just as the excesses of 1983 resulted in substantial investor losses and a poor IPO market in the following few years, so (and the authors feel confident on this point) the IPO boom of 1991 and 1992 is likely to lead to a poor IPO market in the mid-1990s.

RETURNS REQUIRED BY THE PROVIDERS OF DEBT AND EQUITY

A key factor in determining the level of venture capital activity in any market are the rates of return required by the providers of funds to the firm. Indeed, this return is critical to the decision as to whether the prospective reward is commensurate with the risk. We now turn to the concept of the nominal pretax rate of return, as it applies to venture capital, in a little more detail.

When a stable government of a leading nation issues debt (bonds), the repayment of that debt in due course is as near to a financial certainty as it is possible to get. The rate of return that a purchaser of those bonds receives, based on the purchase price, is often referred to as the 'risk-free' rate, since there is essentially no risk of not being paid either the annual/biannual 'coupons' on the bond or, if held to redemption, the bond's capital value. Similarly, a first class, blue-chip company can also borrow money from a bank (overnight, say) at a rate of interest (return) that is very close to this risk-free rate.

As the risk associated with being paid the interest, or being repaid the capital, increases (for example if the loan is made to an individual with no assets for the purpose of buying a house, or to a small company for capital investment), then so does the interest rate. This is reasonable from the bank's point of view, since the returns obtained on its good loans (in the form of interest) must compensate for losses from its occasional bad debts.

With the sort of companies/opportunities that are financed by venture capital, however, the risks are so high that no bank will provide loan finance, irrespective of the rate of interest that the companies are willing or able to pay. Hence, the use of equity-based instruments to finance such companies. But what is the nominal pretax return 'charged' for providing equity? As a logical extension of the idea that the pretax return should increase with the risk of receiving a return on that capital, the return must be much higher than that of debt, but by how much? In addition, most earlier stage companies pay no dividends ('interest'), so how is the 'return' to be calculated at the time that the capital is supplied?

The answer is that the pretax return 'charged' for the money invested in the venture is the expected or 'target' pretax rate of return that the investor is seeking on this money. To demonstrate this point, consider the following simplified example. An investor is prepared to lend $100,000 to an entrepreneur to start up a new company, based on the *expectation* that in five years time the company can be sold for $2 million (the investor's best estimate of its likely value). The investor believes that an appropriate rate of return on the investment (that is, the 'target' rate) is 50 per cent per annum (see below), taking into account the risk that the venture might come to nothing, in which event all the money might be lost. Thus, in five years time, he or she must expect the investment in the company to be worth $100,000 × $(1.5)^5$ = $0.76 million. Assuming that the investor's only return will be from the sale of shares in the company, he or she will, therefore, require 38 per cent of the company's equity, since 38 per cent of $2 million = $0.76 million.

In this example, based on the best estimate of the company's likely worth in five years, the return 'charged' for the capital that is provided to the company will be that accruing from the 38 per cent equity stake, which is expected to give a pretax rate of return of 50 per cent per annum to the investor. Thus the target rate of return of 50 per cent per annum is analogous to the 'interest rate' on debt.

There are two key considerations that influence the target rate of return, both within the US and elsewhere. First is the stage of the investment. In general, the earlier the stage of the investment, the higher the risk, therefore the higher the target return. Second there are other factors specific to the investment, such as technological risks, competitive threats, plus many others. The target rate is also invariably and materially affected by the negotiating power of either side of the transaction. Having said that, the US venture capital industry tends to have generally accepted ranges for the target rate of return, and they vary as a function of the stage of the investment. Typically these might be 100 per cent for seed, 50–70 per cent for start-ups, 35–50 per cent for early stage and 30–40 per cent for later stage investments.[19]

It should be noted, however, that these target rates of return are *not* the same as the rates of return that will actually be received, any more than the interest rate charge by a bank on risky debt is the actual return the bank will receive. In the case of the bank debt, the return for a large portfolio of such loans is likely to be reduced slightly by bad debts. In the case of venture capital investment, on the other hand, the return on a large portfolio of such investments is likely to be reduced *substantially* by company failures or disappointments relative to expectations.

The principal impact of the rate of return required by debt and equity investors on the success of the firm is through its effect on the motivation of the entrepreneur. Once the provider of the capital has assessed his or her target rate of return, a capital structure is adopted which is consistent with this target rate, albeit also being capable of taking into account deviations from the original expectations of all parties (via ratchets, options, etc.). It is self-evident that the higher the rate of return required by the investors, the lower the ultimate reward will be to the entrepreneur. In the light of this, there comes a point when the rate of return required by investors is so high that the entrepreneur no longer feels that the potential reward is commensurate with the effort required and the risks it is necessary to assume and, therefore, will choose not to undertake the venture.

In addition, if the deal structure is such that the potential returns to the entrepreneur, after the inevitable setback, fall to too low a level (as a result of the investor wishing to retain his or her target rate of return), then the entrepreneur might just decide to call it a day, with the ensuing failure of the company. Furthermore, a high target rate of return by investors also tends to lead to a frequently fatal undercapitalization of the firm, as the entrepreneur tries to minimize the amount of equity that is surrendered and/or the investor reduces the amount of money that he or she is prepared to invest for a given target return.

GOVERNMENT INITIATIVES

The US government, as well as many local state authorities, have taken numerous steps over the last thirty five years or so to help seed, start-up and early stage companies (particularly NTBFs), which have been more or less successful. Among the more important financial measures taken by the government were the 'small business investment companies', which came into being in 1958 after the passing of an Act of the same name. We have noted that the Act was designed to encourage the formation and development of the new and early stage companies which had finally been recognized as a powerhouse of economic growth and development.

As we also saw, however, the 'subsidized debt' nature of the money that the government made available to encourage this activity was incompatible with the nature of the investments that the SBICs needed to make. In due course, this fundamental source of incompatibility often led to unstable capital structures for both the SBICs and their portfolio companies, ultimately resulting in a substantial number of SBIC and portfolio company failures during the middle to late 1960s. Other factors leading to the downfall of many SBICs were the inevitable problems that any form of 'cheap money' brings:

an oversupply of inadequately qualified people trying to take advantage of this cheap money, and financial fraud.

Nevertheless, despite a substantial reduction in their number, from perhaps approaching 700 in the mid-1960s to an estimated 330 today, SBICs played a key role in building the US venture capital industry. Indeed, in numerical terms, SBICs still constitute around half of the current number of US venture capital firms, although they now control only a small fraction of the US venture capital pool.

Probably of greatest importance to the future of SBICs, revisions to the SBIC programme are in the process of being unveiled, following on from the Small Business Equity Enhancement Act of 1992.[20] Two key aspects of the improvements in the way the new SBIC system will operate are:

1. the Small Business Administration will now provide funds in the form of participating preferred equity, rather than as debt, thus removing the need to make fixed and regular interest payments on these funds (a major shortcoming of the old system as it required portfolio companies to generate cash); and
2. since the funds are provided as equity rather than debt, the capital provided by the SBA will no longer cause taxable income to be generated by normally exempt institutional investors (such as pension funds). Thus SBICs are likely to become much more attractive to such investors.

With the implementation of these and other changes in the 1992 Act, SBICs are set to experience a new lease of life.

Another important government intervention was made in response to political pressure to revive the ailing venture capital industry of the middle to late 1970s. Five key legislative changes were enacted between 1978 and 1981.[21] To summarize:

1. the 1978 Revenue Act reduced capital gains tax from 49.5 per cent to 28 per cent;
2. the 1979 revision of the 'prudent man' rule of the Employment Retirement Income Security Act (ERISA) allowed pension funds to pursue higher risk investments;
3. the 1980 Small Business Investment Incentive Act reduced the regulatory burden on venture capitalists;
4. the 1980 ERISA 'safe harbor' regulation encouraged the use of pension fund money in venture capital investment;
5. the 1981 Economic Recovery Tax Act lowered the rate of capital gains tax further, to 20 per cent.

As we will see in the following section on the taxation environment, the impact of any *across-the-board* changes to the rate of CGT (both in absolute terms and relative to the rate applied to ordinary income) is subject to much debate. Indeed, in later periods, across-the-board changes in the rate of CGT have been followed by effects on formal venture capital commitments *opposite* to those simplistically predicted or expected. It should not be forgotten, however, that mostly it is only individual investors who are affected by the rate of CGT, yet these provide relatively little by way of funds to the formal venture capital industry.

It may be, therefore, that it was the non CGT measures which had the largest impact on venture capital commitments in the following years. Furthermore, the observed changes in capital commitments could have resulted from other much more important factors, such as IPO activity and certain high-profile investments of the late 1970s (Genentech, Apple, etc.) which once again captured venture capital investors' imaginations as DEC had done in earlier times. Nevertheless, taken together, the measures listed are believed to have provided a substantial boost to the provision of formal venture capital within the United States over the following decade and, at the very least, they helped to reverse what was seen as the dwindling role played by pension fund investors.

Finally, and in addition to the above measures, there are now a large number of state and government funded, or partially funded, programmes to encourage NTBF development, encompassing a wide range of technology based activities.[22]

THE TAXATION ENVIRONMENT

There are two key areas of taxation related initiatives used by the US government in an attempt to promote venture capital investment: lowering the rate of capital gains tax or increasing the differential between CGT and income tax to favour capital gains; and allowing companies to register as S corporations, along with the provisions relating to Section 1244 stock. We shall look at each of these initiatives in a little more detail.

As noted, one of the key features in the 1978–81 package of measures to promote venture capital investment was an across-the-board reduction in the rate of CGT. For many years now, the rate of CGT has been a political hot potato in the US, and its impact on economic growth in general (or, indeed, the provision of venture capital in particular) has been the subject of a wide range of expert opinion. These expert opinions, however, have varied from a view that the rate of CGT has a substantial impact on venture capital availability,[23] to a view that it has only a minor impact,[24] to a view that it has no impact at all.[25]

There are a number of problems with trying to seek some form of correlation between changes in the rate of CGT and venture capital investment, as many have tried to. They include the fact that a broad brush, across-the-board change in the rate of CGT affects *all* capital gains on *all* forms of investment; that it is the CGT – income tax differential that governs the flow of funds into CGT-type investments; and especially that continual changes in the CGT-income tax differential, or *expectations* thereof, favour the flow of funds into the more liquid CGT-type investments (such as quoted stocks and bonds), so that the money can be more easily switched in the event of a further change in the differential. In the absence of changes in the rate of US CGT *specifically* related to venture capital, therefore, we believe that any views expressed regarding its impact can be subject to refutation (hence the differences in expert opinion).

That the impact of the rate of CGT is difficult to assess by watching investment flows is well exemplified by an observation we owe to Bill Bygrave: California, New York and Massachusetts have high state CGT rates but, as we saw earlier, these are the three states which have the largest amount of venture capital headquartered in them. Indeed, the amounts are highly disproportionate, even in per capita terms.

The second key area of taxation-related initiatives for venture capital investment concerns two important provisions for owners of closely held companies, allowing for the favourable tax treatment of losses in the event that the firm proves to be either initially or terminally unprofitable. They are the 'sub-S' election and the issuance of Section 1244 stock.[26]

With regard to the first provision, companies which make a sub-S election retain their corporate status (in particular with respect to limited liability), but are treated very much like a partnership for tax purposes. The two most important effects of this election are that income and losses flow through to the shareholders and tax is paid or relief received at the shareholder level (subject to certain restrictions); and that undistributed income may increase the basis for calculating capital gains and, hence, reduce the taxation liability on the eventual sale of the company.

As for the second provision, some small corporations are allowed to issue Section 1244 stock, which allows for certain losses to be treated as ordinary rather than capital losses in the event that the stock is ultimately sold at a loss.

Finally on the subject of taxation and US venture capital investment, the 1993 US Tax Bill contained a provision for the reduction of CGT to certain investors. While this reduction is expected to help investment in small-capitalization stocks, it will probably reduce the cashflow (and growth) of successful sub-S corporations. The net effect may be neutral to negative![27]

Notes

1. W. D. Bygrave and J. A. Timmons, *Venture Capital at the Crossroads* (Harvard Business School Press, Boston, 1992); Jane Koloski Morris, 'An overview of the venture capital industry', in *Pratt's Guide to Venture Capital Sources* (Venture Economics, New York), 1992 edn, pp. 7-10.
2. Based on figures in Stanley E. Pratt, 'The organised venture capital community', in *Pratt's Guide to Venture Capital Sources*, 1992 edn, pp. 67-72.
3. As the most authoritative source of venture capital data in the US Venture Economics, Inc. and its *Venture Capital Journal* (*VCJ*) have been invaluable for this chapter. It also benefits again from Bygrave and Timmons, *Venture Capital at the Crossroads*.
4. Kathleen Devlin, 'Decade-long rise In VC pool is over', *Venture Capital Journal*, Oct. 1992, pp.38-43; Koloski Morris, 'An overview of the venture capital industry'.
5. Pratt 'The organized venture capital community'; Devlin, 'Decade-long rise in VC pool is over'.
6. See Bygrave and Timmons, *Venture Capital*, p. 26; Jason Huemer, 'Is this the trough?', *Venture Capital Journal*, Mar. 1992, pp. 32-9; Jason Huemer, 'Fund raising bounces back', *Venture Capital Journal*, July 1992, p. 17; Michael Vachon, 'Venture capital reborn', *Venture Capital Journal*, Jan. 1993, pp. 32-6.
7. Huemer, 'Is this the trough?'; Vachon, 'Venture capital reborn'; Bygrave and Timmons, *Venture Capital*, p.49.
8. Kathleen Devlin, 'Disbursements hit ten-year low', *Venture Capital Journal*, June 1992, pp. 27-31; Kathleen Devlin, 'A surge in disbursements', *Venture Capital Journal*, Dec. 1992, pp. 33-7; Alex Alger, 'Venture capital disbursements rise', *Venture Capital Journal*, June 1993, pp. 31-6.
9. *Venture Capital in Europe: 1993 EVCA Yearbook* (EVCA, Zaventum, 1993), p.65.
10. See sources in note 8.
11. See Bygrave and Timmons, *Venture Capital*, p. 274, and the other sources in note 6.
12. Pratt, 'The organized venture capital community'.
13. J. A. Timmons and H. J. Sapienza, 'Venture capital: more than money?', in *Pratt's Guide to Venture Capital Sources*, 1992 edn, pp. 35-41.
14. Brook H. Byers, 'Relationship between venture capitalist and entrepreneur', in *Pratt's Guide to Venture Capital Sources*, 1992 edn, pp. 81-3.
15. Daniel Riordan, 'The IPO record book rewritten', *Venture Capital Journal*, Jan. 1993, pp. 38-44.
16. Ibid.; Daniel Riordan, 'Too far, too fast', *Venture Capital Journal*, July 1992, pp.27-30; Michael Vachon, 'An uptick in M & A exit activity', *Venture Capital Journal*, Feb. 1993, pp. 30-5; John G. F. Bonnanzio (ed.), 'Time to weigh alternatives for cashing out', *Venture Capital Journal*, Nov. 1990, pp. 19-21.
17. T. A. Soja and J. E. Reyes, *Investment Benchmarks: Venture Capital* (Venture Economics, Inc., Needham, Mass., 1990), p. 191; Bygrave and Timmons, *Venture Capital*, p. 167.
18. Personal communication from Bill Bygrave.
19. William A. Sahlman, 'Insights from the American venture capital organization', Harvard Business School, Nov. 1991.
20. Bruce A. Kinn and Arnold M. Zaff, 'The new SBIC program slowly comes to life', *Venture Capital Journal*, May 1993, pp. 37-40.
21. Bygrave and Timmons, *Venture Capital*, pp. 24-5, 202.
22. Ibid., pp. 246-9.
23. R. Premus, 'Venture capital and innovation', US Congressional Report, Joint Economic Committee, Washington, DC, Dec. 1984.
24. 'Do venture capitalists really need a tax break?', *Business Week*, 8 April 1985.
25. Benjamin M. Friedman, 'A benign tax increase – the myth that won't die', *Business Week*, 9 Jan. 1989, p. 22; Benjamin M. Friedman, 'Don't expect any capital-gains tax cut to nourish startups', *Business Week*, 8 April 1989, p. 20.
26. 'S corporations and small business stocks', Tax information planning series, no. 34, Price Waterhouse, revised May 1992.
27. Ibid.

3

VENTURE CAPITAL FUNDING IN GERMANY

The German venture capital industry is now a little over twenty-five years old. In common with most other venture capital markets, however, much of the growth in the German market has been achieved during the mid to late 1980s, although it has also continued to grow rapidly during the early 1990s, in contrast to several of the more mature national markets.[1] As a result, Germany is now the third largest venture capital market in Europe, after the UK and France, with estimated funds under management of approaching DM 7 billion by the end of 1992.[2]

Despite its recent expansion, the German market is still underdeveloped relative to the size of the economy, with cumulative investment equivalent to only around 0.2 per cent of GDP compared with over 1 per cent in the UK, and it remains almost entirely focused in West Germany.[3] The country possesses, however, many of the attributes which are key requirements for the development of a healthy venture capital industry, in particular a strong technology base and many successful small and medium-sized enterprises. As a result, the German venture capital association, the BVK, believes that there is considerable potential for further growth and has suggested that long-term investment could exceed DM 100 billion.[4]

Historically a mixture of cultural, social and structural factors combined to limit the progress of venture capital. Firstly, there was the posture adopted by the traditional lenders who, far from seeing venture capital as being complementary to their own activities, perceived it as a competitive threat. Secondly, among firms there was a reluctance to provide outside investors with information concerning the firm's objectives and its financial standing. This attitude persists today and is allied to a belief among German firms that their *raison d'être* is to generate cash surpluses in order to remain in business, rather than to maximize profit for distribution to shareholders. Lastly, there was an underlying aversion to external equity investors. This was particularly marked among *mittelstand* (that is, small and medium-sized) firms, who tended to consider drawing on external investors to fund a firm's development as a sign of weakness. (Indeed, external equity investors were usually used *only* by troubled firms, who required the funds to undertake a recovery plan.) As a result, only a total of DM 800 million had been invested in around 900 mittelstand firms by 1983.[5]

During the mid-1980s, however, the psychological resistance to venture capital weakened. This change in attitude towards venture capital was perceived as being driven by a number of factors:[6]

1 A Bundesbank survey showed that the proportion of equity in the balance sheets of German firms had fallen from an average of over 30 per cent during the 1960s to only 18 per cent by the end of 1982. In addition, this high gearing (usually composed of long-term loans) tended to be worse among the mittelstand and has persisted until today.
2 There was a growing appreciation of the success of venture capital in the USA and in certain European countries (the UK, France and the Netherlands), both in generating large profits for investors and in rejuvenating industry. Indeed, Germany's low interest rates made the 20 per cent returns being reported for venture capital very attractive to the banks, leading to an increased supply of both capital and firms willing to take advantage of such financing.
3 Continuing domestic economic growth, coupled with the need to prepare for the single European market, created a high demand for new capital to fund investment and new market entry.
4 There was a need to finance a generation change in the ownership of a large number of mittelstand firms, many of which were founded in the postwar period, with the new owners being drawn from the existing management.

Today, the recipients of venture capital are largely mittelstand firms, defined broadly as companies with between 20 and 500 employees. It is interesting to note that in contrast to many other countries, such firms are very powerful (both politically and economically) in Germany. For example, the German machine tool industry, which is comprised almost exclusively of mittelstand firms, is the leading manufacturer of machine tools in the world, employs over one million people, achieves an annual turnover of approaching DM 200 billion, and is Germany's second biggest exporter after the auto industry. The future success of the mittelstand, therefore, is recognized as being vital to the success of the whole economy.

Also interesting is the fact that increasing evidence suggests that the German venture capital industry is developing in a manner which is both more flexible and more closely aligned to the needs of its customers than elsewhere in Europe, helped by government-backed initiatives and the availability of tax efficient methods of investment. In addition, the dominant role played by the bank-owned venture capital groups, supported by the Länder banks, is leading to quicker integration of the industry into the financial infrastructure of the country.

Much of the data relating to the German market, outlined in the following sections of the chapter, has been sourced from the BVK and/or the EVCA. It should be noted, however, that the degree of detail available in this data is rather less than that for the more mature markets of the US or the UK

MARKET SIZE AND GROWTH

As was noted above, most of the industry's present size has been derived from a period of dramatic growth after the mid-1980s. Although this pattern is a common one for many of the European markets, what is perhaps surprising is the apparent increase in momentum of this growth over the last few years. Figure 3.1 shows our estimate of the total capital under management for the German venture capital industry over the last five years. The figures have generally been calculated from data appearing in the EVCA yearbooks for the period in question, by taking the year-end portfolio value and adding to it the estimated funds still available for investment.[7] Having said this, we have made certain estimated adjustments to the EVCA data appearing for the first two years, in order to try to show data which is comparable across the years.

One notable feature of the funds under management is the rapid increase in the amount of funds estimated by EVCA to be still available for investment at the year end, from DM 0.5 billion in 1990, to DM 1.0 billion in 1991, to DM 1.5 billion in 1992. That the above really represents a recent acceleration in the rate of growth can be seen by comparing the growth in the venture capital pool, shown in Fig. 3.1 (which relates to funds under management by both BVK members and non-BVK members), with the growth in the total amount *invested* in portfolio companies by BVK members (which, prior to 1988, probably followed the growth in the total pool quite closely).[8] This appears in Fig. 3.2. After eighteen years of extremely slow growth, the total investment portfolio of BVK members grew fivefold between 1983 and 1991, from DM 785 million to DM 4.1 billion. Over this period, the number of firms in which BVK members invested doubled to 2230, and the average size of investments rose by over two and a half times to DM 1.7 million.

Venture Capital Funding in Germany 71

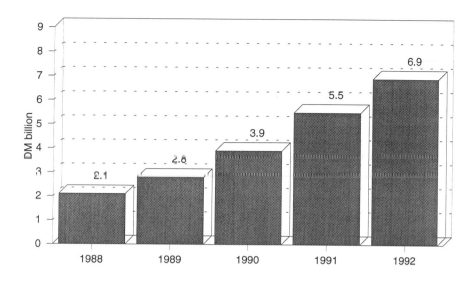

Figure 3.1 Estimated total capital under management as at year end, 1988–1992
(*Source*: adjusted EVCA data)

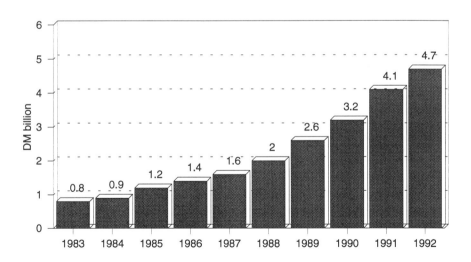

Figure 3.2 Total size of investment portfolio of BVK members as at year end, 1983–1992
(*Source*: BVK)

Consequently, although it took the German venture capital industry twenty years to reach a total portfolio figure of DM 1 billion in 1985, it took only another four years to increase the portfolio size to DM 2 billion, two further years to reach DM 3 billion, and one additional year to reach DM 4 billion. The total funds available for investment by BVK members rose to over DM 6 billion by the end of 1991.[9] Initial statistics from the BVK for 1992 suggest that the investment portfolio of BVK members rose to DM 4.7 billion in 2477 mittelstand firms by the end of 1992.[10]

As an explanation of the steep rise in the German venture capital pool over the last few years, capital commitments have been maintained at about DM 1.5 billion or so in each of 1990, 1991 and 1992, despite the recessionary environment among non-German investors.[11] In the geographical analysis in Fig. 3.3, it can be seen that a significant proportion of the capital committed had non-domestic sources. Principal among these were the Netherlands, the UK and France, within Europe, and the USA, outside Europe. This seems to support the view that investors from outside the country (who are presumably less partisan than the BVK and its members might quite naturally be) can also see the substantial potential for the role of venture capital within Germany.

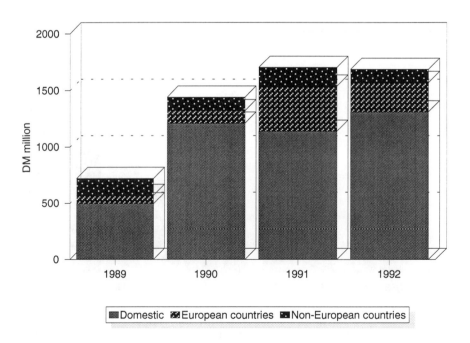

Figure 3.3 Capital commitments by geographical source, 1989–1992
(*Source*: EVCA)

Venture Capital Funding in Germany 73

As might be surmised from the increasing cash component of the venture capital pool, disbursements have tended to lag capital commitments somewhat in recent years. Nevertheless, the level of disbursements has remained healthy over the last three years, at around the DM 1.2 billion level, see Fig. 3.4.[12] In contrast to the situation seen in the USA, disbursements within Germany have been concentrated in the first round stage of investments. On the face of it, this would appear to be a quite reasonable occurrence, considering that the industry is still seeking to expand rapidly the portfolio of investee companies. Having said this, the bias towards first round investments could also be due to the industry investing a much larger proportion of its funds in companies which are unlikely to require further venture capital financing, such as later stage expansions and management buy-outs (MBOs). Indeed, we would suggest that this second possibility is at least a significant factor. In terms of the number of companies, however, there does appear to be an increasing proportion of follow-on investments as shown in Fig. 3.5.

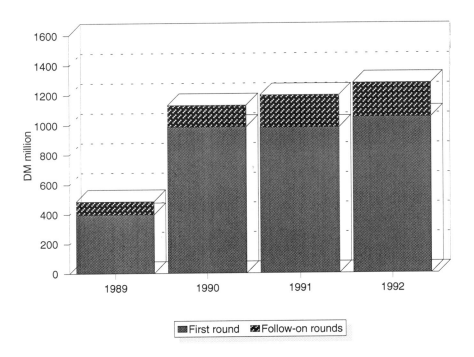

Figure 3.4 Total disbursements by round of financing, 1989–1992
(*Source*: EVCA)

74 The Funding Environment in Four Key Countries

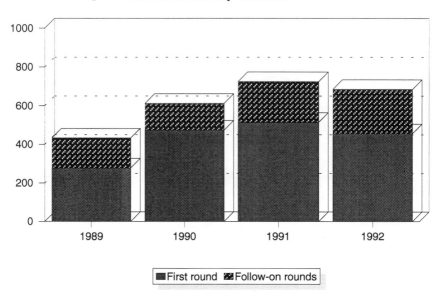

Figure 3.5 Numbers of companies financed by round of financing, 1989–1992
(*Source*: EVCA)

BREAKDOWN BY FUNDING STAGE

In Chapter 1 we noted that European venture capitalists as a whole appeared very unwilling to finance seed, start-up and early stage investments, relative to their US counterparts. In this regard, the German industry appears to be typical.[13] In considering Fig. 3.6 on disbursements by funding stage, it should be noted that the German definition of the 'seed stage' differs from the Anglo-American one. Seed capital in the German sense does not refer to capital required to explore a technical idea, but to capital required to prepare business plans, research potential markets and complete product development.[14] It is thus more akin to the Anglo-American 'start-up' stage.

Important points to note from Fig. 3.6 are:

1 expansion stage financing has dominated disbursements over the period;
2 after accounting for a declining share of disbursements between 1989 and 1991, the MBO share increased sharply in 1992. Driven by the 'generation change' occurring within the mittelstand, the proportion of disbursements represented by MBOs is expected to rise during the rest of the 1990s as MBOs play an increasing part in solving many mittelstand succession problems; and

3 seed and start-up financing, taken together, have seen a slightly increasing share of total disbursements since falling back from the high 1989 level.

When considered in terms of the number of companies financed, however, a slightly different and less volatile picture of disbursement by funding stage is seen (Fig. 3.7).

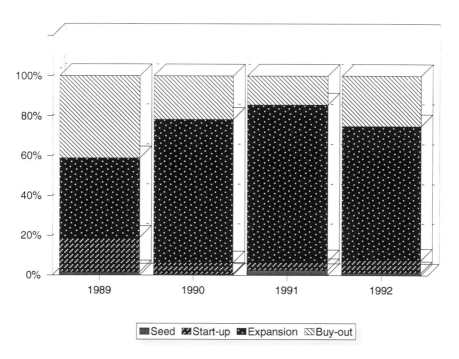

Figure 3.6 Disbursements by funding stage as a proportion of total amount disbursed, 1989–1992
(*Source*: EVCA)

INDUSTRY SECTORS ATTRACTING INVESTMENT

In our chapter on the USA we saw how it was possible to discern clear and rational trends in industry sector investment by US venture capitalists over a fourteen-year period (Fig. 2.11). Unfortunately, such long-term data is not available for industry sector investment by venture capitalists within Germany, and we have had to rely on annual data relating only to relatively recent years. This has had the effect of making any trends more difficult to perceive and less certain.

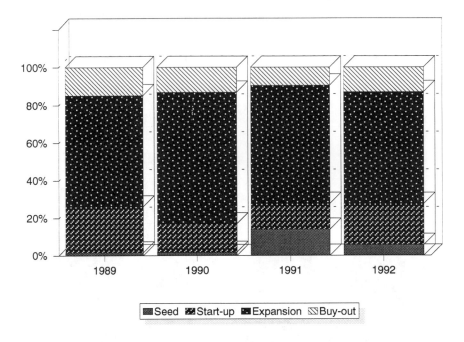

Figure 3.7 Disbursements by funding stage as a porportion of total number of disbursements, 1989–1992
(*Source*: EVCA)

Figure 3.8 shows the amount disbursed to each industry sector, as a percentage of the total amount invested, for each of the four years 1989 to 1992. Because of the relatively short timescale, individual sectoral investment trends are difficult to spot in many cases. A more interesting trend emerges, however, when sectors are grouped. By adding together the total *number* of companies financed within the first six categories of Fig. 3.8 (communications, computer-related products, other electronics, biotechnology/medical/healthcare, chemicals/materials and industrial automation), which one might regard as being the technology-based sectors, and expressing this number as a percentage of the total number of companies financed during each year, the picture in Fig. 3.9 can be observed. It shows a trend (admittedly somewhat short term) *away* from technology-based investments. This would seem to be the exact opposite to the long-term trend within the US, moving increasingly *towards* technology-based investments.

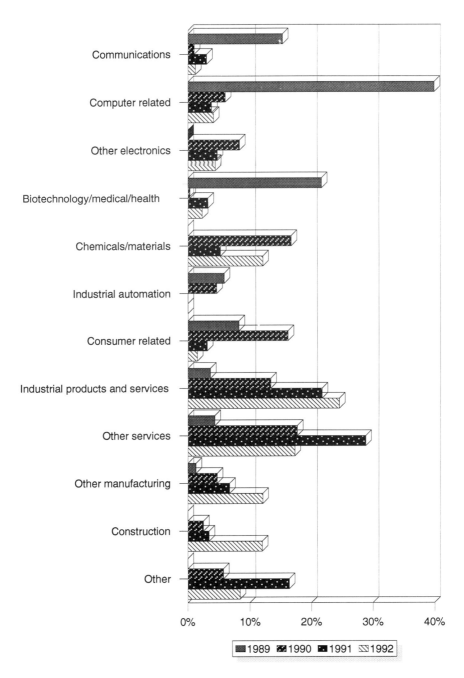

Figure 3.8 Disbursements by industry sector as a proportion of total amount disbursed, 1989–1992
(*Source*: EVCA)

78   The Funding Environment in Four Key Countries

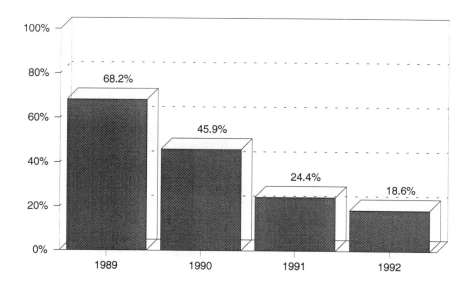

Figure 3.9 Number of technology-based companies financed as a percentage of all financings, 1989–1992
(*Source*: derived from EVCA data)

Having said this, repeating the above exercise in 'disbursement' terms shows a modest increase for 1992 (24.1 per cent) over 1991 (19.9 per cent). Nevertheless, the 1992 technology-based disbursement share is still at less than two-thirds of the 1990 level (39.8 per cent) and less than one-third of the 1989 level (82.6 per cent).

In summary, therefore, the technology-based investment trend within Germany is entirely in accordance with the view expressed earlier, that European venture capital investment in technology-based areas has been on a declining trend of late. Indeed, it is perhaps remarkable that this should be the case in arguably the most technologically advanced country within Western Europe.

INVESTMENT SIZE

The average amount disbursed per transaction has remained at around DM 1.75 million over the last three years.[15] This followed the steep jump between 1989 and 1990 caused by a sharp hike in the average amount disbursed to expansion stage investments (which, as we saw earlier, came to constitute

60–70 per cent of all financings). The changes can be seen in Fig. 3.10. One other trend which is apparent from the figure, and which contrasts to the situation with expansion stage investments, is that the average amount disbursed to start-up and (particularly) seed transactions has fallen significantly.

One explanation for these two trends could be that the venture capitalists sought to reduce their 'up-front' exposure to the more risky investments (that is, seed and start-up), while increasing their exposure to good, lower risk expansion financings. Since venture capitalists probably had less control over the number of good deals they were offered than they had over the amount invested in each deal, they opted to reduce the average *size* of seed and start-up disbursements while seeking to put more money into each expansion transaction. In order to achieve the size reduction for seed and start-up deals, it is believed that these transactions became subject to a much greater degree of syndication than had hitherto been practised.

Finally, it should be remembered that the venture capitalists had a large amount of funds to invest, which could be more easily achieved by simply raising the size of later stage deals.

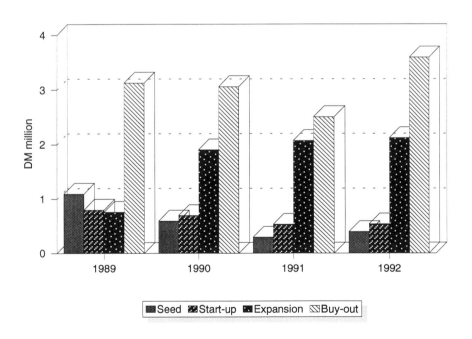

Figure 3.10 Average size of disbursement by stage of investment, 1989–1992
(*Source*: derived from EVCA data)

CHARACTERISTICS OF INVESTORS

German venture capital fund investors can be classified into the following: banks; insurance companies; corporations; private individuals; government agencies; and other investors. Notably absent from this list are pension funds which, although forming the backbone of investment in the Anglo-Saxon economies, play little or no direct role in Germany. It is believed, however, that the risk-averse pension funds buy bank bonds which can be thought of as financing the banks' venture capital funds. Figures 3.11 and 3.12 outline the relative importance to venture capital fund financing of each of these investor types over the last four years. What is immediately obvious is that the banking community has stepped in to fill the void left by the absence of direct pension fund investors, accounting as it does for over half of total capital commitments. The rise in the importance of insurance companies and the decline in importance of government agencies are also notable trends.

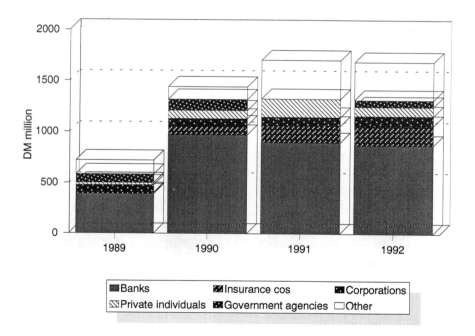

Figure 3.11 Capital commitments by source in value terms, 1989–1992
(*Source*: EVCA)

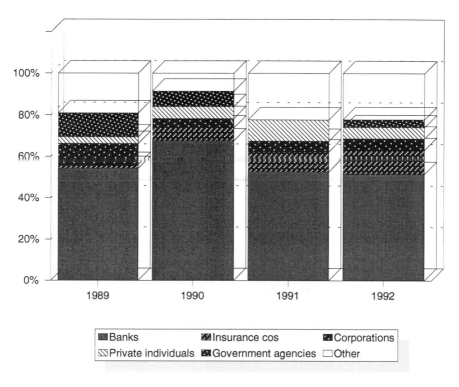

Figure 3.12 Capital commitments by source as a proportion of total amount commited, 1989–1992
(*Source*: EVCA)

FUNDING SOURCES AND METHODS

The eighty-five active venture capital investors in Germany fall into six categories.[16] There are the Kapitalbeteiligungsgesellschaften (KBGs) of the large banks and insurance companies (that is, their venture capital subsidiaries); the KBGs of local banks; venture capital groups; the Mittelständische Beteiligungsgesellschaften (MBGs/Länderfonds – see below); seed capital funds; and other capital investment companies. Furthermore, each of these groups can in turn be characterized along a number of dimensions, including the purpose of the investment, the method of making the investment (direct or 'silent'), whether management support is provided or not, and the phase of investment undertaken.

Before we discuss each in more detail, Figs. 3.13 and 3.14 outline the importance of these types of venture capital investor, both in terms of the total venture capital portfolio and the number of portfolio companies.

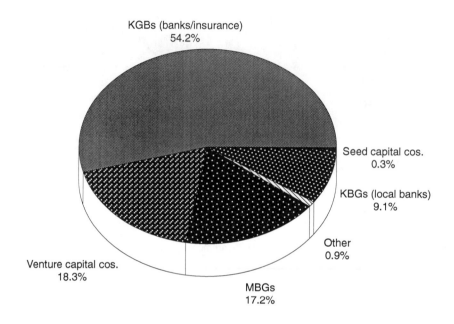

Figure 3.13 Shares of total venture capital portfolio by type of investor (cumulative to mid-1992)
(*Source*: Fraunhofer-Institut)

KBGs of the large banks and insurance companies

The Kapitalbeteiligungsgesellschaften of the large banks and insurance companies (their venture capital subsidiaries) constitute the most important group of companies, accounting for roughly 30 per cent of investment institutions and no less than 50 per cent of the total venture capital portfolio value. These organizations focus solely on the yield from their investments and only become involved in the management of a company within their portfolio in the event of a crisis situation arising. As a result, they tend to favour large investments in expansion stage firms, the average size of investment being over DM 4 million. The form of investment used is a mixture of direct equity and silent partnerships.

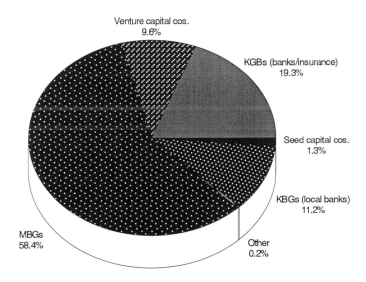

Figure 3.14 Shares of total number of portfolio companies by type of investor (cumulative to mid-1992)
(*Source*: Fraunhofer-Institut)

By way of example, the Deutsche Beteiligungsgesellschaft (DBG), which is the venture capital arm of the Deutsche Bank, is the largest provider of venture capital in Germany, with six funds and DM 640 million invested in 176 companies in 1992.[17] Its most common method of investment is to place one-third of the investment in direct equity and two-thirds in the form of a silent partnership. Only 10 per cent or so of its investment portfolio, however, is in early stage firms. Other large KBGs include the subsidiaries of the Dresdner Bank and the Westdeutsche Landesbank.

In the past these groups have also provided investment capital to new independent venture capital funds, but they are now focusing on their own subsidiaries. Emphasis is being placed on integrating venture capital operations into the broad range of banking services offered and the banks are becoming less passive in their outlook. In addition, DBG for example has been employing the management consultancy Roland Berger with a view to providing active management support for its portfolio companies.

The bank-owned KBGs have traditionally been long-term investors although, in due course, they are willing to consider any exit method and frequently use the management buy-back to achieve this goal. As the banks have become more exposed to financial risk in the former East Germany, however, they have begun to impose tighter financial discipline on their existing corporate customers in the West.

KBGs of local banks

The second most numerous group of venture capital providers, representing roughly a quarter of the total, are the KBGs of the Sparkassen, Genossenschaftsbanken and Volksbanken, that is to say, the local banks. In spite of their numbers they account for less than 10 per cent of the venture capital portfolio. For these players, the *economic* aspects of their investments (that is, the benefits accruing to the local economy and the provision of new customer groups), in addition to the return achieved, are important considerations. The silent partnership form of investment is preferred but, as with the KBGs of the large banks and insurance companies, a mixture of the direct and silent forms is often used. The activities of these institutions, however, are limited to the region in which they are based.

In general, both kinds of KBG operate largely as open funds which draw money from their parent organizations as required, although in some cases funds are also drawn from industrial companies. This makes access to funds straightforward, but leaves the KBGs exposed to relatively harsh treatment by the German tax system.

It should be noted that although KBGs do make investments in early stage companies, the value of these investments is small in relation to their overall portfolios. Indeed, it is generally considered that the banks do not understand the requirements of early stage investment and the ways they differ from those of the expansion stage. As a consequence, the international venture capital groups, who have foreign experience of early stage investing, and the specialist seed capital funds, founded more recently to focus on early stage companies, tend to serve this market more effectively.

Venture capital groups

Pure venture capital companies form the third largest group of firms, accounting for approaching 20 per cent of the total. A significant proportion of these firms are part of international groupings or networks, such as Advent, Apax, Atlas and Euroventures, although probably the largest is TVM with a DM 355 million portfolio (DM 41 million of which is invested in NTBFs).[18] These organizations attempt to bring their wider US or European experience to bear in Germany and seek high returns through capital gains, as is the case in the

UK or the US. They adopt a much more active approach to investing than the KBGs (via the provision of management support to their investee firms) and, generally speaking, use the direct equity form of investment. The investment period is most often between seven and ten years, with exit being achieved through a trade sale or flotation.

Far from hindering their progress, being a purely foreign venture capital group can have distinct advantages. It is possible for certain types of investors to avoid a German tax system which can be tough in its treatment of venture capital investments. International groups can also use overseas contacts to put together international syndicates of investors, to conduct market research and even to help investee firms open overseas subsidiaries.

The first German independent venture capital firm, Wagnisfinanzierungs Gesellschaft (WFG), was set up in 1975 on the initiative of two government ministries and the German industry association. It was intended that WFG should supplement the activities of the KBGs and thus its initial capital was provided by twenty-nine German banks. After restructuring under the ownership of five banks in 1982, however, WFG was finally bought by Deutsche Bank in 1988 and has since been integrated into DBG.

Most other independent German venture capital companies have been set up since 1982. Although they invariably have a broad shareholder base, such firms frequently have strong links to one or more banks and/or major corporate investors. By way of example, the principal shareholders in International Venture Capital Managers, a fund managed by GENES (one of the first independent German firms) included Chase Manhattan Bank, Elf Acquitaine, 3i plc, Johnson and Johnson Development Corporation and Prudential Venture Capital Management.

The strong grip of the banks on all aspects of business makes it hard for truly independent firms to become established. The banks now regard provision of venture capital as part of an overall package of services which they offer to corporate clients and, as a result, they look on the independent firms as competition for their services. In addition, most companies seeking finance will go to their banker in the first instance and only seek financing elsewhere if it is refused by the banks (which are unlikely to refer work to these perceived competitors).

With regard to the provision of venture capital to early stage companies, one of the most active firms has been Technologieholding GmbH, based in Munich. Technologieholding has made twenty investments in early-stage, technology-based firms over the past two years and has been one of the major users of the BJTU scheme (described below).

Finally, the last type of firm in the pure venture capital group are the foreign owned buy-out specialists such as Citicorp Venture Capital. Citicorp, like other firms of this type, generally attempts to apply the traditional, standard US MBO/MBI approach to German companies. It is expected that because of the 'generation change' described earlier this type of firm will increase its market share during the 1990s.

MBGs/Länderfonds

The Mittelständische Beteiligungsgesellschaften add up to 13 per cent of the total number of firms. These organizations were founded as a result of the German government's Programm zur Förderung der Beteiligungsfinanzierung bei kleinen und mittelständischen Unternehmen ('programme to promote venture capital for small and medium-sized firms'), initiated in 1970. It was designed along the lines of 'help for self-help' and it was the intention that it would largely be funded by the Länder. The Länder, in turn, would primarily draw their funds for such financing from the European Recovery Program (a throwback to the Marshall Plan era), which disburses several DM billion each year for investment in small and medium-sized firms.

The MBGs, therefore, have clear economic and political objectives and are now supported by local government funds. Their 'hands-off' investments (there is usually no management support provided) are made using almost exclusively the silent partnership form of investment and in 1992 their total portfolio stood at DM 500 million. Most of this investment has been in expansion stage firms, while the exit method used is almost exclusively through management buy-backs.

Typical of the way MBGs operate is the scheme in Bavaria. In 1972 the Bavarian state ministry for the economy and the Bavarian state agency for development financing (the LfA) founded two new organizations: 'die KBG für die mittelständische Wirtschaft Bayerns mbH' (KBG for the Bavarian mittelstand economic community), in effect an MBG; and 'die Bayerische Garantiegesellschaft mbH für mittelständische Beteiligungen' (BGG), the Bavarian credit guaranty organization for investments in mittelstand firms. Today the former organization is charged with investing in mittelstand businesses (most frequently in the form of a silent partnership), while the BGG offers 70 per cent guarantees on investments made by the MBG, based on guarantees received from both the national and state governments. These guarantees last for up to ten years, although a further ten-year extension is possible.

Such a financing structure can hold the cost of MBG funding at very low levels and, indeed, it was recently estimated to be around 9.5 per cent.[19] The

LfA also offers to provide further low interest loans either instead of, or in addition to, the credit backed investment by the MBG.

The Länder of Baden-Württemberg, Hessen, Hamburg, Saarland, Nordrhein-Westfalen and Rheinland-Pfalz also operate schemes which are in principle similar to that in Bavaria, although the MBGs in Baden-Württemberg, Hessen and Bavaria are the most active. For example, during 1991 the MBG in Baden-Württemberg made 166 investments, mostly ranging between DM 50,000 and DM 100,000, but some as high as DM 1 million.

Seed capital funds

Eight organizations, roughly 10 per cent of the total, are fundamentally seed capital investors. These companies operate regionally, with most investments being 'within an hour's drive from the office', and they are ready to offer management advice should it be required. Some of the better known of these organizations are Seed Capital Fund GmbH in Berlin (a BVK member, although most are not), Refit GmbH in Bavaria, and Technostart based in Stuttgart. The majority of the seed capitalists are based in southern Germany, where high technology activity in Germany is focused.

These seed capital companies manage open funds which are often provided by a local bank, although they seek similar rates of return to the venture capital groups. They have extremely close ties to their main sources of capital and operate, essentially, as their autonomous subsidiaries. The seed funds are mostly very small and fundraising/refinancing can present a particular problem for them. Generally only a small number of investments are made each year; for example by September 1992 Seed Capital Fund GmbH had made only six investments since it was established in April 1990.[20]

It should be remembered, however, that although such firms run so-called 'seed capital' funds, in Germany the term 'seed capital' is sometimes used to refer to a company which is at or around the start-up phase. Thus a company in which a seed capital fund invests may already have a product (which could have been developed in a technology centre, for example) and requires the funds to bring this product to market. In the light of this, 'seed capital funds' should be thought of as handling both seed *and* start-up investments.

Early stage venture capital investing is reported to be experiencing something of a revival in Germany at present, based on support from both German government and EC initiatives, particularly the BJTU pilot scheme which is described in detail later. The seed capital funds are a very important factor in this revival.

Other capital investment companies

Organizations in our last category operate using funds supplied by private individuals or industrial companies. Often they are based around an individual with investment experience, who uses personal contacts to source deals and obtain funding. Little is known about the extent of their activities, but at the end of 1990 the Fraunhofer-Institut had identified four which were active.

The focus of these investment companies is on profit orientated investments in innovative growth companies, with exit being usually achieved through a trade sale. Investments are made either directly (via equity) or sometimes using an atypical silent partnership, which permits a greater degree of investor participation in the management of the company than the typical form. These firms are willing to invest in companies purely to support product development, in other words, to support true seed stage investments in the Anglo-American sense. It is notable that they avoid the BJTU scheme, however, because the administrative overhead and amount of effort involved in applying for this kind of funding is too high for them to bear.[21]

The silent partnership method of investment

There are two principal methods in Germany by which venture capital investments are made: a direct investment in equity, or an investment using a 'stille beteiligung' or silent partnership (although often a mixture of the two methods is used). While equity investment is essentially the same as in the UK, the silent partnership is unique to Germany and, therefore, requires further explanation.

German venture capital firms, the KBGs in particular, are anxious not to hold majority stakes in companies. This would be looked on very unfavourably by the entrepreneurs, who would not wish to let an external investor have control over their business, especially one who wants to exit in a few years' time. In the case of the KBGs, which do not wish to share in the management of the company, a majority stake would also not be consistent with their investment objectives. The solution to this problem is the silent partnership method of investment.

One of the essential features of a silent partnership is that it allows the venture capitalist to make a large investment in a firm without becoming the majority shareholder. In addition, and probably more importantly from the point of view of most investors, it also offers tax benefits which can reduce the aftertax financing costs considerably for both the investor and the entrepreneur. In particular, while the banks view a silent partnership investment as equity, for tax purposes it is viewed as debt. As a result, the investor is able to claim losses in a silent partnership investment as expense items for tax purposes. The case studies in the Appendix at the end of this chapter indicate how a silent partnership would be used as part of an investment.

There are two forms of silent partnership, a 'typical' and an 'atypical' form, each having different implications for the investor with respect to the taxation and management of the business. Not surprisingly, the typical form of silent partnership is the one most commonly used, particularly by the KBGs and MBGs. The following are the key features of an investment made using this form.[22]

1 It is a fixed, low interest rate loan (due to the investor's ability to obtain tax relief on financing costs), with profit participation. In this sense it can be considered a hybrid between loan and equity capital.
2 It also 'participates' in the losses of the company (which can then be offset against the investor's own tax liability), but only up to the extent of the investment. It does not participate in any equity growth, however, and it is typically due to be paid back at par after five to ten years.
3 It ranks between loan and equity in the balance sheet, but is unsecured, so that the silent partner's rights are no better than those of any other unsecured creditor in the event of the company becoming insolvent.
4 It is viewed as equity by the banks, but is treated as a loan for tax purposes. As a result, the income of a silent partner is treated as income from capital. From the company's point of view, the profit participation of the silent partner, in addition to the fixed interest payments, is deductible for tax purposes.
5 A silent partner need not be disclosed, but is not *entitled* to be actively involved in the management of the company.

The atypical form of silent partnership has recently been brought to life, as investment institutions have sought a means to access the large pool of private (business angel) financial assets in Germany, estimated at over DM 100 billion in 1990.[23] A higher level of risk compared with the typical form is offset by the chance for higher returns and certain tax advantages. For tax purposes, the atypical form allows income from a silent partnership to be treated as business income, not income from capital. As a result the silent partner achieves the same tax position as a partner of a commercial partnership. For the investor using the atypical form, this means that any payments made to the investor are subject to half the average tax rate which would otherwise apply.

Specifically, the most important differences between the atypical form and the typical form are as follows.[24]

1 The silent partner is granted certain rights and entitlements with regard to their role in the *active* management of the business.

2 The silent partner can also 'participate' in the equity/asset growth of the business through various arrangements which do not involve the ownership of either equity or assets. Following on from this, the atypical form can be seen as being somewhat closer to equity than the typical form.
3 For taxation purposes, the atypical form is treated in a similar manner to a partner in a commercial partnership, hence income is taxed as 'business income'. As such, capital gains are tax-free after the investment has been held for six months, and income from the investment is taxed at only half the normal rate.

THE VENTURE CAPITALIST/ENTREPRENEUR RELATIONSHIP

The nature of the relationship between the entrepreneur and the venture capital firm will depend very much on the operating style of the latter. We saw above that KBGs and MBGs are passive investors, who make a large part (if not all) of their investment in the form of a silent partnership. On the other hand, the independent venture capital firms and the seed capitalists (who invariably invest only via equity) are much more active investors and believe that they are able to offer hands-on management expertise.

Given the position of the banks within the German economy, the KBG subsidiary of a bank is often the first place for an entrepreneur to go when seeking venture capital funds for a business. For the majority of entrepreneurs the fact that the banks will support the ultimate management buy-back of any equity purchased by the KBG is considered an advantage. In addition, the banks are also willing to continue being long-term partners after the KBG has exited, and believe that they are able to offer significant and helpful advice, although in reality the bank assumes very much a monitoring role.

Once it has invested in a business, a KBG will supervise its investment using formal quarterly meetings with the entrepreneur and will often take an advisory seat on the supervisory board of the company. In practice, the business and the KBG will often be in contact monthly, to discuss the most important results and events. For the early-stage, technology-based firm, however, it is less likely that a KBG will fully understand the challenges to be faced. As a result, this is an area where the more specialist venture capital firms and the seed capital funds believe that they can add value.

In contrast to the KBGs and MBGs, seed capital funds seek to invest in situations where they give more than just financial help and will be proactive in sourcing deals (often relying on a network of previous contacts built up by their partners). Typically they will tend to look for firms in the process of being formed to exploit inventions from a local technology centre, or new firms emerging from public support programmes for NTBFs. As such, seed capital firms tend to undertake an investment strategy which has a much higher dependence on their belief in the potential of NTBFs than do the bank KBGs and MBGs. After the investment has been made, they frequently become actively involved in the management of the company and will help it to prepare materials for trade fairs, for marketing launches, etc. Often they will undertake negotiations with the firm's bank on its behalf and may even offer the firm direct help in selling its products.

Finally, firms which are willing to entertain a venture capitalist may typically have sought bank financing without success or be looking for a different product from that offered by the banks, for example the provision of active management support. They will, therefore, usually require an equity investor to take them forward and the finance will frequently be required quickly.

PERIOD OF INVESTMENT, EXIT OPPORTUNITIES AND VALUATION

The total amount of divestments by the German venture capital industry over the last four years is shown in Fig. 3.15. Note that the figures shown represent the *historical cost* of the divestments and not the actual amount of cash received by the venture capitalists.

The average period of investment in Germany varies considerably, depending on the type of investor and investee. On the one hand, the independent venture capital firms tend to look for an exit timeframe of seven to ten years from the time of the initial investment, similar to the Anglo-American model. On the other hand the KBGs and MBGs, with easy access to open funds, are able and willing to invest for much longer periods. For example, DBG typically expects to exit after a period of up to ten years, but has had investments which have lasted for over twenty years.

Once an exit is sought, however, four principal exit mechanisms are used: a management buy-back (sometimes phased); a sale to an institutional investor; a trade sale to an industrial company; a flotation.

If the investee firm is very successful, the option of a management buy-back can usually be discounted as a commercial possibility, as the founders would not be able to afford a market price for the company. Consequently, the independent venture capital firms have tended to use management buy-backs as an exit method for the 'living dead' (the less successful and modestly

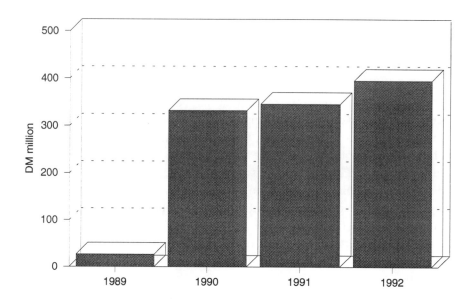

Figure 3.15 Amounts divested by venture capitalists (at historical cost), 1989–1992
(*Source*: EVCA)

unsuccessful companies). However, KBG investors in particular are now looking at management buy-backs as a method of reducing risk in the form of phased buy-back deals. In addition, the MBGs use management buy-backs almost exclusively, although industrial promotion, not profit, is their principal motive for doing so.

Sale to an institutional investor is generally the least attractive route, as institutional investors usually seek to reduce the purchase price so that their yield requirements are more easily met. A trade sale to an industrial company is usually likely to achieve the highest price (especially for NTBFs) in Germany, as the buyer will tend to pay a premium for strategic control. Often the buyer will be drawn from the existing contacts of the venture capital company or the investee firm. As a result, many of the smaller seed capital firms are careful, right from the beginning of their investment in the company, to cultivate contacts with large corporations that may provide an exit route.

Finally, flotations remain relatively unpopular. In this regard, the BVK has noted that the existing means for achieving flotations are sufficient but are just not used; that in comparison with many other countries flotation is not more difficult in Germany, only more unpopular; that the banks have set the size of firms they will consider for flotation too high; and that the large banks prefer to float large companies, because these carry a lower risk. As noted earlier, however, German companies' dislike of flotation as an exit route is probably principally caused by a wish to avoid the publicity and disclosure requirements associated with it. (Having said this, a number of venture capital groups, including Atlas, Barings and TVM, have developed methods to float German NTBFs on the US Nasdaq.)[25] Providing an additional disincentive is the cost of flotation in Germany, which is very high, often amounting to around 9 per cent of the revenues generated from the issue (compared with perhaps between a half and two-thirds of that in the US, UK and Japan).

Some of the problems above, such as the minimum size of firm the banks will consider for flotation and the high cost, can be alleviated to some extent by opting for a listing on Germany's second or third markets (the 'regulated market' and 'free market', respectively). These markets invariably suffer, however, from liquidity problems. (The three levels of market listing are described in more detail in the Appendix to this chapter.)

In summary, the resistance to flotation and the difficulties associated with valuing companies for trade sale have made exits particularly problematic in Germany. As a consequence of the predominance of MBG investments, however, management buy-backs, a mechanism seldom used in the Anglo-American world, account for the majority of exits achieved in Germany.

Where valuation is concerned, one particular problem with German trade sales is the ability to strike a fair price, as the markets for trading companies (both listed and corporate) are very thin. In consequence, parties usually reach an agreement based on the perceived future earnings potential of the firm, coupled with a limited 'earn-out' component which allows for the contract price to be adjusted according to specified criteria. Having said this, exit multiples of *aftertax* earnings for similar firms are reported to be comparable to those for UK companies.[26]

RETURNS REQUIRED BY THE PROVIDERS OF DEBT AND EQUITY

The rates of return required by the providers of funds in Germany are much more difficult to calculate than that for the United States. This is principally due to the various taxation arrangements (such as silent partnerships) and other government supported schemes, coupled with a broader variety of types of venture capital investor, a significant number having other than purely return related objectives. Nevertheless, it would appear that the required returns are in general significantly lower on many comparable investments than those we saw for the United States.

Defining the required pretax rate of return in the same way as we did for the US, as the target nominal pretax return on equity investment, or nominal pretax cost for debt-like instruments, Table 3.1 summarizes the required return for each provider.[27] It should be noted, however, that because of the favourable taxation treatment of silent partnerships, the *effective/equivalent* pretax returns on investments made using such instruments are estimated to be at least 4–5 per cent higher.

Particular considerations which influence the required/target return in Germany are the stage of investment, so that the earlier the stage the higher the required/target return; the type of investor and the form of investment; and then other factors specific to the individual investment, such as negotiating strengths, technological risks and so on. With regard to early stage financing, typically a seed or start-up firm would expect (in the absence of subsidies) to rely largely on funding from a seed capitalist for its first round of financing, which would usually take the form of equity. As a result, the target nominal pretax return might be of the order of 40–45 per cent.

Although, theoretically, the BJTU scheme described below is designed for the first and second rounds of financing, the length of the application procedure will often preclude this kind of financing in the first round. If BJTU funding is secured by the second round, however, it will generally be possible for seed capitalist investment to be matched up to and including that round. As can be seen from Table 3.1, the presence of BJTU capital dramatically reduces the weighted average returns required on funds provided to the early stage company.

Following on from the above, a venture capital group would tend to become involved in financing from the second round onwards, although the target rate of return is likely to be at least as high from this source, possibly driven by the more 'international' expectations of returns of this group of providers. Finally, KBGs and MBGs may become involved in early stage financing (particularly an MBG if this is the policy of the Länder in which it is based), but their participation will be limited. The target rate of return shown for these sources, therefore, is weighted towards later stage transactions.

One of the most important aspects of the provision of venture capital within Germany is that the various schemes which exist to provide essentially mezzanine type financing, particularly with regard to early stage companies, lead to a significant reduction in the weighted target returns on venture capital backed investments.

Table 3.1 Estimated nominal target return on funds by source, mid-1993

Source	Form of investment	Nominal target return
Bank	Overdraft	Base rate + 2–5 % (8.5–11.5 %)
Bank	Long-term loan	Base rate + 0.5–1.5% (7–8 %)
MBG	Silent partnership	9.5 %
KBG	Silent partnership and /or equity	10–20 %
Seed capital fund	Equity (occasionally silent partnership)	Broadly aiming to exit on multiple of 10 after 6 or 7 years. Therefore 40–45 %
Venture capital group	Equity (for early stage companies)	Broadly aiming to exit on multiple of 5 after 4 years. Therefore 50 %
BJTU (TBG or KfW)	Silent partnership	Base rate –2.5 % (currently 5 %) + profit participation Therefore approx. 9 %

GOVERNMENT INITIATIVES

As part of the German government's philosophy it believes that small and medium-sized enterprises (and NTBFs in particular) must receive help to overcome the difficulties they face as a result of their initially weaker market position. Indeed, the extent of this help can be seen from an Anglo-German Foundation estimate, which noted that during the 1988–9 period, the German government devoted around £1.8 billion of dedicated resources to the SME sector. By way of comparison, the figure for Britain was at most £500 million (indeed, the true figure might be as low as £150 million).[28]

The first serious attempt to promote NTBFs within Germany began in 1975, when the Bundesministerium für Forschung und Technologie (BMFT – the Federal Ministry for Research and Technology) created a pilot venture capital scheme under the Deutsche Wagnisfinanzierung GmbH. This scheme (in operation until 1984) was essentially an attempt to create a private sector risk financing system which would specifically seek to make the results of state-supported R&D available for general use.

The next attempt, the Technologie Unternehmensgründungen (TOU) scheme, was initiated in 1983 and operated until December 1988. Under the TOU, direct government subsidies were provided to NTBFs, with the intention that this would facilitate understanding of the various aspects of early stage financing. Following its termination, and based on its findings, it was superseded in 1989 by the Beteiligungskapital für junge Technologieunternehmen (BJTU) scheme.

During the 1980s the government also brought in laws to permit the formation of another new type of organization, known as an Unternehmensbeteiligungsgesellschaft (UBG). These UBGs were given certain tax advantages designed to encourage venture capital investment, although they were not successful in encouraging new funding and have since become almost indistinguishable from KBGs – indeed, for our purposes, no distinction between UBGs and KBGs has been drawn.

The BJTU scheme

As the German venture capital industry expanded in the late 1980s, the proportion of investments represented by early stage companies dropped sharply. According to one report, whereas in 1986 12 per cent of total investment was in seed and start-up businesses, this proportion had fallen to only 7 per cent by 1991.[29] Given that the improved profile of venture capital within Germany had arisen largely from a recognition of the benefits enjoyed in the US from early stage investments in computer and electronics firms, this situation caused considerable concern. As a result the German government (as well as the EC) concluded that, without some form of state intervention, private early stage investing would soon no longer be deemed a viable proposition.

In 1989, therefore, the BMFT started the BJTU pilot scheme in an effort to encourage the provision of venture capital for young technology-based firms. This scheme supplanted and evolved from the TOU initiative, being heavily influenced by the experience gained during that programme. The scheme was designed to operate for five years, until 1994, and to have access to around DM 300 million of funds with which to provide *indirect* subsidies (as against *direct* subsidies under the TOU).[30] The BJTU is focused on technology-based early-stage firms which are less than three years old; it aims to create a supply of risk capital which will facilitate investment for R&D and market entry by such firms.

It is generally agreed that the BJTU scheme is one of the most generous programmes operating within Europe, not only because of the cheap financing it provides, but also because of the exit options which are provided to venture capital investors. Unfortunately, the BJTU suffers from one major drawback, in the form of its time-consuming and complex application procedure, which can take up to a year to complete. In consequence, as we noted earlier, the administrative burden has deterred many smaller firms from using the scheme.

The BJTU has three principal objectives:

1 to encourage venture capital and business investment in early stage, technology-based companies;
2 to facilitate the learning process among investors to enable them to develop best practice for the assessment and acquisition of early-stage, technology-based firms, and for providing management assistance to them;
3 to assess the level of public involvement required to ensure an adequate supply of capital for early stage investments.

Because of the different investment methods used in Germany (silent, direct, or a mixture), the BJTU has two forms: the coinvestment form, and the refinancing form. Each offers a different method of access to the venture capital firms.

The coinvestment form is operated by the Technologie Beteiligungsgesellschaft (TBG), the technology investment subsidiary of the Deutsche Ausgleichsbank. Under this scheme, the TBG makes an investment equal to that of the venture capitalist investor (subject to a ceiling of DM 1 million) in the form of a silent partnership, although investors are free to use their preferred investment method. In addition, the TBG will secure up to 60 per cent of the investor's investment for up to three years, leaving the venture capitalist exposed to only 20–30 per cent of the investment risk for this period (providing, of course, that the investment amount is less than the DM 1 million ceiling).[31] Under the terms of the scheme, venture capitalists may choose during the first three years to sell their investment in the venture to the TBG, at a discount of 40–60 per cent. This provides the venture capitalist with an exit route should the investment prove to be a poor one. Alternatively, the venture capitalist may choose to purchase the TBG's stake during this period, subject to a surcharge of around 25 per cent.

The coinvestment form thus grants the venture capitalist two intrinsically valuable options: a 'put' option to sell its investment for at least 40 per cent of the amount invested; and a 'call' option to buy the TBG's investment for a 25 per cent premium to the amount invested. While it is difficult to calculate the precise value of these options to the venture capitalist, a back of the envelope spreadsheet calculation, using a modified Black & Scholes model, suggests that they might reasonably be worth roughly one-quarter of the amount invested by the venture capitalist (although they are provided at *no cost* to this investor)!

The conditions attached to the coinvestment form are:

1. the TBG investment is limited to DM 1 million;
2. there can be *no* participation in the losses of the firm;
3. the maximum investment period is set at ten years;
4. there is an option for a premature cancellation of the agreement by the firm;
5. there are conditions, specific to each investment, relating to the fixed interest rate on the investment and an additional profit dependent payment.

The alternative refinancing form is operated by the Kreditanstalt für Wiederaufbau (KfW), the German government agency for economic redevelopment. This scheme allows the venture capitalist to obtain an interest-free refinancing loan (which comes with a 90 per cent guarantee), limited to DM 1 million per investment, for a period of up to ten years. In return for this refinancing loan, the KfW receives 40 per cent of the income which the venture capitalist derives from the investment. The net effect of the refinancing scheme, therefore, is that the venture capitalist risks 10 per cent of the amount invested (subject once again to a ceiling of DM1 million) in return for 60 per cent of the income from the investment. One of the most important features of the refinancing form is that it overcomes the liquidity problem of early stage investors.

Of the two alternatives, the refinancing form has proved to be the more popular, not least because it is not necessarily linked to individual investments. The venture capitalist can, for example, obtain the loan for a portfolio of investments and is, therefore, saved the cost of administering an application to the BJTU each time an investment is made. As another point in its favour, the refinancing form also avoids introducing another investor into the syndicate and hence the associated complications. Having said this, there are nevertheless clear preferences for one form or another between different investors.

Up until 31 August 1992, 143 investments had been made using the BJTU provisions, of which 99 had used the refinancing form and 44 the coinvestment form. The total of finance provided under the BJTU scheme by that date, including the commitment of the venture capital investors, had reached DM 114.8 million. A sum of DM 87.5 million was authorized for use by the

KfW and a further DM 76 million for use by the TBG.[32]

The Fraunhofer-Institut, a technology institute which is partially funded by the German government, has analysed investments made under the scheme and found that seed capital investors with refinancing problems, MBGs and the KBG arms of the banks make investments almost exclusively using the refinancing variant. Venture capital companies, seed capital investors without refinancing problems, private and corporate investors, in contrast, mostly use the coinvestment form.

While it is still too early to determine what the enduring effects of the scheme will be, so far the signs have been encouraging. Of the 143 investments referred to above, only 11 firms have fallen into bankruptcy, and the decline of funds being invested in the seed and start-up stage has been reversed.

The Fraunhofer-Institut has had the opportunity to analyse the results of the BJTU scheme up until 31 December 1991 in rather more detail. By that time only 93 investments had been made. Nevertheless, 40 of these investments were in the seed stage, where money had been used to fund product or process development, while the remaining investments provided finance for production or market entry. In addition, 29 investment companies (roughly one-third of those operating in Germany), as well as 5 private investors or companies, had made use of the scheme by the end of 1991. These 29 investment companies included all the seed capital funds then operating in Germany, 7 of the venture capital groups, 4 MBGs, 6 KBGs of local banks, 3 KBGs of large banks and insurance companies, and one large bank. Table 3.2 shows the commitments of individual investor types in more detail. Finally, around two-thirds of the participating investment companies had used the scheme only once or twice, while 5 companies accounted for around 50 per cent of the total BJTU supported investments. Those firms that made most use of the scheme generally had some prior experience of investment in early stage companies, an example being the MBG for Baden-Württemberg.

The UBG law

Following the Bundesbank's report on company capital structure, a new law was introduced, Unternehmensbeteiligungsgesellschaften Gesetze, which was intended to encourage small firms to strengthen their capital base.[33] This law authorized a new type of investment vehicle, an Unternehmensbeteiligungsgesellschaft (UBG), which was afforded more favourable tax status than other investment firms. In particular, UBGs were not required to pay municipal or net worth tax, thus reducing the overall tax burden by around 15

Table 3.2 Investor commitments to the BJTU scheme by investor type, end 1991

Investor type	Coinvestment model	Refinancing model	Share of scheme participation
Seed capital funds	16	11	27 %
Venture capital groups	8	4	12 %
KBGs of banks and insurance cos	0	5	5 %
KBGs of local banks	3	13	16 %
MBGs	4	21	25 %
Banks	0	10	10 %
Other firms	5	0	5 %
Total	360	640	100 %

Source: Fraunhofer-Institut

per cent. In order to qualify for this favourable status, a UBG must meet a number of criteria:

1 it must either be publicly quoted or achieve a public quotation within ten years of its formation;
2 it must invest only in unquoted companies;
3 it can only hold minority stakes;
4 it has to invest in ten or more companies (after some allowance has been made for the time necessary to build up such a portfolio); and
5 its investee companies must be in Germany.

The UBG law is understood to be the only government tax incentive scheme *specifically* designed to encourage the supply of venture capital. Nevertheless, while the government had hoped that maybe as much as 25 per cent of new venture capital funds would be supplied by UBGs, the results to date have been disappointing. One reason is that the banks used UBGs as a way to restructure their *existing* unquoted equity investment activities into a more favourable taxation environment. Furthermore, the need for investment vehicles to be listed within ten years of formation has been a disincentive to German investment firms, who generally do not like the publicity and disclosure requirements associated with a listing. In addition, such vehicles do not appear to make attractive investments for conservative German stock-market investors.

The ESCFN

In 1989, the European commission also responded to the reduction in early stage investments by announcing its intention to support twenty-four seed capital funds within Europe, and the scheme has subsequently been expanded. Up until December 1991, three German funds had received support from the European Seed Capital Fund Network (ESCFN).[34] This consists of a subsidy of up to 50 per cent of the management costs of the fund for the first three to five years, subject to a maximum contribution of DM 1.1 million per firm. The rationale behind this subsidy of management costs is the one we outlined in Chapter 1, that early stage investments involve much higher relative investment costs than later stage investments.

THE TAXATION ENVIRONMENT

We have touched on how the German government has created a favourable taxation environment for the financing of small business (through both formal and informal venture capital) in two ways: by allowing investment in the form of typical and atypical silent partnerships, which have favourable taxation status; and by passing the UBG law. It should also be noted, however, that the taxes on share ownership create a heavy bias towards capital gains for individual shareholders. For example, individual shareholders are able to avoid capital gains altogether if: they own less than 25 per cent of the share capital of the company; the shares are held for at least six months; and no prior contract to sell the shares is entered into before they are purchased. Having said this, however, corporate shareholders must treat capital gains as part of ordinary income.

To appreciate the effects of the German taxation system on a new business, it is helpful to consider the tax position of an entrepreneur at three stages – when a business is formed, as the business operates, and when an exit is made – under the following scenario.[35] The entrepreneur invests capital received from a venture capitalist in the shares of a new company, which becomes the entrepreneur's full-time employer. When the company is formed, the entrepreneur, on condition of having taken part in its incorporation, will not be subject to taxes arising from incorporation.

During employment, the entrepreneur will be liable to personal income tax, which rises on a sliding scale from 22 per cent to 53 per cent, and church tax of around 8 per cent depending on the state in which the individual resides. Several deductions, however, can be made against this taxable income. For instance, interest paid on loans received from the venture capital fund can be offset, and if a silent partnership arrangement is used for the entrepreneur's investment, the entrepreneur can offset a proportion of any losses made by the company against personal income.

On the sale of the entrepreneur's shares, any capital gains arising are tax-free, providing that the individual has held the shares for at least six months and owns less than 25 per cent of the company; any losses can only be offset against gains in the same financial year. If the shares are held for less than six months, capital gains are treated as normal income. If the shareholding exceeds 25 per cent, then the taxation environment becomes significantly harsher. In this latter case, a seller of shares who has held over 25 per cent of the company's equity during the preceding five years is given a tax allowance equivalent to only DM 20,000 on the sale of 100 per cent of the company's equity.

By way of example, if a seller held 50 per cent of the shares and sold them all at once, the tax allowance entitlement would be just DM 10,000. If half of these shares were sold, that is 25 per cent of the company, the vendor would be entitled to a tax allowance of only DM 5,000. In addition to the above, should the gain on the sale be more than DM 80,000, then the DM 20,000 allowance (for 100 per cent of the equity) is reduced by the difference between the gain on the sale and DM 80,000. The gain above the tax allowance is taxed at normal income rates.

ECONOMIC AND SOCIAL RETURNS ON INVESTMENT

The support which the German government has given towards the encouragement of early-stage, technology-based firms has been based on the belief that: 'In the highly industrialised German economy, mastery and exploitation of innovative technologies – and with this the development of innovative products and processes – constitute a major prerequisite for lasting structural change as well as for the retention and expansion of international competitiveness.'[36] In this respect, the government perceived that there were too few new high-growth companies in some of the most important high technology areas.

Studies by the Fraunhofer-Institut showed that in 1990 58 firms funded under the TOU scheme generated a turnover of DM 280 million and employed 1300 people.[37] This data suggests that a firm which survives five years will generate an average turnover of DM 5 million and employ around twenty people. The institute has estimated that the potential exists for the creation of around 300 NTBFs in Germany annually. In addition, based on the TOU's experience, five-year failure rates would be expected to be in the 30–40 per cent range (say, 35 per cent).

Assuming a failure rate of 35 per cent, the annual creation of 300 NTBFs would appear to offer the potential, after five years, of generating around 4000 jobs and a turnover in the region of DM 1 billion. It should be noted, however, that these figures are highly speculative and use empirical data from a government programme which (on average) funded 75 per cent of firms' development costs during the first two years of their life. Nevertheless, they give a good indication of the wealth and employment-creating potential of even a relatively small number of NTBFs. Additionally, these figures relate only to *direct benefits*, and ignore indirect creation of wealth and employment, as well as the beneficial effects on national competitiveness of the presence of such firms.

GROWTH AND PERFORMANCE OF NTBFs

As was indicated above, the detailed performance of NTBFs in Germany has been most comprehensively examined by the Fraunhofer-Institut, which has closely studied both the TOU and BJTU schemes. While it is still too early to draw conclusions from the BJTU scheme, the closing date for participation in the TOU scheme was 31 December 1988, and the Fraunhofer-Institut has documented the performance to date of firms funded under this initiative. The description which follows relies on their interim report of December 1991.[38]

The TOU scheme

The TOU programme was set up to offer three different elements of support, aimed at firms in different phases of development and taking the form of: advice and help for the founder to develop a feasible business concept for his firm (Phase 1); non-repayable subsidies to finance development costs (Phase 2); and credit guarantees to support bank lending to finance the setting up of production and market entry (Phase 3). DM 325 million was made available for the TOU programme by the BMFT, to be distributed as direct subsidies and to provide credit guarantees for loans made by the Deutsche Ausgleichsbank. Between 1984 and 1988, 399 firms received funding from the scheme, including many which received funding for more than one phase. This funding could be broken down as follows:

- DM 8.6 million of non-repayable subsidies to support development of a business concept (258 firms funded);
- DM 242 million of non-repayable subsidies for development work on innovative products or processes (319 firms funded);
- DM 5.2 million of credit guarantees to support loans by the Deutsche Ausgleichsbank to firms in the product development stage (54 firms supported);

- DM 91 million of credit guarantees to support loans by the Deutsche Ausgleichsbank to finance the setting up of production and/or market entry (98 firms supported).

By the end of 1991, three years after the TOU scheme closed to new participants, 85 per cent of the firms supported by Phase 2 of the TOU programme had completed their participation. Of these firms 11 per cent had fallen into bankruptcy and a further 12 per cent had 'failed' in the sense that they were no longer involved in the development or marketing of innovative products. In the broadest possible sense, therefore, 23 per cent of firms could be considered to have failed. Although this rate of failure is considerably lower than would generally be expected for new firms, it is distorted by the relative youth of the firms included in the sample. For example, the 'failure' rate of firms around seven years old rose to 40 per cent, while that for firms founded in the period 1981–3 (which subsequently entered the TOU scheme) was 55 per cent. The highest rates of failure occurred between the third and seventh year after the founding of the firms.

Roughly one third of the failures in the TOU scheme occurred during product development, half at market entry and the remainder following market entry. The Fraunhofer-Institut found that the reasons for business failure varied considerably and that in most cases it was not possible to isolate one factor as the ultimate cause. The following observations were made.

1. In a very few cases, firms were forced to change their goals due to changes in their markets which had not been foreseen by the founder. In almost all cases, however, the development goals were met and, perhaps contrary to expectations, product complexity appeared to have little effect on the rate of failure.
2. Failures appeared to be largely due to lack of knowledge on the part of the founder as to how to manage and develop a business. Consistent with this finding, founders whose experience was not purely technical tended to be more successful, as were firms with more than one founder.
3. The failure rate among firms involved only in Phase 3 of the programme was disproportionately high at over 50 per cent. Reasons for failure largely concerned an inability to judge the market and/or severe difficulties in implementing efficient systems for recording and controlling costs.
4. Interestingly, founders who were formerly employees of universities or of state R&D institutions were disproportionately successful. Those from large organizations or from service organizations, on the other hand, proved to be disproportionately unsuccessful.

Figure 3.16 shows an attribution of TOU failures to five fundamental problems: founder, management, marketing, R&D and financing. With respect to financing, it was found that most firms failed for one of three reasons: (1) the firm did not, or could not, find an additional risk sharing investor; (2) the financial basis of the firm was weak, often due to a thin equity base; (3) financial resources were used inefficiently because of poor financial management, which was sometimes not even conducted seriously.

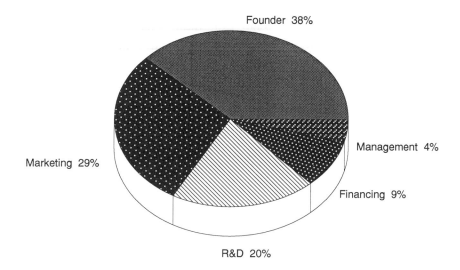

Figure 3.16 Attributed causes of TOU failures
(*Source*: Fraunhofer-Institut)

A number of conclusions were drawn by the Fraunhofer-Institut on the TOU scheme. They found that the scheme enabled the NTBFs, with certain exceptions, to develop independently once TOU support had ended and that the overwhelming majority of firms in the scheme, even after the termination of support from the TOU, maintained a high level of R&D and continued to offer innovative products in the marketplace. They also observed that the majority of founders required support to address non-technical questions arising during the development of their business. However, the goal of achieving an unsubsidized reservoir of sources of advice which specifically addressed the non-technical problems of NTBFs was *not* achieved and, during the operation of the TOU, a sustainable independent supply of risk-bearing capital to support NTBFs did *not* emerge.

APPENDICES

Illustrative case studies

Seed Capital Fund GmbH

Typical of the new generation of venture capital groups which specialize in early stage investment in Germany is Seed Capital Fund GmbH (SCF) in Berlin.[39] The fund draws its money from the Berliner Industriebank, with whom it has an agreement for the provision of DM 5 million. SCF's managers are from the Berlin technology centre VDI/VDE-IT. This is one of Germany's largest technology centres in the information technology field, having supported 220 business start-ups since it was set up in 1978. It thus provides an excellent base for SCF's activities.

SCF is able to utilize both the BJTU and the ESCFN schemes (the latter of which it can use to cover up to half of its management cost for the first three years of its operations). In SCF's view, these two schemes (taken together) considerably increase the viability of seed investments. For SCF's seed stage investing to be viable, however, it is also necessary to supplement help from these sources with support from private investors, the local KBG (which has state supported funds for equity investment in small businesses) and a bank which can provide overdraft facilities.

A typical deal for SCF could involve an overall investment of DM 1 million, with individual parties contributing as follows:

- SCF would invest around DM 250,000 for a 20 per cent equity stake;
- the KBG (or the BJTU) would invest another DM 250,000 in the form of a silent partnership, in return for interest payments and a profit participation;
- private investors would invest DM 100,000;
- a bank would provide a four-year loan of DM 150,000;
- an overdraft facility of DM 250,000 will be secured from another bank.

In addition, SCF would typically support its own investment with a refinancing loan from the KfW (under the BJTU refinancing scheme). In doing so it would receive an interest-free loan for ten years equal to the amount that it invests and a 90 per cent credit guarantee. This loan would thus enable SCF to remain liquid and to cover its management costs over the investment period.

SCF aims to forge relationships with larger companies, which are capable of providing an exit route via a trade sale. The majority of investments made by SCF, however, contain a provision for the entrepreneur to buy back shares in the company.

Morphosys GmbH

Morphosys was set up in July 1992 using a dedicated German investment vehicle financed jointly by Korda & Co., which provided 60 per cent of the fund's money from its seed capital fund, and Technostart (based in Stuttgart), which provided the remaining 40 per cent of the finance.[40] The second round of financing has drawn on the BJTU coinvestment scheme.

Morphosys is a Munich-based antibody engineering venture, with a German/New Zealand founding team with links to the Max Planck Institute for Biochemistry. The firm is developing intellectual property for random mutagenesis of antibodies. Initially, the core business of Morphosys is to develop high affinity therapeutic/diagnostic antibodies as a service for third parties. This business, however, is being carried out as a short-term measure in order to sustain the firm. In the long run, it is hoped that the firm will develop its own proprietary therapeutic antibodies, which would cause the value of the firm to increase significantly, and is the reason for the venture capitalists' interest and investment.

So far, two rounds of financing have been completed. The first round provided financing of DM 360,000, the founders providing DM 172,000 for 48 per cent of the equity, Korda & Co. DM 120,000 for 33 per cent of the equity, and Technostart DM 68,000 for 19 per cent of the equity. For Korda & Co., which prefers to invest at least £250,000 in the first round, this was an unusually small investment. For Technostart, on the other hand, which at present has only DM 1 million of funds under management, it is a normal amount. The venture capital firms hope that in six or seven years time they will be able to exit on a multiple of ten or more times their first round investments. Korda also expects that by the time of exit it will be diluted to below 25 per cent ownership and will, therefore, avoid paying capital gains tax.

The second round of investment raised the total funding to DM 2 million and drew on BJTU financing using the TBG coinvestment option. In this round, Korda invested an extra DM 630,000 (to raise its total commitment to DM 750,000), while the BJTU agreed to match the total investment by other parties to date with DM 1 million of finance. The interest rate of the TBG money was set at 5 per cent and, on exit, the TBG would also receive back up to 150 per cent of its principal. In order to obtain financing from the BJTU, the credit guarantees normally provided by the TBG were waived, as was the option to sell the investment back to the TBG after three years.

Clearly the involvement of the BJTU scheme has reduced the cost of capital to Morphosys significantly. The DM 1 million committed by the venture capital firms and the founders must generate an IRR of roughly 43 per cent to satisfy their expectations. In contrast, the DM 1 million invested by the BJTU must pay a fixed interest rate of 5 per cent and generate an IRR of around 6.5 per cent to repay 150 per cent of the principal in six to seven years time. The weighted average cost of capital to Morphosys is, therefore, about 33 per cent.

Deutsche Beteiligungsgesellschaft (DBG)

The Deutsche Beteiligungsgesellschaft, the venture capital arm of Deutsche Bank, has been operating in Germany for over twenty-five years and is presently considered to be the market leader, with funds under management of DM 640 million.[41] In 1991, DBG invested DM 152 million in 33 companies and achieved 16 exits for a total of DM 37 million.

DBG invests across all industry groups, with about 10 per cent of its investment flow going into early stage companies. Its investments include a number of computer, software, electronics and biotechnology companies, which account for roughly 20 per cent of its total portfolio (by value). DBG operates an 'open fund', by virtue of the fact that it draws money from its parent as and when required. It has a network of regional offices, which it uses to source most of its deal flow, and generally does not syndicate out its investments.

With an early stage company, DBG would seek to make roughly one-third of its investment in the form of equity and the remaining two-thirds in the form of a silent partnership. The silent partnership would be unsecured, carry a high rate of fixed interest, and sometimes have the option of conversion into equity. This investment structure allows DBG to take a large stake in an investee company without becoming the majority shareholder, as it is a policy of DBG to invest only as a minority shareholder.

The 'management buy-back' is becoming an ever more popular exit route for DBG. For example, in 1990 exits were split roughly equally between trade sales and management buy-backs, but in 1991 the majority of exits were achieved via management buy-backs. As a result, DBG is now structuring its deals to allow for a phased management buy-back, which it believes can reduce its risk substantially (indeed, to such an extent that it is willing to consider an IRR of only around 13 per cent on such deals).

The German stock markets

There are three publicly traded stock markets in Germany. In the first two markets, listings are secured by law and monitored by the Stock Exchange Commission. The third market, however, has very limited regulation and no rules governing the minimum capital necessary for an issue, or the minimum period of existence for a company. In more detail the three markets are:

The Official List – operated by the regional stock exchanges, which are presently in the process of being amalgamated into the Deutsche Börse. The Official List contains around 650 companies.

The Regulated Market (Der geregelte Markt) – active since 1987 and roughly the equivalent of the London USM.

The Freiverkehr – the 'free' market, in the sense that it is unregulated. The Freiverkehr has 480 participating companies, is very loosely regulated and there is no obligation to produce company reports. Unfortunately, although it is the easiest capital market from the regulatory point of view, this has resulted in the market being very thin.

Notes

1. 'BVK statistics for 1991', in *BVK Jahrbuch*, 1992.
2. Based on figures in *Venture Capital in Europe: 1993 EVCA yearbook* (EVCA, Zaventum, 1993), p. 98.
3. EVCA yearbook for 1992; *The world in figures 1992* (The Economist Publications, London, 1992).
4. Günter Leopold, *Venture capital in Deutschland*, in *BVK Jahrbuch*, 1992.
5. Ibid.
6. Ibid.
7. EVCA yearbooks for 1991, 1992 and 1993.
8. Udo Wupperfeld, 'The role of various types of German investment companies for the financing of new technology-based firms (NTBF)', Fraunhofer-Institut, Sept. 1992.
9. 'BVK statistics for 1991'.
10. BVK press release of 1992 statistics, BVK, April 1993.
11. Leopold, 'Venture capital in Deutschland'.
12. EVCA yearbooks for 1991, 1992 and 1993.
13. Ibid.
14. 'BVK statistics for 1991'.
15. EVCA yearbooks for 1991, 1992 and 1993.
16. Udo Wupperfeld, 'The role of various types of German investment companies for the financing of new technology-based firms'.
17. Personal communication from Udo Wupperfeld.
18. Ibid.
19. Hans Kellndorfer, 'Mittelstandsförderung ', *BVK Jahrbuch*, 1992.
20. 'Proceedings of the Anglo-German seed-capital workshop', Warwick Business School, Dec. 1992.
21. Personal communications from Thomas Schwarz and Rick Armitage.
22. Paragraph 4, 22. Partnership Law – 22.04 Silent Partnership.
23. 'Unternehmensbeteiligungen', *Frankfurter Allgemeine*, 26 Apr. 1993.
24. Ibid., Partnership Law – 22.04.
25. Personal communication from Dirk Kanngiesser.
26. Personal communications from Thomas Schwarz and Rolf Dienst.

27. The table draws on personal communications from Udo Wupperfeld, Thomas Schwarz, Rick Armitage, Rolf Dienst, William Stevens; also Kellndorfer, 'Mittelstandsförderung'; 'Proceedings of the Anglo-German seed-capital workshop'; 'Focus on venture capital in Germany', *European Venture Capital Journal*, Mar. 1992; 'Venture capital firms', *Impulse*, Nov. 1991.
28. Graham Bannock and Horst Albach, 'Small business policy in Europe', Anglo-German Foundation, 1991.
29. Roger Bendisch, 'Seed und start-up beteiligung', in *BVK Jahrbuch*, 1992.
30. 'Beteiligungskapital für junge technologieunternehmen', BMFT, Aug. 1991.
31. Ibid.
32. Wupperfeld, 'The role of various types of German investment companies for the financing of new technology-based firms'; Monika Harnischfeger, Marianne Kulicke and Udo Wupperfeld 'Zum Stand des Modellversuchs "Beteiligungskapital für junge Technologieunternehmen" (BJTU), Zwischenbericht zum 31.12.1991', Fraunhofer-Institut, 1992.
33. Peter Köhler, 'Glanz und Elend der UBG', *BVK Jahrbuch*, 1992.
34. 'Assistance to small and medium sized businesses', EVCA Early Stage Committee, Oct. 1992.
35. 'Focus on European taxation of entrepreneurs', *European Venture Capital Journal*, Dec. 1991.
36. Marianne Kulicke, Udo Wupperfeld and Günter H. Walter, 'Modellversuch "Förderung Technologie-orientierter Unternehmensgründungen" (TOU). Zwischenbilanz zum 31.12.1991', Fraunhofer-Institut, 1992.
37. Ibid.
38. Ibid.
39. 'Proceedings of the Anglo-German seed-capital workshop'; 'Focus on venture capital in Germany'.
40. Personal communication from Rolf Dienst.
41. Personal communications from Udo Wupperfeld and William Stevens; 'Focus on venture capital in Germany'; DBG Geschäftsbericht (company report), 1990.

4
VENTURE CAPITAL FUNDING IN JAPAN

The Japanese 'venture capital' market is so different from those in the Western world, including the other three national markets that we describe, that it is appropriate to have a rather more extensive introductory section to this chapter to provide a clearer framework and context for our subsequent remarks and observations.

INTRODUCTION AND BACKGROUND

Definition of venture enterprise

Perhaps the first key difference between the Japanese and Western markets is that the meaning of the term 'new venture' or 'venture enterprise' (VE) is very different. According to the Venture Enterprise Centre, a semi-public foundation established by the Ministry of International Trade and Industry (MITI) in 1974, new ventures are companies which satisfy at least four out of the following six criteria.[1]

- *High growth*: average annual growth should have been in excess of 15 per cent per annum for the previous three years.
- *High return*: profit margins should be greater than 15 per cent of sales.
- *Technical originality*: R&D costs should exceed 3 per cent of sales *or* involve more than 15 per cent of the company's employees.
- *Independence*: no larger firm should be holding over 25 per cent of the company's shares.
- *Newness*: the company should be less than ten years old, or have over 40 per cent of its sales accounted for by products launched within the previous three years.
- *Flotation orientation*: it should be the company's *explicit* intention to become publicly quoted.

112 The Funding Environment in Four Key Countries

As a result of these definitional parameters, new venture companies are much older than in the West (indeed, companies such as Glaxo and Intel would probably satisfy the first four of the above criteria). For example, a survey carried out in 1984 by the Venture Enterprise Centre, noted that the 206 new venture companies that took part in the survey had the age distribution in Fig. 4.1, that is, 36 per cent of them were more than ten years old. One possible reason underlying the inclusion of such 'elderly' companies (in Western eyes) within the 'new venture' definition is that Japanese companies tend to take a much longer time after formation to reach the point of 'take-off'.

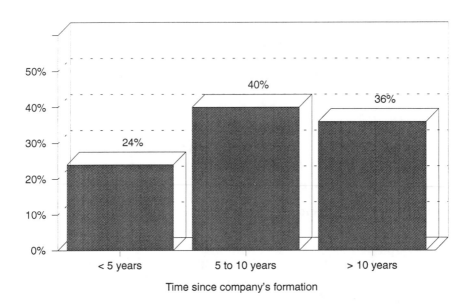

Figure 4.1 Age distribution of new ventures in a Venture Enterprise Centre survey, 1984
(*Source*: Venture Enterprise Centre)

Characteristics of venture capitalists

While the investments of venture capitalists in Japan are motivated by the prospect of making substantial capital gains on their portfolio company investments, in much the same way as most Western venture capitalists, they generally differ in a number of other characteristics.

1 They tend to be tied to large financial, associated companies, such as securities companies and banks (which, for all intents and purposes, are their

parent companies, although an equivalent law to the US Glass–Steagall Act restricts banks from owning more than 5 per cent of the equity in securities companies). These companies provide substantial funds to the venture capitalists to invest in their portfolio companies (cf. 3i in the UK, but with only one bank providing the funds).

2 A second source of venture capital funds is essentially coinvestment funds, referred to as Investment Enterprise Partnerships (IEPs or 'partnership funds'). These funds are more or less analogous to the independent private funds of the Western markets, although they tend to contain a relatively large percentage of funds sourced from Japanese industrial corporate investors and a significant amount of the venture capital firm's own money. As with Western funds, however, the firm receives management fees on the fund and a percentage of the capital gains accruing to the partners (in addition, of course, to all the capital gain on their own portion of the funds).

3 Unlike their Western counterparts, Japanese venture capitalists also commonly generate earnings from making loans, leasing and factoring activities and so on, both with respect to their own portfolio companies and by actively seeking third-party business. They use the steadier stream of earnings from these sources to finance the running costs of their VE investment activities.

4 As a result of the flotation focus of venture capital investing, Japanese venture capitalists have a specialized staff for 'financial consulting'. These staff are experts in listing procedures and securities evaluation, as well as taxation, accounting and other financially related matters.

Cultural, social and industrial obstacles

There are a number of particularly Japanese cultural, social and industrial obstacles to VE formation and growth.[2] First there is the impact of 'lifetime employment' policies. Historically, the Japanese system of lifetime employment has meant that the large companies have sought to recruit the best school or university students, and they would then retain them until retirement at fifty-five or sixty. These employees would usually be remunerated and promoted on the basis of their age and length of service with the company. This acts as a disincentive to potential entrepreneurs. On the one hand, leaving their current employer means giving up almost certain promotion prospects and a high or rising pay scale, while if their new business fails, finding employment again is likely to be hard. On the other, young individuals with the energy and expertise required to succeed with their own businesses, are unlikely to be able to save sufficient capital under a system of age-related pay (especially with the high metropolitan land and property values).

The disincentive to leave an existing position also makes the task of hiring sufficient skilled staff and high quality managers extremely difficult for a small or new business, since they cannot offer either a lifetime employment guarantee or the same high pay as an experienced manager would be able to get from a large company. Indeed, entrepreneurs perceive the recruitment of technical staff, in particular, to be perhaps their biggest problem. According to a 1991 survey by the Japanese Small and Medium Enterprise Agency, nearly 50 per cent of new venture companies think their human resources are poorer than those of large companies.[3]

A further problem arises from societal attitudes to entrepreneurial success and failure. By comparison with a US entrepreneur, for example, success for the Japanese entrepreneur is less likely to bring social prestige, since big company 'family' values and much less emphasis on individualism are continuing themes throughout Japanese culture and society. At the same time, failure results in deep humiliation and loss of face in Japanese society.

Fear of this kind of humiliation strongly discourages risk-taking and encourages conformity. Indeed, this aversion to risk, arising from fear of failure, permeates big company activities too. For example, if a US engineer makes a mistake during the development stage of a new product, but corrects the mistake, that is usually the end of the matter. In Japan, however, the engineer's manager will tend to remember the mistake regardless. Similarly, whereas US R&D may be focused on 'breakthrough' technology, which will as a matter of course involve a high risk of failure, Japanese R&D tends to be focused on goals that appear achievable using currently available technologies.

Due to the inherent conservatism and caution that risk aversion promotes, VEs tend to grow somewhat more slowly than, say, their US equivalents. As a result, it is perhaps not surprising that it commonly takes at least fifteen years before a VE can become listed on the securities market, producing a barrier to early stage venture capital investment.

The relationship between large companies and small companies also has to be taken into account in Japan. Because of its size and bargaining power, a large company is often able to control smaller companies by hiring them as subcontractors on terms which effectively prevent them from trading with the large company's competitors. These industrial groupings are known as *keiretsu*. Although the small companies can gain access to large financial resources, technical assistance, secure orders and so on in this way, it comes at the expense of limiting their growth to the desires of their (essentially) parent company.

In addition, large companies often wait for SMEs to develop new technologies, then quickly catch up with them by applying their much greater resources once the technology has become established. This has the effect of reducing the returns on VE innovations in the Japanese marketplace.

Finally, the regulatory environment within Japan makes US style, hands-on CVC activity difficult, if not impossible. Japanese anti-trust law does not permit a venture capital firm to appoint directors to the board of a VE in which it has invested and, as a result, the firm finds it difficult to influence and monitor its investments closely. The firms are also prevented by the 'administrative guidance' of the Fair Trade Commission from providing managers or directors to work in the enterprises in which they have invested.

History of venture capital in Japan

Although Japan established three Small Business Investment Companies (SBICs) in 1963 in order to provide equity finance for small firms, there was no real concept of venture capital in Japan at that time. Indeed it was not until 1970 that the word 'venture' first appeared in the Japanese business press – in referring to the first US 'venture boom' of the period. There were, however, many 'new venture' companies emerging in Japan by then, such as Kyocera. In order to help these companies become established, eight private venture capitalists were formed between November 1972 and August 1974, seven of which were capitalized by large banks or securities houses.[4]

The next step came in 1975, with the establishment of the Venture Enterprise Centre on the initiative of MITI. Although the centre would not make equity investments in VEs, it was prepared to provide them with loan guarantees. Unfortunately, the impact of the first oil price crisis of 1974, which hit Japan rather harder than most Western countries, resulted in many VEs facing financial difficulties and in a substantial number becoming insolvent. This, in turn, proved an almost fatal blow to the fledgling venture capital industry.

Exacerbating these difficulties for the young industry were a number of other factors. In particular, the Japanese Stock Exchange had not yet matured (the requirements for listing, for example, were very severe) and over-the-counter (OTC) dealings were inactive; and mergers and acquisitions (M&A) activity, particularly hostile M&A, was very rare. As a result, the two most profitable forms of exit for the Western venture capital industry, the IPO and the trade sale, were not in practice available in Japan. It was thus almost impossible to achieve a satisfactory exit for Japanese venture capital investments and the 1970s venture capital boom in Japan soon ended.

As a consequence of such problems, only a few venture capitalists were able to continue with long-term investments in VEs. Some of those that were unable to continue on the former basis left the market altogether, while others began to target only those VEs capable of going public within a few years of the investment being made. In addition, several companies started to offer many other financial services, especially loans, leasing and factoring.

At the start of the 1980s, in common with many other national markets, the environment for both VEs and venture capitalists in Japan started to become more favourable, leading to the second venture boom. This time, however, the major banks and securities companies that had established affiliated venture capital companies during the first boom were joined by other participants. These were the regional banks (usually through joint ventures with securities firms); manufacturing firms (such as Techno-venture); trading companies (such as Marubeni Development); foreign venture capitalists (such as Pacific Technology Ventures); and even venture capital subsidiaries of 'new venture' companies (such as Magnum Venture Capital). Shortly after the start of this pick-up of venture capital activity in Japan, in April 1982, the first of the Toushi Jigyo Kumiai funds or Investment Enterprise Partnerships were started by the Japan Associated Finance Company (JAFCO).[5]

Current overview

At the end of 1992, there were nearly 120 'venture capital' firms in Japan. Furthermore, as at the end of March 1992, the total portfolio size of the largest 67 of these firms, according to a survey carried out by the *Nikkei Venture* magazine, amounted to Yen 911 billion.[6] Most of the money invested in portfolio companies tends to be invested in the form of either equity or, perhaps more frequently, in equity-like instruments, such as convertible bonds ('convertibles') or warrants. In addition, of the total funds made available to the venture capital companies (consisting of the investment portfolio plus any non-invested funds), around half is used to make loans, to both investee and non-investee firms, in order to generate income to cover the funds' running costs.

It should be noted that the venture capital firms are generally not independently referred to as 'venture capitalists', but can instead almost be looked on as tightly associated 'venture capital departments' of their financial institutional backers (especially when these are the banks and securities companies), since they tend to work closely with and solely for these affiliates. For example, venture capitalists associated with banks search for VEs that the banks will be able to do lucrative businesses with, as their main trading banks, after they go public. Indeed, as an important Japanese business practice, they usually keep all their shares in the portfolio companies after the IPO. In contrast, venture capital firms associated with securities houses tend to look for a quick exit via an IPO, so that they can crystallize the capital gain, and their affiliated securities houses can get the listing business (and the associated fees). In either case, there is now a focus on later stage VEs, rather than making high-risk/high-return type investments.

MARKET SIZE AND GROWTH

During the 1980s and early 1990s total capital under management by the Japanese industry showed the sort of explosive growth seen elsewhere (although there is evidence that the pool may have recently plateaued for at least the time being).[7] Indeed, those firms with securities houses as 'parents' are understood to have been keen to increase their VE equity investments in the early 1990s, in anticipation of a 'bull' market in Japanese equities which would provide substantial capital gains on these investments. It should be noted, however, that the amounts described as being 'under management' do not include any of the funds associated with the venture capitalists' other activities, such as loans, leasing and factoring. The amount of loans, in particular, are substantial in comparison, having reached over Yen 1600 billion during 1992.[8]

Figure 4.2 indicates the most recent trends in the total capital under management by the industry, although the figures shown for 1991 and 1992 are

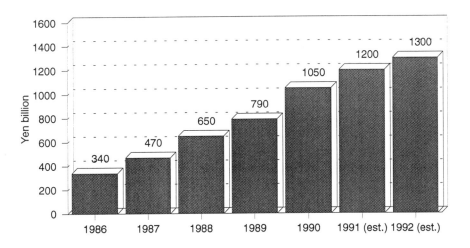

Figure 4.2 Total capital under management, 1986–1992
(*Sources*: Bygrave and Timmons, *Venture Capital*; *Asian VCJ*)

118   The Funding Environment in Four Key Countries

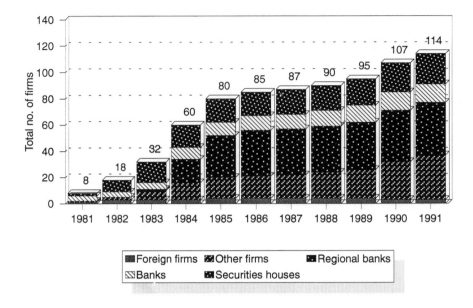

Figure 4.3 Numbers of venture capital firms and their associations, 1981–1991
(*Source*: JAFCO)

our estimates.[9] Between 1986 and 1990, the Japanese venture capital pool more than tripled from roughly Yen 340 billion to around Yen 1050 billion. The rate of growth in the pool is believed to have recently come to a halt, partly due to recession effects and partly due to the high IPO-exit activity of recent years. As might be expected, when the size of the pool was increasing, the number of firms managing it increased as well (see Fig. 4.3).[10] The steepest rise in the number of firms came in the first half of the 1980s, led by the large banks and the securities houses, but followed by the more numerous regional banks and other types of firms.

It is interesting to note that the number of foreign firms in the market has remained more or less constant (and at a low level) since 1982, perhaps indicative of the fundamental differences in the meaning of the term 'venture capital' between Japan and the Western countries (in addition to the well documented difficulties of any foreign firm operating in Japan). In particular, and for the reasons previously outlined, Japan does not really have any CVC/early stage investing, or for that matter any MBO or M&A activity, both of which involve key Western venture capital skills. On the other hand, the foreign venture capitalists are poorly placed to offer advice and assistance on either Japanese IPOs or banking activity, the key areas of Japanese venture capital

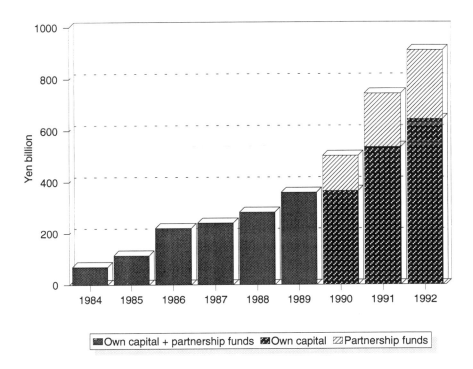

Figure 4.4 Total portfolio of VE investments, 1984–1992, including shares of partnership funds 1990–1992
(*Source*: Nikkei Venture Capital Survey 1992)

skills, or indeed to have the required contacts with potential VE companies.

The growth in the total portfolio of equity and equity-like investments in VE firms since 1984 is shown in Fig. 4.4. For 1990 to 1992 only, it shows the shares of partnership funds and the venture capitalists' own funds. One point worth noting is the apparent stalling of portfolio growth over the 1986–7 period. As a result of the rapid growth in funds flowing into venture capital during the early 1980s, a situation arose of too much money chasing too few good deals. This ultimately resulted in a number of spectacular bankruptcies among venture capital backed VEs in the mid-1980s, causing the temporary setback observed.

While there are now understood to be approaching 120 venture capital firms in Japan, the industry's portfolio is concentrated in the top ten companies, which account for almost two-thirds of the total portfolio (see the

Appendix at the end of the chapter for the most recent reported portfolio sizes and number of portfolio investments for the top twenty firms in these categories). Foremost among these firms is JAFCO, an associate of the Nomura Securities house, which accounts for roughly one quarter of the total Japanese portfolio and is roughly three times larger than its nearest rival.

In geographical terms, following the removal of exchange controls in Japan during 1980 Japanese firms have invested substantial and (until recently) rapidly increasing amounts overseas, primarily in the US, but also in Europe.[11] For example, during the 1989–90 period Japanese corporations were investing at the rate of nearly US$ 500 million annually in the US. This represented a threefold increase from 1987 and a tenfold increase from 1985. This investment took the form of both direct investment in portfolio companies (especially by trading and manufacturing companies investing directly in high technology firms) and indirect investment via US venture capital firms.

According to a report in the *European Venture Capital Journal*, in carrying out these venture capital investments the major Japanese corporations were seeking to gain both a 'window on high technology' (and access to US NTBF R&D) and strategic business partners to facilitate their expansion into the US. With the more recent domestic economic difficulties and finding access to US NTBF R&D difficult, Japanese investment in US venture capital partnerships dropped from a high of US$ 82.4 million in 1988 to virtually zero in 1991, along with a more general slowing down in overseas investment during 1991 and 1992.[12] Nevertheless, foreign investments still account for a significant portion of the Japanese venture capital portfolio, 13.6 per cent of the total value of Yen 910.7 billion in mid-1992.[13] In addition to their venture capital activity, we also noted that the Japanese venture capitalists carried out a substantial amount of lending business. Indeed, in this respect, 28 out of the 66 venture capital firms participating in the 1992 Nikkei Venture Capital Survey have a larger loan than venture capital portfolio (see the Appendix), occasionally substantially so as in the case of Yamaichi Finance. For the most part, however, these loans are generally not made to the venture capitalist's portfolio companies. The 1992 Nikkei Venture Capital Survey showed that 89 per cent of the value of loans made by Japanese venture capital firms went to non-investees. That most loans are made to third parties is probably driven by the fact that the venture capitalists are looking for a dependable, lower risk source of income to finance their operations.

Finally, it should be noted that the first half of 1992 saw a decline in both disbursements and loan activity for the first time in many years, as Japan's current economic problems took their toll on venture capital investment.[14]

BREAKDOWN BY FUNDING STAGE

The majority of Japanese venture capitalists have focused on investing in VEs that are almost ready to go public and rarely invest in companies that have not reached this 'pre-IPO' stage, let alone in early stage firms. A number of factors helped to determine this venture capital investment strategy.

1 Most of the funds invested by the venture capitalists came from their own equity capital and bank loans, usually borrowed from their parent companies. Since the cashflow required to service the loan finance component of their portfolio usually exceeded the cashflow from their investment portfolio, the venture capitalists needed to receive rapid and reasonably certain capital gains from their investments in order to make up for the cashflow shortfall. Hence their propensity to invest in pre-IPO firms.
2 To all intents and purposes, the only practical exit route for successful venture capital investments in Japan is the IPO, as the M&A market is inactive, with the possible exception of friendly transactions. On the other hand, the listing requirements are so severe and the environment is so unconducive to small company growth that investors in new companies and start-ups would often have to wait for twenty years or more before they could go public. This is far too long because of the constraints in our first point.
3 In almost all cases, most venture capital employees come from either the parent company or financial institutions. In consequence, they do not have the technical knowledge required to be able to evaluate high-technology, early-stage VEs, nor do they have appropriate industrial experience to be able to add value in other 'hands-on' ways. The venture capitalists need, therefore, to be able to invest in later stage VEs that can be dealt with on a 'hands-off' basis.
4 Related to the above, venture capital firms cannot easily control or influence the management of the investees because of the Japanese antitrust regulations (which stipulate that the firm cannot hold board seats of its portfolio companies and cannot own more than 49 per cent of the equity of a VE) and 'administrative guidance' from the Fair Trade Commission.

In addition, Japanese venture capitalists have been attracted to investing in later stage VEs because of the sheer numbers of well-performing but as yet unlisted companies in this category within Japan.[15]

Thus, as far as the majority of venture capitalists are concerned (that is to say the banks and securities companies which constitute around 80 per cent of the membership of the Venture Enterprise Centre), there is effectively considered to be only one 'stage' of venture capital investment, 'pre-IPO'. Among the remaining venture capital firms, however, those affiliated to industrial corporations tend to consider financial returns and liquidity to be of less interest, while the strategic relevance of exposure to new technologies and markets, and the potential to manufacture or market new products, is of prime importance. For these firms, early stage investments in high technology businesses are the norm and, indeed, such investments formed a very large part of Japanese venture capital investment within the US.

INDUSTRY SECTORS ATTRACTING INVESTMENT

Although there is a marked concentration within the Japanese venture capital portfolio with regard to the stage of investment (pre-IPO), these investments are made in a very wide range of industries, with much less evidence of significant concentration as a result of a sustained preference for a particular industry or industries. According to the 1992 Nikkei Venture Capital Survey, the relative number of investments made in the top six industry categories were more or less the same in 1992 as in 1991, although 'housing, construction and real estate' dropped down the rankings as a result of the collapse in property prices, see Table 4.1. The survey noted, however, that there did appear to be target industries for venture capital investments, although of course the actual investments made depend on the particular investment opportunities arising. The five most preferred industries were: (1) life sciences; (2) biotechnology/medical/healthcare; (3) environmental technology; (4) factory automation; (5) electrical and electronic technologies.

Table 4.1 Ranking of industries according to number of investments received

Industry	1992	1991
Electrical and electronics	1	1
Machinery	2	2
Services	3	6
Wholesaling	4	4
Information processing	5	5
Housing, construction, real estate	6	3

Source: Nikkei Venture Capital Survey 1992.

As an example of the relative lack of industry focus of venture capital portfolios, Fig. 4.5 shows how JAFCO's portfolio is partitioned between the various industry categories. The percentage shares for each sector relate to its worldwide portfolio as at 31 March 1992.

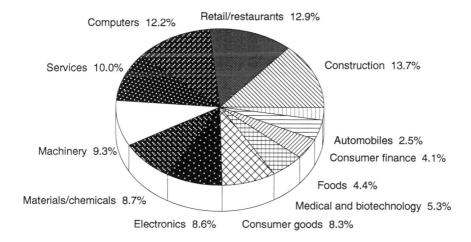

Figure 4.5 JAFCO's cumulative portfolio investments by industry, March 1992
(*Source*: JAFCO)

INVESTMENT SIZE

Because of the essentially pre-IPO nature of the majority of Japanese venture capital investments, the average size of the disbursements made tends to be relatively large and similar in size to the later stage development capital deals (or even smaller MBOs) of the Western markets. Figure 4.6 estimates the average disbursement per investee by JAFCO for four accounting periods up to 31 March 1992.

CHARACTERISTICS OF INVESTORS

There are two principal sources of funds for Japanese private venture capital firms, depending on the type of fund. General investment funds, the venture capitalists' *own* funds, are formed from the initial equity capital contributed

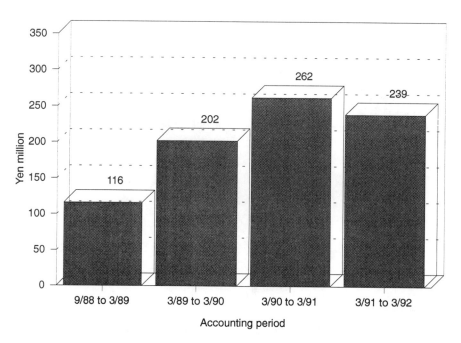

Figure 4.6 Estimation of JAFCO's average size of disbursement, 1988–1992
(*Source*: based on JAFCO data)

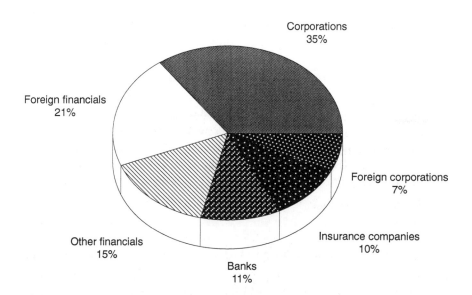

Figure 4.7 Types of investors in JAFCO partnership funds, March 1992
(*Source*: JAFCO)

Venture Capital Funding in Japan 125

by the parent company (and any other investors), in addition to loans from the parent bank, securities house, etc. Partnership funds, on the other hand, are composed of capital from industrial corporations, foreign financial companies, insurance companies, and so on. It is interesting to note that the majority of Japanese pension funds consider investments in venture capital funds to be too risky and, as a result, pension fund capital is estimated to account for only 5 per cent or so of the venture capital pool.

With regard to the partnership funds, these are still dominated by JAFCO, who set up the first in 1982 based on the way that venture capital funds were established in the US. Since then, JAFCO has set up no fewer than forty such funds which now have a combined investment portfolio of over Yen 100 billion. Figures 4.7 and 4.8 show the composition of these JAFCO partnership funds by investor type and by geographical source. These partnership funds are formed by selling 'personal bonds' to the limited investors, but only after the investors taking part in a particular IEP have been finalized. The number of investors in any fund is invariably forty-nine or fewer, since Japanese securities law requires that such a fund must be raised publicly in the event that the number of investors reaches fifty or more.

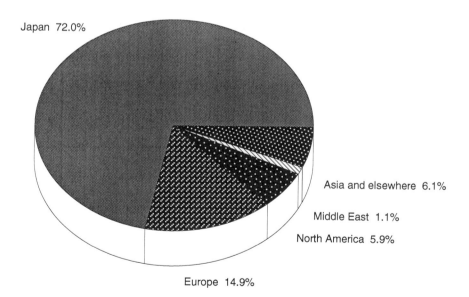

Figure 4.8 Geographical origins of investors in JAFCO partnership funds, April 1992
(*Source*: JAFCO)

126 The Funding Environment in Four Key Countries

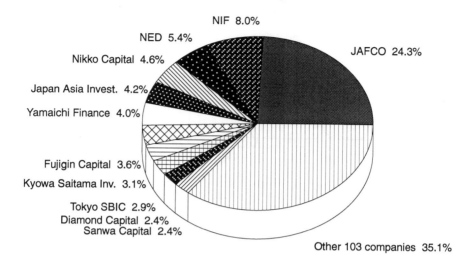

Figure 4.9 Shares of companies in the total venture capital portfolio, mid-1992
(*Source*: Nikkei Venture Capital Survey)

With regard to the majority of venture capital firms, which consist either primarily or solely of general investment funds, the firm can often make losses for a long period after commencing trading and thus requires substantial commitment from the parent firm to survive. For example, Mitsubishi Bank formed its venture capital associate, Diamond Capital Corporation, in 1974. Diamond remained unprofitable for its first seven years, until capital gains generated from its portfolio had risen to a sufficient level to cover its cost base. Throughout this period Mitsubishi financed Diamond with loans carrying a commercial rate of interest. Today, Diamond still has only one partnership fund.[16]

Finally, in addition to the private venture capital firms, there are also a few private/semi-public SBICs. These firms are analogous to their US counterparts in that they borrow money from the government (and banks) in order to invest in Japanese SMEs.

FUNDING SOURCES AND METHODS

We have seen how the Japanese venture capital market tends to concentrate on the financing of pre-IPO companies. For most businesses prior to this

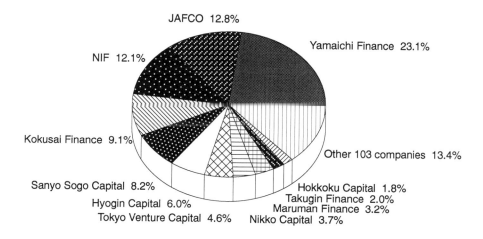

Figure 4.10 Shares of companies in the total loan portfolio, mid-1992
(*Source*: Nikkei Venture Capital Survey)

stage, there usually tends to be little interest shown by the majority of the formal venture capital industry (with the possible exception of certain high technology categories of company, such as biotechnology). As a result, the primary sources of venture capital for earlier stage VEs are generally families and relatives, other SMEs with interests in the VE's product area, the Venture Enterprise Centre's loan guarantee scheme, local and national government grants and subsidies (see the Appendix at the end of the chapter for a fuller description), and – when the VE's products are ready for production and marketing – the company's customers (in the form of advanced payments).

With regard to the later stage financing of VEs by the formal venture capital industry, however, according to JAFCO there were 114 venture capital firms operating in Japan at the end of 1991. These firms could be categorized as follows: associates of securities houses (23 firms); associates of large/city banks (14 firms); associates of regional banks (40 firms); other Japanese organizations (34 firms); foreign organizations (3 firms). Since 1991 the total may have risen to about 120.

Figures 4.9 and 4.10 outline the relative importance of the key players in terms of their shares of the total venture capital portfolio and the total loan portfolio. It should be remembered that the majority of the equity portfolio consists of general fund investments, although partnership funds appear to be on the increase, while loans are principally made to non-investees. As can be seen, there is a great degree of concentration in both the venture capital and the loan portfolios, with the top eleven companies in each case accounting for approaching two-thirds of the former and over 86 per cent of the latter. In addition, the securities houses and banks dominate both types of capital. We shall now look at the various sources of venture capital funding in a little more detail.

Key public and semi-public organizations

We have summarized in the Appendix the main formal funding support systems for early stage (R&D) companies in Japan, many of which are public or semi-public in nature. Two particular organizations or types of organization are worth further comment: the Small Business Investment Companies or SBICs, and the Venture Enterprise Centre.

Japanese SBICs, set up in Tokyo, Osaka and Nagoya, came into being following the 1963 Japanese Small Business Investment Law. They are semi-public in the sense that they tend to have the local governments among their shareholders, and can also borrow government money to supplement their bank loans. In contrast to the US SBICs, the Japanese firms were set up to invest in small and medium-sized firms rather than to finance new ventures (although since the early 1980s they have also invested in the latter). In this respect, the specific intention of the 1963 law was to help these companies to:

- modernize their equipment and facilities;
- improve the technology on which their products are based;
- rationalize their management structure;
- upgrade their operational structure;
- help rectify sources of competitive disadvantage;
- stimulate demand for the company's products;
- help secure fair opportunities for business development;
- assist with employee relations, employee welfare and ensure an adequate supply of labour.

The Japanese SBICs also have a number of restrictions placed on their investments:[17]

- they are only permitted to invest in equity and equity-like instruments (such as convertible bonds);
- they should look to receive between 15 per cent and 50 per cent of the investee's equity in return for their investment;

- following the investment, the nominal share capital of the investee may not exceed Yen 300 million;
- the investee must have audited accounts, be profitable, dividend paying and fall into one of 28 business types;
- the investments have to be made on a commercial basis;
- the investee must intend to offer shares to the public at some future date.

As at March 1992, the three SBICs accounted for just over 10 per cent of the total value of the venture capital portfolio and had over 2000 investees (more than twice the number of investees in the JAFCO portfolio). The average disbursement was only about Yen 45 million, less than 20 per cent of that for the industry as a whole.[18] The annual investment rate by the SBICs is currently running at approaching Yen 6 billion in over a hundred companies, roughly three-quarters of which are first round investments. In contrast to the affiliates of banks and securities houses, the present focus for investment is understood to be in the area of new start-up companies and the overseas expansion of later stage SMEs.[19]

The Venture Enterprise Centre was established by MITI in 1974 as another semi-public organization. Its main activities are twofold. Firstly, it provides loan guarantees to help small, advanced technology companies undertake R&D activities. These guarantees are limited to 80 per cent of the loan or Yen 80 million, whichever is the larger, and last for eight years. By the end of March 1991, the Centre had guaranteed 364 loans amounting to Yen 14.4 billion and 22 R&D projects had become commercially successful. Secondly, it is also intended to act as the main source of information on venture capital within Japan, and indeed it publishes a monthly journal, *Venture Forum*.

Private venture capital firms

For the purpose of this discussion, private venture capital firms can be divided into those which are tied to securities houses; those which are tied to either the large, city or regional banks; and independent venture capital firms.

According to the 1992 Nikkei Venture Capital Survey, associates of the big four securities houses dominate both the venture capital portfolio and the loan portfolio. Their respective portfolio shares are as shown in Table 4.2. Clearly, the key area of relevant expertise possessed by the securities house associates lies in the area of advice on and assistance with the investee's IPO. In this regard, the venture capital firms are seen as a source of new IPOs by the parent. In this way, the securities house and its associate venture capital firm have a symbiotic relationship. The securities house can earn generous listing fees from effecting the IPO on behalf of the venture capital firm's portfolio companies, while the venture capital firm gains a substantial enhancement to its exit mechanism (due to the sheer market power of the leading securities houses), improving both the liquidity of its investments and, in all likelihood, the actual magnitude of its capital gain.

Table 4.2 Portfolio shares of associates of the 'big four' securities houses

Securities house	Associate company	Share of VC portfolio	Share of loan portfolio
Nomura	JAFCO	24.3%	12.8%
Daiwa	NIF	8.0%	12.1%
Nikko	Nikko Capital	4.6%	3.7%
	Central Capital	2.3%	n.a.
Yamaichi	Yamaichi Finance	4.0%	23.1%
Total		43.2%	51.7%

Source: Nikkei Venture Capital Survey

Possibly the main reason that so many banks have chosen to set up associated venture capital firms, making them the second largest group of private venture capital firms, is due to the fact that Japanese anti-trust law prohibits banks from owning more than 5 per cent of the issued share capital of a company. Since corporate shareholdings are indicative in Japanese business of long-term business relationships, the banks use their associate firms to obtain such shareholdings. As a result, however, the associate's primary objective is not to crystallize a capital gain following the IPO, but to become a long-term holder of the investee's shares.

While the number of large or city bank associates increased steadily throughout the 1980s, the venture capital firms set up by the smaller, regional banks increased rapidly after 1984. Having said this, it is understood that nearly 90 per cent of these regional firms were set up in the form of joint ventures with securities houses. It is an arrangement that is mutually beneficial to both companies, since the large securities houses only have branches in the main cities, and therefore rely on the regional banks' associates for a source of IPO deal flow from the regions, while once again the associate venture capital firm benefits from the securities house's IPO expertise.[20]

Finally, as regards independent private venture capital firms, these tend either to fill the financing gaps left in the market by the banks, securities houses and SBICs, or to be strategically focused. As an example of the former case, the foreign venture capitalists have tried to carry out CVC-type venture capital activities in Japan. To date, however, they have met with only very limited success because of the social, cultural and economic factors discussed earlier, in addition to difficulties experienced in both sourcing and exiting deals. As a result, the number of foreign firms has remained at only three or four throughout the 1980s.

With respect to strategic funds, there have been a number of firms set up by industrial/trading companies (such as Techno-venture in 1974 and Magnum Venture Capital in 1983). These funds tend to have a 'window on technology' investment motivation.[21]

Debt versus equity financing

A 1991 survey by Japan's Small and Medium Enterprise Agency showed that over three-quarters of SMEs prefer loan financing to the issue of equity and that, whenever possible, they sought these loans from government associated institutions who would provide them at a low rate of interest.[22] There are, of course, the expected factors accounting for this preference: the lower 'cost' of loan financing compared with equity, due to its inherently lower risk nature; and the unwillingness of equity holders to have their holdings diluted. There is, however, a further factor operating in Japan, in that it is more tax effective to pay interest on debt out of pretax income (which is allowable for tax purposes) than to pay dividends out of aftertax income.

It is understood that the Japanese operate a modified version of the UK's 'imputation tax' system, so that although the effective rate of corporation tax paid at the company level on dividends is around 50 per cent or so of the gross dividend, the 'tax credit' received ('imputed' to have been paid) by the individual shareholder is only 10 per cent of the net dividend.[23] Indeed, it may in part be the fact that the taxation system favours debt over equity (admittedly among other factors) that makes convertibles and bonds with warrants attached so popular in Japan (that is, debt instruments with equity-like features). Indeed, the Venture Enterprise Centre has estimated that its members' 'equity' portfolio, as at the end of 1990, was composed of roughly 69 per cent ordinary shares, 28 per cent bonds with warrants attached and 3 per cent convertibles.

THE VENTURE CAPITALIST/ENTREPRENEUR RELATIONSHIP

By far the most common type of entrepreneurial enterprise/venture capitalist relationship in Japan covers a situation whereby a venture capital firm takes an equity or equity-like stake in a VE, perhaps three to five years before it will be ready to become publicly quoted, and helps and advises the VE in a hands-off manner (as far as the VE's operations are concerned) through both the pre-IPO and IPO stage. In order to describe the investment process and nature of the relationship between the investor and the investee, we shall outline the procedure for a typical investment by JAFCO.

Approximately one-third of JAFCO's 320 employees worldwide are involved with seeking out and researching companies in which to invest. The sources of information used can vary from JAFCO's regional banking contacts, through to personal contacts of the employees, through to scanning trade magazines or newspapers.[24] When it is believed that a suitable company has been identified, there are four stages the investment candidate must go through (usually sequentially) before an investment can be made:

1 the investment committee, where a proposal to invest in the investment candidate is drawn up;
2 the planning committee, where the initial capital structure and the likely timing of JAFCO's investments up to the time of flotation are established;
3 the investment evaluation department, which provides an *independent* appraisal (an appraisal from other than the investment candidate's internal sponsor) of the investment opportunity and the required investigative 'due diligence' before the deal can take place; and finally
4 referral to the executive committee for approval.

As a result of this careful screening process, in addition to the disproportionate emphasis that JAFCO places on the strength of the investee's management team (relative to most other Japanese venture capitalists), it has experienced a very low bankruptcy rate among its investments.

While JAFCO invariably takes a hands-off role in the running of the company (except in the relatively few problem companies), it does offer its portfolio companies a range of consultancy services in the areas of finance and taxation, business development, preparation for the IPO on the Japanese markets, and personnel recruitment services (through its 'JAFCO Brains Company' subsidiary).

Before an investment is made, therefore, the investment candidate may already have been working with JAFCO for a year or so. A diagrammatic representation of the investment process, from identification of the investment candidate through to the IPO and beyond, is given in Fig. 4.11.

Following on from the IPO, as a general rule, JAFCO will usually keep the equity in which its own (general investment) funds have invested, while selling equity held in the partnership funds. It should be noted that the IEPs are invariably set up as a form of time-limited investment trust and, as such, are required to liquidate their holdings within a defined period (commonly ten years). As a result of this requirement to sell their holding within a specified period, JAFCO needs to exercise a great deal of skill, both during the IPO and in the 'aftermarket', in order to manage the natural downward pricing pressure that the market will attempt to impose on the post-IPO share price in the presence of a perceived 'forced seller' of the shares.

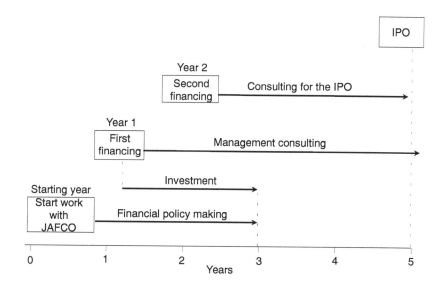

Figure 4.11 Typical investment process for JAFCO's venture investments
(*Source*: JAFCO)

PERIOD OF INVESTMENT, EXIT OPPORTUNITIES AND VALUATION

In Japan, the question of exit is not quite as straightforward as in most of the Western markets. As part of the Japanese business culture, the buying of shares in one company by another is used as a gesture to show that a long-term business relationship exists between the two companies. As such, the converse also tends to be true, in that the selling of such a shareholding signifies the end of the relationship. In the light of this, the Western venture capital practice of buying part of a company's equity for a limited period of, say, five years, followed by a total 'exit' from that shareholding on, say, flotation, is culturally incongruent. As a result, the venture capital subsidiaries of the securities houses and especially banks often hold on to their own shareholdings following an investee's flotation. The main exception to this tendency, as noted above, occurs with shares held in the partnership funds, which are usually required to sell all shareholdings as a result of their trust status.

As will be evident from our comments, the period of venture capital investment in Japan will depend very much on the nature of the relationship between the investee and the investor and its associate(s). We have seen that JAFCO tends to have a typical 'investment cycle' for its Japanese investments (encompassing the pre-investment evaluation, investment and pre-IPO period) of around four to five years on average, which is believed to be somewhat shorter than many other Japanese venture capital firms. Having said this, JAFCO usually retains the investee's equity contained within its own (General Investment) portfolio beyond the point of IPO. When banking associated venture capitalists invest in VEs, a key investment motivation is to obtain the long-term banking business of these companies. In consequence, equity tends to be retained by the venture capitalist following an IPO. Thus the period of investment in Japan can vary from perhaps four or five years up to a more or less indefinite shareholding.

For a long time, one of the key obstacles to venture capital investment in Japan was the lack of an effective exit method. On the one hand, a number of factors effectively inhibit M&A activity, while on the other, it was very difficult indeed to obtain a quotation on the public securities markets.

We have touched on reasons for the inactive Japanese M&A market. They include cultural factors related to the Japanese view of the company as being, in some senses, a family. Hence selling such a company 'family' meets with psychological resistance.[25] Partly as a result of the above, hostile acquisitions are almost non-existent and most acquisitions involve the sale of an SME to a larger company that may be either a supplier or a customer of that SME. Typical reasons for merging in this way might be failure by the SME to keep up with competitors' innovations; a wish by the larger company to diversify; or insufficient funds being available to the SME to cover its required R&D expenditure.[26] In addition, Japanese law does not permit the formation of holding companies, which hinders M&A activity through share purchases.

In contrast to the above, it is estimated that perhaps two-thirds of all VEs want to go public at some stage, not least because public companies tend to have a better corporate image and get greater access to credit. A December 1991 survey by the Small and Medium Enterprise Agency gave the following reasons mentioned by SMEs for going public:[27]

- to make going public the managerial target (mentioned by 74.3 per cent of SMEs);
- to obtain access to capital (69.4 per cent);
- because a securities house recommended going public (32.8 per cent);
- because a venture capital firm recommended going public (9.5 per cent);
- because a bank recommended going public (4.7 per cent).

Historically, however, one of the main problems for both the VE and the venture capitalist in obtaining a public quotation is that it is normal for publicly quoted companies to be well established, in order to be able to comply with the very demanding quotation requirements. For example, in recent times, 92 per cent of OTC companies were fifteen or more years old when they went public and less than 1 per cent were under ten years old.[28]

The two principal types of public market for IPOs are the over-the-counter market and the main Stock Exchange markets. Initially, the requirements to obtain a quotation on the OTC market were exceptionally tough and, in addition, companies were not permitted to raise further capital by issuing shares at the market price. Between 1983 and 1985, however, the government brought in legislation to relax restrictions relating to dealing, sale of stock, listing and disclosure requirements for the OTC market. In consequence of these changes, the number of companies going public through the OTC market mushroomed, as can be seen in Fig. 4.12.

Also acting to improve the OTC market, an automatic quotation transmission system, QUICK, was introduced in July 1984, which ultimately led to the development of Jasdaq (Japanese Association of Stock Dealers Automated Quotation – in many ways analogous to the US Nasdaq) in October 1991.

In addition to the OTC market, Japan also has three main Stock Exchange markets, based in Tokyo, Osaka and Nagoya and five other regional markets. Furthermore, the three main markets are split into two parts, the First Section, where the larger companies are traded, and the Second Section. Since the OTC changes were implemented, however, these Stock Exchange markets have lost a substantial amount of IPO market share to the OTC market. Indeed, this situation occurred even though a third market (called the New Second Section for Specially Selected Stocks) was started, with less demanding listing requirements, in the Second Section of the Osaka Stock Exchange in an attempt to attract this business.

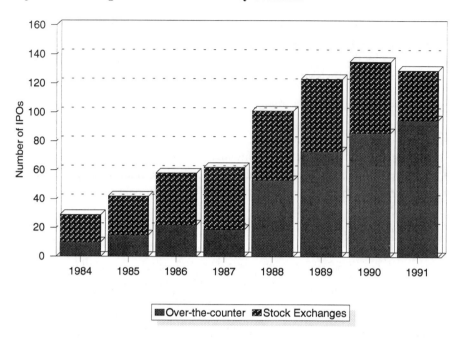

Figure 4.12 Venture-backed IPOs vis the OTC and Stock Exchange markets, 1984–1991
(*Source*: JAFCO)

Because the majority of exits are achieved using the IPO route, coupled with the well-functioning and liquid equity markets, valuing a company for an IPO exit is a relatively straightforward affair (although it still requires a great deal of experience). It will involve, among other things, an assessment by the sponsoring securities house of the likely demand for the company's shares at a price set in comparison with similar companies already being traded on the markets. Built into the IPO price will be a discount to the perceived 'fair' post-IPO price in order to provide an incentive to those buying the shares.

RETURNS REQUIRED BY THE PROVIDERS OF DEBT AND EQUITY

The rate of return required by the providers of venture capital in Japan is, once again, a very difficult question to address. Although the venture capitalists do appear to have target rates of return up until at least the time of the

IPO, the fact that the affiliates of the securities houses and (in particular) the banks tend to hold on to their equity for an indefinite period following the IPO muddies the picture somewhat. Having said that, defining the required rate of return as before to be the target nominal pretax return on equity, or the nominal pretax cost for debt-like instruments, Table 4.3 summarizes the estimated return required by each provider.

Table 4.3 Estimated nominal target return on funds by source

Source	Form of investment	Nominal target return
Bank	Short-term loan	The short-term prime lending rate (4.5%) + (a) 0–0.25% for large companies (b) 0.2–0.5% for SMEs
Bank	Long-term loan	The long-term prime lending rate (= to the short-term rate + 0.5–1%) + (a) or (b) above
Securities house affiliates	Mainly equity	Understood to be around 25–35% over the 3 to 5 pre-IPO years
Bank affiliates	Mainly equity	Understood to be around 25–35% over the 3 to 5 pre-IPO years
Corporate investors	Equity	Unknown, probably both company specific and implicit rather than explicit
SBICs	Equity only	Unknown, although the rate is probably less than those quoted for the securities houses and banks, because of the various government-derived subsidies and debt guarantees
Foreign venture capitalists	Equity	As per their domestic rates (see US and UK chapters)

Where short and long-term loans are concerned, the banks set the rates in accordance with the 'short-term prime lending rate' (SPLR) for loans of less than one year, and the 'long-term prime lending rate' (LPLR) for loans of over one year duration. The SPLR has been calculated by reference to the value-weighted average of several banks' borrowing rates since January 1989, while the LPLR has been based on the former rate plus some premium since 1991.

138 The Funding Environment in Four Key Countries

Fundamentally, however, the SPLR tends to vary in a manner which is linked to the general level of interest rates prevailing in the economy at any one time. Unfortunately, as far as SMEs are concerned, such variability is unattractive from the point of view of both financial planning and the additional risk premium that the banks apply to act as a cushion against this rate movement. As a result, SMEs tend to go for fixed-rate government loans whenever possible. In order to demonstrate the likely variability of the SPLR and LPLR as a function of the general level of interest rates in the economy, Fig. 4.13 shows how these have varied over time.

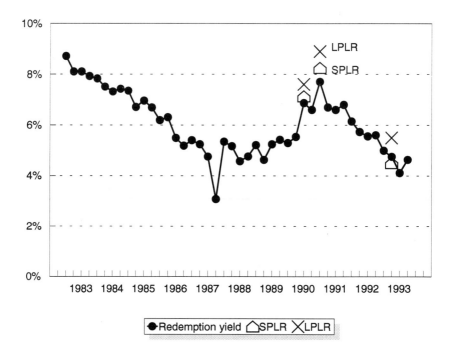

Figure 4.13 Long-term and short-term prime lending rates in relation to the general level of interest rates in the economy (benchmark bond redemption yield)
(*Source*: Datastream)

With respect to the returns required by the affiliates of the securities houses and banks, these are also likely to be influenced (to a rather less extent) by the general level of interest rates, since most source a significant proportion of their capital in the form of loans from their associated banks and securities houses. However, their required returns are unlikely to deviate significantly from the range shown for their usual pre-IPO type of transaction.

GOVERNMENT INITIATIVES

The Japanese government has undertaken a wide range of initiatives to assist SMEs. They include government-sponsored organizations to promote the development of SMEs, government influence on third party lenders and taxation incentives. The main focus of government activity, however, has been to help and improve the performance of existing SMEs, rather than specifically to promote the formation of new ventures. Nevertheless, new ventures are able to take advantage of a number of the initiatives. The following are some of the more important national government-sponsored organizations active in the SME field.[29]

Organization	Outline of activities
Small and Medium Enterprise Agency	Indirect promotion and guidance, provides planning and helps coordinate other agencies
Japan Small Business Corporation	Primary responsibility for implementing MITI measures directed towards SMEs
Small Business Finance Corporation	Extends loans (generally secured) for plant, equipment and long-term operations to SMEs
National Finance Corporation	Makes loans to individuals and certain types of business capitalized at less than Yen 10 million, or with fewer than 100 employees
Shoko Chukin Bank	Provides finance for business cooperatives and their members and/or for the establishment of cooperatives
Small Business Credit Insurance Corporation	Provides insurance for credit guarantees
Small Business Investment Company	Provides equity and consultancy to joint stock corporations with less than Yen 100 million of capital

Although, in general terms, the government has not sought to take specific measures to help start-up and early stage businesses, in April 1993 the Small and Medium Enterprise Agency established a fund dedicated to helping such companies. The purpose of this fund is to make interest-free loans to companies less than three years old, for the purchase of equipment. The initial size of this fund was set at Yen 2.1 billion. (See also the Appendix to this chapter.)

With respect to the influence of government on third party lenders, a good example was seen in February 1993 when the Ministry of Finance officially asked the commercial banks 'not to refrain from lending to small businesses'. This action was taken in response to the worsening prospects for bank lending to such businesses as a result of the recession.

140   The Funding Environment in Four Key Countries

Finally, special taxation incentives designed to help SMEs are usually limited to fixed time periods, and generally focus on assisting R&D and capital investment. As an example, where taxation help for R&D investment is concerned, SMEs have had the following options: *either* between 1985 and 1992 the SME could receive a tax deduction equivalent to 6 per cent of the annual R&D expenditure, up to a limit of 15 per cent of the corporation tax bill, *or* for 1992 *only*, the SME could make a tax deduction of 20 per cent of the highest annual R&D expenditure ever incurred, up to a limit of 10 per cent of the corporation tax bill. Regarding taxation help for capital investment, *either* for 1993 *only*, the SME could make a tax deduction of 7 per cent of the acquisition cost of high-technology machines (such as manufacturing robots, computers), *or* it could depreciate 30 per cent of its acquisition cost.

THE TAXATION ENVIRONMENT

Having looked at the types of government taxation incentives that exist specifically to assist SMEs, we summarize the key elements of the Japanese tax system which affect investor and entrepreneur returns in general.[30]

In the event that a joint stock company is set up by a group of Japanese individuals, the main tax features of interest will be:

- there are *no* tax allowances relating to the initial investment in the company's shares;
- the entrepreneurs should have a similar size of remuneration package to their previous employment in order to avoid being liable to any additional taxes;
- a capital gains liability will arise on the sale of the investors' and entrepreneurs' shares.

In relation to capital gains tax, gains by individuals will normally be subject to tax at 26 per cent (CGT of 20 per cent + a local tax of 6 per cent). Alternatively, one can elect to pay 1 per cent of the gross proceeds for publicly traded stocks. Any capital losses can be offset by capital gains elsewhere, but cannot be deducted from earned income. It is interesting to note that before April 1989 individuals were not subject to CGT in Japan and therefore had an incentive to invest in venture capital funds. This incentive did not apply to corporate stakeholders in venture capital funds, however, who were subject to CGT at 50 per cent.

ECONOMIC AND SOCIAL RETURNS ON INVESTMENT

In contrast to the United States and a few of the European countries, the Japanese venture capital industry does not appear to be unduly concerned with measuring financial returns on its investments and, to the best of our knowledge, no work has been carried out in this area. Similarly, it is very difficult to get any feel for the wider returns on venture capital investment, except in isolated circumstances such as in the case of the Venture Enterprise Centre, where 22 R&D projects out of 364 investments had become 'commercially successful' as at the end of March 1991. It is felt unlikely, however, that the main activity of the Japanese venture capital industry, that is the 'hands-off' assistance to relatively mature pre-IPO companies to go public, will provide substantial social returns. On the other hand, it is believed that the activities of the SBICs, the Venture Enterprise Centre and other government initiatives are likely to do so.

GROWTH AND PERFORMANCE OF NTBFs

In order to understand the factors influencing the growth in Japanese NTBFs and their performance, it is useful to obtain an overview of the structure of Japanese industry as a whole. Of particular relevance are the relative importance of the contributions made by firms of different sizes to the economy, and the relationship between SMEs and large firms in the functioning of the economy.

According to statistics obtained from the Ministry of Finance, there are approximately 2 million registered joint stock companies in Japan. Of these companies, perhaps around 45 per cent were estimated to be manufacturing concerns. A valuable insight into the relative importance of small, medium and large firms to the Japanese manufacturing economy can be obtained from considering Fig. 4.14. As can be seen, the manufacturing part of the Japanese economy (which probably contains most of the NTBFs) is dominated by companies which are small (fewer than 20 employees) and medium-sized (20–300 employees). Indeed, even in value-added terms, SMEs account for approaching 55 per cent of the Japanese total.

According to a 1987 survey by the Small and Medium Enterprise Agency, however, 56 per cent of all SMEs act as dedicated subcontractors of only one larger firm (that is, operate as part of a Keiretsu) and are therefore, in all but name, subsidiaries of this larger firm. (That more of them are not absorbed by the larger company may be due, at least in part, to the prohibition of holding company structures by Japanese law.) Adjusting for this distortion more than halves the number of truly independent SMEs and probably has a similar effect on their contribution to the value-added total.

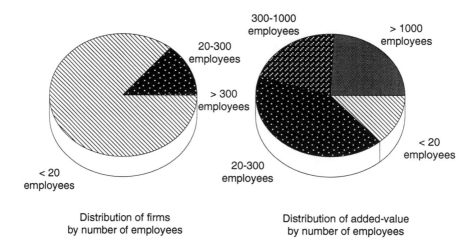

Figure 4.14 Distribution and added value of manufacturing companies of different sizes, 1989
(*Sources*: Ministry of Finance; MITI Management and Coordination Agency)

Nevertheless, there remains a substantial number of truly independent small manufacturing firms which supply many more than one larger company. It is understood that a significant proportion of these could be considered to be NTBFs, whose R&D expenditure as a percentage of sales (typically 7–10 per cent) is a multiple of the average amount spent by the larger companies (perhaps only 2 per cent).[31]

There are some interconnected reasons for the relatively large number of NTBFs in Japan. In the first place, Japan has a significant number of large and medium-sized technology-based companies to act as customers of the NTBFs. Secondly, the product life-cycle of technology-based products in Japan tends to be very short, and large company structures are not flexible enough to maintain their competitive edge. As a result, there is a lot of 'farming out' of product development to the smaller, more responsive NTBFs, who can develop products faster and more cost-effectively. Thirdly, although R&D expenditure by NTBFs is much greater as a percentage of sales than the larger firms, it tends to be concentrated on the less risky 'D' side. This appears to be a consequence of the general Japanese aversion to business risk, which leads firms to focus on the incremental improvement of products rather than to attempt 'trail-blazing' product innovation. One side effect of this approach is that it is invariably much less costly to develop a new product, which thus lowers the barrier to entry for new firms. Hence, a higher number of NTBFs come into being.

To conclude, as a consequence of the relationship between the independent NTBFs and the larger firms, in addition to the 'incremental' nature of their products, NTBFs in Japan are, on average, likely to grow much more slowly than, say, their counterparts in the United States; be more numerous; and have lower overall growth potential.

APPENDICES

Funding R&D: a case study

D Electron & Electric Wire Ltd

The company was established in 1984, has a share capital of Yen 85 million and achieved sales of Yen 470 million in its fiscal 1990 year. Subsequent to its formation, it spent heavily on R&D, resulting in the development of over 60 types of trial products.

Since it was founded, the company has used no fewer than seven sources of finance to support its R&D activities, in addition to the share capital subscribed by the founders. These are outlined in the following list.[32]

Year	Type of finance	Source
1985	Subsidy	Promotion Fund for Medium and Small Venture Firms
	Debt guarantee	Venture Enterprise Centre
1986	Subsidy	New Technology Development Foundation
1987	Subsidy	MITI (subsidy for technology improvement)
1989	Low interest loan	Osaka Prefecture/Frontier Industry Promotion Fund
1990	Debt guarantee	Venture Enterprise Centre
	Warrant (venture capital)	Osaka R&D Type Firms Promotion Foundation
1991	Subsidy	Sanwa Venture Fostering Fund

The total amount of funding received from these sources has so far amounted to approximately Yen 300 million, with the vast majority taking the form of subsidies. In addition, the receipt of these funds has allowed the company to achieve sufficient status for the banks to become willing to make loans.

Venture Capital Funding in Japan

Characteristics of leading firms, mid-1992

Table A4.1 Top twenty firms by venture capital portfolio size

Rank (last year)	Venture capital firm	Total portfolio (Yen million)	General Portfolio	Firms	Partnership Portfolio	Firms
1 (1)	Japan Assoc. Finance (JAFCO)	221,311	117,659	865	103,652	568
2 (2)	Nippon Invest. & Finance (NIF)	72,894	39,912	434	32,982	253
3 (3)	Nippon Enterprise Dev. (NED)	48,931	47,525	416	1,406	36
4 (4)	Nikko Capital	41,891	33,240	347	8,651	104
5 (6)	Japan Asia Investment	37,830	2,266	37	35,564	81
6 (8)	Yamaichi Finance	36,729	22,106	174	14,623	159
7 (5)	Fujigin Capital	32,581	32,581	278		
8 (12)	Kyowa Saitama Investment	28,175	28,175	203		
9 (7)	Tokyo SBIC	26,823	26,823	565		
10 (10)	Diamond Capital	22,104	20,945	303	1,159	23
11 (9)	Sanwa Capital	22,100	22,100	282		
12 (11)	Osaka SBIC	21,422	21,422	482		
13 (13)	Central Capital	20,835	20,835	234		
14 (16)	Tokyo Venture Capital	20,202	20,202	426		
15 (19)	Maruman Finance	18,865	18,865	206		
16 (15)	Techno-venture	17,043	225	11	16,818	99
17 (18)	Kokusai Finance	16,840	6,104	139	10,736	84
18 (17)	Daiwagin Investment	16,218	6,853	107	9,365	146
19 (14)	Sanyo Sogo Capital	14,021	12,322	241	1,699	26
20 (24)	New Japan Finance	12,994	9,308	185	3,686	49

Source: Nikkei Venture Capital Survey 1992.

Table A4.2 Top twenty firms by number of investees

Rank (last year)	Venture capital firm	No. of investees (new investments)
1 (1)	Japan Associated Finance Co (JAFCO)	201 (36)
2 (3)	Nippon Investment & Finance (NIF)	114 (17)
3 (2)	Yamaichi Finance	93 (12)
4 (6)	Tokyo Venture Capital	92 (13)
5 (4)	Nippon Enterprise Development (NED)	91 (12)
6 (5)	Diamond Capital	81 (7)
7 (7)	Central Capital	75 (15)
8 (9)	Nikko Capital	67 (18)
9 (8)	Kankaku Investment	61 (12)
10 (25)	Techno-venture	55 (22)
11 (11)	Fujigin Capital	49 (13)
12 (11)	Sanwa Capital	45 (11)
12 (10)	New Japan Finance	45 (9)
14 (15)	Maruman Finance	44 (17)
15 (14)	Kokusai Finance	39 (10)
15 (13)	Sanyo Sogo Capital	39 (6)
17 (-)	Okasan Finance	38 (14)
18 (19)	Daiwagin Kigyo Yushi	27 (13)
19 (17)	Tokyo SBIC	25 (4)
20 (15)	Mitsui Finance Service	24 (5)

Source: Nikkei Venture Capital Survey 1992.

Table A4.3 Top twenty firms by loan portfolio size

Rank	Venture capital firm	Loans 1992 (Yen million)	Loans 1991 (Yen million)	Growth (%)	No. of borrowers
1	Yamaichi Finance	373,314	361,052	3.4	154
2	JAFCO	206,469	238,249	−13.3	39
3	NIF	195,000	214,588	−9.1	64
4	Kokusai Finance	147,221	157,748	−6.7	66
5	Sanyo Sogo Capital	131,810	178,541	−26.2	91
6	Hyogin Capital	96,801	100,025	−3.2	189
7	Tokyo Venture Capital	74,816	74,807	0.0	35
8	Nikko Capital	59,754	60,300	−0.9	38
9	Maruman Finance	51,624	57,562	−10.3	37
10	Takugin Finance	32,877	37,869	−13.2	65
11	Hokkoku Capital	28,942	28,520	1.5	316
12	New Japan Finance	24,944	14,634	70.5	12
13	Kyushu Capital	21,203	24,090	−12.0	40
14	NED	18,593	27,630	−32.7	38
15	Japan Asia Investment	15,120	19,781	−23.6	10
16	Kyoto Investment Finance	12,790	12,383	3.3	67
17	Cosmo Sogo Finance	11,810	10,100	16.9	13
18	Daiichi Capital	10,290	4,484	129.5	8
19	Kyowa Saitama Investment	10,257	19,426	−47.2	32
20	Izumigin Finance	9,925	7,453	33.2	29

Source: Nikkei Venture Capital Survey 1992.

Summary of R&D support for SMEs

Fund	Outline	Subsidy value, etc.	Remarks
MITI: Technology Improvement Subsidy	General subsidy for the following firms: medium and small firms (defined as public firms capitalized at less than Y100m or employing fewer than 300 and private firms with fewer than 300 employees) under the Medium and Small Enterprise Fundamental Law; • unlisted firms; • firms with R&D expenditure of over 3% of sales for the last 2 years. 2 R&D type Medium and Small Enterprise Technology Development subsidy. 3 Subcontractors Promotion Technology subsidy.	1 Y5–20m; 2 Y7–30m; 3 Y5–30m; all with a limit of 50% of R&D expenditure	With the subsidy by MITI, local governments may add some more funds.
New Technology Development Foundation	1 Only for the development of new utility models that can be brought into practical use within one year. 2 Unlisted firms including individuals.	Up to Y10m.	Started from private fund.
Promotion Fund for Medium and Small Venture Firms	1 Subsidy for R&D. 2 Subsidy for R&D with foreign institutions. 3 Subsidy for human resource development.	1 and 2 up to Y3m; 3 up to Y1m; all with a limit of 50% of the R&D cost.	Organised by 3 SBICs.
Sanwa Venture Fostering Fund	1 R&D subsidy for firms who have less than 5 years experience in a new field or are < 5 years old, for projects that can be commercialized within two years. 2 Debt guarantee for R&D projects.	1 up to Y5m with a limit of 50% of the R&D cost; 2 80% of debt, up to Y80m for 5 years.	After getting subsidy, debt guarantee is also available.
Kyusyu and Yamaguchi Districts Firms Promotion Fund	1 R&D subsidy for projects that can be commercialized within two years. 2 Subsidy for human resource development for firms who have less than 10 years experience in a new field or are < 5 years old.	1 up to Y5m; 2 up to Y1m: both with a limit of 50% of the R&D cost.	Established by Fukuoka Bank.
Osaka R&D Type Firms Promotion Foundation	Indirect Venture Capital System for firms in the Osaka area. (This foundation organizes and controls all funds raised by 18 venture capitalists. Offered to R&D type firms between 7 and 25 years old with capital of less than Y1,000m, or small firms of less than 7 years old with capital smaller than Y15m.)	Up to Y50m.	Established in 1990.
Venture Enterprise Centre	Debt guarantee for R&D type firms that are: • capitalized at less than Y500m; • employing fewer than 500; and • private, but not subsidiaries of larger firms.	80% of debt, up to Y80m for 8 years.	Established in 1974 by MITI.

m = million
y = yen
Source: Small and Medium Enterprise Agency.

Notes

1. Rodney Clark, 'Venture capital in Japan', in Clark, *Venture Capital in Britain, America and Japan* (Croom Helm, 1987), pp. 27-64; see page 33. Clark's work represents the most comprehensive overview of the Japanese venture capital market available in English.
2. Ibid., pp. 28-9.
3. Chusho Kigyo Hakusho (Small and Medium Enterprise Agency), 1992.
4. Clark, 'Venture capital in Japan'.
5. 'JAFCO', *European Venture Capital Journal*, Nov.-Dec. 1990.
6. 'Financial Times survey: venture and development capital', *Financial Times*, 24 Sept. 1993.
7. Ibid.
8. 'Nikkei venture capital survey 1992', *Nikkei Venture*, June 1992.
9. Ibid.; W. D. Bygrave and J. A. Timmons, *Venture Capital at the Crossroads* (Harvard Business School Press, Boston, 1992), p. 70.
10. Based on information supplied by JAFCO.
11. 'Japanese investment in US ventures on the increase', *European Venture Capital Journal*, July–Aug. 1989.
12. *Venture Capital Journal*, Apr. 1992; Mijojo Kaisha-ban, "Kaisha Shiki-ho', *Toyo Keizai Shinposha*, 1992.
13. Nikkei Venture Capital Survey 1992.
14. *Nihon Keizai Shinbun*, cf. *Financial Times*, 18 Jan. 1993.
15. Based on information supplied by JAFCO.
16. Clark, 'Venture capital in Japan', p. 37.
17. Clark, *Venture Capital in Japan*, p 41.
18. 'Nikkei Venture Capital Survey 1992', *Nikkei Venture*, June 1992.
19. *Nihon Keizai Shinbun*, 19 Apr. 1993.
20. Based on information supplied by JAFCO.
21. Clark, 'Venture capital in Japan'.
22. Chusho Kigyo Hakusho, 1992.
23. 'Focus on European taxation of entrepreneurs', *European Venture Capital Journal*, Nov.–Dec. 1991.
24. 'JAFCO', *European Venture Capital Journal*, Nov.–Dec. 1990; JAFCO.
25. W. Carl Kester, *Japanese Takeovers* (Harvard Business School Press, Boston, 1991), pp. 8-13.
26. *Nikkan Kogyo Shinbun*, 10 July 1987.
27. Clark, 'Venture capital in Japan'; Chusho Kigyo Hakusho, 1992.
28. 'Nikkei Venture Capital Survey 1992', *Nikkei Venture*, June 1992.
29. D. Hawkins, 'New business entrepreneurship in the Japanese economy', *Journal of Business Venturing*, Mar. 1993.
30. 'Focus on European taxation of entrepreneurs', *European Venture Capital Journal*, Nov.–Dec. 1991.
31. 'Nikkei Venture Capital Survey 1992', *Nikkei Venture*, June 1992.
32. Sourced from *Nikkei Venture*.

5
VENTURE CAPITAL FUNDING IN THE UK

Following the emergence of a formally distinct venture capital industry during the latter part of the 1970s, the UK industry has grown dramatically since the beginning of the 1980s, and is now clearly the largest within Europe and second only to the United States globally.

By far the largest and most established firm operating in the UK venture capital market is 3i which, according to the 1993–4 edition of the British Venture Capital Association (BVCA) directory, has some £2 billion of funds under management, invested in around 4,000 companies. Including 3i, the BVCA had 117 full members in 1992 who were active in making long–term equity investments, primarily in unquoted companies. All in all, the UK industry today probably has funds either invested (at cost) or available to invest of the order of £7.5 billion.[1]

UK venture capital firms can be categorized as: *independent firms*, who manage one or more funds raised from external sources, the funds they manage being private, institutionally backed, publicly listed, business expansion scheme, or some combination thereof; *captive groups*, which are often specialist and wholly owned venture capital operations (subsidiaries or divisions) of banks, pension funds, insurance companies, industrial corporations or fund management groups; *semi–captive groups*, which operate as autonomous associates of larger groups such as insurance companies, and tend to be owned jointly by the associated company and the managers, who raise and manage third party funds; and *government sector* operations, which manage capital supplied from public sector sources (often with other than purely financial objectives, such as job creation).

Much of the numerical data below has come from the BVCA itself and from articles in the *UK Venture Capital Journal* (UKVCJ) which in turn has sourced most material from Venture Economics and the BVCA. In addition, we have also drawn on the EVCA's annual yearbooks. Although data from these sources tends to differ (for instance, Venture Economics usually excludes 3i from its analysis to avoid distorting the UK picture as a whole, whereas the BVCA and EVCA include 3i), together they provide by far the best information about the UK industry. To the extent that data presented here differs between these sources, an attempt has been made to reconcile the differences in order to obtain a coherent overview. It should be remembered, however, that one has to proceed with very great caution when attempting to interpret *any* venture capital data.

MARKET SIZE AND GROWTH

As was seen for the US, the UK venture capital industry is now experiencing a period of consolidation and slow growth. To begin to examine the market trends accompanying this slow–down, we look at total capital under management. Here the most recently available and consistent data has been produced in the EVCA yearbooks. A summary of the trend over the five years from 1988 to 1992 is shown in Fig. 5.1.

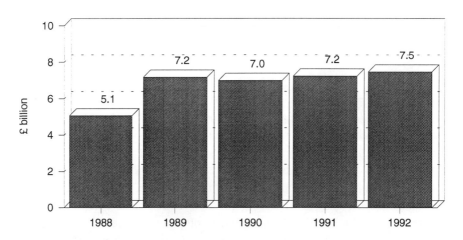

Figure 5.1 Total capital under management (including portfolio valued at cost), 1988–1992
(*Sources*: 1991, 1992, 1993 EVCA yearbooks)

The relatively low rate of growth in the UK venture capital pool, certainly when compared to that seen for Germany and Japan, is of course due to its greater maturity and relative size. The reduction in the estimated cash component of the UK pool since 1989, however, has tended to hide a stronger underlying growth of the UK invested portfolio (see Fig. 5.2). This continuation in the rate of growth of the invested portfolio is understandable though as having raised a fund, the venture capitalist is under pressure to invest the money in order to achieve the high 'venture capital' returns that the investors are seeking.

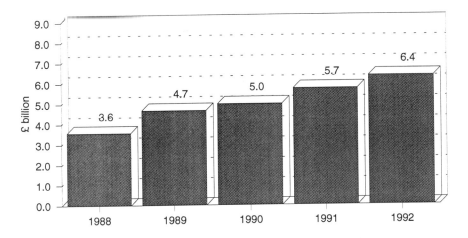

Figure 5.2 Total size of investment portfolio (valued at cost), 1988–1992
(*Sources*: EVCA yearbooks)

Accompanying the slow–down in growth of the venture capital pool, there may also have been an increase in the number of larger funds, with the *UKVCJ* reporting 12 funds having more than £200 million under management in 1990, compared with only 7 in 1989.[2]

Next, we examine the two key aspects of venture capital fund management, raising the capital and investing the capital. The 1980s saw a dramatic rise in the annual amount of capital committed to (raised by) independent venture capital funds; it peaked in 1989 before falling back to the levels of the mid–1980s during the early 1990s. (Note that usually captive funds are not really 'raised' from third parties.) Figure 5.3 shows this rapid rise and subsequent fall in capital commitments.[3]

In this chart, money committed to 'dedicated pools' by captive funds has been included from 1987 onwards. These dedicated pools are managed at arms length on behalf of the institutional investors by the independent venture capital group.

Three categories of independent fund have been distinguished in the

152 The Funding Environment in Four Key Countries

analysis, namely *private* funds, which raise capital primarily from institutional investors; *BES/BSS* funds, which raised capital from individuals investing under the Business Expansion Scheme (BES) or its forerunner the Business Start–up Scheme (BSS); and *public* funds, which are publicly listed investment firms. Having said that, it can be seen that private independent funds represent the vast majority of funds raised, accounting for around 92 per cent (£5.1 billion) of the cumulative funds total over the period (£5.5 billion).

It should be noted that the amount raised by the independent venture capitalists, however, is supplemented by substantial inflows into the pool from captive organizations (that is, the amount invested by them) and from realized capital gains which are available for reinvestment (see Fig. 5.4). It can also be seen that these have remained a relatively stable supply of investments into the venture capital pool, despite the sharp fall–off in the amount raised by the independents as the economy entered into recession.

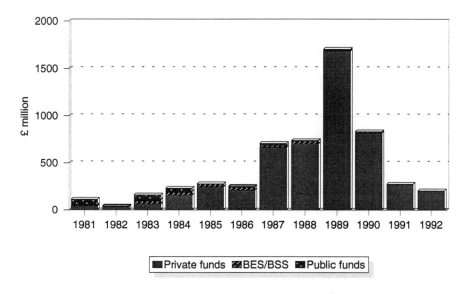

Figure 5.3 Capital commitments by type of fund (not including captive funds or 3i), 1981–1992
(Source: UKVCJ)

In terms of the number of new independent funds raised, the BES funds were more significant than suggested by their total value.[4] It should be noted, however, that the number of new BES funds raised showed a dramatic decline between 1987 and 1992, principally due to the changes brought about in 1988, which allowed 'assured tenancies' to be covered under the

Business Expansion Scheme. As a result, trading companies, such as those normally financed by the formal venture capital industry, found it very difficult indeed to compete for BES funds. Nevertheless, after the 1988 rule change, over £2 billion of BES funds were raised from private investors for assured tenancies.[5]

On the investment side, total disbursements by venture capitalists have roughly followed the pattern of funds being raised, although disbursement levels were significantly higher than the amount of funds raised in 1991 and 1992, being mainly financed by the fundraising excess of the late 1980s (particularly 1989).[6] While most of the funds were invested in UK firms (see Fig. 5.6), a small amount went to US companies, and more recently a significant amount has gone into European businesses (although the European figures are distorted slightly by a definitional change).

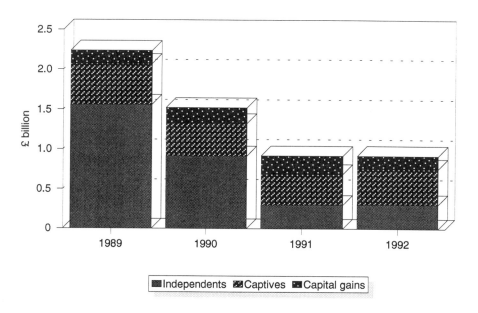

Figure 5.4 Venture capital 'raised' by source, 1989–1992
(*Source*: EVCA yearbooks)

According to BVCA statistics, during the 1989–92 period, the number of UK company financings has remained at around 1200 per annum, although this total also includes follow-on financing rounds. Nevertheless, the BVCA numbers suggest that 78 per cent of the funds disbursed in 1992 went into new investments, with the remainder being follow-on financings.

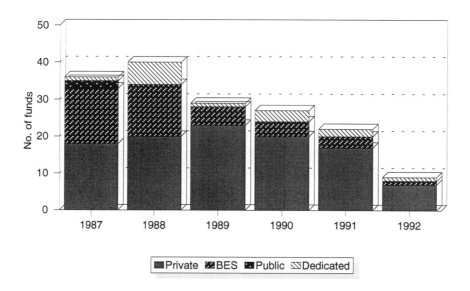

Figure 5.5 Number of new funds raised by type of fund, 1987–1992
(Source: UKVCJ)

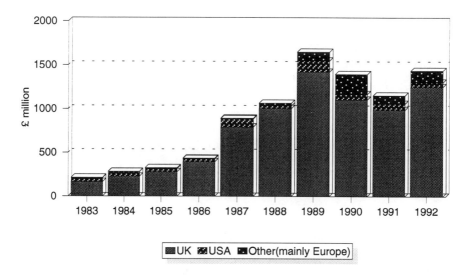

Figure 5.6 Total disbursements by geographical region, 1983–1992
(Sources: UKVCJ; BVCA)

BREAKDOWN BY FUNDING STAGE

There are, in principle, three key dimensions along which venture capital firms can choose to specialise, if they so wish. They are by *funding stage*, that is seed, start–up, expansion, buy–out, etc.; by *industry sector*, that is technology, manufacturing, service, etc.; and/or by *geographical region*, whether UK, regional or international. Since the focus of this chapter is principally the UK venture capital market, we concentrate on the first two of these dimensions.

With regard to investment preference by funding stage, the most recent surveys of UK firms indicate the pattern shown in Fig. 5.7.[7] While it is difficult to infer too much from these surveys, it does appear that a number of firms shifted their investment preferences between 1989 and 1990 (perhaps as the recession began to bite), away from early stage investments and towards either broad base or later stage investing. In addition, anecdotal evidence would seem to suggest that a number of broad base funds became focused on later stage investments.

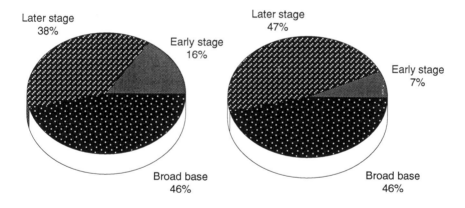

Figure 5.7 Investment preferences of firms by funding stage, end 1989 and end 1990
(Source: UKVCJ)

Somewhat in contrast to that evidence of a possible shift away from early stage investments between 1989 and 1990, the number of new funds being raised with a focus on early stage investments appears to have been much more resilient to macroeconomic factors, with two or three new early stage funds being raised every year between 1988 and 1992.[8] In comparison, the number of new funds focusing on all other stages of investment (including 'all stages' funds) dropped from twenty-one in 1989 to only six in 1992. By way of a rider to the above remarks, there appears to be some correlation between new funds having an early stage investment focus and new funds having a technology focus.

In terms of actual financings carried out between 1984 and 1992, the data from the *UKVCJ* and the BVCA appears to be slightly at odds, particularly with regard to the disbursement share accounted for by buy–outs and buy–ins.[9] The main reason for the difference between the two data sets, however, is that 3i's investments are included in the BVCA figures, but are omitted from the *UKVCJ*'s data. The impact of the inclusion of 3i's investments is to reduce the amount of money flowing into buy–outs and buy–ins, and to increase the emphasis on expansion and (to a lesser extent) 'other early stage'. In Fig. 5.8 and Fig. 5.9 we have presented only the BVCA data.

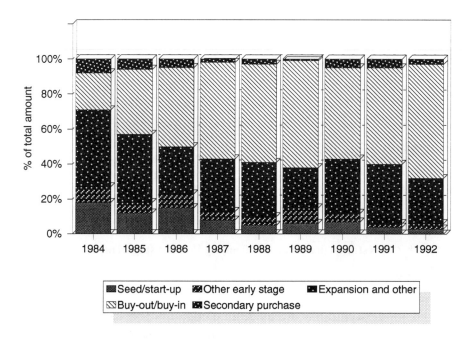

Figure 5.8 Disbursements by funding stage as a proportion of total amount disbursed, 1984–1992
(Source: BVCA)

Venture Capital Funding in the UK 157

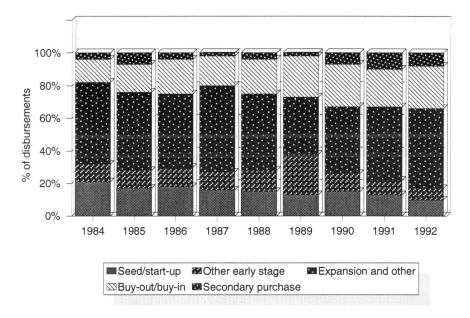

Figure 5.9 Disbursements by funding stage as a proportion of total number of disbursements, 1984–1992
(*Source*: BVCA)

A number of points are worth noting.

1 The amount of funds flowing into buy–out/buy–in activities, as a percentage of the total number of investments/total amount invested, increased dramatically over the period. Indeed, in 1992 MBOs/MBIs accounted for a quarter of all deals and two-thirds of the total amount disbursed.
2 'Expansion and other' funding (including the refinancing of bank debt in the BVCA figures), after declining in relative importance during the late 1980s, appears to have picked up in the early 1990s. This is principally due to this area holding its level of funding during the recession (because of low exit activity and distressed financing, as we saw earlier for the USA), while other areas declined.
3 Secondary purchases have grown since 1989, especially as a percentage of the number of disbursements, a phenomenon which is probably also 'recession refinancing' related.
4 Seed/start–up and other early stage financings have suffered a continual erosion of market share, particularly in terms of the total value of disbursements.

5 The average size of disbursements in seed, start–up and other early stage investments picked up in 1992, breaking the downward trend of the preceding three years.

Overall, the data paints a picture of a boom period for venture capital from 1984 to 1989, characterized by increasing MBO/MBI activity and investment, followed by a period of venture capital recession in 1990–1, characterized by reinvestment in existing portfolio companies, lessening MBO/MBI activity and a somewhat sharper fall–off in seed/start–up and early stage financing.

INDUSTRY SECTORS ATTRACTING INVESTMENT

The second dimension along which UK venture capitalists can choose to specialize is by industry sector. In this regard, 'sector specialization' tends to go only so far as 'technology preference' or 'non–technology preference', at least in terms of the available data, and probably in operational terms too.

It is interesting to set any discussion of industry sector specialization in the context of the former business experience of the fund's executives. In this respect, a sample of 227 venture capital executives in 1989 showed that roughly half had finance–type backgrounds and only 19 per cent had technology-related backgrounds (see Fig. 5.10).[10] Since technology-related investment probably requires more industry-specific knowledge and skills than any other sector, at least in terms of investment evaluation, it would not be surprising for investment preferences to be in line with the availability of these technology-related skills. Having said this, the venture capitalist skills most likely to be needed by NTBFs are those of industrial experience and finance.

Figure 5.11 shows the investment preferences of venture capital firms between sectors in 1989 and 1990. We noted earlier an apparent shift in investment preference in these years away from early stage investments and towards later stage deals. A degree of correlation between early stage investments and technology focus was also noted. Thus it is not surprising that Fig. 5.11 indicates a move away from a preference for technology-based investments between 1989 and 1990.

Industry sectors are examined in more detail in Figs 5.12 and 5.13. Disbursements since 1984 have been broken down into four technology-related sectors: computer-related investments; electronics and related investments; medical technology and biotechnology investments; and communications-related investments. In addition, the non–technology sector disbursements have been segmented into a further four categories: consumer-related investments; industrial investments; other manufacturing investments; and other service investments. (The BVCA data does not include MBOs, MBIs, acquisitions and secondary purchases in the 1984–6 figures.)

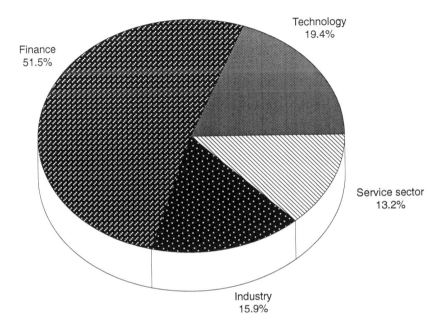

Figure 5.10 Backgrounds of venture capital executives, 1989 (total sample = 227)
(*Source*: *UKVCJ*)

Analysed in this way, a number of trends become evident.

1 Consumer sector investment (both in absolute terms and as a percentage of the total amount) has declined significantly from the 1989 peak, as has the number of deals. This is only to be expected, however, as the economy entered recession.
2 The non–technology 'other service' sector has become an increasingly important part of venture capital investment since 1989, while 'other manufacturing' has declined from its peak during 1988.
3 The number of investments in (relatively) non–technology related industrial companies has picked up slightly in absolute terms and more markedly as a percentage of the total number of investments.
4 Finally, the four technology-related investment sectors have shown dramatic declines in terms of both relative and absolute importance over

the period. This trend is in all probability linked to the apparent move away from seed, start–up and early stage investing noted earlier in this chapter.

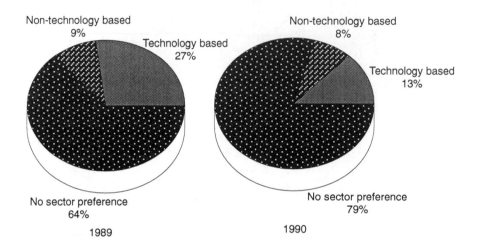

Figure 5.11 Investment preferences of venture capital firms between industry sectors, end 1989 and end 1990
(Source: UKVCJ)

This fourth trend is particularly worrying, as it does not appear to be solely due to the impact of the economic recession. If so, then technology–based investment would not be expected to recover as economic conditions improve. This trend is perhaps easier to see in Fig. 5.14, which shows only the share of technology–based investment in the total number of venture capital deals. (In this case we have supplied estimates for the impact of including MBOs, MBIs, acquisitions and secondary purchases in the 1984–6 data.)

Note that although the unadjusted data for the first three years of the period excludes MBOs, MBIs, acquisitions and secondary purchases, the *trend* was still down from 1984 to 1986. We have estimated that, on the same basis as the later years, the 1984–6 figures would have been between 5 and 8 percentage points lower.

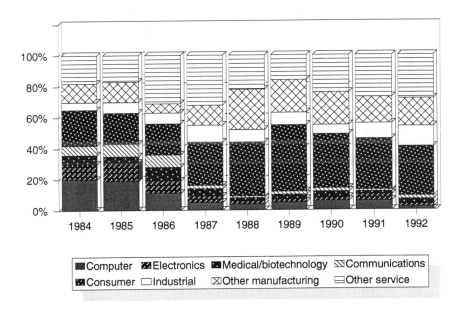

Figure 5.12 Disbursements by industry sector as a proportion of total amount disbursed, 1984–1992 (1984–6 excludes MBOs, MBIs, acquisitions and secondary purchases)
(*Source*: BVCA)

INVESTMENT SIZE

Analyzing the size *distribution* of disbursements per transaction yields an interesting insight into the changing nature of venture capital investment in the UK. We shall consider first the distribution of disbursements into a number of size bands. As can be seen from Fig. 5.15, between 1985 and 1989 there was a dramatic increase in the proportion of transactions involving amounts of over £500,000, in particular for the 'over £2 million' segment. Note also that the proportion of deals falling into the 'under £100,000' segment fell particularly sharply.

162 The Funding Environment in Four Key Countries

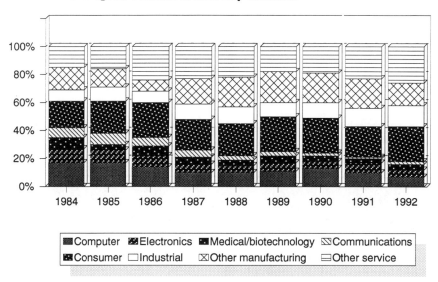

Figure 5.13 Disbursements by industry sector as a proportion of total number of disbursements (1984–6 excludes MBOs, MBIs, acquisitions and secondary purchases)
(Source: BVCA)

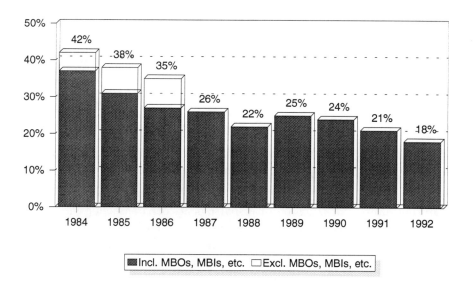

Figure 5.14 Technology-related disbursements as a proportion of total number of disbursements, 1984–1992
(Sources: BVCA, with adjusted data for 1984–6)

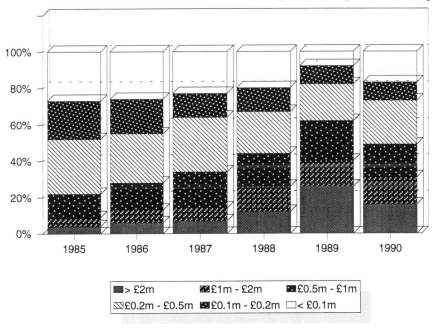

Figure 5.15 Disbursements by size as a proprtion of total number of disbursements, 1985-1990
(*Source*: UKVCJ/Venture Economics)

While one would expect the general level of price inflation over the 1985-9 period to have pushed some transactions into the next highest size band, this does not explain the observed trend. Instead, the explanation has probably two key and related components. The first was the industry's ability to raise ever-increasing amounts of money, which leads to a requirement to find more and, more importantly, larger homes for the available cash; and the second was the industry's inability to charge substantially higher fees to investors in order to compensate for the extra effort of managing a more fragmented portfolio of smaller investments, which lead to a requirement to minimize the number of companies that a given amount was invested in. This explanation finds further support when the distribution of the total amount invested between the various size categories is analyzed (see Fig. 5.16).

Finally, although analogous data for 1991 and 1992 was not available, a comparison of the average size of disbursement per transaction is believed to act as a good guide to the likely distribution of disbursement sizes (see Fig. 5.17). It would thus appear that, after some degree of 'shrinkage' in disbursement sizes in both 1990 and 1991, there was a sharp increase during 1992. Following the end of the venture capital bull market of 1989, funds became scarcer in 1990 and 1991. This combined with the perceived increase in risk associated with very large and highly leveraged MBOs, etc. (which accounted for a substantial proportion of the late 1980s investments) at the start of a recession, and caused a reversal in the trend of increasing investment concentration on larger deals during 1990. With the UK economy showing signs of emerging from the recession during 1992, however, the MBOs started to return and with them the larger transaction sizes. The poor economics of investing smaller amounts in companies during the earlier stages of their development remains a major problem within the industry.

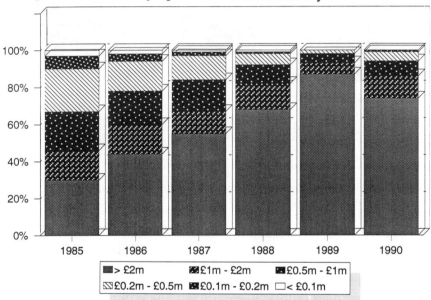

Figure 5.16 Disbursements by size as a proportion of total amount disbursed, 1985–1990
(*Source*: *UKVCJ*/Venture Economics)

CHARACTERISTICS OF INVESTORS

We shall analyse contributions made to the venture capital funds by different categories of investors in two stages: investors in independent venture capital funds, and investors in independent and captive venture capital funds combined. As we saw earlier (Fig. 5.4), the funds 'raised' from investors in captive funds exceeded those of the independents after 1990, as the amounts raised by independents fell dramatically.

UK independent venture capital fund investors, the ultimate sources of venture capital, fall into one of the following groups: UK pension funds; foreign institutions; UK insurance companies; private individuals and family trusts; industrial corporations; UK fund management groups; academic institutions; UK banks; government and local authorities; and others. The relative historic importance of investors in these categories (combining four of them into two groups) is indicated for 1986 to 1990 in Fig. 5.18.[11]

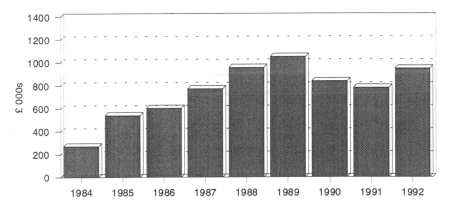

Figure 5.17 Average amount disbursed per investment, 1984–1992 (1984–6 excludes MBOs, MBIs, acquisitions and secondary purchases)
(*Source*: BVCA)

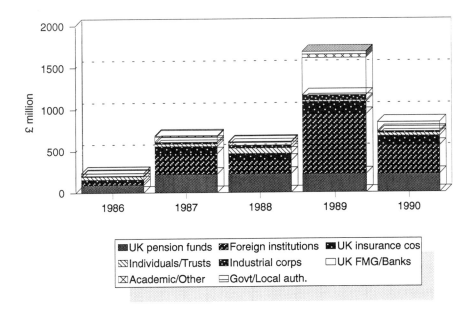

Figure 5.18 Value of capital committed to independent funds by source, 1986–1990
(*Source*: UKVCJ)

Key features worth noting in Fig. 5.18 are that:

1. UK pension funds form a substantial and, perhaps more importantly, stable source of funds for independent venture capitalists. As a group, they have contributed over £200 million in each of the last four years shown;
2. foreign institutions account for a large proportion of the capital invested in most years, although these investment flows appear to be highly volatile;
3. other mainline UK institutional investors (insurance and fund management companies) have also been a significant, if again somewhat volatile, source of funds;
4. UK corporations have provided only a relatively modest proportion of the total (between 2 and 6 per cent);
5. government and local authorities contribute little or nothing to the independent funds.

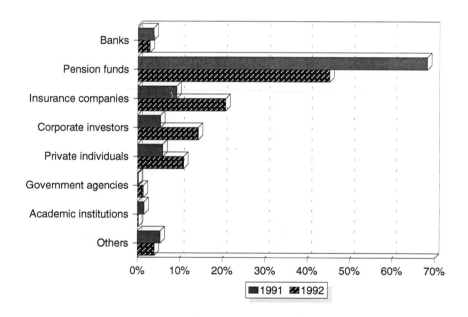

Figure 5.19 Sources of independent funds as a proportion of total amount raised, 1991 and 1992
(*Source*: BVCA)

The fact that pension funds appear to be the only reliable source of funds for the independent venture capitalists, through both 'bull' and 'bear' phases of the market, is amply demonstrated by the BVCA's figures for the following two years (1991 and 1992) – a period when venture capital fundraising by independents fell off dramatically.[12] It has to be said, however, that more recently there has been a perceived increase in the amount of money being channelled into captive funds, *including* money from the pension funds.

Although the BVCA data does not separate out foreign institutions in its analysis, which distorts comparisons with the previous *UKVCJ* (Venture Economics) data, funding from most non–pension related sources fell sharply in 1991, while even pension funds' contributions fell in 1992. Funds sourced from outside the UK (particularly those from North America and Europe) remained substantial, however, in both 1991 and 1992 (see Fig. 5.20).[13]

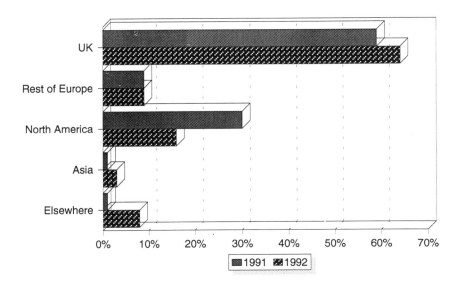

Figure 5.20 Geographical sources of independent funds as a proportion of total amount raised, 1991 and 1992
(*Source*: BVCA)

When the sources of funds provided to captive venture capital firms and 3i are included in the figures for 1989 to 1992, the contribution from the banks significantly increases (banks owned over 97 per cent of 3i's shares in issue).[14]

168 The Funding Environment in Four Key Countries

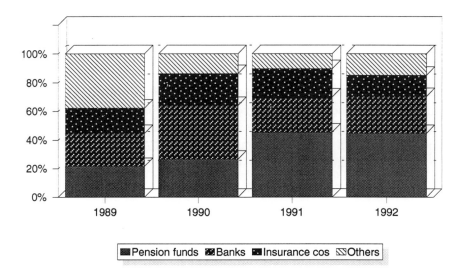

Figure 5.21 Sources of capital for captive and independent funds as a proportion of total amount, 1989–1992
(*Sources*: 1991, 1992, 1993 EVCA yearbooks)

FUNDING SOURCES AND METHODS

In terms of the number of venture capital transactions, the market shares enjoyed by each of the main types of investment vehicles over the period 1985 to 1990 is shown in Fig. 5.22.[15] A number of observations can be made for that period:

1 the government/local authority share of the number of deals has been low and more or less stable;
2 the BES share rapidly declined from 25 per cent in 1985 to only 2 per cent in 1990 (for reasons previously explained);
3 after increasing from 1985 to 1987, largely at the expense of BES and (to some extent) captive funds, the market share of independent funds eased back a little in the following three years; and
4 captive funds grew strongly following 1987, more than regaining any lost market share of the previous period, as independent funds were hit by capital-raising problems.

Venture Capital Funding in the UK 169

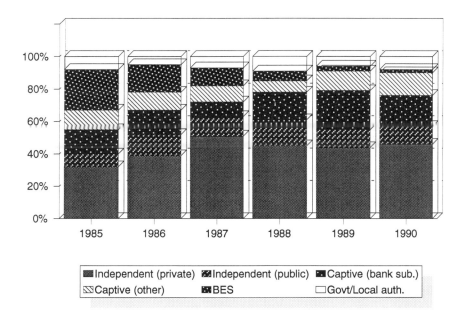

Figure 5.22 Disbursements made by type of investment vehicle as a proportion of total number of disbursements, 1985– 1990
(*Source: UKVCJ*)

In terms of the total amount invested by each category of fund, similar (if not somewhat more exaggerated) trends are evident (see Fig. 5.23). Note in particular that by 1990 government, local authority and BES funds had declined in importance to such an extent that they, together, accounted for only 2 per cent of the total amount invested.

In terms of the relationship between independent and captive funds, however, recent BVCA data, for 1989 to 1992, suggests large annual swings in market share, first one way, then the other.[16]

So far, the venture capitalists have been categorized essentially according to the *nature* of their source of capital – third–party, associated company, BES, government, etc. In the following sections, we shall attempt to flesh out the details of the venture capital players in the UK market according to the scale, scope or nature of their activities and, in particular, group them into: 3i, the venture 'supercapitalist'; the venture capitalists; the seed capitalists.

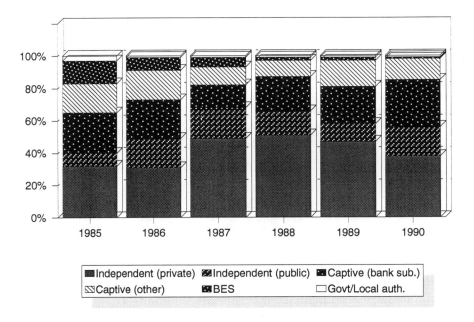

Figure 5.23 Disbursements made by type of investment vehicle as a proportion of total amount disbursed, 1985–1990
(*Source*: UKVCJ)

3i, the venture 'supercapitalist'

Until 1994, 3i was a private company owned by the major UK banks, including the Bank of England, the shareholdings being in accordance with Table 5.1. The company was set up in 1945 and as of 1993, had invested around £6 billion in over 11,800 companies,[17] approaching 40 per cent of these companies still forming part of its portfolio. The company has eighteen offices in the UK, and international offices in France, Germany, Italy, Spain and the USA, supplemented with joint ventures in Australia, India, Japan, Netherlands and Portugal. In 3i's 1992–3 financial year, it invested in around 560 private UK SMEs (almost half of the UK market). The company sourced its capital from its banking shareholders and, as such, could be regarded as captive. Since then, however, 3i has raised two funds in association with third parties and has gone public.

Table 5.1 Shareholdings in 3i Group plc, 1993

Bank of England	14.61%
Bank of Scotland	3.03%
Barclays Bank plc	18.35%
Lloyds Bank plc	13.33%
Midland Bank plc	17.54%
The Royal Bank of Scotland plc	7.38%
National Westminster Bank plc	22.37%
Coutts & Co. (owned by National Westminster)	0.68%
Staff of 3i	2.71%
Total	100.0%

To give some idea of the importance of the firms in which 3i invests to the economy as a whole, the aggregate sales of its portfolio companies are estimated to be £60 billion (of which £9 billion are exports), or 11–12 per cent of GDP, and they collectively employ about 1 million people, that is, 4–5 per cent of the UK workforce. In recent years, in common with other UK venture capitalists, 3i's investments have become increasingly focused on 'growth capital' (expansion capital) and MBOs/MBIs, as can be seen from its disbursement record over the years 1990–3 in Fig. 5.24.[18] One key feature to note is that the amount invested by 3i in start–up companies, in both absolute and relative terms, has decreased over the period, from £38 million in fiscal 1990 to only £15 million in fiscal 1993. As might be expected from its emphasis on later stage deals, 3i adopts a hands–off approach to its investments, although involvement might be a little more hands–on with start–up situations.

Finally, unlike other venture capitalists, 3i makes a large number of investments in the 'equity gap' (under £250,000) (see Fig. 5.25). This said, such investments are believed to be much more debt–like than equity.

The venture capitalists

Of the remaining 116 members of the BVCA, according to the 1993–4 BVCA directory, 68 companies have a preference for later stage deals and have no interest in seed, start–up or, usually, early stage deals. A further 41 firms appear to be willing to consider both early and later stage deals, although most of these specifically exclude seed investments. Finally, only 7 firms have chosen to focus upon seed, start–up and early stage businesses, which we shall collectively refer to as the 'seed capitalists'. The remaining 109 firms we shall refer to as the 'venture capitalists'.

172 The Funding Environment in Four Key Countries

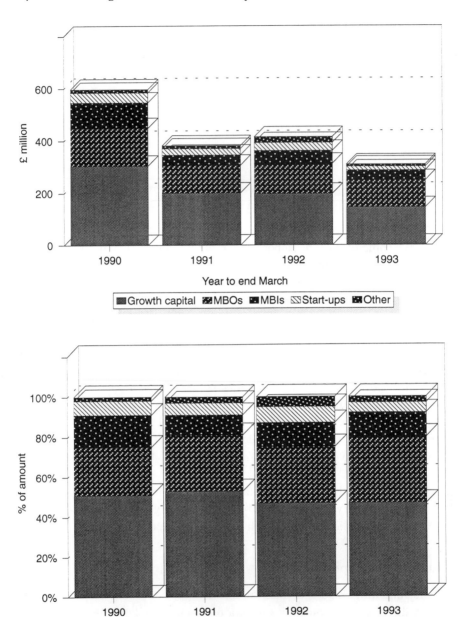

Figure 5.24 3i: disbursements by investment stage, in value and percentage terms, 1990–1993
(*Source*: 3i)

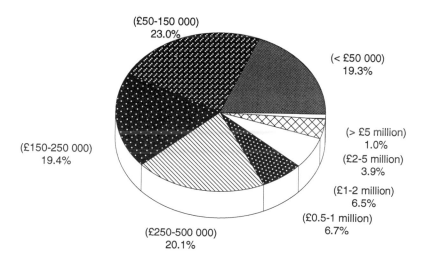

Figure 5.25 3i: disbursements by size range (the number of companies in each range), fiscal 1993
(*Source*: 3i)

The venture capitalists divide into the groups shown in Fig. 5.26. While government-related firms might be motivated to some extent by other than purely financial considerations, the remaining 103 venture capitalists are similar in that they are motivated by the capital gain that they hope to make on their investments. There are differences between captive and independent firms in two main respects: captives do not have to raise capital from third parties and captives tend to focus more on income from their investees than do independents. Otherwise there are relatively few differences in the methods of operation of the captive and the independent funds.

A key dimension along which there are variations among venture capital firms is in their 'minimum investment size'. According to the figures quoted by firms in the 1993–4 BVCA directory, the distribution of minimum investment size for the venture capitalists is in accordance with Fig. 5.27 (some amounts quoted have been included in the total for the nearest available figure). In this regard, we believe that minimum figures below £250,000 are in all probability rather misleading. We suspect that in most cases investments significantly smaller than £250,000 are only made in circumstances where either: additional follow–on investments are likely to be required to increase the total investment beyond this level; or the investment is made as part of a syndicated deal, whereby the total investment of the syndicate is much larger than the amount invested; or, far more rarely, small investments are made in companies with explosive growth potential but little requirement for cash beyond the initial investment. In addition, it is also likely that the sizes quoted in the BVCA directory are somewhat lower than the actual figures, so as to capture marginal size candidates for consideration.

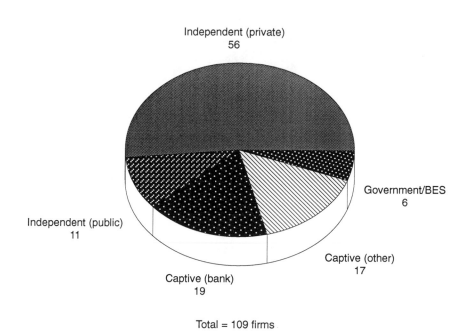

Figure 5.26 'Venture capitalists' by type of firm, 1993–4
(*Source*: 1993–4 BVCA directory)

Finally, it is understood that the majority of investments made by the venture capitalists are dealt with on a hands–off basis and often in a wide range of industries, because of the concentration of investment in later stage companies.

The seed capitalists

Among the seven seed capitalist BVCA members, one is a government-associated firm, one is captive and the rest are independents. There are several important contrasts with the venture capitalists. Those relevant in this context are that the *actual* minimum deal size is smaller than £250,000 for six out of the seven companies, although at least one of the six prefers to invest a cumulative minimum of £250,000 over the first and subsequent financing rounds; and investments are undertaken on very much more of a hands–on (CVC) basis and are focused on NTBFs. We will see differences relating to investment period and rates of return in later sections.

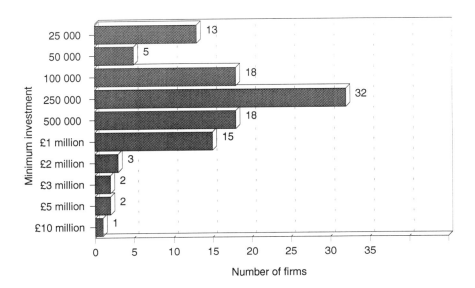

Figure 5.27 'Venture capitalists': minimum investment sizes quoted by firms, 1993–4
(*Source*: 1993–4 BVCA directory)

THE VENTURE CAPITALIST/ENTREPRENEUR RELATIONSHIP

Whereas the industry was initially modelled on the US system, the boom in the UK venture capital market has taken it away from the relatively high proportion of CVC-type transactions (and CVC-type, hands-on investor/investee relationships) of the US. Today, with the notable exception of the seed capitalists and the relatively few venture capitalists who still invest significant amounts in early stage deals, the industry has moved towards the hands–off provision of capital to later stage companies.

In early stage deals, the nature of the relationship between the investor and the investee is similar to that in the US (see Chapter 2). With the more numerous later stage deals, however, there tend to be only three types of investor/investee interactions. The first occurs in the period immediately prior to the transaction, when there is a period of intense contact during the shaping and negotiation of the deal. This can also involve a third–party vendor in the case of an MBO/MBI. Then, in the period between the completion of the transaction and exit, it is common for interactions to consist of little more than 'trading updates' and 'reconciliation against budget' types of interactions, perhaps monthly. Since later stage companies invariably have complete management teams with good track records and operate in established markets with established products, and so on, there can be only a very limited capacity in which the venture capitalist can add value to an investee company that is performing well. In the event of something going wrong with the investee's trading, however, the venture capitalist is well placed as an external monitor and shareholder of the business to effect appropriate changes. Finally, in the period leading up to the exit for investors, the venture capitalist once again acquires a role in providing the relevant exit expertise and contacts.

PERIOD OF INVESTMENT, EXIT OPPORTUNITIES AND VALUATION

The total amount of divestments by the UK venture capital industry over the four years from 1989 to 1992 is shown in Fig. 5.28 in value terms. However, the figures shown represent the *historical cost* of those companies divested and, as such, do not represent the actual amounts received by the venture capitalists. For example, the figures include the historical cost of investments written off, which would act to depress actual cash receipts relative to the figures shown. On the other hand, they do not include realized cash profits on investments, which would act to increase cash receipts.

The distribution of exits between the various divestment methods is shown in Fig. 5.29. As can be seen, in those two years, approaching half of all divestments were achieved through write–offs; roughly one–quarter of investments proceeded to a trade sale; and trade sales outnumbered IPOs by 2 or 3 to 1.

Venture Capital Funding in the UK 177

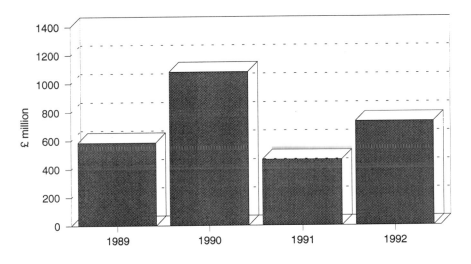

Figure 5.28 Total divestments by UK venture capitalists, 1989–1992
(*Sources*: 1991, 1992, 1993 EVCA yearbooks)

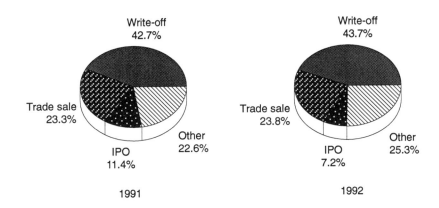

Figure 5.29 Companies divested according to method of divestment, 1991 and 1992
(*Source*: 1993 EVCA yearbook)

At the time of investment, it is said that UK venture capitalists are seeking to exit in three to five years, although seed, start–up and early stage investors may be more in step with their US counterparts at around five to seven years. The most recently available data for the average time interval between the first venture investment and the exit date would appear to be entirely consistent with this time horizon.[19] Indeed, the data suggests that the investment period is pretty much independent of the exit route. Tables 5.2 and 5.3 outline the average period of investment for divestments achieved via either acquisitions (trade sales) or via IPOs over the period 1987 to 1989.

Table 5.2 Average investment period (in years) preceding trade sales, according to stage of company at time of investment

Year of trade sale	Early	Expansions	MBO/I	Secondary	All stages
1987	2.6	2.8	2.8	3.4	2.8
1988	4.5	3.3	3.1	4.0	3.6
1989	3.4	3.8	3.3	4.0	3.6
Average	3.6	3.3	3.1	3.9	3.4

Table 5.3 Average investment period (in years) preceding IPOs, according to stage of company at time of investment

Year of IPO	Early	Expansions	MBO/I	Secondary	All stages
1987	3.0	5.2	3.7	2.5	4.1
1988	4.1	3.6	3.1	4.3	3.3
1989	4.0	3.3	3.2	1.0	3.2
Average	3.4	4.1	3.3	2.9	3.6

As seen above, there are two principal means of exit in the UK for successful companies, the trade sale and the IPO. We also saw that for 1991 and 1992, the trade sale outweighed the IPO as an exit route by a factor of 2 or 3 to 1. Earlier data from Venture Economics, however, appears to suggest that this bias towards trade sales as an exit route might be a relatively recent phenomenon.[20] Having said this, the main problem is that although IPOs are publicly reported events, trade sales are often discreet affairs. Thus the earlier data from Venture Economics may have failed to capture the true level of divestments via trade sales. With these above caveats in mind, Fig. 5.30 shows the relative importance of the two exit routes for venture–backed companies.

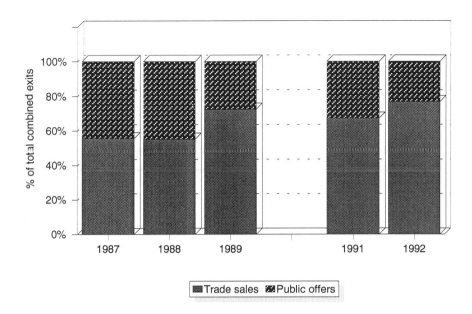

Figure 5.30 Relative shares of trade sales and IPOs as exits from venture-backed companies, 1987–1989 and 1991–1992
(*Sources*: UKVCJ for 1987–9; 1993 EVCA yearbook for 1991–2)

Much has been said in recent years on the subject of the relative difficulty of achieving IPOs in the UK (and, indeed, Europe) compared with the US. It is perhaps appropriate, therefore, to outline here the situation with regard to IPOs of UK venture-backed companies. There are, at present, two formally regulated markets in the UK, the main market or 'Official List' and the Unlisted Securities Market (USM). During the late 1980s there was also an even less regulated Third Market.

The USM was established in November 1980, in response to the Wilson Committee report on 'The financing of small firms', published in the same year. It had two main purposes:[21] to provide a formally regulated market for SMEs which were either unlikely, or unable, to apply for a full listing on the Official List; and to bring under Stock Exchange control those unlisted companies whose securities had formerly been freely traded under Stock Exchange Rule 163(2).

In theory, the USM was the ideal public market for venture capital investment exits, not least because of the reduced requirements for obtaining a quotation relative to the main market. Indeed, the theory was borne out in practice for the first few years of its life, as Fig. 5.31 shows. Nevertheless, between 1982 and 1988, the average new issue size rose from £2 million to £9 million, as MBOs and expansion deals formed an increasing proportion of IPO exits. This led, in turn, to more IPOs via the main market. The final blow to the USM, however, came in 1989 when, in response to an EC Directive, regulatory differences between the two markets were narrowed considerably and new USM IPOs fell dramatically (see Fig. 5.32). (The lowering of regulatory requirements for both the Official List and the USM also led to the demise of the Third Market, which had only been in existence for three to four years.) Following this decline in activity, which was also accompanied by a similar fall in trading volumes (from £24 million per day in 1987 to £5.6 million per day in 1991), the future of the USM was placed under review, with initial indications that it would be closed. After representations from, in particular, those in the venture capital industry, however, the market gained a stay of execution until 1996.[22]

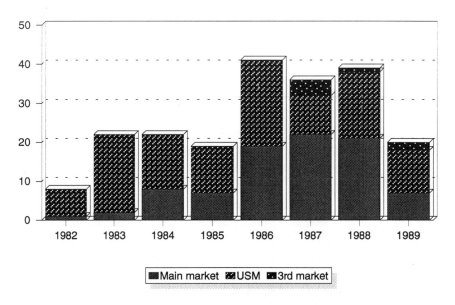

Figure 5.31 Number of venture-backed IPOs by market, 1982–1989
(*Source: UKVCJ*)

The valuation of companies upon exit by venture capitalists is likely to be dependent on the exit method used, in pretty much the same way that we saw was the case in the US, for more or less all of the same reasons (although the UK's substantially less well functioning equity markets for small companies must also be taken into consideration).

Venture Capital Funding in the UK 181

The best guide to value regarding trade sales is probably that given by Stoy Hayward in *Acquisitions Monthly* (which in turn has been estimated from AMDATA III price/earnings (P/E) data).[23] Figure 5.33 shows that, between 1987 and 1991, private companies were invariably sold at P/Es which were below the average for companies in the FT 500 Index (on occasion, substantially so). In addition, this discount appears to have increased somewhat as the economy entered recession and company owners became prepared to accept rather lower valuations for their companies.

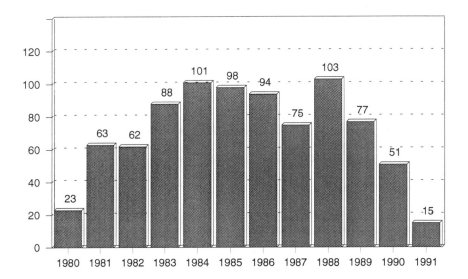

Figure 5.32 Number of new companies joining the Unlisted Securities Market, 1980–1991
(*Source*: Stock Exchange)

IPOs, on the other hand, may have enjoyed P/E ratings nearer to the FT 500 Index multiples for most of this period. For example, the weighted average P/E for those venture–backed IPOs going public during 1988, at 12.3, was very close to both the FT 500 and private company P/E averages (of 12.6 and 12.5 respectively). In 1989, however, while the private company P/E fell significantly to around 10.2, the venture–backed IPO P/E (12.6) remained up with that of the FT 500 Index (12.4).[24]

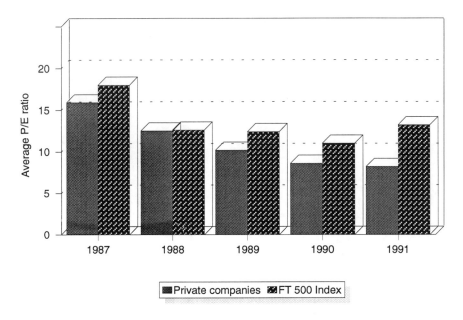

Figure 5.33 Comparison of price/earnings ratios of private and quoted UK companies, 1987–1991
(*Sources*: Stoy Hayward/AMDATA/*Acquisitions Monthly*; Datastream)

RETURNS REQUIRED BY THE PROVIDERS OF DEBT AND EQUITY

Due to interest rates which have been historically significantly higher than the other three countries we have considered, the nominal pretax return on debt capital has traditionally been somewhat higher in the UK. The target pretax return on venture capital, however, has been maintained at or slightly below US levels on a like–for–like basis (particularly for early stage investments). Defining the required pretax rate of return as for the US, Table 5.4 summarizes the required return from each provider.

Venture Capital Funding in the UK 183

Table 5.4 Estimated nominal target return on funds by source

Source	Form of investment	Nominal target return
Bank	Overdraft	Base rate + 2%–5% (8%–11%)
Bank	Long–term loan	Base rate + 3%–4% (9%–10%)
Loan guarantee scheme	Loan (2 to 7 years) of up to £0.25m usually guaranteed as to 70% of the principal	Base rate + 3%–3½% (9%–9½%)
BES	Equity only	Equivalent to 20%–25% (40% tax payer) Equivalent to 25%–30% (25% tax payer)
Venture capital group	Equity, equity package, mezzanine, loan	35% (MBOs, expansion) Up to 50% (early stage)
Seed capital group	Equity only (usually)	40% to 50%+ (early stage to seed)

It is perhaps worth adding, by way of explanation, how the estimated nominal target return has been arrived at for investments made under the Business Expansion Scheme. Consider the following illustrative calculation for a 40% taxpayer BES investor. Let us assume that the BES investor wants to receive the same sort of *post–tax* returns on the investment as the formal seed capitalists, equivalent to a *pre–tax* return of ten times the initial investment in six to seven years (although it is noted that BES investors are *allowed* to divest with full tax relief after five years). Thus we have:

- for a 40 per cent taxpayer, therefore, for every £1 *gross* invested under the scheme, the *net* investment is only £0.6;
- a seed capitalist who receives ten times the initial investment and is subject to CGT at 40 per cent actually receives only 1 + 9 × 0.6 = 6.4 times the initial investment *post–tax*;
- since CGT is not paid under the BES, the pre–tax return is the same as the post–tax return. As a result, the BES investor requires a return of only 0.6 × 6.4 = 3.84 times the initial *gross* investment to enjoy the same *post–tax* returns as the seed capitalists;
- 3.84 times the initial gross investment is equivalent to 21.2 per cent per annum (compounded over seven years) or 25.1 per cent per annum

(compounded over six years), hence the rounded range for the BES target return.

The factors influencing the target returns from the various sources are similar to those noted for the other countries. Bank debt financing is largely influenced by the base rate prevailing at the time, in addition to the 'quality of the lender' (factors such as available security, the performance of the company, the quality of the company's management, etc.); loan guarantee scheme lending is principally influenced by the above factors, plus the location of the business (whether it is, for instance, in an Inner City Task Force Area); BES investment is largely influenced by the marginal tax rate of the investor; and seed and venture capital required rates of return are dependent on the stage of the investment and other factors specific to the investment.

GOVERNMENT INITIATIVES

The UK government has undertaken a range of finance related initiatives to help promote SMEs. Some of the more important measures, particularly intended to help smaller firms, have included: the Business Expansion Scheme (BES); the Loan Guarantee Scheme (LGS); Small firms Merit Award for Research and Technology, known as the SMART award; and smaller scale initiatives to promote the supply of capital from 'business angels'. In addition, regional enterprise boards were also set up on the initiatives of five of the county councils.

The Business Expansion Scheme

The Business Expansion Scheme was introduced in 1983, as a follow-on to the Business Start-up Scheme (BSS), which had been in operation for the previous two years. After various revisions over the course of the following ten years, in an effort either to curb abuse of the scheme or to expand its scope to other activities that became considered as being worthy of its support, the following are the main features of the scheme as it stood in 1993, according to the Inland Revenue leaflets.[25]

(i) The Scheme gives an investor relief at his or her highest income tax rates on the amount invested (up to a maximum of £40,000 a year). When the shares are sold, no capital gains tax is payable if they have been held for at least five years.

(ii) The relief is given for investment in shares in unquoted companies. This

means companies whose shares are not dealt in on the Stock Exchange or the Unlisted Securities Market.
(iii) It covers most kinds of companies trading wholly or mainly in the UK – including manufacturing, service, construction, retail and wholesale distribution. But some companies are excluded, for example those involved in financial services or overseas companies. Companies with substantial property backing are also excluded.
(iv) The Scheme applies to companies which specialise in letting properties on assured tenancies. The properties can be houses, bungalows, flats or bedsitters. The company can acquire existing properties or it can buy new ones. The properties must be in the United Kingdom.
(v) The relief is for genuinely additional investment in unquoted companies.
(vi) Only investors who are not closely connected with the company qualify for relief. It is not available to people putting money into their own business.
(vii) Qualifying investment must be in newly issued shares held on a long-term basis. This means investment in new ordinary shares which have no special rights and which are held for at least five years.
(viii) The relief is withdrawn in whole or in part if the investor withdraws his or her money from the company (or sells the shares) within five years. The relief is also withdrawn if the company fails to meet any of the conditions of the Scheme within three years.
(ix) An investor must invest at least £500 per company unless the investment is made through an approved investment fund.

In addition to the above, it should be noted that the maximum amount on which a BES fund could obtain relief in any one year was limited in most cases to £0.75 million, but up to £5 million in the case of shipping companies and 'assured tenancies'.

Although it had been the clear intention of the government to encourage the provision of risk capital to young and start-up companies (hence the very generous tax incentives), this was not the outcome and many property and other asset-backed deals were dreamt up by the financial community, particularly following the 1988 amendment to allow 'assured tenancy' investments. For example, in the five years prior to the 1988 amendment, just under £700 million had been raised by BES funded schemes.[26] In the five years after the amendment, over £2 billion was raised for assured tenancy schemes alone.[27]

The fact that possibly over £1 billion of taxpayers' money has been given by way of tax breaks *on the invested money alone* (not to mention CGT reliefs), most of which has been channelled into activities of questionable economic benefit, goes some way towards explaining the Inland Revenue's dislike of the scheme. In light of this, we believe that the government's decision to terminate the BES (at least in the existing form) at the end of 1993 was more than justified. In its place, however, the Enterprise Investment Scheme (EIS), announced in the November 1993 budget, appears to be very BES–like although the assured tenancy tax loophole has been removed.

The Loan Guarantee Scheme

Probably the second most substantial government–backed initiative, the Loan Guarantee Scheme, was introduced in 1981. It is run as a joint venture between the Department of Trade and Industry (DTI), and a number of banking and similar lenders (including 3i and some of the enterprise boards).[28] The scheme is designed to help in circumstances where a bank is unable to make a conventional loan to a small firm with a viable business proposition, because of a lack of adequate security for the loan or lack of an adequate trading record, or both.

The LGS provides a government guarantee to the lending institution for amounts between £5000 and £100,000 for both start–up and existing businesses, rising to £250,000 for established businesses (two years trading record). The extent of this guarantee is normally for 70 per cent of the amount loaned, rising to 85 per cent for established businesses and those operating in Inner City Task Force (ICTF) or City Challenge (CC) areas, and lasts for a period of between two and seven years. For variable rate loans, a premium will be payable to the DTI for the guarantee, equivalent to 1.5 per cent per annum on the loaned amount. For fixed rate loans and loans made to companies operating in ICTF or CC areas, on the other hand, this premium is reduced to only 0.5 per cent per annum. (This premium is in addition to the lender's normal loan rate.)

According to the DTI, since the LGS was brought in, more than 33,000 small firms have benefited from it and an aggregate amount of over £1 billion has been loaned using the scheme. To emphasise the higher risk nature of LGS loans, Table 5.5 shows typical failure rates of businesses taking advantage of the scheme, over the seven years following the granting of the loan.[29]

Table 5.5 Typical cumulative default rates under the Loan Guarantee Scheme (percentage of defaults within each time period)

	1 year	2 years	3 years	4 years	5 years	6 years	7 years
1981–4	10%	26%	34%	37%	38%	39%	40%

Sources: based on VCR, NERA, Department of Employment and DTI data.

SMART awards

The SMART scheme is essentially a DTI–funded competition, open to firms with fewer than fifty employees. The aims of the scheme are essentially three-fold:[30] to facilitate highly innovative projects which, despite being commercially viable, cannot find sources of finance; to encourage the formation of NTBFs; to help such firms to reach a stage of sufficient maturity for traditional sources of finance to become available. The competition is held annually, with (in 1991) 180 awards on offer. In February 1992 a new three-year programme started, worth a total of £42 million.

The awards are made available in two stages. Stage 1 is intended to provide funds of up to £45,000 (equivalent to 75 per cent of the project's total cost) to support a feasibility study of a project and stage 2 (normally around twelve months later) is intended to provide funds of up to a further £60,000 (equivalent to 50 per cent of the project's phase 2 cost) to support the development of, say, a prototype product. Roughly half to two–thirds of companies receiving stage 1 support go on to receive stage 2 support.

Informal investors: 'business angels'

At the beginning of 1992 the government launched a scheme to provide small amounts of 'pump-priming money' through five development projects which were designed to bring together business angels and small businesses looking for money. These projects are being led by five of the Training and Enterprise Councils. As yet, however, it is far too early to judge the success or otherwise of this initiative.

Enterprise boards

In 1982 five of the county councils launched their own regional schemes, in an effort to help local businesses recover from the effects of the recession.[31] These enterprise boards, which were set up by the councils using third-party money, were intended to provide long-term funds to manufacturing industry, thus ensuring their long–term survival, and to plug the 'equity gap' for amounts of less than £250,000.

Today, four out of the five still survive, although all have evolved from their original form, not least because of the abolition of the county councils. The funds available from these sources in 1992 are shown in Table 5.6.[32] It is interesting to note that, with regard to the investment performance of these enterprise boards, Greater London Enterprises is understood to have 'put in a relatively good performance', while Yorkshire Enterprise has managed a gross return on its investments of 35 per cent .

Table 5.6 Funds available from regional enterprise boards in 1992

Fund	Investment range	Type of project
Yorkshire Enterprise Ltd		
Yorkshire Fund	£50,000–£1.25m	Manufacturing and service MBOs and restructurings (esp. MBOs from receiver).
Yorkshire Enterprise Fund	£50,000–£0.25m	All except early stage.
West Yorkshire Small Firms Fund	£15,000 max.	SMEs in manufacturing or allied to tourism.
West Midlands Enterprise Board		
WMEB	£50,000 max.	Firms with between 50 and 1000 employees. All except start-ups.
West Midlands Growth Fund	£0.1m–£0.75m	All types.
Black Country Venture Capital Fund	Under £0.1m	All types.
Lancashire Enterprises		
LE Ventures	£0.15m–£0.5m	All types.
Lancashire BIC Investment Fund	£2000–£50,000	All types.
Rosebud Fund	£1000–£50,000	Start–up, reorganization, development and MBO.
Greater London Enterprises		
GLE Development Capital	£50,000–£0.5m	All types.
London Television Growth Fund	Up to £1m	All areas of the media industry.
Kickstart	£5000–£25,000	Seedcorn for high tech.

THE TAXATION ENVIRONMENT

We have outlined how the taxation incentives contained within the BES had a material impact on lowering the cost of capital to those firms taking advantage of it (equivalent to increasing returns to investors in BES enterprises). In addition, it should not be forgotten that small companies are also subject to a reduced rate of income tax (initially 25 per cent) relative to their larger brethren. Other key elements of the UK taxation system which affect investor and entrepreneur returns are the following.[33]

Venture Capital Funding in the UK 189

1 Neither the entrepreneur nor the investor is allowed to deduct their initial investment in the company from their taxable income/capital gains, except (to a limited extent) in the case of a 'serial entrepreneur' who wishes to reinvest part of the capital gain from a previous venture into a further enterprise.
2 If entrepreneurs borrow money to buy shares in their new company, then the interest charged on those funds will be offsetable against their income (earned and passive) if the company is either 'close' or 'employee controlled'. *Interest relief is not available, however, to other investors.*
3 Although the rules governing taxation resulting from share ownership are complex, broadly speaking:

    (a) gains (after making allowance for inflation) made on founder shares, rights issue shares, etc., over and above an annual exemption limit of around £6000, are subject to CGT at the individual's marginal income tax rate; while
    (b) gains from share options (unless under an approved scheme), are treated as income, as are dividends;
    (c) capital losses may only be offset against gains in the year in which they are made, unless (ordinary) shares were subscribed for in a qualifying, unquoted trading company (including USM companies), in which case losses can be offset against income.

4 The entrepreneur should be able to have the same sort of remuneration package as obtained from his previous firm, without giving rise to additional tax liabilities.

ECONOMIC AND SOCIAL RETURNS ON INVESTMENT

Publicly available data relating to returns on venture capital investment is relatively scarce within the UK and, even in circumstances where it is available, is often of questionable validity. In an attempt to overcome this shortcoming, the BVCA is in the process of carrying out a pilot study in order to be able to provide such information. Unfortunately, it is likely to take several years at least following this study before anything like the sort of output obtainable from Venture Economics in the US can be achieved.

At present, much of the calculated returns-on-investment information relates to 3i, with the occasional returns vignette from other specific funds (usually when they have done well and wish to attract further capital). The following is a summary of the most recent data that we have managed to accumulate.

(1) Prior to the initial aborted flotation of 3i, a leading firm of stockbrokers, Smith New Court, analysed the 'performance' of 3i against that of four major

investment trusts, Candover, Drayton Consolidated, Electra and Murray Ventures.[34] Although such a comparison is somewhat suspect because of the context in which it was made, the broker generated the five-year compound rates of return and volatilities (up to the end of January 1991) given in Table 5.7.

Table 5.7 A comparison of performance of 3i and four major investment trusts (to end January 1991)

Firm	5-year ROR	Annual volatility
3i	15.0%	10.2
Candover	32.3%	11.4
Drayton	4.8%	18.4
Electra	14.3%	15.3
Murray	7.4%	17.2
All share index	12.4%	10.7

Source: Smith New Court

(2) Hambro Advanced Technology Trust, which specializes in NTBF–type investments, achieved a cash-on-cash return of around 33 per cent over the period 1982–9.[35]

(3) 3i's investment returns, based on published reports and making adjustments to allow for its atypical structure, have been estimated in a paper by Brown, revealing a trend of decreasing returns, as shown in Fig. 5.34.[36] (It is the trend, rather than the magnitude, of the returns that is likely to be the most accurate approximation of reality, since estimated returns based on published data must be viewed with caution.) Since 3i accounts for a substantial part of the UK venture capital market, and also invests across more or less all stages and sizes of investment, it might be reasonable to assume that the above will mirror the returns from ' UK Venture Capital Industry plc'.

(4) Finally, a preliminary review by the DTI of the SMART awards scheme calculated that the 1988 round of awards would eventually give rise to profits of around £20 million in *present value* terms (see later), for an outlay of only £9 million.[37] This would represent an exceptionally good return in venture capital terms if achieved.

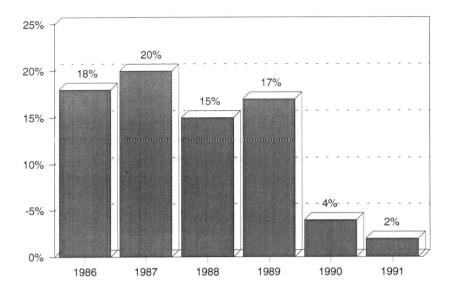

Figure 5.34 Estimated returns on 3i's investments, 1986–1991
(*Sources*: D. Brown; Bygrave, Hay and Peeters (eds, *Realizing Investment Value*, 1994)

With regard to social returns, no comprehensive public data has yet been accumulated to demonstrate any of the social benefits to the economy of UK venture capital activity. One should bear in mind, however, the figures quoted earlier for 3i, that is, that its portfolio companies' sales are equal to around 11–12 per cent of UK GDP and they employ equivalent to 4–5 per cent of the workforce.

We shall revisit the question of social returns resulting from venture capital activities, when we analyse the case studies at a later stage.

GROWTH AND PERFORMANCE OF NTBFs

A relatively recent study of the UK carried out by Daly et al. focused on producing the sort of information generated by Birch's US study of the role that SMEs play in the growth of the economy.[38] Two of the key findings of this work, which related to the 1987–9 period, are worth noting. Daly et al. found that firms with fewer than ten employees created half a million jobs, or roughly half of the total net growth in employment, while employing less than 20 per cent of the UK workforce; and that, taken together with the findings of earlier studies, it would appear that the overall job creation ability of small firms is less affected by the economic cycle than that for large firms and, indeed, appears remarkably stable.

We shall specifically address the question of job creation by NTBFs in both Part III and Part IV, especially with regard to our portfolio of UK case studies.

Notes

1. Based upon figures appearing in *Venture Capital in Europe: 1993 EVCA Yearbook* (EVCA, Zaventum, 1993), p. 156.
2. 'Special report: resources of the UK venture capital industry', *UK Venture Capital Journal*, July 1990, pp. 8–14; 'Special report: resources of the UK venture capital industry', *UK Venture Capital Journal*, July 1991, pp. 15–19.
3. 'Special report: capital commitments to UK venture capital funds in 1988', *UK Venture Capital Journal*, Jan. 1989, pp. 8–17; 'Special report: capital commitments to UK venture capital funds in 1990', *UK Venture Capital Journal*, Jan. 1991, pp. 12–20; 'Special report: capital commitments to UK venture capital funds in 1991', *UK Venture Capital Journal*, Jan. 1992, pp. 13–18; 'Special report: capital commitments to UK venture capital funds in 1992', *UK Venture Capital Journal*, Jan. 1993, pp. 17–21.
4. Ibid.
5. 'Myth versus reality: a simple guide to assured tenancy BES investment', Johnson Fry, July 1993, p.1.
6. 'Special report: review of 1988 investment activity', *UK Venture Capital Journal*, May 1989, pp. 9–16; 'Special report: review of 1989 investment activity', *UK Venture Capital Journal*, May 1990, pp. 6–13; 'Special report: review of 1990 investment activity', *UK Venture Capital Journal*, May 1991, pp. 10–16; .'Special report: review of 1991 investment activity', *UK Venture Capital Journal*, May 1992, pp. 12–17; British Venture Capital Association, 'Report on investment activity', 1984 to 1992 inclusive.
7. 'Special report: resources', *UKVCJ*, July 1990, pp. 8–14; 'Special report: resources', *UKVCJ*, July 1991, pp. 15–19.
8. 'Special report: capital', *UKVCJ*, Jan. 1991, pp. 12–20; 'Special report: capital', *UKVCJ*, Jan. 1992, pp. 13–18; 'Special report: capital', *UKVCJ*, Jan. 1993, pp. 17–21.
9. 'Special report: review', *UKVCJ*, May 1989, pp. 9–16; 'Special report: review', *UKVCJ*, May 1990, pp. 6–13; 'Special report: review', *UKVCJ*, May 1991, pp. 10–16; 'Special report: review', *UKVCJ*, May 1992, pp. 12–17; BVCA, 'Report on investment activity', 1984 to 1992 inclusive.
10. 'Special report: resources', *UKVCJ*, July 1990, pp. 8–14.
11. 'Special report: capital', *UKVCJ*, Jan. 1989, pp. 8–17; 'Special report: capital', *UKVCJ*, Jan. 1991, pp. 12–20.
12. British Venture Capital Association, 'Report on investment activity 1992', 1993, p. 15.
13. Ibid., p. 16.
14. 3i, '3i Group plc: company facts 1993', 1993.
15. 'Special report: review', *UKVCJ*, May 1989, pp. 9–16; 'Special report: review', *UKVCJ*, May 1991, pp. 10–16.
16. 3i, '3i Group plc: company facts 1993'; BVCA, 'Report on investment activity 1992', p. 14.
17. 3i, '3i Group plc: company facts 1993'.
18. Ibid.; 'Proceedings of the Anglo–German seed capital workshop held at the Oxford Science Park on 30 September/1 October 1992', Fraunhofer–Institut (ISI) and Warwick Business School, 22 Dec. 1992.
19. 'Special report: venture-backed new issues 1988–1989', *UK Venture Capital Journal*, Sept.

1989, pp 7–17; 'Special report: exiting venture capital investments: patterns in trade sales and new issues', *UK Venture Capital Journal*, Sept. 1990, pp 7–16.
20. 'Special report: exciting', *UKVCJ*, Sept. 1990, pp. 7–16.
21. 'The USM – an appraisal', Business Development Group, Smaller Companies Review, Report no. 3, London Stock Exchange, June 1992.
22. 'Small–firms market considered', *Financial Times*, 16 June 1993.
23. Rick Sopher (of Stoy Hayward), 'Prices remain surprisingly steady', *Acquisitions Monthly*, Feb. 1992.
24. Ibid., 'Small-firms market considered'.
25. 'IR 51: The Business Expansion Scheme', Inland Revenue, May 1989, p.2; 'IR 85: The Business Expansion Scheme – private rented housing', Inland Revenue, Jan. 1989, p. 3.
26. John Spiers, 'Full circle for the Business Expansion Scheme ?', *Venture Capital Report*, 1988.
27. 'Myth versus reality'.
28. 'Loan Guarantee Scheme', DTI, March 1993; 'Change to Small Firms Loan Guarantee Scheme', DTI, April 1993.
29. '*Venture Capital Report* guide', *Venture Capital Report*, 1993, p. 39.
30. Ibid.
31. Keith Butterick, 'Focus: ten years on – the enterprise board experience', *UK Venture Capital Journal*, May 1992, pp. 18–21.
32. Ibid.
33. 'Focus on European taxation of entrepreneurs', *European Venture Capital Journal*, Nov.–Dec. 1991, pp. 12–31.
34. 'Broker runs the rule over 3i's performance', *UK Venture Capital Journal*, Mar. 1992, pp. 7–8.
35. William D. Bygrave, Michael Hay and Jos B. Peeters (eds), *Realizing Investment Value* (Pitman/Financial Times, 1994), p. 35; G. Bannock, *Venture Capital and the Equity Gap* (Graham Bannock and Partners, London, 1991).
36. Presentation at the 1992 Venture Symposium by D. Brown, Madrid, June 1992.
37. 'The SMART scheme evaluation report', DTI Assessment Paper 13, Research and Technology Policy Division, Department of Trade and Industry, Jan. 1991.
38. David L. Birch, *Choosing a Place to Grow: Business Location Decisions in the 1970s*, (Cambridge, Mass.: MIT Program on Neighborhood and Regional Changes, 1981); Michael Daly, Martin Campbell, Geoffrey Robson and Colin Gallagher, 'Job creation 1987–89: the contributions of small and large firms', *Employment Gazette*, Nov. 1991, pp. 589–96.

Part III

DIMENSIONS OF NATIONAL DIFFERENCE

We have given a preliminary outline of the funding environment and the main features of the venture capital systems operating in the UK and in three of its key competitor nations, the USA, Germany and Japan. It has been clear that the nature of 'venture capital' varies very substantially between the four countries. At one end of the spectrum is the United States, with its highly technology-orientated venture capital industry in which CVC still constitutes a significant area of activity, albeit a rather smaller portion than it represented perhaps fifteen years ago. At the other extreme, what is referred to as the Japanese venture capital industry is almost unrecognizable as such in Western eyes, being for the most part essentially an 'IPO machine'. Somewhere in the middle, although superficially rather closer to the US industry, are the systems in the UK and Germany. However, venture capitalists in these countries, unlike in the US, have become increasingly averse to both early stage deals (including the seed and start-up stages) and technology-related companies.

In Part III, we shall contrast and compare the most important aspects of 'venture capital' in these national markets. In particular we shall seek to examine national differences in the characteristics and impact of their venture capital activities, and the factors affecting the 'cost' and availability of venture capital to firms operating in the four economies.

6

NATIONAL DIFFERENCES IN THE CHARACTERISTICS AND IMPACT OF VENTURE CAPITAL

To compare and contrast national market characteristics described in the previous four chapters we have used the rates of exchange prevailing at the time of the study to convert local currencies into sterling:

$$£1.00 = \$1.50 = DM\ 2.50 = Yen\ 156$$

Note that since the UK's exit from the Exchange Rate Mechanism, sterling has fallen in value significantly against the other currencies. This has had the effect of inflating the sterling values of comparative amounts (perhaps by around 15–25 per cent) for the other countries, relative to the pre-devaluation period (when most of the money was invested).

MARKET AND INVESTMENT CHARACTERISTICS

The principal quantitative measures of differences between the four venture capital markets can be categorized as:

- *market size* related factors, such as total funds under management and growth rate;
- allocation of investment according to *funding stage*;
- allocation of investment according to *industry sector*;
- the average amount invested, that is, *disbursement size*;
- the degree of dependence of the venture capitalists on capital committed by the various types of *fund investors*.

When making comparisons, however, it is crucial to note that the data on which these comparisons are made has not been obtained on a consistent, like-for-like basis. Any conclusions drawn from the data, therefore, would need to consider whether apparent differences are in fact real, or only due to variations in definitions or methods of collection. Bearing this in mind, the following five figures and their associated notes outline the principal differences between the markets in each of these quantitative aspects.[1]

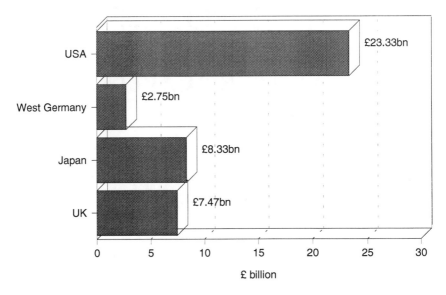

Figure 6.1 Market sizes: comparison of estimates of total funds under management, 1992

Figure 6.1 deals with market size. The first key point to note in this respect is that, despite the recent apparent flattening-off in total US funds under management, the US pool is still very much larger than the next largest. Indeed, reported venture capital figures for the US by Venture Economics usually exclude funds held by the specialist buy-out firms (such as Kohlberg, Kravis, Roberts and Co.). Although the size of funds held by the specialist buy-out firms is highly volatile, they can be substantial. For example, following the LBO 'feeding frenzy' of 1988, when KKR alone raised a $5.6 billion fund, including such firms in the venture capital pool would have increased the pool size by nearly $13 billion (£8.5 billion).[2]

Secondly, partly due to the recent weakness of sterling, the Japanese venture capital pool is now believed to have overtaken that of the UK. As was noted in Chapter 4, however, the vast majority of the pool is made up of 'pre-IPO' investments.

Thirdly, the most rapidly growing of the pools in Fig. 6.1 is that of West Germany, although there appears to have been an appreciable build up

Characteristics and Impact of Venture Capital 199

in liquidity in the early 1990s, as venture capitalists have struggled to invest sufficient amounts to keep up with capital commitments. In contrast, the relatively mature US and UK pools have remained fairly flat resulting, in the UK's case at least, in an erosion of the degree of fund liquidity over the last few years.

Finally, the numbers of venture capital firms and their increase tend to have mirrored changes in the pool. In particular, the number of US firms (640) and UK firms (115) have both declined from their end-1980s peaks, while in both Japan (114) and West Germany (85) the trend is still upwards.

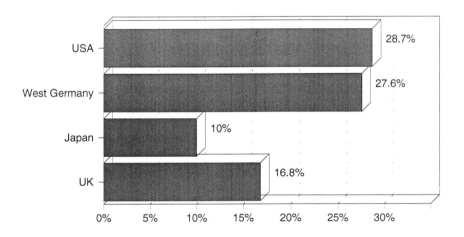

Figure 6.2 Funding stage: comparison of estimates of disbursements to early stage companies as a proportion of all disbursements, 1992

Figure 6.2 relates to funding stage. Here it can be noted that between 1 in 3 and 1 in 4 of all disbursements in both the US and West Germany during 1992 are believed to have been made to early stage companies (that is, seed, start-up and other early stage firms). While the West German share has remained fairly static over the last few years, the US proportion has declined. In the UK, early stage firms accounted for only 1 in 6 of all disbursements, having rapidly declined from some 2 in 5 disbursements only four years previously. This decline has been in both relative terms (as a percentage of the total) and absolute terms (in number of deals). Early stage investments in Japan account for less than an estimated 1 in 10 of all transactions. In addition, it is understood that many of these investments are made outside Japan, in particular in US NTBFs.

200 Dimensions of National Difference

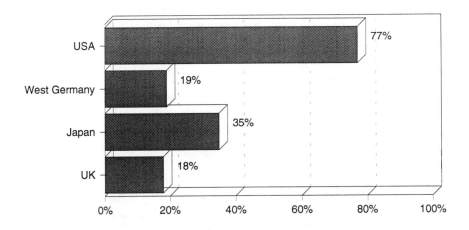

Figure 6.3 Industry sector: comparison of estimates of disbursements to technology-based companies as a proportion of all disbursements, 1992

Figure 6.3 compares the four countries with regard to industry sector. It shows that US venture capital is highly focused on investing in technology-based firms and not only in those firms which are in the early stages of their development. The 1992 figure, showing that over three-quarters of all investments made were to technology-based firms, is understood to have represented a steady increase from around half of all disbursements at the end of the 1970s. The Japanese data, showing that roughly one-third of investments are to firms in technology-related areas, hide the fact that a higher proportion of these are to later stage companies than elsewhere. Due to the 'pre-IPO' nature of Japanese venture capital, it seems that the focus is biased neither towards nor against technology-based investment.

In both West Germany and the UK, fewer than 1 in 5 of investments were made in technology-based firms during 1992. In the UK, technology-based investment appears to have been on a declining trend for at least the latter part of the 1980s and the early 1990s. There does, however, appear to be a correlation between technology investments and early stage companies (in contrast to the US and Japan). In Germany, on the other hand, the change of emphasis away from technology-based investments has been dramatic over only the 1989–92 period from a level approaching that of the US in 1989.

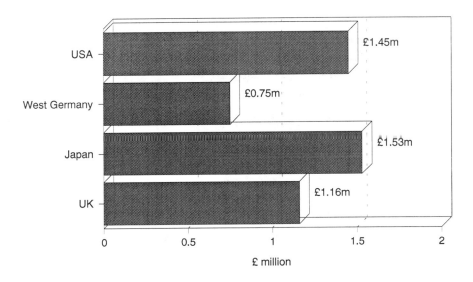

Figure 6.4 Disbursement size: comparison of estimates of average amount per disbursement, 1992

Figure 6.4 shows average sizes of disbursements. A key point to note in this regard is that in all four countries, the average amount disbursed in any one year appears to correlate more or less closely with the amount of funds raised during that year. There are two main reasons for this. First, in good fundraising years there tends to be an increase in the proportion of funds being raised to invest specifically in later stage deals. These later stage deals invariably involve significantly larger average disbursement amounts than earlier stage transactions. Second, having raised the money, the funds are under pressure to invest it, in order to achieve the promised 'venture capital' type returns to their investors. Since it is hard to find more good deals, the funds compensate by increasing the average amount disbursed per transaction.

With regard to West Germany, irrespective of the financing stage of the company receiving the finance, disbursement sizes appear to be generally smaller than their counterparts in the other three countries. This is probably due to the relative availability of 'loan like' finance in West Germany, which tends to reduce the overall level of equity required from the venture capitalist in any particular transaction.

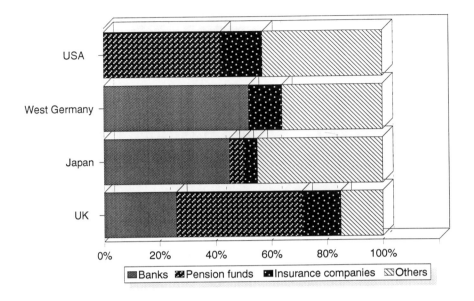

Figure 6.5 Fund investors: comparison of estimated sources of capital commitments to venture capital funds (as share of total amount committed), 1992

Figure 6.5 compares fund investors. Here we can comment that in the US, banks play virtually no role in investing in venture capital funds because of the Glass-Steagall Act, although other institutional sources of investment funds such as the pension funds (in particular) and insurance companies tend to fill the void left by the banks. In West Germany, which lacks the *direct* large independent pension fund investment of the US and UK, the banks dominate commitments to the venture funds. Japanese venture capital commitments are dominated by institutional funds, in particular the banks (which, through indirect investments in associated venture capital firms, account for an estimated 45 per cent of the whole) and securities houses (30 per cent). While Japan has many large pension and insurance companies, these invariably consider 'venture capital' investment to be too risky. As a result, such funds each account for perhaps only around 5 per cent or so of commitments. As with Japan, the vast majority of UK venture capital commitments are institutional in nature, with the pension funds, banks and insurance companies accounting for over 85 per cent of commitments.

FUNDING SOURCES AND METHODS

The nature of the venture capital players tends to vary considerably between the countries, although there are several points of similarity between the US and UK industries. Table 6.1 summarizes the key characteristics of funding from each of the source categories within the four countries. It should be noted, however, that the details of particular government schemes or tax-efficient methods of investing (such as West Germany's silent partnerships or the UK's BES) will be discussed in the following chapter.

In the USA, the main sources of funds (particularly in value terms) are the private independent venture capital firms, which tend to make equity and/or equity related investments across the entire range of investment stages. These firms concentrate on investing in technology-based firms and usually have significant hands-on involvement with their investees particularly with early stage companies.

While private independent firms also comprise the largest part of the UK venture capital industry, there are also a substantial number of 'captive' companies, roughly half of which are tied to a bank. Although both independent and captive firms provide similar types of funding packages to those in the US (such as equity/equity related investments), they have become increasingly averse to both early stage and technology-based investments, consistent with their normally hands-off investment style. The main exceptions to this general trend are the seed capitalists, whose investment methods are more akin to those of the early stage US venture capitalists.

In contrast to both of these countries, the provision of venture capital within West Germany is dominated by the KBGs of the banks and insurance companies (particularly in terms of the total amount invested) and the MBGs supported by local government (accounting for approaching 60 per cent of investee companies). In comparison, the traditional US/UK style venture and seed capitalists play a much reduced role. KBGs and MBGs have in common their preference for later stage (particularly expansion) transactions in a broad range of industries, which can be managed in a hands-off fashion. Where they differ, however, is in their method of investment and their motivations for investing. In this regard, the KBGs might typically invest through a mixture of direct equity investment and a silent partnership, and be motivated by the prospect of a significant capital gain and the future banking business of the investee company. The MBGs, on the other hand, invest almost exclusively through silent partnerships and have clear political and economic objectives (since their funds are sourced from the local government).

Table 6.1 Summary of funding sources and methods

Country	Source of funds	Estimated no. of firms	Type of funding	Stage of investment	Technology preference?	Hands-on/hands-off preference
USA	Private independent firms	510	Equity, pseudo-equity	All stages	Technology	Hands-on
	Corporate industrial firms	80	Equity, pseudo-equity	Earlier stage	Technology	Hands-on
	Corporate financial firms	50	Equity, pseudo-equity mezzanine/debt	Later stage	No preference	Hands-off
	Bank and non-bank SBICs	(included above)	Equity and debt	Usually earlier stage	No preference	Usually hands-off
West Germany	KBGs (of large banks and insurance companies)	25	Equity and silent partnership mixture	Later stage	No preference	Hands-off
	KBGs (local banks)	21	Equity and silent partnership mixture	Later stage	No preference	Hands-off
	Venture capital groups	16	Equity, pseudo-equity	All stages	No preference	Hands-off
	MBGs/Länderfonds	11	Silent partnership	Later stage	No preference	Hands-off
	Seed capital funds	8	Equity (occasionally silent partnership)	seed, start-up	Technology	Hands-on
	Other capital investment companies	4	Equity and atypical silent partnership	'True' seed	Technology	Hands-on
Japan	Securities house associates	23	Equity, pseudo-equity and debt	Pre-IPO	No preference	Hands-off
	Large/City bank associates	14	Equity, Pseudo-equity and debt	Pre-IPO	No preference	Hands-off
	Regional bank associates	40	Equity, pseudo-equity and debt	Pre-IPO	No preference	Hands-off
	Other Japanese organizations	31	Various	All stages	No preference	Hands-on and hands-off
	Foreign organizations	3	Equity, pseudo-equity	All stages	No preference	Hands-on and hands-off
	Japanese SBICs	3	Equity, pseudo-equity	All stages	No preference	Hands-on and hands-off
UK	3i – The venture 'supercapitalist'	1	Equity, pseudo-equity and debt	All stages (mainly later stage)	Non-technology	Hands-off
	Venture capitalists	109	Equity, pseudo-equity and debt	Later stage (some early, no seed)	Often prefer non-technology	Hands-off
	Seed capitalists	7	Equity, pseudo-equity	Seed, start-up	Technology	Hands-on

Finally, the vast majority of the Japanese 'venture capital' industry is not involved with the provision of venture capital in the Western sense at all, being primarily focused on what we have termed 'pre-IPO' investment and dominated by securities houses and banks (which, in turn, have usually developed links with the securities houses).

We have chosen to characterize most of the Japanese market as being 'pre-IPO' in nature, and have not done so in the other markets where the IPO is a common exit route, for three reasons:

1. the securities house and bank associates selectively invest in those firms wishing to exit via an IPO and which are capable of doing so within a five-year time frame (hence the relative maturity of the investee companies, which are almost always over ten years old);
2. the focus of the interaction between the investor and investee, from the start of the relationship, is on preparing the investee for the IPO. This is particularly true in the case of the securities house associates, but is also usual with the bank associates, since banking business with quoted companies is generally perceived as being of lower risk (not least because of the access to equity funding);
3. the equity and debt supplied by the securities house and bank associates is usually either 'expansion' or 'replacement' funding (certainly not early stage, or for the purposes of an MBO/MBI, turnaround, etc.). Indeed, it is understood that it is not unknown for the investee not to actually require any of the money invested, and for the sole purpose of the investment to be to secure the IPO services of the investor.

It is interesting to note that one thing which the Japanese securities house and bank associates have in common with the West German KBGs is that a significant motivating factor for making the initial investment is capturing the longer-term investee business for the venture capitalists' parent companies.

PERIOD OF INVESTMENT, EXIT OPPORTUNITIES AND VALUATION

There are three dimensions to the process of harvesting venture capital investments, which together have a material impact on the rate of return obtained from this activity. These are the period of investment; the method of exit; and the valuation of the investment at the time of exit. A summary of the variations in these key parameters between the four countries is given in Table 6.2. At the same time, we describe this variation in a little more detail.

Table 6.2 shows a twofold variation in the average period of investment between the UK's 3–4 years and Germany's 7 years. There are, however, a number of differences and caveats in the way that these periods have been calculated that materially distort the comparison, and the following should be noted in particular.

1. The UK average has been calculated from data covering the years 1987 to 1989 and it is likely that there will be some variation in this average when measured over a different time period (indeed, the US IPO exit data show significant annual variation). It also contains data relating to investment periods for all stages and types of investment, which were exited via both the acquisition and IPO routes.
2. The US average, in contrast, contains only data on those companies choosing the IPO exit route. Nevertheless, if the UK experience is anything to go by (where the period of investment for both trade sales and IPOs was almost identical), then the IPO data are likely to provide a good guide to the period of investment prior to trade sales too.
3. In practice, however, in both the UK and the US, the venture capitalists tend to retain some or all of their equity holding after the IPO (particularly in the US), sometimes for a number of years. This is done either because of regulatory requirements to do so, or because they believe that there is still considerable scope for appreciation in the share price (it must be remembered that there is a need to convince the new public-market shareholders that this is the case). Such a further holding period is not included in the IPO period data and, therefore, the true average IPO holding period is likely to be extended by at least a year or two.
4. In Japan the 4–5 years holding period prior to the IPO can be very misleading, since both the securities house and (in particular) bank associates can hold investee shares more or less indefinitely after the IPO. In this way, the investors can consolidate the relationship between the investee company and the venture capitalists' parent companies, thus allowing the parent to capture further long-term business from the investee.
5. Finally, the situation in West Germany can be similar in some ways to that in Japan, and shares may be retained by (say) the KBG well beyond the time of the IPO, so as to capture the long-term banking business.

In summary, therefore, the actual average periods of investment in the UK and US are possibly a year or two longer than shown in the table, while the holding periods in West Germany and Japan are likely to be considerably longer than indicated.

Table 6.2 Summary of period of investment, exit opportunities (in rank order) and valuation

Country	Average period of investment	Most important exit methods	Valuation
USA	5 years	(= 1) Trade sale (= 1) IPO (= 3) Secondary sale (= 3) Management buy-backs	IPOs tend to produce the highest company valuations, by virtue of the fact that the better companies have a preference for this exit method. As a corollary to this, the remaining exit methods usually result in lower valuations.
West Germany	Probably over 7 years	(1) Management buy-backs (2) Trade sale (3) IPO (4) Secondary sale	The thin German equity markets mean that company valuation is a difficult task. As a result, MBBs and trade sales often use an 'earn out' type of approach, in order to achieve a fair exit price.
Japan	4–5 years	(1) IPO	IPOs are priced at a reasonable discount to likely 'fair' post-IPO trading price.
UK	3–4 years	(1) Trade sale (2) IPO	Trade sales are usually priced at lower P/Es than the corresponding similar quoted firms (sometimes markedly so). In contrast, IPOs often command P/E ratios at or around those of similar FT 500 stocks.

Following on from what we describe as the 'pre-IPO' nature of venture capital investment in Japan, it will come as no surprise to learn that exits are achieved pretty much exclusively via IPOs. An increasing proportion of these IPOs are achieved through the country's OTC market, particularly since the regulation of these markets was relaxed by the government during the 1983-5 period and automated systems such as QUICK and (more recently) Jasdaq were brought in. Elsewhere, the popularity of the IPO exit route decreases rapidly as one goes from the US (where it shares 'pole position' with trade sales), to the UK, to West Germany.

Part of the difficulty in assessing the relative importance of exit methods other than IPOs, which are publicly recorded, lies in what is believed to be a significant under-reporting of trade sales, etc., because of the (usually) private nature of such transactions. Thus, allowing for a degree of under-reporting, trade sales may in fact be significantly more popular than IPOs in the US. What is certainly apparent, however, is that the importance of IPOs in the three Western markets diminishes with the size and liquidity of their share markets. Table 6.3 gives a comparison of the three Western secondary share markets which are considered as being particularly apposite to the trading of shares in small companies, that is, NASDAQ in the US, the USM in the UK, and the Geregelter Markt in West Germany.[3]

Table 6.3 A comparison of three Western secondary share markets

Market	Peak Annual Share Volume (Year)	Peak Market Capitalization (Year)	Number Of Companies (Year)
NASDAQ	462,600 (1991)	£338,900m (1991)	4,000+ (1991)
USM	6,000 (1987)	£10,000m (1989)	450 (1989)
Geregelter Markt	2,200 (1989)	£2,100m (1991)	150 (1991)

As can be seen, the electronic screen-based US NASDAQ market, which in fact grew out of a thriving OTC market for smaller companies over twenty years ago, has trading volumes nearly 80 times larger than the peak for the London USM and over 210 times greater than the peak for the West German second market (although the number of companies traded are only 9 and 27 times larger, respectively). These dramatically greater levels of US secondary market liquidity, which facilitate US IPOs, are the prime reason for the enhanced profile of IPOs as an exit route in the US relative to the UK and West Germany.

One of the underlying causes of this liquidity is the greater degree and depth of share ownership among the US population relative to the other two markets. In contrast, despite the popularity of the government's privatization programme, which had been intended to promote wider share ownership, the number of non-privatization shareholders in the UK remains at around a relatively low 1.5 million people.[4] In the case of West Germany, public share ownership still meets with cultural resistance. As a result, IPOs account for a very much lower proportion of exits in the UK, not least because of the atrophy of the USM in recent years, while in West Germany they rank as a poor third.

Leading the exits in the UK are trade sales, which outnumber IPOs by a factor of two or three to one. Although more frequently used than IPOs in West Germany, trade sales there still form only the second most numerous category, coming after management buy-backs (MBBs). The picture in West Germany is affected, however, by the exits involving investees of the MBGs, who favour MBBs as their almost exclusive exit mechanism, probably for political reasons. Since MBGs account for nearly 60 per cent of the total number of venture-backed companies, the distorting effect is substantial.

Where the valuation of the investment at the time of exit is concerned, evidence from both the US and the UK suggests that companies exiting via IPOs do so at rather higher average valuations than those exiting via a trade sale. It appears, however, that this is likely to be partly due to the fact that companies using this exit method tend to be, *on average*, of a better quality than those involved in trade sales, since this latter route is also frequently used to 'bail out' companies with problems.

In all markets, IPO prices are usually set, where possible, by reference to three criteria:

1 the valuations (commonly, but not always, P/E based) of similar firms already traded in the domestic market place;
2 an upward or downward valuation adjustment relative to these comparator companies, depending on whether the prospects for the IPO company are better or worse than those of the comparator(s); and most importantly,
3 an assessment by the sponsoring securities house of the likely demand for the company's shares at a particular price.

It is also usual, in order for the stock to be 'well received' by the market (and thus trade at a level above the issue price), for the IPO price to be set at a discount to the perceived 'fair' price that the stock is anticipated to trade at in the aftermarket.

With regard to trade sales, the valuation of similar companies on both the public equity markets and in the private mergers and acquisitions market will be taken into consideration, but the eventual price is likely to be most strongly influenced by the relative strength of the bargaining positions of the acquirer and acquiree (that is, a strong, rapidly growing company with many potential suitors will generally strike a better price than a company in which only one potential acquirer expresses an interest, etc.). Having said that, in cases where there are either few or no comparable companies (especially in West Germany), or where the company's prospects are uncertain, trade sales can be carried out using an 'earn out' type of approach, whereby the final price paid by the acquirer is dependent on the acquiree company's post-acquisition performance.

Finally, management buy-backs tend to be reserved (outside of West Germany) for the relatively unsuccessful companies, since the managements of the more successful companies are rarely able to raise sufficient funds to buy the company back from the venture capitalists.

Within West Germany, however, the MBB is used by the MBGs in an effort to preserve the independence of their investee companies. In doing so, it is thought unlikely that this raises the maximum exit price. It is also understood that phased MBBs, over a number of years, are increasingly being used by the KBGs as a way of minimizing the KBGs' exposure to equity risk.

RETURN ON INVESTMENT

In the earlier chapters we have considered a number of different aspects of the 'returns' generated by venture capital investment. In essence, these can be considered as having two components: the narrowly defined (financial/economic) investment returns accruing to the providers of the capital to the venture enterprise, that is, the entrepreneurs, venture capitalists, business angels, etc.; and the wider (economic/social) returns accruing to others, including those closely connected with the company's activities (such as employees, suppliers and customers) and those who are more remote (through jobs created in the surrounding communities or in the economy as a whole, or by way of improvements in the government's finances from higher tax receipts, etc.).

With regard to the financial returns accruing to investors, we noted earlier that there has been relatively little work done outside the US and none that has produced the sort of industry-wide annual returns data provided by Venture Economics for the US. Within our four-country sample, the annual returns for 3i calculated by Brown over the period 1986–9 (inclusive) are broadly in accord with the 'top quartile' data provided by Soja & Reyes in *Investment Benchmarks*.[5] If 3i's returns, as adjusted by Brown, are truly representative of average UK returns as a whole, then it would appear that venture capital activity within the UK is capable of being as profitable as it is in the US (albeit that the UK has a later-stage, non-technology investment focus).

As far as returns on UK government schemes are concerned, an evaluation of the SMART award scheme undertaken by the DTI suggested that break-even would be achieved if only 1 in 35 of the 1988 stage 1 winners achieved their predicted growth.[6]

So far as we know, there is no corresponding data relating to financial investment returns within the public domain for either Japan or West Germany. Indeed, the situation is complicated by the fact that a large proportion of the key investors in these countries have motives which extend well beyond the financial gains resulting from the original 'venture capital' investment, and often hold shares for very long periods in order to cement relationships and capture other business. In light of this, it is questionable whether returns data for these countries would either have much meaning or even be capable of being calculated.

In respect of the wider economic and social returns resulting from venture capital investment, once again the subject has perhaps been most widely researched for the US market. For example the Coopers & Lybrand survey of 235 venture-backed companies which generated 36,000 new jobs (in direct employment alone), $800 million of exports, spent $700 million on R&D and paid $170 million in corporate taxes, yet had only been trading for an average of just under two years.[7]

Within West Germany, a comprehensive study by the Fraunhofer-Institut of the completed TOU scheme suggested rather more modest, although still impressive, levels of achievement. This study calculated that 58 firms funded under the TOU scheme had generated a total of DM 280 million and (direct) employment for 1300 people. The average age of the sample, in contrast to the US, was understood to be around five years.[8]

It should be noted, however, that the results of the US Coopers & Lybrand survey related to 235 respondents out of 1650 companies who were sent the survey, and it could easily be that it was predominantly the largest and most successful companies that responded.

For Japan, as was the case with financial returns, so it is also with economic and social returns, and the authors are unaware of any studies of such returns in Japan.

Finally, in the UK a number of studies of the economic and social returns attributable to NTBF activities have been made, and two in particular are worth noting here. The first has been carried out by Garnsey et al. and consists of extensive academic analysis specifically related to the growth in NTBFs in and around the Cambridge area.[9] In brief, it has been estimated that as of 1992 there were somewhere between 700 and 900 NTBFs in and around the Cambridge area, which collectively employed roughly 22,000 people, up from 14,000 in 1984 (although perhaps 1500 down on the 1990 peak due to recessionary forces). In addition, earlier work by Moore and Spires, estimated that for every job created in direct employment by these NTBFs, an additional job had been created in indirect employment.[10]

While these numbers are still more than an order of magnitude less than the 330 000 employees in the USA's Silicon Valley, it must be remembered that the first Silicon Valley firms arrived in 1955, possibly twenty years before the beginnings of what has come to be referred to as 'the Cambridge phenomenon'.

The other study is the January 1991 evaluation of the SMART awards by the DTI, which showed that the *self-projected* annual sales of the 1988 stage 2 award winners averaged £0.33m one year after the completion of stage 2, £0.72m two years after and £4.5m five years after.[11] These figures appear to be around 2.5 times the rate of growth of those West German firms financed under the TOU scheme and were thought by the DTI to be (perhaps understandably) overoptimistic. We feel that the actual outcome is likely to be more in line with the West German experience.

Notes

1. Figures 6.1 to 6.5 rely on the sources and data presented in Part II.
2. 'Focus on global statistics', *European Venture Capital Journal*, Sept.–Oct. 1989, pp. 3–7.
3. Business Development Group, Smaller Companies Review, 'The USM – an appraisal', report no. 3, and 'a comparative study of overseas second tier markets', report no.4, London Stock Exchange, June 1992.
4. Based on figures supplied by ProShare, July 1993.
5. D. Brown, presentation at the 1992 Venture Symposium, Madrid, June 1992; T. A. Soja and J. E. Reyes, *Investment Benchmarks: Venture Capital* (Venture Economics, Inc., Needham, Mass., 1990), p.118; William D. Bygrave and Jeffry A. Timmons, *Venture Capital at the Crossroads* (Harvard Business School Press, Cambridge, Mass.,1992), p.157.
6. 'The SMART scheme evaluation report', DTI Assessment Paper 13, Research and Technology Policy Division, Department of Trade and Industry, Jan. 1991.
7. 'The economic impact of venture capital', a joint study by Coopers & Lybrand, Strategic Management Services and Venture Economics, presented by Joseph Schlosser at Venture Forum '90, San Francisco, 25 Oct., 1990.
8. Dr. Marianne Kulicke, Udo Wupperfeld and Günter H. Walter, 'Modellversuch `Förderung Technologie-orientierter Unternehmensgründungen' (TOU). Zwischenbilanz zum 31.12. 1991' (Pilot project TOU. Interim report 31.12.1991), Fraunhofer-Institut, 1992.
9. E.W. Garnsey, S.C. Galloway and S.H. Mathisen, 'Flexibility and specialisation in question', Department of Engineering and Judge Institute of Management Studies, Cambridge, July 1993;

Elizabeth Garnsey and Andrew Cannon-Brookes, 'The "Cambridge phenomenon" revisited : aggregate change among Cambridge high-technology companies since 1985', *Entrepreneurship and Regional Development*, 5 (1993), pp.179–207; Ian Moore and Elizabeth Garnsey, 'Funding for innovation in small firms: the role of government', Judge Institute of Management Studies, June 1993; Elizabeth Garnsey, Helen Alford and John Roberts, 'Acquisition as long-term venture: cases from high technology industry', *Journal of General Management*, 18: 1 (autumn 1992).
10. B. Moore and R. Spires, 'The role of high technology complexes and science parks in regional development', OECD Seminar on Science Parks and Technology Complexes, Venice, 3 June 1986.
11. 'The SMART scheme evaluation report'.

7

NATIONAL DIFFERENCES IN THE COST OF CAPITAL, GOVERNMENT INITIATIVES AND THE TAXATION ENVIRONMENT

In comparing some of the prime influences on venture capital funding in the four countries, we shall look in particular at variations in the 'cost of capital' to corporations, at the various government schemes, and at the differing taxation environments from the point of view of the entrepreneurs and investors.

COST OF CAPITAL

In Chapters 2 to 5 we indicated the typical nominal pretax rates of return required by investors who provide the various types of funding available to SMEs and venture-backed firms. While being useful from the point of view of their ease of understanding, such nominal pretax investor returns are of little use when attempting to provide an international comparison of differences in the cost of capital to corporations. This is because the *real, post-tax* returns to the provider of capital in any particular country are affected by both the taxation environment (in the broadest sense) and the national rate of inflation. In addition, the average cost of an individual company's funding also depends on the precise mixture and form of debt, equity, etc. which make up that funding, and due to taxation and other factors the *post-tax cost* to the company is not necessarily the same as the *post-tax return* to investors.

In the following analysis, which relies heavily on work carried out by McCauley and Zimmer at the Federal Reserve Bank of New York in 1989, we shall attempt to arrive at some view of the relative differences in corporate costs of capital between the four countries.[1]

Cost of Capital, Government Initiatives and the Taxation Environment 215

Definitions

McCauley and Zimmer used the following definitions (either explicitly or implicitly) of the four key elements which together help describe comparable capital costs within each country.

1 The *cost of debt* was defined as 'the real aftertax rate of interest faced by non-financial corporate borrowers'. Essentially, this rate was calculated by starting with the weighted average of nominal rates on corporate bank and bond debt, subtracting inflation effects and correcting for tax allowances on corporate interest payments.
2 The *cost of equity* was implicitly taken as being equivalent to the inverse of the P/E ratio or 'post-tax earnings yield' on each of the countries' equity markets, after adjusting for differences in inflation, depreciation allowances, accounting conventions, etc., in order to make the real aftertax yields on equity comparable.
3 The *cost of funds* was defined as the 'weighted average of a firm's debt and equity costs'.
4 Finally, the *cost of capital* was defined as 'the minimum before-tax real rate of return that an investment project must generate in order to pay its financing costs after tax liabilities'.

It should be noted that the work by McCauley and Zimmer only calculated the *average* cost of capital for *quoted corporations* within each country, over the twelve-year period 1977–88. This will need to be borne in mind, although we consider that the general findings of the analysis contain a number of conclusions which are relevant to the cost of venture capital funding.

In summary, therefore, the definitions are related as follows:

(a) weighted average cost of debt + weighted average cost of equity = cost of funds
(b) cost of funds + net tax liabilities = cost of capital.

Cost of debt

For most of the 1977–88 period, the effective (pretax) nominal cost of debt in the UK has tended to be either equivalent to or above that in the US. In turn, the costs of debt in these countries have always been above the nominal rates in both West Germany and Japan, which have tended to shadow each other. After adjusting the nominal interest rates on debt for the effects of inflation and the allowable tax deductions on corporate interest payments, however, a rather different picture emerges, whereby the effective real aftertax cost of debt in each country has been very similar over the 1982–8 period (see Fig. 7.1).

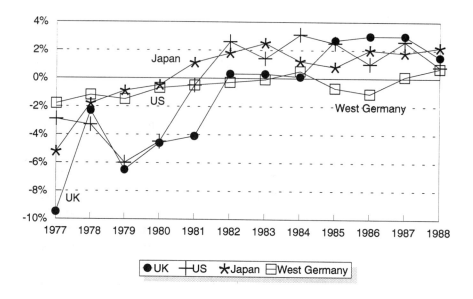

Figure 7.1 Effective real aftertax cost of debt, 1977–1988
(*Source*: Federal Reserve Bank of New York)

Two points are worth noting with regard to Fig. 7.1. The first is that prior to 1982 the relative cost of debt was distorted by high levels of inflation. On a post-tax basis, however, those economies with high levels of inflation improve their relative cost of debt, by virtue of the fact that the entire *nominal* interest payment on the debt is deductible for tax purposes. The second is that from 1982 (inclusive) the average effective real post-tax costs of debt are almost identical for the UK (1.82 per cent), the US (1.85 per cent) and Japan (1.82 per cent). West Germany, on the other hand, has enjoyed an average cost of debt advantage (at –0.05 per cent) of nearly two full percentage points.

Cost of equity

Due to the nature of equity, the effective real post-tax cost of equity funding is necessarily more complex to calculate. The approach used by McCauley and Zimmer is based on the fundamental assumption that the equity market value of post-tax earnings (the 'post-tax earnings yield') implies a 'correct' value for the average post-tax cost of equity. In order to make valid international comparisons, however, the earnings yield derived from the inverse of each market's P/E ratio was adjusted by McCauley and Zimmer to take account of a number of both common and country-specific factors affecting the average post-tax earnings yield. The result of their analysis is given in Fig. 7.2.

Cost of Capital, Government Initiatives and the Taxation Environment 217

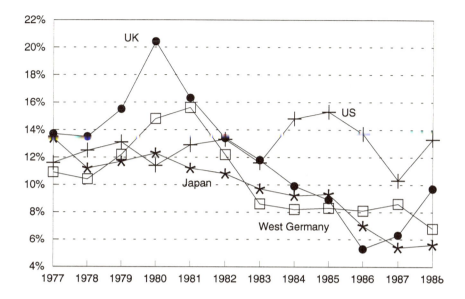

Figure 7.2 Effective real aftertax cost of equity, 1977–1988
(*Source*: Federal Reserve Bank of New York)

While equity costs have generally declined over the period, as a result of very 'bullish' equity markets (except for the US which has remained roughly constant), the differentials between the countries are far more marked than was the case with debt. It should also be noted that equity is far more expensive, in real post-tax terms, than was debt and that, as a consequence, gearing levels will be critical to national cost of capital differences.

Cost of funds

McCauley and Zimmer estimated the average gearing levels of the corporate (non-financial) sector by taking the average ratio of the book value of a company's debt to the market value of its equity. While this approach is not precise, it is believed to be accurate enough for the purposes of calculating the cost of funds.

It is interesting to note from Fig. 7.3 that Japanese and West German levels of gearing are much higher than those for the US and UK. It is noticeable, however, that over the period shown, the average level of Japanese gearing has more than halved, although this is almost certainly principally due to increases in the market value of equity relative to debt than to debt retirement.

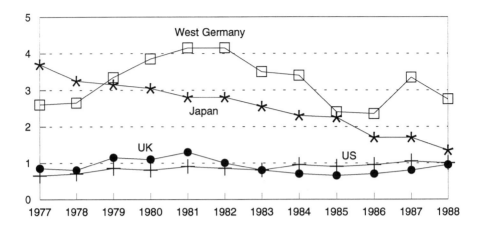

Figure 7.3 Average corporate gearing levels: ratio of book debt to market value of equity, 1977–1988
(*Source*: Federal Reserve Bank of New York)

The differences in average gearing levels between the countries have a dramatic impact on the average real post-tax cost of funds, as can be seen in Fig. 7.4. During the period, the US has had the highest average cost of funds (5.4 per cent) followed by the UK (4.7 per cent). Funding costs in both countries, however, are around two or three times those prevailing in Japan (2.0 per cent) and West Germany (1.6 per cent). In this regard, Japan has benefited from the relatively cheap cost of both equity and debt, while West Germany's low funding cost is permitted by the combination of high gearing with very cheap debt. At a more fundamental level, however, it is the nature of the relationship between industry, banks and government in these countries, which so reduces default risk to allow high gearing at low risk premia.

Cost of capital

The cost of funds (as defined above) provides a picture of what, in real after-tax terms, corporations must pay for their capital. The cost of capital, however, is a measure of the real *minimum* rate of return that a company (or project) needs to generate *before tax*, in order to be able to pay for both the cost of funds *and* its tax obligations/liabilities, having taken into account the value of any investment tax credit and/or depreciation allowance.

Cost of Capital, Government Initiatives and the Taxation Environment 219

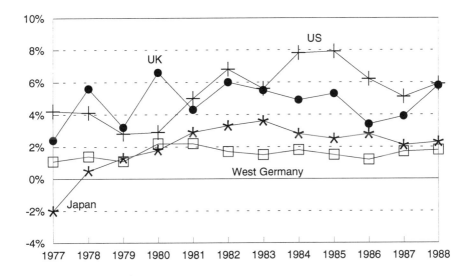

Figure 7.4 Effective real aftertax cost of funds, 1977–1988
(*Source*: Federal Reserve Bank of New York)

McCauley and Zimmer calculated for a number of different project types how the cost of capital varied between the four countries. In doing so, they produced two general results which explained the observed trends. They found that the relatively low cost of funds gave Japanese and West German firms the largest cost of capital advantage with respect to long-term projects, while for short-term projects (three years), their cost of capital advantage was eroded significantly by the lower US and UK corporate tax rates.

One of the most interesting results to come out of the cost of capital analysis relates to the cost of capital calculated for an R&D project, where the returns are generated ten years after the initial investment. While not strictly comparable, this situation is in many ways analogous to NTBF venture capital investment. As can be seen from Fig. 7.5, the UK cost of capital for such a project was the highest throughout the period, although its differential relative to the rates for other countries was reduced during the later years. In contrast, the US cost of capital rose substantially during the period, from a level below that of West Germany prior to 1982, to a level significantly above it. By far the lowest cost of capital throughout the period was that of Japan which, although rising from the levels of the late 1970s, has remained below 10 per cent throughout (compared with an average rate of 14.3 per cent for the next lowest country, West Germany).

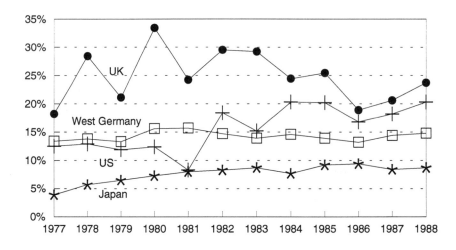

Figure 7.5 Real cost of capital for an R&D project with a ten-year pay-off lag, 1977–1988
(*Source*: Federal Reserve Bank of New York)

Inferences for the relative cost of venture capital

While the period covered by the analysis carried out by the Federal Reserve Bank of New York finished in 1988, and the work was not specifically focused on the provision of venture capital, we believe that there are a number of conclusions relating to the work which are relevant to assessing the differences in the cost of venture capital between the four countries.

The *cost of debt* for corporations as a whole is currently believed to be more or less in line with that seen over the latter part of the period covered by McCauley and Zimmer. Although not strictly comparable to their calculations, we can make an assessment for 1993 based on the minimum lending rates prevailing in each country;[2] their approximate rates of inflation;[3] and the effective estimated tax rates for SMEs. This produces a cost of debt for each country of roughly:

US	1.7%
UK	2.0%
West Germany	−1.6%
Japan	1.2%

It should be noted, however, that when loans, etc. are made available to SME companies (including venture-backed firms), they often carry significant premia to the minimum lending rate. Adjusting for the likely premia would give an estimated 'SME' cost of debt of:

US	4.6%
UK	5.0%
West Germany	−1.0%
Japan	1.5%

Adding these premia opens up a substantial gap between the cost of debt to SME firms in the US and UK markets, and those in the West German and Japanese markets.

One factor missing from the analysis so far, however, is the amount of debt that banks permit such companies to have relative to their equity capital. In this regard, the West German (in particular) and Japanese banks would seem to permit much higher levels of gearing compared with those in the US and UK. This is because of the much greater integration of the banking and industrial sectors, and to a lesser extent government support, in a way which permits higher gearing without much higher bankruptcy rates than in the UK and US.

The *cost of equity* to young venture-backed firms is more complex to calculate than for quoted companies, not least because many such companies do not have a positive 'earnings yield' for the first few years and the cost of equity can change very rapidly as a company progresses from seed, to start-up, to early stage. Nevertheless, we shall consider the case whereby an early stage company obtains equity capital from one of the venture capitalists operating in each country. We shall also assume that this is obtained on the basis of an expected nominal pretax return *to the venture capitalist* of 40 per cent (for, say, a five-year investment period). For the moment, we shall ignore any differences between the countries for the cost of *direct* equity capital investment and the 'tax advantageous' schemes (such as BES), since we are seeking to obtain a 'ball park' estimate of the cost of equity for CVC-type activities, in order to see how the overall cost of venture capital funding varies as a function of the permitted gearing levels.

Assuming that the company pays no dividends and that the investor's sole source of return on the investment is the expected capital gain obtained on sale of the shareholding, then the *nominal* aftertax cost of venture capital equity *to the company* is equivalent to the 40 per cent required rate of return (since the annual growth in share value is composed of the post-tax earnings yield *plus* the expected average compound growth in post-tax earnings over the period, cf. the McCauley and Zimmer calculations). Subtracting the national inflation rates from this total gives 'quick and dirty' estimates of the real cost of early stage venture capital equity in each country as:

US	37.4%
UK	37.5%
West Germany	35.0%
Japan	38.5%

The *cost of funding* can now be calculated as a function of the debt/equity ratio, which varies as shown in Fig. 7.6.

What we believe can be concluded from the above is that even relatively large national differences in the cost of equity for (say) early stage venture capital purposes are of significantly less importance in determining the overall cost of funding than the level of gearing that will be tolerated. For example, the cost of UK funds is 21.3 per cent at a debt/equity ratio of 1, which is roughly twice as expensive as West German funds at a debt/equity ratio of 2 (11.0 per cent). The debt/equity ratios used in this example for the UK and West Germany should be compared with the ratios calculated for quoted companies by McCauley and Zimmer during 1988 of 0.95 and 2.75, respectively.

In summary, therefore, the cost of funds for early stage firms, which is a principal element in determining the overall cost of capital, is likely to be most influenced by what we consider to be three separable factors: the cost of equity; the cost of debt; and the degree of leverage/gearing. When discussing the various government initiatives and the taxation environment during the remainder of this chapter, we shall also consider (where appropriate) the impact that they may have on these factors.

GOVERNMENT INITIATIVES AND THE TAXATION ENVIRONMENT

Table 7.1 summarizes the focus of the various government-based initiatives in each of the four countries, highlights their impact on lowering the cost of funds and/or improving the supply of capital to SMEs (including venture-backed companies), and notes whether or not they are broadly taxation related in nature. We have also noted the European Seed Capital Network (ESCN) initiative, which has provided support to a number of West German and British seed capitalists. (Note that the initiatives in the table are by no means a comprehensive set.)

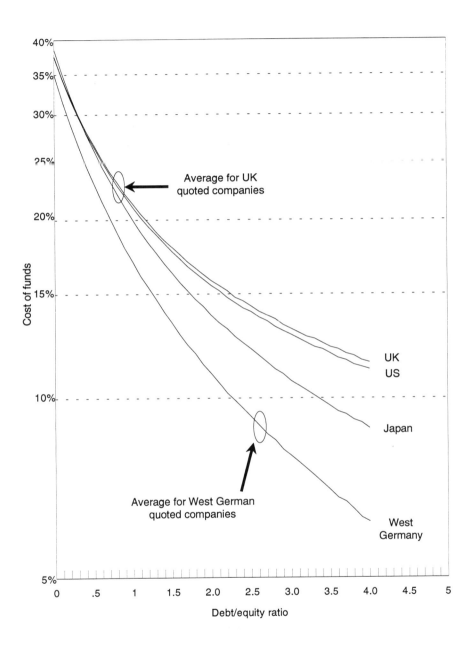

Figure 7.6 Cost of venture capital funds as a function of the debt/equity ratio, 1993

224 Dimensions of National Difference

Table 7.1 Summary of the focus of government initiatives and the taxation environment

Country	Scheme/Action	Lowers the cost of funds via			Providing a subsidy	Improves the supply of capital?
		Lowering the cost of equity	Lowering the cost of debt	Raising leverage		
USA	• SBICs	Yes (non-tax related)	Yes (non-tax related)			Yes (equity and debt)
	• CGT reductions of 1978 and 1981	Yes (tax related)				Yes (equity)
	• ERISA and other regulatory changes during 1979–1980					Yes (equity)
West Germany	• 'Silent partnership' investment vehicle	Yes (tax related)	Yes (tax related)			Yes (equity and debt)
	• TOU scheme				Yes (non-tax related)	Yes (subsidy)
	• BJTU scheme	Yes (non-tax related)	Yes (non-tax related)			Yes (equity and debt)
	• UBG initiative	Yes (tax related)	Yes (tax related)			Yes (equity anddebt)
	• CGT exemption for <25% shareholding	Yes (tax related)				Yes (equity)
Japan	• Small Business Finance Corporation			Yes (non-tax related)		Yes (debt)
	• National Finance Corporation			Yes (non-tax related)		Yes (debt)
	• SBICs	Yes (non-tax related)	Yes (non-tax related)			Yes (equity and debt)
	• Government influence on lenders			Yes (non-tax related)		Yes (debt)
UK	• BES	Yes (tax related)				Yes (equity)
	• Loan Guarantee Scheme			Yes (non-tax related)		Yes (debt)
	• SMART awards				Yes (non-tax related)	Yes (subsidy)
	• TEC 'business angels' initiative					Yes (equity)
	• Enterprise boards					Yes (equity)
	• 'Serial entrepreneur' CGT relief	Yes (tax related)				Yes (equity)
	• Interest relief for entrepreneurial equity borrowings	Yes (tax related)				Yes (equity)
Europe	• ESCN				Yes (non-tax related)	Yes (equity)

Cost of Capital, Government Initiatives and the Taxation Environment   225

It is interesting to observe that although the various government initiatives and taxation measures have sought to improve the supply of capital, there appear to be characteristic national differences in focus on the *type* of capital that the measures seek to encourage. By way of example, the three US measures are almost solely focused on improving the supply of equity capital. Similarly, the UK initiatives, with the very notable exception of the Loan Guarantee Scheme, are also predominantly concerned with improving the supply of equity. In contrast, the West German schemes tend to be seeking to improve the flow of both debt and equity, although the bias this time is towards debt. Indeed, the financing usually takes the shape of 'participating debt'. Finally, the Japanese initiatives appear to be mainly concentrated on improving the availability of debt to SMEs.

It would appear, therefore, that the countries exhibit a tendency to encourage the supply of the type of capital that they are most familiar with in the financing of SMEs. In terms of the various methodologies used to improve the supply of capital, these can be categorized into three groups: improving access to funds; measures unrelated to taxation to lower the cost of funds; and taxation-related measures to lower the cost of funds. We shall now discuss these approaches in a little more detail.

Improving access to funds

Typical of the approach which aims to improve access to funds are the US ERISA 'prudent man' and 'safe harbor' changes, and other regulatory changes brought about during 1979 and 1980; the provision of 'pump-priming' money to the UK TECs in order to facilitate business angel activities; and the setting up of enterprise boards by the UK local authorities.

In the first case, prior to 1979 the large US pension funds were constrained from venture capital investment by virtue of the fact that they had a fiduciary duty to avoid 'risky' investments. It was also unclear whether venture capitalists, through accepting pension fund money, would be constrained by the same fiduciary duty. In addition, venture capitalists needed to register with the Securities and Exchange Commission and conform to the associated 'investment advisor' regulations, which could severely hamper their activities. Thus there were substantial barriers to the provision of funds via venture capital activities. Allowing pension funds to invest in higher risk investments and specifically insulating the venture capitalists from the pension funds' fiduciary duties, while at the same time removing the need for venture capitalists to register with the SEC, substantially improved the supply of capital to the venture capitalists from the pension funds and eased the onward investment of those funds by the venture capitalists. As a mark of the success and impact of these regulatory changes, it should be remembered that today pension funds as a whole provide by far the largest single source of formal venture capital investment in the US.

Both the pump-priming through UK TECs and the enterprise board initiatives were intended to fill the 'equity gap' in the UK, that is to provide money in amounts smaller than £250,000 to early stage companies and SMEs. The first scheme was focused on improving the flow of funds from the informal venture capital market by attempting to network those companies seeking funds with those business angels capable of providing them. The second sought to improve the provision of small amounts of venture capital by setting up a number of regional sources, at that time under the aegis of the local authorities. Although the enterprise boards changed somewhat from their original form, on balance the majority achieved a degree of success in respect of most of their original objectives.

Measures unrelated to taxation to lower the cost of funds

Examples of measures not related to taxation and designed to lower the cost of funds include (1) the US and Japanese SBICs; (2) the West German BJTU scheme, the remaining Japanese initiatives and the British Loan Guarantee Scheme; and (3) the West German TOU scheme and the British SMART awards. We have chosen to categorize the various initiatives into three groups, since each group acts in a different way in lowering the cost of funds.

SBICs in the US and Japan have access to substantial government loans at preferential rates of interest, so that they essentially receive a subsidy from the government which in effect they are able to pass on to some extent to their investee companies.

All the initiatives outlined in (2), however, either directly or indirectly allow their investees to enjoy a higher degree of leverage than would otherwise be the case, thus lowering the cost of funds. This is achieved in the UK (LGS) and West Germany (BJTU) by providing various government-sourced guarantees on either straight debt or debt/(pseudo)equity packages.

Finally, both the former TOU scheme, which has now been superseded by the BJTU scheme, and the SMART awards provided direct (and non-repayable) subsidies to help finance the development of innovative products and processes (although the TOU scheme also provided a lesser quantity of credit guarantees).

Taxation-related measures to lower the cost of funds

Taxation-related incentives to lower the cost of funds can be categorized according to the point in the investment cycle which they are *primarily*

Cost of Capital, Government Initiatives and the Taxation Environment

designed to act on. They may be designed to act at the start of the investment cycle, for instance by reducing the amount of funds provided by the investor, net of the tax incentive; during the course of the investment, by lowering the net cost of funds; at the point of exit, by reducing/eliminating net taxable gains.

It is also possible for the measures to be designed to act on more than one part of the investment cycle, such as the BES, which allows income tax relief on the initial investment and capital gains relief at the time of exit. In addition, the UK 'serial entrepreneur' relief allows capital gains at the point of exit of one investment cycle (company) to be partially or wholly sheltered from CGT through reinvestment at the beginning of another investment cycle (company).

In Table 7.2 we have divided the various schemes which act to lower the cost of funds, related or unrelated to taxation, according to the point or points in the investment cycle on which they are principally designed to act.

Table 7.2 Point of action in the investment cycle of schemes lowering the cost of funds

Country	Scheme/Action	Lowers the cost of funds by acting principally		
		At the point of investment	During the investment	At the point of exit
USA	● SBICs		Yes (non-tax related)	
	● CGT reductions of 1978 and 1981			Yes (tax related)
West Germany	● 'Silent partnership' investment vehicle		Yes (tax related)	
	● TOU scheme	Yes (non-tax related)		
	● BJTU scheme		Yes (non-tax related)	
	● UBG initiative		Yes (tax related)	
	● CGT exemption for <25% shareholding			Yes (tax related)
Japan	● Small Business Finance Corporation		Yes (non-tax related)	
	● National Finance Corporation		Yes (non-tax related)	
	● SBICs		Yes (non-tax related)	
	● Government influence on lenders		Yes (non-tax related)	
UK	● BES	Yes (tax related)		Yes (tax related)
	● Loan Guarantee Scheme		Yes (non-tax related)	
	● SMART awards	Yes (non-tax related)		
	● 'Serial entrepreneur' CGT relief	Yes (tax related)		Yes (tax related)
	● Interest relief for entrepreneurial equity borrowings		Yes (tax related)	
Europe	● ESCN		Yes (non-tax related)	

Notes

1. Robert N. McCauley and Steven A. Zimmer, 'Explaining international differences in the cost of capital', *Federal Reserve Bank of New York Quarterly Review*, summer 1989, pp. 7–28.
2. *Financial Times*, 4–5 Sept. 1993, p. 11.
3. *Financial Times*, 2 July 1993, p. 4.

Part IV

VENTURE CAPITAL FUNDING: RECOMMENDATIONS FOR THE UK

In Part III the venture capital funding environments of the four countries outlined in Part II have been compared and contrasted. In addition, we have also considered at length differences in the cost of capital between these nations, since this is of critical importance to the type and extent of venture capital investment, or indeed economic activity as a whole.

With regard to the cost of capital, we presented data generated by the Federal Reserve Bank of New York in 1989, which showed that the substantially higher real aftertax cost of funds in the UK and the US led to a very substantial cost of capital disadvantage for long-term investment projects (R&D, NTBF start-ups, etc.) relative to Germany and Japan. By way of example, in 1988 the real cost of capital for an R&D project with a ten-year pay-off lag in the UK was 60 per cent higher than in Germany and almost three times that for a comparable Japanese project! Furthermore, differentials of this order of magnitude are expected to have persisted to the present time. While Germany benefited from a slightly lower cost of debt over the period covered by the analysis, and both Germany and Japan had relatively low equity costs, the main driver for the differential on long-term pay-off projects was the high level of gearing permitted in Japan and (especially) Germany.

In Part IV we shall analyse the case for taxation-related incentives and proceed to propose specific measures which, among other things, should help to 'level the playing field' with regard to the UK's substantial cost of capital disadvantage for the financing of NTBFs. These will include modifications of existing UK incentives; incentives taken from the examples of the other countries studied, and modified in order for them to become congruent with the UK taxation system; and new incentives.

8

THE CASE FOR ADDITIONAL TAXATION-RELATED INCENTIVES FOR THE CREATION AND DEVELOPMENT OF NTBFs

In this chapter we shall seek to set out, both in qualitative and (to the maximum extent possible) quantitative terms, key elements of the rationale for providing additional taxation and related incentives to assist the creation and early stage development of NTBFs within the UK. Because of the complexity and diversity of the UK economy, its system of taxation, and the interactions of NTBFs with each of these, any quantitative model must necessarily represent a greatly simplified version of the real world. Nevertheless, the same can also be said for the discipline of management accounting, yet who would consider running a company of any size without implementing such a system of accounting to aid decision-making, planning and control of the business? The fact that a numerical model of the real world can only be somewhat simplistic, therefore, does not mean that it cannot contribute invaluable insights (for decision-making, planning or control purposes) into the process or system that it is seeking to describe, or that one should not attempt to produce such a model because its results will be necessarily flawed. It does mean, however, that the model's output should be viewed with caution and checked for its reasonableness, and that any numbers produced should not be relied on as being in any way exact or precise.

In brief, therefore, the primary objectives of the chapter will be to:

1 attempt to produce simplified quantitative financial models of the interaction between NTBFs and, in particular, the rest of the UK economy;
2 use these models to make a case for providing additional taxation and related financial incentives, in a manner which is consistent with government policy relating to the provision of incentives;
3 look to quantify the impact of such incentives on investment in NTBFs and the benefits accruing to the economy as a whole (and especially to the

government's finances, henceforth referred to as the Exchequer); and finally to
4 consider the output from these numerical financial models in the context of the results obtained from other theoretical and practical work.

GOVERNMENT POLICY ON SUPPORT

There has been a great deal of high profile discussion in government circles, in industry and in the media concerning the subject of how best to achieve and improve the commercial exploitation of the UK's science, engineering and technology (SE&T) base. In particular, the White Paper 'Realising our potential: a strategy for science, engineering and technology' of May 1993 discussed proposed changes and government policy relating to this area of economic activity.[1]

A principal concern of the White Paper was how to improve the flow of SE&T knowhow into marketable products, thus improving the economic return on the approximately £5.3 billion of annual government-funded science and technology expenditure. It is with this concern in mind that we shall seek to address the question of how the government might enhance the flow of SE&T-based products to the marketplace via an already established route, namely the formation and subsequent growth of SE&T-based companies. In doing so, however, we have chosen to limit the scope of the discussion to the provision of taxation and related incentives to entrepreneurs and investors involved with such companies, as the effects of such measures alone are anticipated to provide an effective solution to surmount the main barriers to the creation and growth of NTBFs.

Before commencing the discussion, it is essential that the following two extracts from the White Paper are noted, since they provide important guidance regarding government policy on providing support (for our purposes, on taxation and related incentives). First:

> Even where market failure may prevent a worthwhile project from going ahead, Government support is only justified where the additional benefits are expected to exceed the costs of support.[2]

Secondly, although the White Paper notes that the government is generally unwilling to support 'near-market' research:

> Nevertheless, there will be instances where this general rule breaks down – for example, where the research is generic and points the way towards a range of new applications or where the market is characterised by small firms which can some-

times experience difficulty in raising external finance for potentially worthwhile research and development projects ... An important test here will be the extent to which all the benefits of support can be captured by an individual firm or venture, which might therefore be expected to pay for the work itself, or by a wide group of firms or society generally.[3]

Therefore, it would seem reasonable that government support for a NTBF during the seed, start-up and early stage of its development would be deemed justifiable if it can be clearly demonstrated that in all likelihood:

1. the benefits (to the Exchequer) accruing from that support are expected to exceed the costs (to the Exchequer) of that support;
2. additional benefits accrue, in substantial measure, to parties other than the immediate stakeholders (such as to shareholders, entrepreneurs, employees); and
3. that difficulty is being experienced by NTBFs in raising external finance for potentially worthwhile projects.

For the purpose of the following analysis, it will be taken as read that the third in the list can be easily demonstrated for seed, start-up and other early stage NTBF ventures (for example, see the analysis by the Department of Trade and Industry of the SMART awards scheme, which we shall consider later).[4]

ANALYSIS OF THE DISTRIBUTION OF WEALTH CREATED BY NTBFs

In this section we shall attempt to apportion the wealth created by a NTBF among the shareholders/entrepreneur, the employees, the company's suppliers and the Exchequer. In order to do so, we shall assume and consider a simplified model of the key economic interactions between the NTBF and the UK economy, in accordance with the diagrammatic representation in Fig. 8.1. (There it is assumed that no dividends are paid and that no interest is either paid or received by the NTBF.) Over and above any numerical results that the financial model of this system might yield, our primary goal will be to demonstrate that '*in all likelihood, additional benefits accrue, in substantial measure, to parties other than the immediate stakeholders (such as to shareholders, entrepreneurs, employees)*', that is, that condition (2) above holds true for NTBFs.

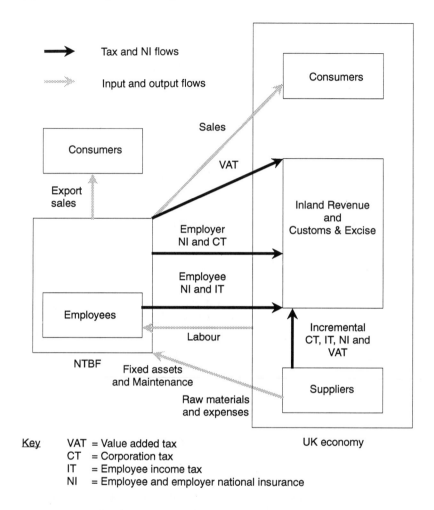

Figure 8.1 Simplified diagram of key operational and fiscal interactions between an NTBF after start-up and the UK economy

Structure and approach of the financial model

For the sake of simplicity, the model will deal with the financial components of wealth created by the NTBF in 'present value' (PV) terms. For those unfamiliar with this concept, a simplified introduction is provided in the Appendix to the chapter. Suffice to say, however, that the PV of (for example) cash generated by all of the firm's future sales can be looked on as the amount of cash that would need to be offered today in fair exchange for the right to receive the cash from those future sales.

Having reduced all the future cashflows associated with the key parameters of the model to their PV equivalents, the subsequent numerical manipulation of the model is greatly simplified. In addition, this approach facilitates conceptualizing the total of all future wealth created by the NTBF as being a 'cake', which one can then 'slice' into its various components. Of particular concern to the analysis will be the size of the Exchequer's slice(s) of the total cake, which will include some or all of the following four main components: value added tax (VAT); corporation tax (CT); employee income tax (IT); and employee and employer National Insurance (NI).

We shall now consider and attempt to quantify these 'taxes' (a term which from now on will be taken to include NI, unless stated otherwise) arising as a result of the NTBF's formation and growth. For the purpose of the calculations we shall assume that the PV of cashflows (or cash) from a NTBF's future sales = 100 units. By expressing the PV of sales in terms of units, the model can be generally applied to any PV of sales expressed in £ sterling. We shall also assume that the 100 units of sales are made up of the PVs of 'operating profit' (10 units), 'employment costs' (40 units), 'raw materials and expenses' (35 units) and 'fixed assets and maintenance' (15 units). It should be noted in this breakdown that employment costs include employee gross salaries plus the employer's NI contribution. For a more detailed discussion of the split and definitions of each component, see the Appendix on p. 254.

Finally, and perhaps more importantly, we shall assume that if the NTBF is *not* set up in the UK to satisfy the *latent* demand for its products from either UK end-consumers (if it is a producer of final goods, that is, finished products such as compact disc players), or a UK industrial downstream user chain (if it is a producer of intermediate goods, such as electronic components), then sooner or later, and probably sooner, similar products will be produced in a competing foreign nation, which will export them into the UK to satisfy this latent UK market demand. In addition, and in a similar way, the foreign nation will also satisfy the *latent* non-UK market for these products. In our subsequent remarks we shall refer to this assumption as the 'import/export substitution assumption'.

That this assumption is reasonable finds support from the vast quantities of anecdotal evidence relating to the highly – and *internationally* – competitive nature of many technology-based markets. This international competitiveness is particularly well characterized:

- where a need or target problem is widely recognized (for example, a disease or medical condition, bottlenecks in computer and communications data transfer, processing and storage, new materials or equipment to solve common manufacturing/process problems, etc.);

- where knowledge of the fundamental technological techniques/knowhow is widely dispersed (such as those of biotechnology, computer programming, engineering design, etc.); and/or
- where the target market is global in nature and thus large (as in pharmaceuticals, computers, communications, consumer electronics, etc.).

One very important consequence of the import/export substitution assumption relates to concerns that products developed by a UK-based NTBF might *displace* other products produced by existing UK firms (through obsolescence, or otherwise), and that, in so far as they do so, the NTBF's output should not *all* be considered as being incremental to that of the UK economy as a whole. This is *not* the case, however, since under the import/export substitution assumption these products would have been displaced to *exactly the same extent* by imports had the UK-based NTBF not come into being. As a result, the NTBF's *total* output can be considered as being incremental to that of the UK economy as a whole, *in comparison with the scenario in which it had not come into being*.

Value added tax

All but the very smallest of companies are required to register for VAT. Having done so, it is normal for the company to pay each quarter to Customs and Excise the difference between the VAT it has charged its customers on sales (or, to be more precise, its 'taxable outputs') and the amount it has incurred on its purchases ('taxable inputs'). Unfortunately, any attempt to calculate the amount of VAT due on 100 units of NTBF sales is complicated by the fact that not all inputs and outputs bear VAT at the standard rate of 17.5 per cent (by virtue of the fact that they are either 'zero rated for' or 'outside the scope of' VAT). In this respect, since NTBFs tend to have a substantial export bias in their sales (particularly towards the US market), which are usually zero rated for VAT, the export to home sales ratio is critical to the calculation of VAT generated on taxable outputs.

Having said that, for the purpose of the analysis and the model the question we really need to address when considering the impact of a NTBF coming into being within the UK is 'what will be the *difference* in Customs and Excise net VAT receipts *between* the situation in which a UK NTBF is formed and the situation in which it is not formed?' In order to address this question, let us consider the two possible situations (denoted from now on as 'with UK NTBF' and 'without UK NTBF'), as outlined in Fig. 8.2.

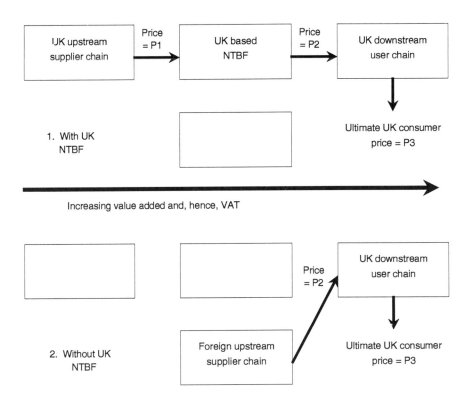

Figure 8.2 The pattern of the flow of VAT to Customs and Excise with and without a UK NTBF

As shown in Fig. 8.2, in the first situation, 'with UK NTBF', the UK-based NTBF forms part of the 'value added' chain between its suppliers (the 'UK upstream supplier chain') and its customers (the 'UK downstream user chain'). We have denoted the price at which it sells its product(s) to its customers as P2. Because of the way the UK VAT system works, the ultimate UK consumer of the final goods (who will not be registered for VAT and can, therefore, not reclaim it) must bear the net cost of *all* VAT generated in the value added chain of the final goods consumed. In this way, the ultimate UK consumer of the final goods which the NTBF's products cause to be generated by the downstream user chain will pay VAT of P3 × 17.5 per cent (if, for example, they are standard rated).

In the situation in which a UK-based NTBF is *not* formed, 'without UK NTBF', however, the import/export substitution assumption suggests that the potential UK downstream user chain will be satisfied by foreign-based imports. The net amount of VAT paid, however, will remain the same at P3 x 17.5 per cent. In summary, therefore, based on our simplified model and the import/export substitution assumption, there is *no difference* in net VAT received by the Exchequer between the two situations. (In reality, of course, any *delay* in satisfying the downstream need with imports will cause some reduction in net VAT receipts.)

Corporation tax

NTBFs commonly operate as loss makers in the seed, start-up and early stage of their development, often due to the high R&D costs of product development. Nevertheless, if they survive they eventually use up these early tax losses and start to pay corporation tax on their profits at, initially, 25 per cent (the 'small companies' rate) rising to 33 per cent. We shall assume, once again for the purpose of simplifying the analysis, that: the NTBF is all-equity financed, but no dividends are paid; the PV of any net interest paid or received is zero; CT is paid at the small companies rate of 25 per cent (on the 10 units of operating profit assumed); and the PV of capital allowances = 50 per cent of the fixed asset and maintenance total.

Using these assumptions, one can calculate that the CT generated should amount to 0.625 units, leaving a post-tax cash profit of 9.375 units, accruing to the shareholders/entrepreneur. Does this represent a genuine gain to the Exchequer, compared to the 'without UK NTBF' scenario, or is it an illusory taxation gain, as was reasoned to be the case for VAT? The answer is that it is a genuine taxation gain since, unlike the case with VAT, in the 'without UK NTBF' scenario the CT (and, indeed, other value added components) will accrue to the foreign nation and its government, rather than to the UK as in the 'with UK NTBF' situation.

In summary, therefore, the benefit to the Exchequer of the NTBF's formation is likely to be around the calculated figure of 0.625 units. In addition, the nation's wealth is also likely to benefit from the 9.375 units of post-tax cashflow accruing to the entrepreneurs and shareholders of the NTBF.

Income tax and National Insurance

There are essentially three principal taxes on employment in the UK, IT, the employee's NI contribution and the employer's NI contribution. In the UK, the progressive income tax regime, coupled with various allowances and taxation schedules, means that the effective tax rate applied to an employee's gross earnings varies from person to person. Nevertheless, for employees with gross earnings in the range of £10,000 to £30,000, the average tax paid as a percentage of gross earnings is estimated to hover around 20 per cent. By way of comparison, the employer's NI contribution is around 10 per cent, while the employee's NI contribution tends to be in the region of 5.5 per cent.

Given that the PV of the NTBF's total employment costs is assumed to be 40 units, then its employees' gross earnings (after removing the employer's NI costs) would be 36.36 units, from which they will pay 7.27 units of IT. As we reasoned above for CT, this also represents a real gain to the Exchequer, because otherwise the employees' earnings and the taxes on them would accrue to a foreign nation and its government.

It was noted that the employer's NI contribution amounts to 10 per cent of gross employee salary for the likely range of salaries pertaining to the NTBF. This tax can thus be calculated as being 3.64 units, which once again represents a real gain to the UK Exchequer. Similarly, the employees' NI contributions, based on an estimated 5.5 per cent of gross salaries, represent a real gain to the Exchequer of approximately 2.00 units.

Additional taxes generated by suppliers to the NTBF and their employees

In addition to the taxes calculated above, the NTBF's suppliers and their employees are also likely to generate incremental taxes (CT, IT and NI), if they are based in the UK. In the following calculation, we assume that the NTBF's suppliers are all UK based, and that supplies made to the NTBF represent additional turnover for the suppliers. We shall also assume that: the suppliers' marginal cost (employment, raw materials, fixed assets, etc.) and profit components of its sales to the NTBF are in the same proportion as those outlined previously for the NTBF; the suppliers' marginal CT rate = 33 per cent; capital allowance, IT and NI rates are as for the NTBF; marginal taxes generated by the suppliers' suppliers amount to 35 per cent of the total taxes on the supplier.

Based on these assumptions, we can calculate that additional taxes generated by suppliers (of both raw materials and expenses, and fixed assets and maintenance) in the supply chain amount to 13.73 units (all assumed to be lost if the NTBF is not formed). While that figure is dependent on the NTBF's suppliers being UK based (or, more precisely, being subject to UK taxes), we believe that this is a reasonable first assumption since:

1 particularly during their early days, NTBFs are likely to seek suppliers local to their operations wherever possible, in order to have access in the event of supply problems;

2 local sources of supply are also likely to be their first port of call, since there is invariably more information available regarding local (or UK) sources than imports; and
3 from a logistics point of view, when NTBFs have to source supplies which have either a partial or substantial non-UK component, they are likely to deal through a UK subsidiary, agent or distributor, which in turn will capture at least some additional taxes for the UK. However, it should be recognised that this assumption could be one potential source of inaccuracy in the model's output.

Summary of taxes resulting from NTBF's creation and a 'reality check'

Summarizing the results of our analysis, the total incremental taxes generated by the NTBF, under the base case assumptions, are as follows:

NTBF CT	0.63 units
NTBF employment-related taxes	12.91 units
Incremental supply-chain taxes	13.73 units
Total taxes generated	27.27 units

Thus, the share of the NTBF's 100 units of PV sales 'cake' attributable to the various parties is as shown in Fig. 8.3.

We cautioned at the start that it was necessary to test the model's output for reasonableness, whenever possible. It is appropriate at this stage, therefore, to try to assess if our estimate of the Exchequer's share of the NTBF's output (in the form of taxes) appears to be reasonable, when compared against any available and appropriate macroeconomic data. While there is no macroeconomic data which is expressed in PV terms (for obvious reasons) we can compare the calculated PV taxation/PV sales percentage against the annual taxation/sales percentage for the economy as a whole. Although the latter is not in PV terms, and is subject to a number of other distorting factors, it should roughly correspond to the average annual taxation/sales percentage for UK companies. If our model is sound, this percentage should not be *radically* different from our calculated percentage of NTBF sales appropriated by taxes (in PV terms), although it should be remembered that the figure for the UK economy as a whole *includes* VAT which has been excluded from the NTBF calculation.

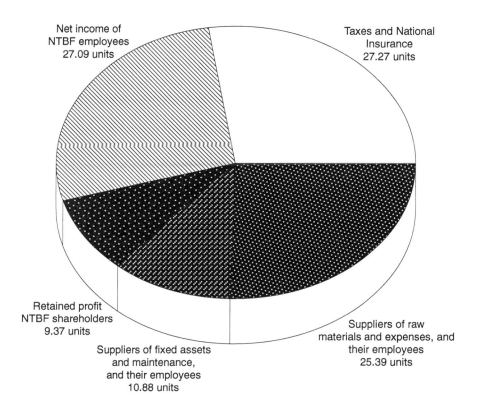

Figure 8.3 Distribution of benefit from NTBF sales (total = 100 units)

Figure 8.4 shows the UK's total taxation receipts, including National Insurance, as a percentage of UK GDP (= UK 'sales'), for the thirty-five years to 1992. As can be seen, during the latter years which, due to changes in tax rates etc., is really the only period over which valid comparison can be made, the total taxation percentage has been between 40 per cent and 44 per cent of UK 'sales'. Stripping out an estimate of the proportion due to VAT, which was only relatively recently raised to 17.5 per cent from 15 per cent, and does not apply to all 'sales', it is likely that total CT, IT and NI taxation receipts as a percentage of GDP have averaged between 25 per cent and 30 per cent. While this analysis produces a range which is numerically similar to the 27 per cent or so that the model produces, it is not regarded as *validating* our estimate, only as suggesting that the model's output and our analysis so far is *not unreasonable* or at odds with reality.

Impact of employment creation

In Fig. 8.3 the benefit to the Exchequer of NTBF formation and subsequent growth was shown as taking the form of *additional* taxes, amounting to roughly 27 units per 100 units of NTBF sales. As a consequence of the import/export substitution assumption, however, the *jobs* created by the UK-based NTBF can also be looked on as being *additional* UK jobs. Following this reasoning, the Exchequer's finances can be considered as benefiting from the removal of these employees from the unemployed pool (note that this is *not* saying that the NTBF's employees *themselves* were necessarily previously unemployed), thus saving the cost of providing benefits, such as earnings-related unemployment benefit, social security, etc.

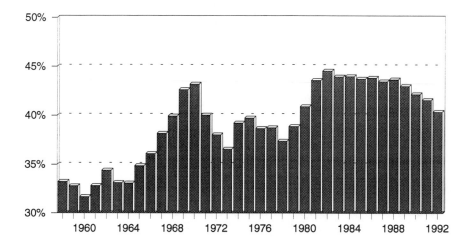

Figure 8.4 Total taxation receipts (including NI and VAT) as a percentage of GDP, 1958–1992
(*Source*: Datastream)

We believe that it is reasonable to assume that the saving to the Exchequer is likely to be of the order of 80 per cent to 90 per cent of the NTBF employees' net earnings (say 85 per cent), or roughly 23 units. Thus, the net benefit to the Exchequer is estimated to be around 50 units, as shown in the modified pie chart in Fig. 8.5.

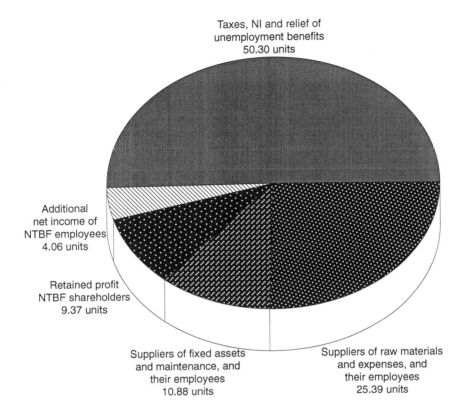

Figure 8.5 Distribution of benefit from NTBF sales with the impact of employment creation included (total = 100 units)

Summary

We have analysed the distribution of wealth created by the formation and growth of an NTBF, and have estimated that roughly 27 per cent of the present value of the NTBF's future sales accrues to the Exchequer via taxes, although the net benefit to the Exchequer could be considered as being around 50 per cent after taking into account the impact of the creation of employment. Critical to the accuracy of the quantitative part of this analysis, is that the import/export substitution assumption holds true (or at least approximately so). We believe, however, that this assumption is based on a very likely scenario, as the history of a whole plethora of examples of technology-based products shows that technical and proprietary knowhow tends to diffuse rapidly outside the country of its origin (computers, software, semiconductors, biotechnology, etc.).

More important than the quantitative results generated by the previous calculations, however, we have achieved the primary goal of this analysis, namely to demonstrate that 'in all likelihood, additional benefits accrue, in substantial measure, to parties other than the immediate stakeholders (such as to shareholders, entrepreneurs, employees), and have thus shown that NBTFs tend to satisfy this necessary criterion (condition (2)) for warranting government support. (For the more detailed quantitative analysis, see the Appendix on p. 257.)

EXPECTED RETURNS TO THE EXCHEQUER ON SUPPORT COSTS

In this section we shall attempt to calculate the expected returns to the Exchequer on a generalized tax incentive. The primary goal here, however, is to demonstrate that 'in all likelihood, the benefits (to the Exchequer) accruing from that support are expected to exceed the costs (to the Exchequer) of that support', that is, that condition (1) for government support is satisfied for taxation incentives granted to NTBFs.

In order to calculate the return to the Exchequer on a generalized tax incentive, we shall use a PV model similar to that outlined for the NTBF in the previous section, and continue to deal in PV terms throughout the analysis. To be able to consider the tax incentive's impact on the economy as a whole, however, we shall apply the following analysis to a *portfolio* containing *all* of the NTBFs in the UK economy. The methodology of the analysis and the associated key assumptions will be taken step by step.

We shall first consider a portfolio containing *all* UK NTBFs which qualify for a 'tax credit' (outlined below). Let the total sales of this NTBF portfolio ('the portfolio') be 100 units. We shall assume that the Exchequer receives 50 units of benefit per 100 units of sales of the portfolio (as calculated in the previous section), and that the amount of equity invested by the entrepreneurs and other shareholders of the portfolio businesses (the 'equity holders') = 15 units.

Next, we shall consider a situation whereby the government grants a general 'tax credit' of 5 units per 15 units of *gross* investment by equity holders, so that their *net* investment in the portfolio becomes 10 units (since 5 units can be claimed back from the Exchequer). This has the effect of boosting expected investment returns for an identical portfolio by a half, since the amount invested by the equity holders has effectively been reduced by a third. A diagrammatic representation of this and subsequent effects is given in Fig. 8.6.

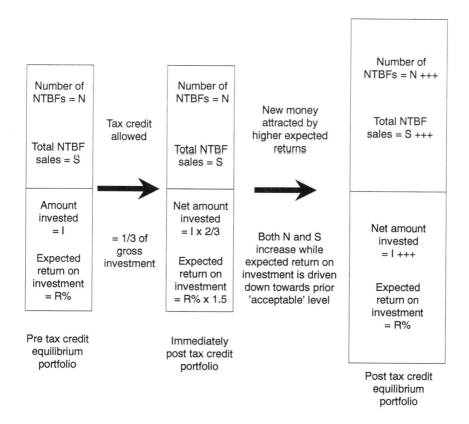

Figure 8.6 NTBF portfolio response to 'tax credit'

Such a substantial rise in expected returns would be likely to cause a flow of funds from the private sector into NTBF investments, with two main consequences: the return on the net amount invested will tend to be driven down towards the previous 'acceptable' level; and the number of companies in the portfolio is likely to grow and, thus, the portfolio's total sales.

Finally, we shall assume that half of the net new money flowing into NTBF investment acts to increase the total number of investments made (that is, is invested in *additional* firms that would otherwise not have been financed), while the remaining half acts to drive investment returns down towards the previous level (by bidding up prices for firms that would have been financed without the benefit of the tax credit). Under this assumption of 50 per cent *additionality*, the *net gain* to the Exchequer is 67 per cent of the

246 Venture Capital Funding: Recommendations for the UK

total cost of the 'tax credits'. (For the avoidance of doubt, the gain quoted takes into account the cost of supplying tax credits to investors who would have invested in NTBFs without the tax credit incentive.)

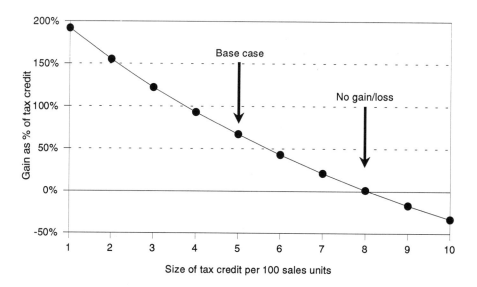

Figure 8.7 Sensitivity of expected Exchequer gain in percentage terms to the size of the 'tax credit' per 100 sales units

As can be seen in Fig. 8.7, sensitizing this result against the key variables of the analysis shows that the Exchequer is likely to show some form of gain in most of the realistic possible scenarios. In particular, varying the size of the credit shows that the smaller the credit the larger the gain as a *percentage* of the cost of the credit. This pattern suggests an optimal size of tax credit, which maximizes the *absolute* tax gain to the Exchequer (rather than the percentage gain), as shown in Fig. 8.8. It is no coincidence that the 5 units of tax credit per 100 units of sales (or 15 units of *gross* investment) is at around the point of peak gain to the Exchequer – we chose it to be so in our base case scenario (although there is little difference between 4 and 6 units of 'tax credit').

Holding the size of the credit constant at 5 units and varying the degree of additionality to allow a greater or lesser proportion of the net new money to act to increase the total number of investments/portfolio sales, we get the result shown in Fig. 8.9. This chart shows what one might expect: the greater the 'efficiency' (additionality) of the tax incentive in increasing sales/NTBF investments (the lower the proportion of the 'tax credit' that is 'wasted' in driving down investment returns), the greater the return to the Exchequer. The point at which the tax credit has *no* net effect ('no gain/loss') occurs when less than 35 per cent of the net new money acts to increase sales/NTBF investments. This point is consistent with only 8 units of net new investment being attracted, which is believed to be a very low amount considering the large increase in returns.

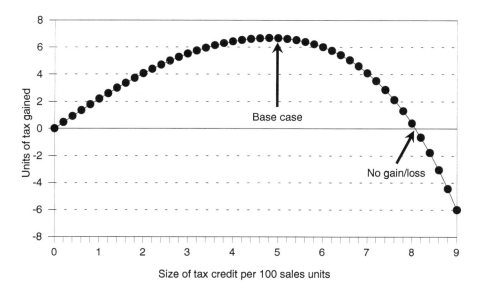

Figure 8.8 Sensitivity of expected Exchequer gain in absolute terms to the size of the 'tax credit' per 100 sales units

Finally, note that we have assumed in the calculations, for the sake of simplicity, that *all* investors can gain the benefit of the 'tax credit'. In the event that certain types of investors cannot benefit from a particular 'tax credit' (for instance, pension funds), and will thus not be motivated to invest more by the incentive, this will not affect the calculated returns on the tax credit.

Summary

The analysis above has demonstrated that the most likely response to a tax incentive will be a gain of some order of magnitude to the Exchequer (QED). This, taken together with the analysis of the distribution of wealth created by NTBFs in the previous section, allows us to conclude that taxation incentives to promote the formation and growth of NTBFs are likely to be consistent with government policy and aims with respect to the science, engineering and technology base.

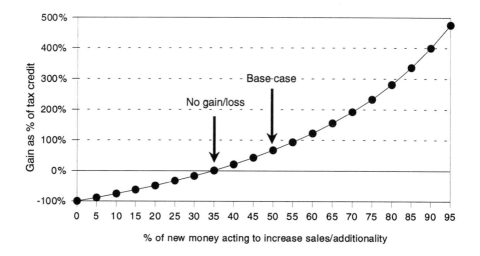

Figure 8.9 Sensitivity of expected Exchequer gain to percentage of new money acting to increase sales (additionality)

A further 'reality check'

The above analysis concludes that the returns to the Exchequer on providing tax incentives to NTBFs will, in all likelihood, outweigh the costs of those incentives. Support for this view can be found in the analysis of two schemes which were specifically targeted at NTBFs, the UK SMART scheme and the West German TOU scheme. Although in neither scheme are incentives taxation based, they both involve government support which can be considered as approximating closely to tax incentives.

In the DTI's analysis of the 1988 round of SMART awards, the following conclusion was drawn:

> On the basis of this and other data we have collected plus some fairly heroic (but conservative) assumptions we have calculated in Annex 4 that the 1988 round of SMART which cost about £9m may give rise eventually to profits of about £20m in present value terms. If only four of the 140 Stage I winners were to achieve their predictions the scheme's contribution to profits might exceed its costs for that round. This allows both for less than total additionality and discounting to present value terms.[5]

In West Germany, on the other hand, the TOU scheme provided an average of £250,000 per company in non-repayable subsidies, to roughly 400 companies during the period 1984–8 (inclusive). The results of the scheme suggested that those companies which survived for five years (approximately 35 per cent of the total) generated an average annual turnover of around £2 million. This should be compared against the average investment per successful company – adjusted for failure rates – of £385,000. As can be seen, if the West German government received only a little over 19 per cent of the fifth year's turnover *alone* in taxes, it would have recovered its investment in nominal terms. The scheme must surely have more than paid for itself in PV terms.

THE OPTIMAL USE OF 'TAX CREDITS'

We have demonstrated that the start-up and subsequent growth of a NTBF is likely to provide substantial benefits to both the Exchequer's finances and to other parties (such as its suppliers). In addition, we have shown that the granting of even reasonably substantial 'tax credits' to investors in these enterprises is likely to more than repay such an 'investment' by the Exchequer, as a result of taxes generated on the NTBF's activities during its lifetime and through the creation of jobs. The question, however, remains: 'how and/or where should this "investment" be applied so as to create the maximum impact on the total return to the Exchequer?' The following comments will seek to answer this question.

Consider the typical stages of development of a successful NTBF, as shown in the idealized diagram in Fig. 8.10 ('units' are *not* in PV terms for the purpose of this diagram). Clearly, and perhaps somewhat simplistically, there would appear to be two ways in which the total sales of the NTBF portfolio could be enhanced: by increasing the number of start-ups; and/or by enhancing the sales/profits growth of each firm.

In order to increase the number of start-ups, 'tax credits' could be given to both seed and start-up NTBF investments. As we saw earlier, although some of this incentive is likely to be 'wasted' (by driving down average returns as a result of making more marginal investments), some is likely to filter through to increasing the overall number of quality investments which are ultimately capable of producing successful enterprises. The key point to note, however, is that *for a given absolute quantity of 'tax incentives'*, because of the substantially smaller amounts generally invested in seed and start-up companies, the leverage in creating new companies – and hence increasing

250 Venture Capital Funding: Recommendations for the UK

the ultimate PV of returns to the Exchequer – is highest at this stage of investment. Indeed, if we refined the model of the previous section to take into account the *investment stage* at which the '15 units' of investment were made, we could quantitatively show this to be the case.

Further support for the view that this might be the optimal point at which to grant incentives, is gained from the fact that seed and start-up investment is at the point in the NTBF life-cycle which is more and more likely to be avoided by investment funds, which have become increasingly risk averse. (A 'risk neutral' investor would *not* avoid such investments, since the risk should be adequately compensated for by enhanced rewards.) This increasing investor risk aversion is a key reason behind the observed fall-off in financing seed, start-up and early stage NTBFs in the UK.

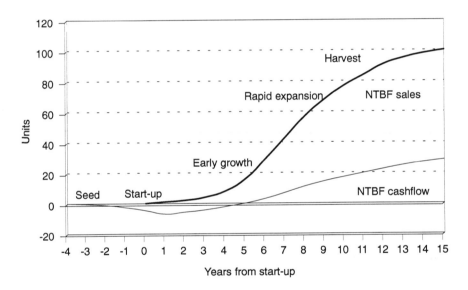

Figure 8.10 Life-cycle of a high-growth NTBF

The most critical factor which is in short supply in start-up and early stage NTBFs and which is likely to have the greatest impact on enhancing the sales, profits, etc., of the NTBF, is hands-on management by persons experienced in the problems of start-up and early stage enterprises. There are four principal aspects to this shortfall.

1. Those making investments in such young enterprises, particularly venture capitalists, appear to have insufficient quantities of experienced personnel to cope with the demand for this area of activity.

2 Investors in venture capital funds are generally unwilling to compensate funds for the extra time and effort required to ensure successful investment in such companies.
3 The personal tax system discourages very experienced managers, in particular, from giving up their usually better paid/more secure jobs in order to manage and build NTBFs. In most cases, the risks are seen as substantially outweighing the rewards.
4 The tax system allows private individuals who are potential NTBF investors, 'business angels', to enjoy (capital gains and income) tax-free investment in alternative (passive) investments, such as home ownership, pension schemes, PEPs, Tessas, etc.

We have established that the Exchequer is likely to get the 'biggest bang for its buck' in providing tax incentives to NTBFs if these are granted to investors (including managers and entrepreneurs) responsible for providing seed, start–up and early stage financing. But this does not mean to say that these incentives need to be provided on an 'all up front' basis or, indeed, that they necessarily need to be implemented by cash outflows from the Exchequer in advance of cash being received by the Exchequer. In Chapter 10 we shall propose a number of particular tax incentives and assess their likely impact on investor returns and Exchequer cashflows.

ADDITIONAL ECONOMIC JUSTIFICATION FOR INCENTIVES

In this chapter we have sought to build a case for taxation related incentives for NTBF investments based on a *financial* analysis of the proposition. In many ways this is the tried and tested approach that would be taken in order to justify (or otherwise) a commercial investment or similar project. We have concluded that in general terms, from the Exchequer's point of view, there appears to be a strong *financial* case for making the 'investment' in the form of taxation-related incentives targeted at NTBFs. There is, however, some extremely pertinent *economics*-related work in the area of 'social' and 'private' returns to innovation, which we believe provides further support in making the case for taxation related incentives for NTBFs.

We saw earlier that one of the government's key criteria for justifying support was 'the extent to which all the benefits of support can be captured by ... society generally.' Probably the most widely known and referred-to series of studies in this area has been carried out by Mansfield et al., who studied a number of US industrial innovations (most of which could be considered to be technology based) and estimated the 'private' and 'social' returns on investment relating to them. In this respect the 'private' return refers to the IRR on investment captured by the innovating company (that is, the IRR on investment as it is normally calculated for commercial projects). The 'social' return, on the other hand, is the return on investment by those who adopted the new products or processes.

What Mansfield et al. found, was that the average return to the innovating firms was around 25 per cent, but that the average social return was more than double this amount at 56 per cent.[6] In addition, it was clear in several of the examples studied 'that no firm with the advantage of hindsight would have invested in the innovation' due to the very poor private returns obtained, although the high social returns meant that society as a whole had benefited significantly. This result has since been widely corroborated by the results of other studies, such as that of Bresnahan which showed that between 1958 and 1972 the benefit to the US financial services sector of adopting mainframe computers was at least five times the cost, and thus exceeded the returns to the innovator.[7] Thus it would appear that society benefits from technology–based industrial innovation in ways additional to those already identified (increased taxation revenues to the Exchequer) in our earlier financial analysis.

We shall close this chapter with a quote from the OECD's 1992 report on 'Technology and the economy': 'The public good nature of much innovation associated with knowledge spillovers implies that the benefit to society exceeds the net benefit to the firms that develop new technologies.'[8]

APPENDICES

The 'present value' concept: a brief introductory outline

In developing the financial models in this chapter, we have described the future cashflows of the NTBF in terms of their 'present value' (PV) equivalents. This Appendix gives a brief outline of the concept of PV for readers who are unfamiliar with it. For a fuller and more thorough discussion of PV and related concepts, the reader is invited to refer to *Principles of Corporate Finance* by Richard A. Brealey and Stewart C. Myers.[9]

A pound today is worth more than a pound tomorrow
Which is worth more, £1 that is given to you today, or £1 that is given to you in a year's time? Answer: £1 that is given to you today. Why? Well, if you receive £1 today you would be able to invest it (in a savings account, say) and earn some form of interest on it. As a result, in a year's time it will have grown in value by the rate of interest, 'r', on the account and thus be worth more than £1, £$(1 + r)$ in fact.

Alternatively, one could ask, 'how much would I need to invest today in order for it to be worth £1 in a year's time?' If we let the amount that we would need to invest today be £x, then the equation that we would have to solve to find out is

$$x(1 + r) = 1$$

giving

$$x = 1/(1 + r)$$

Therefore, we would have to invest £$1/(1 + r)$ today in order for it to be worth £1 in a year's time. Here, £x is referred to as the 'present value' of receiving £1 in a year's time.

In general, £C received in a year's time has a PV of £$C/(1+r)$ and it can be similarly shown that

£C received in two years' time has a PV of £$C/(1+r)^2$
£C received in three years' time has a PV of £$C/(1+r)^3$
£C received in n years' time has a PV of £$C/(1+r)^n$

A safe pound is worth more than a risky pound
Which is worth more, £1 that you know with absolute certainty that you are going to receive in a year's time, or £1 that you only stand (say) a 50 per cent

chance of receiving? In this case the answer is rather more obvious, the 'certain' £1. As a corollary, as the probability that you will receive the £1 falls (or, alternatively, the 'risk' that you might not receive it increases), the value that you perceive it as having falls. People who lend money professionally, such as bank managers, try to compensate for the fact that there is a (usually small) risk that they might not get their money back by increasing the rate of interest that they charge on the money loaned. In this way, the higher the risk, the higher the interest rate charged.

Going back to the PV calculation, this amounts to increasing the rate of interest r, which can in turn be seen to decrease the PV of the future cash receipt. Usually, r is referred to as the 'discount rate', as it is often used to calculate returns on investments other than loans, for instance equity.

Finally, and related to the above, if one adjusts the value of r applied to discount the future series of cashflows received from an investment (for instance, in a company's equity or a commercial project), so that it becomes equal to the PV of that investment, then the r at which this occurs is known as the internal rate of return (IRR) of the investment.

Summary

In order to obtain the PV equivalent of a series of future cashflows (cash receipts or payments), one discounts each cashflow by a risk–adjusted discount rate. Summing up the PVs of each cashflow in the series gives us the PV of the series as a whole. Secondly, the IRR of an investment is the discount rate that must be applied to the cash returns on that investment so that the PV of the returns minus the PV of the investment (or 'net present value', NPV, of the investment) = 0. We are now in a position to build our model of PV equivalents of the components of NTBF future cashflows in the next Appendix.

The 'present value' equivalents of components of NTBF future cashflows

Consider an NTBF which generates the following (much simplified) cashflows over the years of its lifetime, using the definitions we give below.

The Case for Additional Taxation-related Incentives

Year	0	1	2	3	...
Cashflow from sales	s_0	s_1	s_2	s_3	etc.
less, the cash costs of:					
Raw materials and expenses	m_0	m_1	m_2	m_3	etc.
Employment	e_0	e_1	e_2	e_3	etc.
Fixed assets and maintenance	a_0	a_1	a_2	a_3	etc.
gives us the net cash:					
Operating profit	p_0	p_1	p_2	p_3	etc.

Where: $p_0 = s_0 - m_0 - e_0 - a_0$; and similarly for all p_a

The definitions we are using for each of the cashflow components are as follows.

Raw materials and expenses includes the cash costs of: (1) purchased raw materials consumed in the production of finished goods/services; (2) purchased raw materials consumed in the packaging and distribution process; (3) all other purchased consumable materials used within the business (within the administration, sales, marketing, personnel functions, etc.); and (4) expenditure on other 'consumable' items of a revenue nature (rent and rates, heating, lighting, other energy costs, freight, insurance, etc.).

Employment includes the cash costs of: (1) wages and salaries, benefits in kind ('costs' which will attract taxes at the employee level – income tax and the employee's National Insurance contribution); (2) additional pension costs ('costs' which can be considered as attracting no taxes at either the employer or employee level); and (3) other 'employment' costs (employer's National Insurance contribution – an employment tax at the employer level).

Fixed assets and maintenance includes the cash costs of: (1) the purchase of fixed capital and any costs incurred in improving and/or expanding that fixed capital (before accounting for capital allowances); and (2) the costs of maintaining that fixed capital.

Following on from the above, we can denote the present value of each of the cashflow components as follows.

$$S = PV(s_0) + PV(s_1) + PV(s_2) + PV(s_3) + \text{etc.}$$

It should be noted that by using this generalized formula we do not need to know what the appropriate risk-adjusted discount rate(s) is(are) to apply to these cashflows, simply that S represents the PV of future sales cashflows discounted at the appropriate rate(s).

Using a similar approach, we can reduce the other cashflow elements to their PV equivalents to obtain M, E, A and P (with an obvious notation), so that:

$$P = S - M - E - A \text{ or}$$
$$S = M + E + A + P$$

Estimated size of PV components relative to sales

The above equation expresses the PV of the sales of the NTBF as being the algebraic sum of the PVs of the company's raw materials and expenses, employment costs, fixed assets and maintenance expenditure and operating profit (as defined). In order to be able to carry out quantitative analysis based on this PV model of the NTBF, it is necessary to be able to make an estimate of the relative sizes of these PV components of the sales total. We can, however, treat any such estimates we make as forming the 'base case', which can then be subjected to sensitivity analysis to establish the robustness of the models' results to these initial estimates.

Let us assume that $S = 100$ units. By expressing S in terms of a number of 'units', the model can be generally applied to any value of S expressed in £ sterling. If we assume that the cost of raw materials and expenses in most years will tend to average at around 35 per cent of the value of the NTBF's sales in that year (see Chapter 9 for verification of the reasonableness of this and the other assumptions appearing here), then we might expect that $M = 35$ per cent of S, or 35 units. (This result is exact if $m_a = 35$ per cent of s_a in all years – that is, if it is a cost that is perfectly variable with sales.)

Similarly, if we assume that employment costs are 40 per cent of the value of sales in most years, then $E = 40$ per cent of S, or 40 units, would seem reasonable. In making this assumption, it is believed that employment costs for most NTBFs are likely to settle at somewhere between 30 and 50 per cent of sales, once the company has become established (maybe five years or so after start-up). The exact percentage will most probably be dependent on the service/manufacturing characteristics of the business (it is likely to be higher for more service orientated businesses).

As regards operating profit, we believe that NTBFs should be capable of returning average operating margins on sales of perhaps around 10 per cent or so (weighted for successful and unsuccessful firms); therefore we shall start by assuming $P = 10$ per cent of S, or 10 units.

Finally, fixed assets and maintenance is the most difficult parameter to estimate on an a priori basis, since it is anticipated to be fairly 'lumpy' expenditure. Nevertheless, by using the PV approach, it can be deduced, since $S = M + E + A + P$. Thus $A = 15$ units.

Summary

In summary, therefore, our starting or base case assumptions for the allocation (or breakdown) of the PV of the NTBF's sales total are as follows:

PV of raw materials and expenses (M)	35 units
PV of employment costs (E)	40 units
PV of fixed assets and maintenance (A)	15 units
PV of operating profit (P)	10 units
PV of sales (S)	100 units

Quantitative model of the distribution of wealth created by an NTBF

Using the model outline described in the previous Appendix, we can now analyse and estimate how the wealth created by the NTBF is likely to be distributed. Of prime importance, we shall attempt to calculate the tax revenues (including 'pseudo' taxes such as National Insurance) and other benefits accruing to the Exchequer (such as relief from having to make unemployment benefit and social security payments) as a result of the creation and growth of the NTBF. We shall also consider the net financial benefits accruing to all other parties related to the NTBF's business. We shall summarize first and present the formal analysis in spreadsheet form afterwards.

Summary of the distribution of wealth

The 100 PV units of NTBF sales are distributed as in Table A8.1, based on our base case assumptions. (The amount shown as accruing to NTBF employees is only that which would be considered as being additional to the amount that they would have received if they had been unemployed – the 'relief of benefits paid' amount.) As can be seen, by far the greatest beneficiary of the NTBF's formation and growth is likely to be the Exchequer, which is estimated to receive around half of the created wealth. Furthermore, over one-third of the wealth is expected to benefit the NTBF's suppliers in the supply chain. Indeed, shareholders are likely to capture less than 10 per cent of the wealth created by the NTBF's activities, with the employees receiving only around 4 per cent (net).

Table A8.1 Distribution of wealth created by an NTBF

Beneficiary	Units	Units
Exchequer		
Net CT on operating profit	0.63	
IT and NI on employment costs	12.91	
Incremental 'supply chain' taxes	13.73	
Relief of benefits paid	23.03	
Total		50.30
NTBF shareholders		9.37
NTBF employees		4.06
Supply chain		36.27
Total		100.00

The model appears to be fairly robust with respect to the split of the NTBF's sales assumed in the base case calculation (between operating profit, employment costs, raw materials and expenses and fixed asset and maintenance expenditure), when calculating the net benefit to the Exchequer. The calculated Exchequer benefit is least sensitive to the assumptions relating to operating profit and raw materials and expenses, with an *increase* of 10 units in either of these quantities *reducing* the calculated benefit by only 2 or 3 units (and vice versa). The fixed asset and maintenance assumption is a more sensitive figure, since it also leads to changes in capital allowances. Here, a 10 unit *increase, reduces* the Exchequer's net benefit by 6 units or so (and vice versa). The most sensitive assumption is that of employment costs, because of the relatively high tax burden on this component. In this respect, an *increase* of 10 units *increases* the Exchequer's net benefit by some 7 units (and vice versa).

Analysis of incremental taxes and national insurance generated as a result of the formation and subsequent growth of a UK-based NTBF

Preliminary key assumptions:

(a) that the economy is 'open' to the extent that if a NTBF fails to form in the UK, in order to exploit commercially some new technology or technologies, then sooner or later (and probably sooner rather than later) the technology will be commercially exploited by a foreign firm or firms (either through 'leakage' or through independent development).

Thus, the markets for the products of that technology that would have been satisfied by the UK-based NTBF (both domestic and export) would be captured by a foreign firm or firms.

It is assumed likely that the UK market for such products would be satisfied by exports from the foreign firm's home country;

(N.B. *The net effect of assuming that (a) holds true is that one can ignore the impact of the UK-based NTBF upon other companies within the UK economy, e.g. market share erosion of their products, employment levels, etc., since this would have happened anyway in the absence of the NTBF – i.e. as the foreign firm started to import similar products into the UK.*

As regards the model developed herein, the assumptions contained in (a) allow us to consider the activities of the NTBF as representing additional productive economic activity for the UK economy.)

(b) that the PV of the NTBFs future sales = 100 units, split as follows:

PV of cash 'operating profit'	10.00	units.
PV of 'employment' costs	40.00	units.
PV of 'raw materials and expenses'	35.00	units.
PV of 'fixed assets and maintenance' expenditure	15.00	units.

(c) that the effective rate of corporation tax for the NTBF = (i.e. the 'small companies' rate) — 25.0%
that the effective rate of corporation tax for the NTBF's suppliers = 33.0%
that the effective rate of income tax on employee salaries = 20.0%
that the effective rate of employee's national insurance contribution = 5.5%
that the effective rate of employer's national insurance contribution = 10.0%

We can now attempt to estimate the PV of the incremental future tax and NI, generated for the benefit of the UK economy by the NTBF's activities.

Results of analysis

(1) PV of VAT paid on the NTBF's sales

Following on from the preliminary key assumption (a) of the previous analysis, it is assumed that the UK market will be served by imports of similar products to those of the NTBF, if the UK-based NTBF is not formed.

The ultimate end consumer of these products, or products resulting therefrom, is likely to pay the same amount of VAT, whether they are the result of domestic production or of imports.

As a result, the formation and subsequent growth of the UK-based NTBF is expected to have more or less no impact upon the PV of VAT receipts.

(2) PV of CT paid on the NTBF's operating profit

Assuming that:
- (a) the PV operating profit margin on sales = **10.0%**
- (b) the business is all equity financed, although no dividends are paid;
- (c) the PV of any net interest paid or received by the NTBF is zero;
- (d) CT is paid at the small companies rate (see previously);
- (e) the PV of capital allowances on the NTBF's fixed assets expenditure as a % of the PV of the fixed assets and maintenance expenditure total = **50.0%**
- (f) the PV of the NTBF's fixed assets and maintenance expenditure as a % of the PV of the NTBF's sales = **15.0%**

then the PV of CT paid on the NTBF's operating profit, less capital allowances, is as follows:

	CT due before capital allowances	2.5 units.
less:	capital allowances	−1.875 units.
	total net CT due	<u>0.625</u> units.

(3) PV of IT and NI paid on the NTBF's employment costs

Taxes on employment costs are assumed to consist of IT paid by the employee on his/her income, plus the employer's and employee's NI contributions.

Assuming that:
- (a) the effective rates of IT and the employer's and employee's NI contributions are as previously stated; and
- (b) the PV of employment costs as a % of the PV of the NTBF's sales = **40.0%**

then the PVs of the additional income tax and NI contributions are as follows:

income tax	7.27 units.
employee's NI contribution	2.00 units.
employer's NI contribution	3.64 units.
total	<u>12.91</u> units.

(4) PV of additional taxes etc. paid on the NTBF's raw materials and expenses

These are assumed to consist of:
- (a) additional corporation taxes (less capital allowances) borne by the suppliers of the raw materials, etc.
- (b) additional income taxes generated by increased earnings of the supplier's workforces (either by increasing the pay of existing employees, or by increasing the number of employees, or both); and
- (c) the supplier's additional employer and employee NI contributions.

Assuming that:
- (a) the PV of the incremental operating profit made by the supplier, as a % of the PV of the supplies made = 10.0%
- (b) the PV of the incremental salaries paid to supplier employees, as a % of the PV of the supplies made = 40.0%
- (c) the PV of the incremental raw material costs and expenses borne by the supplier as a % of the PV of the supplies made = 35.0% *(also assumed to be the % of the additional taxes etc. borne by the supplier)*
- (d) the PV of the supplier's incremental fixed asset and maintenance expenditure as a % of the PV of the supplies made = 15.0% *(also assumed to be the % of the additional taxes, etc. borne by the supplier)*
- (e) the PV of the supplies made as a % of the PV of the NTBF's sales = 35.0%
- (f) the supplier's effective rate of CT is as noted previously;
- (g) the PV of capital allowances on the supplier's incremental fixed asset expenditure as a % of the PV of the supplier's incremental fixed asset and maintenance expenditure = 50.0%

then the PV of the total additional taxes etc. paid by the supplier and its employees are as follows:

	incremental corporation tax	1.16 units.
less:	incremental capital allowances	−0.87 units.
	incremental taxes, etc. on raw materials and expenses	3.36 units.
	incremental taxes, etc. on capital expenditure and maintenance	1.44 units.
	incremental supplier NI	1.27 units.
	incremental employee NI	0.70 units.
	incremental income tax	2.55 units.
	total	9.61 units.

(5) PV of additional taxes etc. paid on the NTBF's fixed assets and maintenance expenditure

As above, these are essentially assumed to consist of:
- (a) additional corporation taxes (less capital allowances) borne by the suppliers of the fixed assets, etc.
- (b) additional income taxes generated by increased earnings of the supplier's workforces (either by increasing the pay of the existing employees, or by increasing the number of employees, or both); and
- (c) the supplier's additional employer and employee NI contributions.

Assuming that:
- (a) the PV of the incremental operating profit made by the supplier, as a % of the PV of the supplies made = **10.0%**
- (b) the PV of the incremental salaries paid to supplier employees, as a % of the PV of the supplies made = **40.0%**
- (c) the PV of the incremental raw material costs and expenses borne by the supplier as a % of the PV of the supplies made = **35.0%**
  (also assumed to be the % of the additional taxes etc. borne by the supplier)
- (d) the PV of the supplier's incremental fixed asset and maintenance expenditure as a % of the PV of the supplies made = **15.0%**
  (also assumed to be the % of the additional taxes, etc. borne by the supplier)
- (e) the PV of the supplies made as a % of the PV of the NTBF's sales = **15.0%**
- (f) the supplier's effective rate of CT is as noted previously;
- (g) the PV of capital allowances on the supplier's incremental fixed asset expenditure as a % of the PV of the supplier's incremental fixed asset and maintenance expenditure = **50.0%**

then the PV of the total additional taxes etc. paid by the supplier and its employees are as follows:

	incremental corporation tax	0.50 units.
less:	incremental capital allowances	−0.37 units.
	incremental taxes, etc. on raw materials and expenses	1.44 units.
	incremental taxes, etc. on capital expenditure and maintenance	0.62 units.
	incremental supplier NI	0.55 units.
	incremental employee NI	0.30 units.
	incremental income tax	1.09 units.
	total	<u>4.12</u> units.

(6) Relief of benefits paid (to NTBF employees only)

Finally, in addition to the incremental taxes generated by the NTBF, we should also take into account the 'unburdening' of the Exchequer with the need to pay social security and unemployment benefits, etc. to the previously (unproductive) unemployed workers who gain employment as a result of the NTBF's activities.

(N.B. As a consequence of the assumptions contained in 'key preliminary assumption: (a)', we can assume that all employment by the NTBF constitutes additional jobs for the economy as a whole.)

If we assume that the savings to the Exchequer as a % of the net earnings of the NTBF employees = $\boxed{85\%}$
then the benefits in respect of the NTBF's employees alone would be expected to amount to __23.03__ units.

(7) Other taxes and benefits ignored by the model

The foregoing analysis has ignored a number of other factors, including:
- (a) any increase in the corporation tax rate suffered by the NTBF as it grows, from the small company rate (25%) to the normal (33%) rate. This would increase the total incremental amount of tax generated by the NTBF by up to perhaps 1.5 units;
- (b) taxes on additional spending (VAT) or saving (on interest or capital gains) by the NTBF's and its suppliers' employees, as, a result of their higher net disposable income; and
- (c) additional relief of unemployment benefits paid, in the event that the NTBF's suppliers required additional employees.

It should be noted, however, that the net effect of making adjustments for the above factors would be to increase the estimated benefit to the Exchequer.

(8) Summary of the total incremental taxes etc. generated as a result of the NTBF

For each 100 units of PV of NTBF sales, the number of incremental PV units of taxes, etc. generated as a result of the NTBF is:

	Units
NTBF Corporation Tax (less capital allowances)	0.63
NTBF employment-related taxes, etc. (including NI)	12.91
Raw materials and expenses related taxes, etc.	9.61
Fixed capital and maintenance related taxes, etc.	4.12
Relief of benefits paid (to NTBF employees only)	23.03
Total incremental taxes, etc. generated	**50.30**

Sensitivity analysis of total incremental taxes etc. generated, to the NTBF sales' split assumptions

Operating profit per 100 units of NTBF sales

Units	Total	
40	42.79	
35	44.14	
30	45.46	
25	46.74	
20	47.98	
15	49.17	
10	50.30	Base case
5	51.36	
0	52.34	

Employment costs per 100 units of NTBF sales

Units	Total	
80	77.30	
70	70.87	
60	64.28	
50	57.46	
40	50.30	Base case
30	42.58	
20	33.91	
10	23.32	

Raw mats. & expenses per 100 units of NTBF sales

Units	Total	
55	43.27	
50	45.03	
45	46.78	
40	48.54	
35	50.30	Base case
30	52.05	
25	53.81	
20	55.56	
15	57.32	

Fixed assets & maint. per 100 units of NTBF sales

Units	Total	
40	31.01	
35	35.71	
30	39.90	
25	43.68	
20	47.13	
15	50.30	Base case
10	53.24	
5	55.98	

Note: In the above sensitivity analysis, as the sensitized parameter is increased or decreased from its 'base case' level, this is compensated for by decreasing or increasing (respectively) the other three parameters, in proportion to their base case ratios, so as to maintain the overall total at 100 units.

Quantitative model of expected returns to the Exchequer on 'support' costs

Assuming that the base case net benefit to the Exchequer, as calculated in the previous Appendix, is correct (that is, at 50 units per 100 units of NTBF sales), we shall now attempt to analyse the likely range of 'returns' that the Exchequer would be expected to enjoy as a result of supporting the formation and early development of NTBFs via some form of 'tax credit'. For the purpose of this analysis, we shall assume that the PV of the amount of equity invested by the NTBF shareholders = 15 units (gross). Once again we give the summary first and follow with the assumptions and detailed calculations of the likely returns to the Exchequer (including a sensitivity analysis of the returns versus the assumptions) in spreadsheet form. It should be noted, however, that this time the analysis relates to the *entire UK 'portfolio'* of NTBFs.

Summary of results

Although the model used is necessarily a simple one, it does produce a strong indication that there will be a net benefit to the Exchequer from providing even reasonably sizeable tax credits (relative to the amount of equity) on NTBF investments. While some of the credit is clearly 'wasted' by being supplied to NTBFs which would have been financed anyway (a factor which the model takes into account), and a further amount is wasted by driving down the returns on the NTBF portfolio, the amount that does go into *additional* NTBF formation is highly leveraged (nearly sevenfold in the base case) to producing higher NTBF portfolio sales and, thus, higher Exchequer returns (with a more than threefold leverage ratio). It is thought, therefore, that for any reasonable size of tax credit (and here the base case calculates an optimal credit of 5 units per 15 units of *gross* investment), there will be a positive and possibly quite substantial return to the Exchequer on its tax credit 'investment'.

Calculation of expected returns to the Exchequer on 'support costs' – a base case example

Notes: *All of the following amounts are quoted in present value (PV) units. The analysis relates to the entire portfolio of NTBFs.*

Preliminary key assumptions:

(a) that per 100 units of the NTBF portfolio's sales, the Exchequer effectively receives (via taxes, NI and unemployment benefits no longer paid out): 50.00 units.

(b) that the PV of the amount of equity invested by the entrepreneurs and other shareholders (collectively the 'equity holders') in the portfolio of NTBFs = 15.00 units.

(c) that a 'tax credit' of one form or another is allowed to the equity holders of NTBF investments, equivalent to: 5.00 units.

which reduces their net investment to: 10.00 units.
and boosts the return on their net investment by: 50.00%

(d) that following the announcement of the new 'tax credit' availability to equity holders of NTBF investments, the significantly higher returns cause more money to become available from the private sector for investment in NTBFs.

In due course, some of this money is likely to act to drive down average returns on equity holders' net investment in the portfolio as a whole (as eager investors compete to finance new deals), towards the previously 'acceptable' levels.

Some of the money, on the other hand, is likely to increase the total number of NTBFs within the portfolio and, in so doing, increase the total portfolio unit sales.

(e) that the proportion of the new money being invested to drive down portfolio returns = 50.00%

thus, net new equity holder money so doing = 5.00 units.
and new equity holder money acting to increase turnover = 5.00 units.

(f) that sales leverage on net investment = 100/(15.00), i.e. the initial ratio.
therefore, total sales grow by: 33.33 units.
of which the Exchequer effectively receives: 16.67 units.
for a total 'tax credit' investment of: 10.00 units.
and a gain by the Exchequer, as a % of the 'tax credit' of: 67%

The Case for Additional Taxation-related Incentives

'Tax credit' per 100 units of sales	Gain as % of tax credit
10	–33%
9	–17%
8	1%
7	21%
6	43%
5 (Base case)	67%
4	93%
3	122%
2	155%
1	192%

'Tax credit' per 100 units of sales	Absolute' gain (units)	'Tax credit' per 100 units of sales	Absolute gain (units)
0.0	0.00	4.6	6.66
0.2	0.46	4.8	6.68
0.4	0.91	5.0	6.67
0.6	1.35	5.2	6.61
0.8	1.78	5.4	6.53
1.0	2.19	5.6	6.39
1.2	2.59	5.8	6.22
1.4	2.98	6.0	6.00
1.6	3.35	6.2	5.73
1.8	3.71	6.4	5.41
2.0	4.05	6.6	5.03
2.2	4.38	6.8	4.59
2.4	4.69	7.0	4.08
2.6	4.98	7.2	3.51
2.8	5.25	7.4	2.86
3.0	5.50	7.6	2.12
3.2	5.73	7.8	1.30
3.4	5.94	8.0	0.38
3.6	6.13	8.2	–0.64
3.8	6.29	8.4	–1.78
4.0	6.42	8.6	–3.05
4.2	6.53	8.8	–4.45
4.4	6.61	9.0	–6.00

Sensitivity analysis of the gain to the Exchequer to the proportion of new money acting to increase sales

Total new money (units)	Proportion acting to increase sales	Gain as % of tax credit
100.0	95%	476%
50.0	90%	400%
33.3	85%	336%
25.0	80%	281%
20.0	75%	233%
16.7	70%	192%
14.3	65%	155%
12.5	60%	122%
11.1	55%	93%
Base case 10.0	50%	67%
9.1	45%	43%
8.3	40%	21%
7.7	35%	1%
7.1	30%	−17%
6.7	25%	−33%
6.2	20%	−49%
5.9	15%	−63%
5.6	10%	−76%
5.3	5%	−89%
5.0	0%	−100%

Notes

1. 'Realising our potential: a strategy for science, engineering and technology', Cm 2250, HMSO, May 1993. See also for mid-1993, .'Review of allocation, management and use of government expenditure on science and technology', Cabinet Office (OPSS), May 1993; 'An attempt to see the future', 'Hunt for winning ideas heads science research proposals', 'Appliance of UK science' and 'Science to focus on picking winners', *Financial Times*, 27 May 1993; 'Heseltine's plan to help Britain win', *Financial Times*, 26 April 1993; 'The need to build new partnerships', *The Times*, 27 May 1993.
2. 'Realising our potential', ch. 2, p. 15, para. 2.20.
3. Ibid., p. 16, para. 2.22.
4. 'The SMART scheme evaluation report', DTI assessment paper 13, Research and Technology Policy Division, Department of Trade and Industry, Jan. 1991.
5. Ibid., pp. 11–12.
6. E. Mansfield, J. Rapoport, A. Romeo, S. Wagner and G. Beardsley, 'Social and private rates of return from industrial innovations', *Quarterly Journal of Economics*, 77: 2 (1977), pp. 221–40.
7. Cited in 'Technology and the economy: the key relationships', OECD, Paris, 1992, p.59.
8. Ibid.
9. Richard A. Brealey and Stewart C. Myers, *Principles of Corporate Finance*, (McGraw-Hill, 1988).

9
UK NTBF CASE STUDIES AND ANALYSIS

In Chapter 8 we developed a financial model in an attempt to analyse and estimate the distribution of wealth created by NTBFs, particularly that component accruing to the Exchequer.

In calculating the expected proportion of the PV of the NTBF's future sales (UK domestic and UK export only) accruing to the Exchequer in the form of taxes, we assumed values for various key parameters. These fell into two categories.

1 Average percentage taxation rates, estimated from the current UK taxation system, in particular:

   (a) CT = 25 per cent of taxable profits;
   (b) PV of capital allowances = 50 per cent of the fixed asset and maintenance total;
   (c) IT = 20 per cent of employee's gross salary (EGS);
   (d) employer's NI contribution = 10 per cent of EGS;
   (e) employee's NI contribution = 5.5 per cent of EGS.

   These estimates, since they were perceived as being based on the current *known* system of taxation, were not sensitized in the model, although it was accepted that 'reality' would differ to some extent from these central estimates for individual firms.

2 Estimates of how the PV of sales for the NTBF is apportioned between the PVs of (in the base case):

   (a) 'operating profit' = 10 per cent;
   (b) 'employment costs' = 40 per cent;
   (c) 'raw materials and expenses' = 35 per cent;
   (d) 'fixed assets and maintenance' = 15 per cent.

   Since these estimates were made on the basis of perceived 'reasonable' values and were far less certain than those above, they were sensitized over a wide range of possible values to assess the robustness of the result. (The PV of 'equity' invested was also assumed to be 15 per cent.)

In this chapter we shall consider actual data from nine case study firms to see how well the model fits with this data and, in particular, to consider the accuracy of the non-sensitized assumptions contained in (1) above in respect of real world examples. In the next chapter we shall seek to gain insight into other characteristics of these case study firms which we perceive to be more generally pertinent to the financing of NTBFs.

COMPARISON OF CASE STUDY DATA WITH MODEL INPUTS

In Table 9.1 we have summarized key data relating to the nine case study companies, extracted from the fuller accounts contained in the Appendices to this chapter. This data has been substantially obtained from information in the public domain, supplemented by additional input from the companies themselves. (Two of the case study companies have been disguised with invented names, 'Advanced Chemical Intermediates' and 'Servo Integrated Solutions', but the information about the companies is genuine.) In this regard, we would like to express our sincere gratitude for the considerable amount of time-consuming help obtained from the entrepreneurs in question; without which this work would have been very much the poorer. The final case study descriptions and estimates, however, have been produced by the authors, who take sole responsibility for any errors or omissions.

It should be noted when considering the case material that these firms have not been randomly chosen but have, instead, been selected to cover a broad range of company maturities, company sizes, business types and characteristics, financing methods, etc. Nevertheless, it is recognized that the sample carries a substantial bias towards successful and more mature companies, about which data was more freely available. We shall consider and make allowance for how this might affect our *numerically based* conclusions regarding the model developed earlier.

We shall now discuss the data contained in the case studies, with regard to the model's key inputs and outputs.

The apportionment of the PV of NTBF sales

The base case of the model assumes that the PV of NTBF sales is apportioned in accordance with the outline contained in (2) above. When constructing the model in Chapter 8 we indicated that the PVs of the various elements were arrived at by discounting all future cashflows by 'appropriate' discount rates, which remained undefined. In order to calculate PVs based on real data, however, we must first define these discount rates. The problem is not as difficult, however, as it might at first seem. Because we are dealing with *actual* data, there is *no uncertainty* in the values we are discounting. Thus the correct value to apply to all *actual* values is the 'risk-free' rate which, for the purpose of this exercise, we shall assume to be 6 per cent. (Note that a sensitivity analysis of the risk-free rate assumed shows that the discounted percentage of sales PV, in most cases, is very insensitive to changes in the risk-free rate.) Let us now consider each of the assumed base case values outlined in (2) in more detail.

The proportion of sales PV accounted for by the PV of *employment costs* is likely to be approximately equal to the ratio of the PV of gross *accounting* (*not* cash) staff costs to the PV of *accounting* sales. We have shown this percentage for each of the case study firms since their formation in Table 9.1 (with the sole exception of Macro 4, in which the MBO date was taken as being the starting point for the calculation).

In carrying out the calculation, we also used the firms' *total* gross staff costs and their *total* sales, while recognizing that in some cases both totals included non-UK staff and production. Having said this, where data was available (six firms), around 80 per cent of staff were employed in the UK (on average), and probably a similar proportion of sales were accounted for by domestic sales and exports. Thus we believe that the ratio is likely to be a good approximation to the ratio that we would have ideally liked to have calculated, that is

$$\frac{\text{PV of UK gross staff costs}}{\text{PV of UK domestic and UK export sales}}$$

As was expected, what the results show is that there is a very wide range of values for the PV of 'employment costs', between around 16 per cent of sales PV for Psion to 92 per cent of sales PV for the British Bio-Technology Group, with the average for all firms in the sample being around 38 per cent.

A more detailed year by year analysis revealed, however, that it is usual during the first two or three years for the ratio of staff costs to sales to be much higher than that for the subsequent 'mature' years. As a result, the bias of the sample towards more mature companies is likely to have suppressed this ratio relative to all UK NTBFs.

It is interesting to note that despite being seven years from its start-up, British Bio-Technology is still an 'immature' firm, because of the very long R&D times required to develop its products through to the sales stage. This,

Table 9.1 Summary of case study data

Company	Age of company (years)	Annual sales (£m)	Sales analysis - Geographical distribution as a % of total sales			Pretax profit analysis			
			Domestic	Foreign	Export	Year when became profitable	Peak margin	Average margin	
Linx Printing Technologies	7	11.9	21.6%	–	78.4%	3rd	16%	11%	
Domino Printing Sciencies	14	71.6	16.0%	84.0%	n.a.	3rd	26%	15%	
Psion	12	35.1	55.1%	6.4%[b]	38.5%	1st	35%	6%	
Tadpole Technology	9	12.5	6.0%	94.0%	n.a.	3rd	14%	–3%	
Macro 4	9	19.0	21.6%	78.4%	n.a.	n.a.	52%	45%	
Datapaq	8	3.4	13.1%	86.9%	n.a.	3rd	13%	4%	
British Bio-Technology Group	7	5.0	40.5%	59.5%	n.a.	Beyond 7th	–45%	–127%	
'Advanced Chemical Intermediates'	1	0.5	60.0%	–	40.0%	n.a.	n.a.	n.a.	
'Servo Integrated Solutions'	3	0.4	72.4%	–	27.6%	Never	–25%	–56%	

Company	Quoted or unquoted	Peak number of employees		Estimated PVs as a % of total sales					Fixed asset & maintenance
		Total	UK only	CT	Employer/employee NI&T	Gross staff costs	Pretax profit	Equity	
Linx Printing Technologies	Quoted	175	175	0.4%	8.3%[a]	27%	11%	4%	16%
Domino Printing Sciencies	Quoted	820	n.a.	3.6%	8.9%	26%	16%	16%	12%
Psion	Quoted	279	249	2.8%	5.4%	16%	6%	7%	10%
Tadpole Technology	Quoted	134	n.a.	0.2%	8.3%	26%	–4%	9%	12%
Macro 4	Quoted	198	95	11.7%	6.6%[d]	39%	45%	n.a.	18%
Datapaq	Unquoted	53	39	0.2%	10.5%	32%	3%	3%	6%
British Bio-Technology Group	Quoted	260	n.a.	0.0%	30.1%	92%	–124%	373%	110%
'Advanced Chemical Intermediates'	Unquoted	8	8	0.0%	n.a.	n.a.	n.a.	n.a.	n.a.
'Servo Integrated Solutions'	Unquoted	10	10	0.0%	19.5%	48%	–57%	28%	14%

Table notes

[a] In Linx's latest year for which data are available, the actual amounts of employer's NI, employees' NI and employees' IT paid as a % of gross salaries were 8.9%, 5.5% and 19.8% respectively. (Total employer's 'social security' costs have ranged between 9.8% and 10.5% of salary annually since Linx's formation.)

[b] The 6.4% of sales by Psion shown as 'Foreign' are those sales made in markets outside the UK which are not satisfied by UK exports.

[c] Macro 4 has been around much longer than the 9 years shown, but it has been 9 years since the MBO.

[d] For Macro 4's UK employees, the employer's NI contribution has been between 10.2% and 10.4% of gross salary for the last 5 years. Its employees' NI contribution has ranged from 3.8% to (last year) 4.8% of gross salary, however, due to the relatively high salaries of its employees, which exceed the maximum employee NI limit. As an additional result of these relatively high salary levels, the employee IT rate has ranged between 23.3% and 34.6% over the last 7 years for which data are available.

coupled with the unusually high percentage of very highly skilled (and thus expensive) staff, has resulted in the highest of the PV of employment costs/PV of sales ratios. Over the next few years this ratio should fall substantially. In conclusion, we believe that the model's assumption of 40 per cent of the PV of sales accruing to employment costs is a reasonable starting assumption for the base case.

In respect of the proportion of sales PV accounted for by the PV of *operating profit* (as defined for the model), it is not possible to assess this as directly from company accounting data as we did with employment costs. This is because, as used in the model, it represents a measure of the residual 'free' cashflow in the business, before apportionment to the Exchequer (via corporate taxes) and to equity holders (via retained earnings). In addition, the model also assumes that the net amount of any interest income on cash balances less any interest paid to debt holders has a zero PV.

Having said this, it is thought that a check of the reasonableness of the estimate can be obtained in two ways: by reference to the accounting *pretax* profit margins that the case study firms generate (since such profits will have made some allowance for the model's assumption that the PV of debt = 0); and, by implication, based on a comparison of the amount of corporation tax (including advanced corporation tax and net of capital allowances) *actually* paid by the case study companies, against the model's predictions.

With respect to the first of these it is interesting to note in Table 9.1 that the percentage of the PV of sales accounted for by the PV of pretax profits correlates very closely with the *average* pretax margins, calculated on a year by year basis. This is a result of the relatively low, risk-free discount rate (6 per cent) applied to the actual case study data, which allows for the pretax margins in all years to have a significant representation when calculating the PV percentage. As a consequence, however, the question of choosing a 'reasonable' value for the operating profit percentage can be reduced to choosing a reasonable average pretax margin.

Looked at in this way, it would seem reasonable that successful NTBF investments might achieve average pretax margins in the region of 15 per cent or so, mid-range NTBF investments might achieve 0–5 per cent margins, while unsuccessful investments might achieve average margins in the minus 10 per cent to minus 100 per cent range. (We believe it very likely that, among the case studies, Tadpole Technology will start to generate the sort of margin associated with successful investments during the next few years, while in the much longer term British Bio-technology Group may also have the potential to do so.)

While the number of unsuccessful NTBF investments is expected to be more numerous than mid-range investments which, in turn, will number rather more than the successful ones, the PVs of sales and operating profit associated with successful investments are likely to dwarf those of the other two categories. Indeed, this is the whole basis of venture capital investment, that is, that the amount made on the 'winners' outweighs the amount lost on the 'losers' and the 'also rans'.

In sum, therefore, we would expect that the *weighted* PV of operating profit as a percentage of the PV of sales will be much closer to the typical margin of the successful companies than the unsuccessful ones. As a result, an assumption of 10 per cent for this value would appear to be a reasonable one for the base case.

With this value as a base case assumption, does the model generate reasonable output values for the PV of corporation taxes (the second check above)? Well, in the base case, the model estimates the percentage of the PV of sales represented by the PV of CT to be 0.6 per cent. Averaging the percentage for the case studies gives a figure of 2.1 per cent, although after stripping out Macro 4, this percentage falls to 0.9 per cent. We believe that it is valid to remove the Macro 4 'outlier' from the calculation, since the CT rate is generated by virtue of its 45 per cent pretax margins on essentially rental income, which may prove to be unique (or at least almost so) in the area of NTBF investments. Adjusting the 0.9 per cent downwards to take account of the sample bias towards the more mature and successful companies (who pay more CT), means that the model's estimate looks reasonable when compared to reality.

Contained within the model's CT calculation is an assumption for capital allowances on fixed assets. We shall now consider, therefore, the model's *fixed assets and maintenance* assumption. As was the case with the previous two parameters, it is difficult to obtain annual measures of each firm's cash fixed asset and maintenance expenditure from the available accounting data. An adequate approximation of this can be obtained, however. We can take the reported *accounting* increase in the firm's tangible fixed assets over the previous year and add back the depreciation charge for the year. This should give an *accounting* value of the assets purchased during the year, which we shall assume to be equal to the cash spent on fixed assets during the year. We can also assume that the *accounting* depreciation charge on the fixed assets is equal to their *economic* depreciation, then assume that the required 'maintenance' expenditure is equivalent to the economic depreciation of the assets. Using this approach, the PV of fixed asset and maintenance expenditure for each company can be estimated, as demonstrated in the Appendix and summarized in Table 9.1.

Once again eliminating the outlying percentage of British Bio-technology (which would be expected to be reduced dramatically following the launch of its first product) and allowing for the possibility of slightly higher percentage figures from unsuccessful companies (which would be likely to produce poorer sales figures relative to their asset base), the base case assumption that the PV of fixed asset and maintenance expenditure represents 15 per cent of the PV of sales would seem very reasonable.

Finally, the PV of *raw materials and expenses* as a percentage of the PV of sales can be obtained by subtraction (since, in total, the PVs of the components of sales must add up to 100 per cent), to give the 35 per cent assumed in the base case.

In summary, therefore, the base case assumptions of the break-down of the PV of sales into the four specified components seems reasonable and consistent with data obtained in respect of the case studies, after allowing for the sample bias.

Other assumed parameters

There are two remaining areas of input for the model requiring to be checked for their reasonability, the PV of the amount of equity invested as a percentage of the PV of sales, and the general area of actual tax rates, etc. experienced by the case study firms.

With regard to the PV of the amount of *equity* invested as a percentage of the PV of sales, Table 9.1 shows the values for the firms. Ignoring once again the British Bio-technology outlier, the range varies from 3 per cent (Datapaq) to 28 per cent (SIS), with four of the six companies at less than 10 per cent. We believe that the average for successful companies is unlikely to be more than 10 per cent, while that for the less successful and unsuccessful companies could be more likely to be in the 15–30 per cent range, or conceivably more. Taking into account the sample bias, we believe that the base case assumption of 15 per cent looks a reasonable starting point. (Note that if the successful and more mature companies in the sample are self-financing, at least to the extent that they no longer require further *equity* capital, then the percentages shown should continue to fall as further sales are generated. Indeed, in the long run, the PV of 'post-tax' profits for firms needs to exceed the PV of equity invested, in order to get a return on that equity investment!)

As far as actual tax rates experienced by the companies and their employees are concerned, relatively little data was forthcoming, since in many cases reported social security costs etc. include data on non-UK employees. With regard to the rate assumed for the *employer's NI* contribution, the data relating specifically to the UK was provided by Macro 4, which reported a rate of 10.2 to 10.4 per cent of gross salary over the previous six years. Linx, on the other hand, provided data which appeared to suggest that lower rates may have been paid (7.8 per cent in fiscal 1992, 8.9 per cent in fiscal 1993). Since the employer's NI contribution starts at 4.6 per cent of gross salary for employees earning around £3,000 per annum and escalates rapidly to 10.4 per cent for salaries of roughly £10,000 and over (without limit), we believe that the model's assumption of 10 per cent of NTBF employee gross salary is likely to be a reasonable weighted average for most firms.

With regard to the rate assumed for the *employee's NI* contribution, the situation is more complex because of the presence of two rates of NI ('standard' and 'reduced'), a more gradual increase in the rate applied (for 'standard' only) and a limit on the maximum amount of NI payable. The variation in the rate of employee NI with gross salary is shown in Fig. 9.1, based on pre-1994 data. In this respect, by far the most common group of individuals paying the reduced rate of NI will be married women, who are usually entitled to do so.

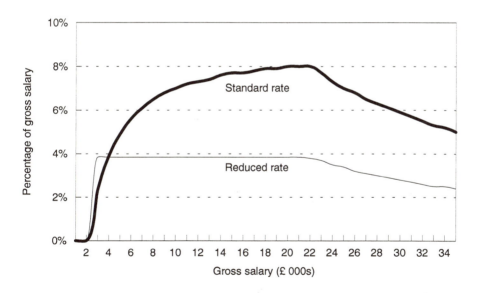

Figure 9.1 Employee National Insurance contribution as a percentage of gross salary (pre-1994 data)
(*Source*: Department of Social Security)

Once again, the best data regarding the actual rate of employee NI paid came from Macro 4 and Linx. Over the last five years for which data was obtained, Macro 4 employees appear to have paid an NI rate of between 3.8 per cent and 4.8 per cent (4.8 per cent most recently). The average salary of its employees, however, rose from £27,000 in 1988 to £34,000 in 1992 and, as a result, an employee earning the firm's average wage would have expected to pay around 5 per cent or so in NI. The slightly lower rate actually paid is likely to be due to reduced rate employees and additional personal taxation reliefs. (Note that the £34,000 average salary for 1992 was by far the highest for the case study firms. Average salaries for the remaining firms ranged from £14,000 (1989) to £24,000.)

Linx, on the other hand, appears to have applied average rates of 5.1 per cent and 5.5 per cent respectively for fiscal 1992 and 1993. The average salary of Linx employees over this period was approaching £17,000, although there were of course a few senior staff with significantly higher salaries than this. The difference between a figure based on the standard rate curve and the average rate actually paid is probably, once again, accounted for by employees paying the reduced rate.

In conclusion, therefore, taking all the various factors affecting the employee NI contribution into consideration and allowing for sample bias, we believe that the model's assumption of an average employee NI rate of 5.5 per cent is reasonable.

The final employment-related tax rate that is capable of comparison with actual data from the case study sample is that of *income tax* as a percentage of gross annual salary. In Fig. 9.2 we outline how the tax rate as a percentage of gross annual salary varies with gross salary for a single person whose only tax relief is the single person's allowance. This graph, if taken as being approximately correct for all employees, would seem to suggest that a firm such as Linx, with an average salary per employee of roughly £17,000 in 1991 and 1992, might be expected to pay somewhere in the region of 19 per cent of salaries in taxes. In reality, it paid 17.0 per cent and 19.8 per cent in these years, respectively. In contrast, Macro 4 would be expected to pay a little over 25 per cent in 1992 on an average salary of £34,000, and actually paid 29.4 per cent (although it paid 26.7 per cent on an average salary of £32,000 in 1991).

Taking the average salary range for the case study companies into consideration, that is, £14,000 (a 1989 figure) to £34,000, it would appear that the model's assumption of a 20 per cent income tax rate, to be applied to gross salaries, is again a reasonable one.

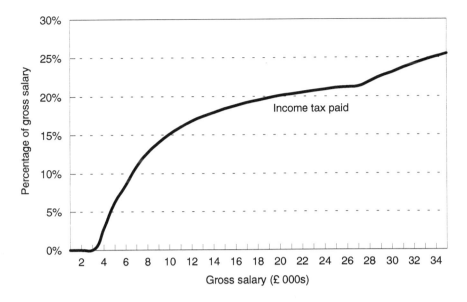

Figure 9.2 Income tax rate as a percentage of gross salary (with single person's allowance only)
(*Source*: Inland Revenue)

CONCLUSIONS

In this chapter we set out to consider some of the key assumptions regarding the values input into the model of Chapter 8 and some of the model's output, in comparison with real data extracted from a number of case studies. Although the firms used as case studies were not randomly chosen and, taken as a whole, were biased towards successful and more mature companies, the sample did include companies with a broad range of characteristics. Having analysed data from these companies and considered the likely impact of the sample bias, we have concluded that the inputs for/outputs of the model which were capable of being compared with 'real' data appear to be reasonable. That the 'real' numbers show, in some circumstances, significant variation from the base case parameter assumptions should not worry us unduly, since the model's output is subject to wide-ranging sensitivity analysis of these parameters.

In short, therefore, the model's inputs and outputs which are capable of being tested against 'real' data appear to compare reasonably well.

APPENDICES

Case Study 1: Linx Printing Technologies

Business profile

Linx Printing Technologies is a Cambridge–based ink–jet printer manufacturer, which has been hailed as 'a venture capital classic' by the *UK Venture Capital Journal*.[1] The company was formed in December 1986 and went public nearly six years later in October 1992. The following passage has been extracted from its IPO ('placing') documentation.[2]

> Linx operates within the growing product identification market. The increasing requirement to identify and code products and their packaging as part of the production process is driven by many requirements, including:
>
> - legislation, demanding 'use by' or 'best before' dates on products;
> - batch coding of products to improve traceability and minimise market impact in the event of product defects;
> - the use of increasingly sophisticated inventory control techniques in factories, warehouses and retail outlets.
>
> Linx's CIJ printers provide a cost–effective method of marking virtually any shape or surface with variable or fixed data at high speed without interrupting the normal production process.

Trading record

Linx's trading record since its formation has been obtained from the company's annual reports,[3] and is summarized in Table A9.1.

Table A9.1 Trading record of Linx Printing Technologies, 1986–1993 (£000s)

	Total sales	Export sales	Domestic sales	Pretax profit	Pretax margin
1986–7 (partial)	1	0	1	(150)	–
1987–8	152	127	25	(496)	–
1988–9	2,431	1,987	444	241	10%
1989–90	3,766	2,864	902	511	14%
1990–1	6,481	4,762	1,719	875	14%
1991–2	10,470	7,421	3,049	1,640	16%
1992–3	11,940	9,362	2,578	1,430	12%

Estimated cashflow to Exchequer

An estimate of the amount of cashflow paid to the Exchequer (in the form of CT, IT and NI) as a result of the company's activities during the seven accounting periods since its formation is given in Fig. A9.1.[4]

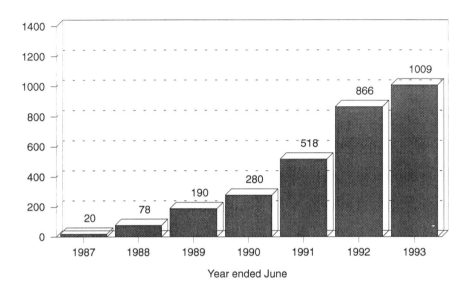

Figure A9.1 Linx: estimated totals of CT, IT and NI paid to the Exchequer, 1987–1993 (£000s)

Growth in number of employees

The growth in the average number of Linx's employees during each fiscal year is shown in Fig. A9.2.[5] It is understood that most, if not all, of these are UK employees.

Equity financing

Part of the rationale for labelling the case of Linx as a 'classic' is that the company was backed by venture capital right from the seed stage. The equity finance was provided in three tranches, with the founders and Managed Technology Investors (MTI) in the first of these and MTI and Paribas providing capital in the two subsequent tranches. The following is a record of the company's pre–IPO *equity* issues.

282 Venture Capital Funding: Recommendations for the UK

Year (fiscal)	Amount (£000s)
1986–7 (partial)	484
1987–8	470
1988–9	8
1989–90	6
1990–1	49
1991–2	99

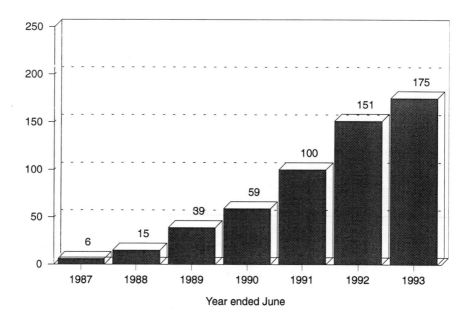

Figure A9.2 Linx: average number of employees, 1987–1993

It should be noted, however, that the venture–capital–provided equity of the first two (fiscal) years was the only *necessary* equity that needed to be provided to the company.

Financing difficulty experienced?
It is understood that the search for seed and start–up finance was 'far from easy' and took the best part of a year to secure.

Exit
Linx went public in October 1992, via a full listing on the UK Stock Exchange. This involved increasing the existing number of shares in the com-

pany by 12 per cent, and the placing of 25 per cent of the enlarged share capital (that is, only a partial exit). The average IRR to investors (based on the October IPO share price) was estimated as being approximately 59 per cent. The estimated maximum CGT liability resulting from the placing (assuming that all investors were subject to CGT), was £1.01 million.

Linx Printing Technologies: more details
Key extracts from P & L and balance sheet

Year ended June	1987 (6 months)	1988	1989	1990	1991	1992	1993
(a) Total sales	£1 335	£151 882	£2 431 000	£3 766 000	£6 481 013	£10 470 255	£11 940 000
UK export sales	£0	£126 882	£1 987 000	£2 864 000	£4 761 638	£7 421 544	£9 362 000
UK domestic sales	£1 335	£25 000	£444 000	£902 000	£1 719 375	£3 048 711	£2 578 000
(b) Staff costs							
wages & salaries	£54 540	£214 128	£518 572	£789 915	£1 445 969	£2 508 911	£2 953 000
social security costs	5 700	£22 123	£54 370	£77 620	£145 829	£259 337	£296 000
other pension costs	£1 449	£7 091	£15 694	£29 400	£42 673	£81 699	£94 000
(c) Employees	6	15	39	59	100	151	175
UK employees	6	15	39	59	100	151	175
(d) Issue of shares (before issue costs)	£483 751	£470 000	£8 073	£6 156	£49 310	£99 275	n.a.
(e) Pretax profit	(150 000)	(£496 000)	£241 000	£511 000	£875 000	£1 640,000	£1 430 000
(% of sales)	–11236%	–327%	10%	14%	14%	16%	12%
Gross staff costs as a % of total sales	4620.9%	160.2%	24.2%	23.8%	25.2%	27.2%	28.0%

Estimate of cash flowing to/(from) Exchequer from taxes and NI (first 7 years)

Year ended June	1987 (6 months)	1988	1989	1990	1991	1992	1993
(a) CT paid	£0	£842	£3 268	£1 396	£3 850	£115 143	n.a.
(b) Employer's NI	£5 700	£22 123	£54 370	£77 620	£145 829	£195 583	£262 242
(% of gross salary)	10.5%	10.3%	10.5%	9.8%	10.1%	7.8%	8.9%
(c) Employees' NI	£3 000	£11 777	£26 521	£43 445	£79 528	£128,557	£163 710
(% of gross salary)	5.5%	5.5%	5.5%	5.5.%	5.5%	5.1%	5.5%
(d) Employees' IT	£10 908	£42 826	£103 714	£157 983	£289 194	£426 572	£583 308
(% of gross salary)	20.0%	20.0%	20.0%	20.0%	20.0%	17.0%	19.8%
Total tax cashflow	£19 608	£77 568	£189 874	£280 444	£518 401	£865 855	£1 009 260
as % of sales	1468.7%	51.1%	7.8%	7.4%	8.0%	8.3%	8.5%
Cumulative cashflow	£19 608	£97 175	£287 049	£567 494	£1 085 895	£1 951 750	£2 961 010
(a) Net VAT received	n.a.	n.a.	£214 984	£236 610	£467 630	£685 990	£830 026
Paid	n.a.	n.a.	(£69 499)	(£134 971)	(£293 002)	(£483 345)	(£486 941)
Received	n.a.	n.a.	£284 483	£371 581	£760 632	£1 169 335	£1 316 967

Denotes an estimated value

Assumed to equal 'social security costs'

PVs of key parameters as a % of total sales (over period shown):

(1) Corporation tax =	0.35%
(2) National insurance (employer and employee) and income taxes =	8.09%
(3) Gross staff costs =	27.38%
(4) Pretax profit =	11.00%
(5) Equity =	3.92%

Case Study 2: Domino Printing Sciences

Business profile

Domino Printing Sciences is another Cambridge-based business (cf. Linx) involved in 'the research and development, manufacture and sale of ink–jet printing systems and related consumables'.[6] The company was formed in September 1978 and went public nearly seven years later in May 1985.[7] Domino launched its first continuous ink–jet printer, 'Unijet', in July of 1979, less than one year after its start-up. The launch of its second printer, 'Solo 1', during 1981, however, coincided with the introduction of a new EEC directive which forced manufacturers of perishable products to label them with a 'sell by' and/or 'best before' date, thus boosting the demand for labelling technology – and the company's potential. Since then, the company has launched a stream of new products and has made several strategic acquisitions in related technological areas, which have also facilitated its geographical expansion.

Trading record

Domino's trading record since its formation has been obtained from the company's annual reports, and is summarized in Table A9.2.[8]

Table A9.2 Trading record of Domino Printing Sciences, 1979–1992 (£000s)

	Total sales	Export sales	Domestic sales	Pretax profit	Pretax margin
1979 (partial)	0	0	0	(36)	–
1980	82	0	82	(69)	–
1981	542	146	396	18	3%
1982	1,126	536	590	120	11%
1983	2,454	802	1,652	263	11%
1984	7,376	4,612	2,764	1,820	25%
1985	11,196	7,582	3,614	2,650	24%
1986	13,672	8,404	5,268	3,606	26%
1987	21,396	15,506	5,890	4,507	21%
1988	32,827	26,525	6,302	5,115	16%
1989	37,976	30,257	7,719	4,711	12%
1990	45,907	34,023	11,884	6,088	13%
1991	60,371	49,860	10,511	9,026	15%
1992	71,611	60,173	11,438	11,939	17%

Estimated cashflow to Exchequer

An estimate of the amount of cashflow paid to the Exchequer (in the form of

286 Venture Capital Funding: Recommendations for the UK

CT, IT and NI), as a result of the company's activities during the fourteen accounting periods since its formation is given in Fig. A9.3.[9]

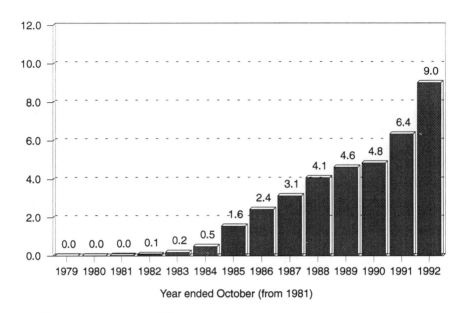

Figure A9.3 Domino: estimated totals of CT, IT and NI paid to the Exchequer, 1979–1992 (£m)

Growth in number of employees

The growth in the average number of Domino's employees during each fiscal year is shown in Fig. A9.4. It includes employees entering the group as a result of acquisitions.[10]

Equity financing

The initial capital (£20,000, including debt and equity), was raised by the founding entrepreneur Graeme Minto by mortgaging his home. In the following month the company won the ICFC (a subsidiary of 3i) Innovator Award (£10,000) which was supplemented by an investment from ICFC in July 1979 of £100,000. Interestingly, only £7,500 of the ICFC capital was equity, the rest being a twenty–years 15.5 per cent fixed rate loan (ultimately paid back early). A critical factor in Domino's success, however, was its relationship with a company called CCL, which carried out an estimated £1 million of development work for Domino in exchange for (uncertain) future royalties. Finally, in 1982, the company won the first prize (£50,000) in the Hill Samuel 150-year Anniversary Awards. Domino's seed and start–up

UK NTBF Case Studies and Analysis   287

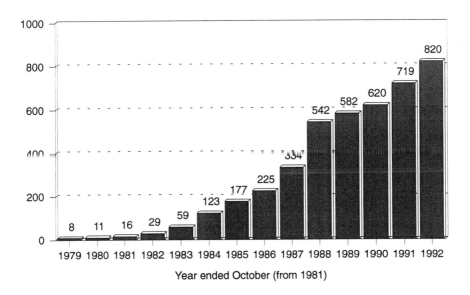

Figure A9.4 Domino: average number of employees, 1979–1992

period was thus financed predominantly by debt, by winning prizes, but most importantly by the development deal with CCL. Its *equity* history, however, was as follows.

Year (fiscal)	Amount (£000s)
1979 (partial)	12
1980	9
1981	1
1982	0
1983	0
1984	15
1985	2,720
1986	14
1987	28,144
1988	128
1989	297
1990	49
1991	402
1992	15,451

Financing difficulty experienced?

No financing difficulty was experienced. The company was fortunate in obtaining an offer from 3i 'within a week or so' of requesting funds. These funds were available to be drawn down after 'around six weeks'.

Exit

Domino went public in May 1985, via a listing on the Stock Exchange. This involved increasing the existing number of shares in the company by 31 per cent, and the placing of 42 per cent of the (thus) enlarged share capital (that is, a partial exit). Roughly half of the new money raised by Domino was in consideration for an acquisition. The estimated maximum CGT liability resulting from the placing (assuming that all investors were subject to CGT), was £1.9 million.

Domino Printing Sciences: more details

Key extracts from P & L and balance sheet (£000s)

Year ended October	1979 (to April)	1980 (to April) (18 months)	1981	1982	1983	1984	1985	1986	1987	1988	1989	1990	1991	1992
(a) Total sales	£0	£82	£542	£1 126	£2 454	£7 376	£11 196	£13 672	£21 396	£32 827	£37 976	£45 907	£60 371	£71 611
Foreign sales	£0	£0	£146	£536	£802	£4 612	£7 582	£8 404	£15 506	£26 525	£30 257	£34 023	£49 860	£60 173
UK domestic sales	£0	£82	£396	£590	£1 652	£2 764	£3 614	£5 268	£5 890	£6 302	£7 719	£11 884	£10 511	£11 438
(b) Staff costs														
wages & salaries	£44	£70	£118	£245	£574	£1 431	£2 037	£2 909	£5 037	£8 171	£9 394	£10 551	£13 260	£15 730
social security costs	£4	£6	£11	£23	£53	£131	£190	£310	£566	£841	£940	£1 129	£1 717	£2 484
other pension costs	£3	£5	£8	£16	£37	£60	£94	£111	£206	£258	£252	£313	£357	£442
(c) Employees														
UK employees	8	11	16	29	59	123	177	225	334	542	582	620	719	820
(d) Issue of shares (before issue costs)	£12	£9	£1	£0	£0	£15	£2 720	£14	£28 144	£128	£97	£49	n.a.	n.a.
(e) Pretax profit	(£36)	(£69)	£18	£120	£263	£1 820	£2 650	£3 606	£4 507	£5 115	£4 711	£6 088	£9 026	£11 939
(% of sales)	n.a.	-84%	3%	11%	11%	25%	24%	26%	21%	16%	12%	13%	15%	17%
Gross staff costs as a % of total sales	n.a.	98.8%	25.3%	25.2%	27.1%	22.0%	20.7%	24.4%	27.1%	28.2%	27.3%	26.1%	25.4%	26.1%

Estimate of cash flowing to/(from) Exchequer from taxes and NI (first 14 years) (£000s)

Year ended October	1979 (to April)	1980 (to April) (18 months)	1981	1982	1983	1984	1985	1986	1987	1988	1989	1990	1991	1992
(a) CT paid	£0	£0	£0	£0	£2	£4	£848	£1 376	£1 297	£1 164	£196	£1 027	£1 263	£2 517
(b) Employer's NI	£4	£6	£11	£23	£53	£131	£190	£310	£566	£841	£940	£1 129	£1 717	£2 484
(% of gross salary)	9.1%	8.6%	9.3%	9.4%	9.2%	9.2%	9.3%	10.7%	11.2%	10.3%	10.3%	10.7%	12.9%	15.8%
(c) Employees' NI	£2	£4	£6	£13	£32	£79	£112	£160	£277	£449	£417	£580	£729	£865
(% of gross salary)	5.5%	5.5%	5.5%	5.5%	5.5%	5.5%	5.5%	5.5%	5.5%	5.5%	5.3%	5.5%	5.5%	5.5%
(d) Employees' IT	£9	£14	£24	£49	£115	£286	£407	£582	£1 007	£1 634	£1 679	£2 110	£2 652	£3 146
(% of gross salary)	20.0%	20.0%	20.0%	20.0%	20.0%	20.0%	20.0%	20.0%	20.0%	20.0%	20.3%	20.0%	20.0%	20.0%
Total tax cashflow	£15	£24	£41	£85	£201	£500	£1 557	£2 428	£3 147	£4 089	£4 631	£4 847	£6 361	£9 012
as % of sales	n.a.	29.1%	7.6%	7.6%	8.2%	6.8%	13.9%	17.8%	14.7%	12.5%	12.2%	10.6%	10.5%	12.6%
Cumulative cashflow	£15	£39	£80	£166	£367	£867	£2 424	£4 852	£8 000	£12 088	£16 720	£21 566	£27 927	£36 940

PVs of key parameters as a % of total sales (over period shown):

(1) Corporation tax = 3.63%
(2) National insurance (employer and employee and income taxes= 8.48%
(3) Gross staff costs = 26.11%
(4) Pretax profit = 16.47%
(5) Equity = 16.29%

☐ Denotes an estimated value
☐ Assumed to equal 'social security costs'

Case Study 3: Psion

Business profile
The principal activities of Psion are 'the research into and development, engineering, marketing and selling of portable computers, datacommunication equipment, business applications and leisure software. In addition, the group is involved in the negotiation, specification and implementation of custom software systems.'[11] The company was formed in October 1980 and went public nearly seven years later in March 1988.

Psion is probably best known for its hand held 'Psion Organiser', and products which have subsequently grown out of this concept. Its latest products are the Psion 3 (launched in late 1991), which might be considered as being a more modern, sophisticated and powerful version of the original organizer, and the MC range of corporate hand–held computers. The company is also involved, however, with games and other custom software, an area in which it generated its initial sales.[12] Finally, Psion has more recently become active in datacommunications, following its 1989 acquisition of Dacom Systems.

Trading record
Psion's trading record since its formation has been obtained from the company's annual reports,[13] and is summarized in Table A9.3.

Table A9.3 Trading record of Psion, 1981–1992 (£000s)

	Total sales	Export sales	Domestic sales	Pretax profit	Pretax margin
1981	120	0	120	15	13%
1982	1,727	400	1,117	613	35%
1983	4,808	1,100	3,028	1,593	33%
1984	4,594	600	3,500	(1,296)	–
1985	4,174	590	3,100	441	11%
1986	5,029	870	4,117	383	8%
1987	11,811	3,450	8,126	1,863	16%
1988	19,226	6,900	11,535	2,758	14%
1989	31,425	9,900	20,620	3,345	11%
1990	31,396	10,800	20,443	546	2%
1991	21,333	8,300	11,704	(2,197)	–
1992	35,088	13,500	19,330	1,420	4%

Estimated cashflow to Exchequer
An estimate of the amount of cashflow paid to the Exchequer (in the form of CT, IT and NI) as a result of the company's activities during the twelve accounting periods since its formation is given in Fig. A9.5.[14]

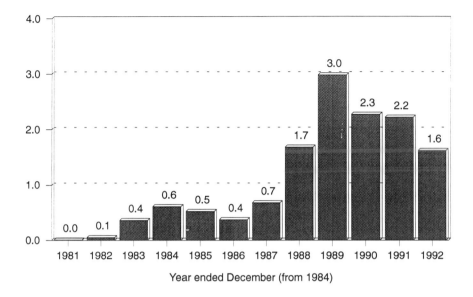

Figure A9.5 Psion: estimated totals of CT, IT and NI paid to the Exchequer, 1981–1992 (£m)

Growth in number of employees

The growth in the average number of Psion's employees during each fiscal year is shown in Fig. A9.6. It includes employees entering the group as a result of acquisitions.[15]

Equity financing

The initial £1,000 share capital came from the founder's own 'free capital' of £50,000, which he used as a loan to Psion, in addition to a personally guaranteed bank loan of £65,000. The next major increase in equity capital came in 1984, when the company raised £800,000 from two business angels (who were personal friends of the founder and are still non–executive directors of the board), in order to secure a greater equity base from which to launch the Psion Organiser and cover against the loss of anticipated business to significant customers (Sinclair and ICL). Following this issue, no additional equity was required until Psion went public in March of 1988, when it raised a further £1.5 million. Its equity history is as follows.

292 Venture Capital Funding: Recommendations for the UK

Year (fiscal)	Amount (£000s)
1981	1
1982	5
1983	0
1984	800
1985	0
1986	0
1987	0
1988	1,478
1989	9,112
1990	18
1991	4
1992	79

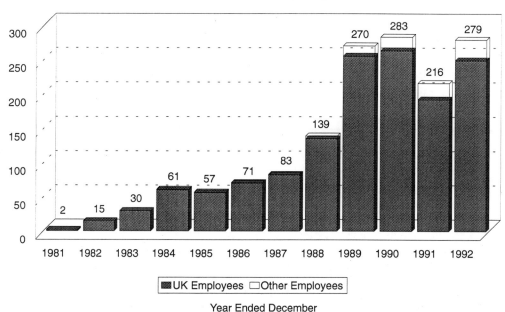

Figure A9.6 Psion: average number of employees, 1981–1992

Financing difficulty experienced?

Psion has not experienced difficulties in raising finance since its formation. The entrepreneur was discouraged, however, from using government-sourced financial assistance by the effort and bureaucracy required, which would have detracted from his running of the business during the critical first few years.

Exit

Psion went public in March 1988, by obtaining a quotation on the Unlisted Securities Market of the UK Stock Exchange. This involved increasing the existing number of shares in the company by 9 per cent, and the placing of 18 per cent of the (thus) enlarged share capital (that is, only a partial exit). The estimated CGT liability resulting from the placing (assuming all investors to be subject to CGT), was £649,000.

Psion: more details

Key extracts from P & L and balance sheet (£000s)

Year ended December	1981 (to Nov)	1982 (to Nov)	1983 (to Nov) (13 months)	1984	1985	1986	1987	1988	1989	1990	1991	1992
(a) Total sales	£120	£1 727	£4 808	£4 594	£4 174	£5 029	£11 811	£19 226	£31 425	£31 396	£21 333	£35 088
Other sales	£0	£210	£680	£494	£484	£42	£235	£791	£905	£153	£1 329	£2 258
UK export sales	£0	£400	£1 100	£600	£590	£870	£3 450	£6 900	£9 900	£10 800	£8 300	£13 500
UK domestic sales	£120	£1 117	£3 028	£3 500	£3 100	£4 117	£8 126	£11 535	£20 620	£20 443	£11 704	£19 330
(b) Staff costs												
wages and salaries	£19	£143	£290	£592	£800	£940	£1 371	£2 162	£4 549	£5 046	£4 075	£4 823
social security costs	£1	£11	£22	£58	£68	£89	£114	£223	£462	£537	£421	£555
other pension costs	£0	£0	£1	£6	£7	£20	£38	£54	£98	£93	£82	£100
(c) Employees	2	15	30	61	57	71	83	139	270	283	216	279
(d) UK employees	2	15	30	60	56	70	82	135	255	263	192	249
Issue of shares	£1	£5	£0	£800	£0	£0	£0	£1 478	£9 112	£18	£4	£79
(e) Pretax profit (before issue costs)	£15	£613	£1 593	(£1 296)	£441	£383	£1 863	£2 758	£3 345	£546	(£2 197)	£1 420
(% of sales)	13%	35%	33%	-28%	11%	8%	16%	14%	11%	2%	-10%	4%
Gross staff costs as a % of total sales	16.7%	8.9%	6.5%	14.3%	21.0%	20.9%	12.9%	12.7%	16.3%	18.1%	21.5%	15.6%

Estimate of cash flowing to/(from) Exchequer from taxes and NI (first 12 years) (£000s)

Year ended December	1981 (to Nov)	1982 (to Nov)	1983 (to Nov) (13 months)	1984	1985	1986	1987	1988	1989	1990	1991	1992
(a) CT paid	£0	£6	£265	£400	£250	£44	£214	£910	£1 360	£452	£761	(£163)
(b) Employer's NI	£2	£11	£22	£58	£68	£89	£114	£223	£462	£537	£421	£555
(% of gross salary)	10.5%	7.7%	7.6%	9.8%	8.5%	9.5%	8.3%	10.3%	10.2%	10.6%	10.3%	11.5%
(c) Employees's NI	£1	£8	£16	£33	£44	£52	£75	£119	£250	£278	£224	£265
(% of gross salary)	5.5%	5.5%	5.5%	5.5%	5.5%	5.5%	5.5%	5.5%	5.5%	5.5%	5.5%	5.5%
(d) Employees IT	£4	£29	£58	£118	£160	£188	£274	£432	£910	£1 009	£815	£965
(% of gross salary)	20.0%	20.0%	20.0%	20.0%	20.0%	20.0%	20.0%	20.0%	20.0%	20.0%	20.0%	20.0%
Total tax cashflow	£7	£53	£361	£609	£522	£373	£678	£1 684	£2 982	£2 276	£2 221	£1 622
as % of sales	5.7%	3.1%	7.5%	13.3%	12.5%	7.4%	5.7%	8.8%	9.5%	7.2%	10.4%	4.6%
Cumulative cashflow	£7	£60	£421	£1 030	£1 552	£1 925	£2 603	£4 287	£7 269	£9 545	£11 766	£13 388

PVs of key parameters as a % of total sales (over period shown):

(1) Corporation tax = 2.83%
(2) National insurance (employer and employee) and income taxes = 5.12%
(3) Gross staff costs = 16.09%
(4) Pretax profit = 6.23%
(5) Equity = 6.96%

☐ Denotes an estimated value
▨ Assumed to equal 'social security costs'

Case Study 4: Tadpole Technology

Business profile

The principal activities of Tadpole are 'the design, development, manufacture and sale of computer systems and components'.[16] The company was formed in November 1983 and went public nine years later in December 1992.

Although Tadpole is still very small indeed by comparison with many of its customers, it offers a development service (in 32/64 bit single board computers and, more recently, complete portable workstation systems) to some of the largest and most prestigious multinational and international companies, including IBM, AT&T, British Telecom, Motorola, Sun Microsystems, and many others.[17] According to the chairman's statement in the 1988 annual report and accounts, 'The pressure of the accelerating rate of technological change leads our customers' managements to make decisions to buy in rather than design internally . . . Tadpole has developed into an internationally respected supplier by exploiting its advantages of speed, innovation and quality.' Since then, Tadpole has developed the world's only notebook–size workstation, the SPARCbook, and has announced an agreement with IBM to develop a notebook workstation based on the new PowerPC microprocessor architecture.

Trading record

Tadpole's trading record since its formation has been obtained from the company's annual reports,[18] and is summarized in Table A9.4.

Table A9.4 Trading record of Tadpole Technology, 1984–1993 (H1) (£000s)

	Total sales	Export sales	Domestic sales	Pretax profit	Pretax margin
1984	77	17	60	(231)	–
1985	787	50	737	(137)	–
1986	1,147	140	1,007	73	6%
1987	2,565	641	1,924	348	14%
1988	4,570	1,727	2,843	462	10%
1989	5,750	3,810	1,940	(935)	–
1990	6,659	4,841	1,818	(269)	–
1991	9,611	9,323	288	684	7%
1992	12,461	11,713	748	(1,690)	–
1993 (H1)	8,905	8,193	712	27	0%

Estimated cashflow to Exchequer

An estimate of the amount of cashflow paid to the Exchequer (in the form of CT, IT and NI) as a result of the company's activities during the nine accounting periods since its formation is given in Fig. A9.7.[19] (Year ends are December except for 1991 and 1992, which are September year ends; 1991 is a nine-month period.)

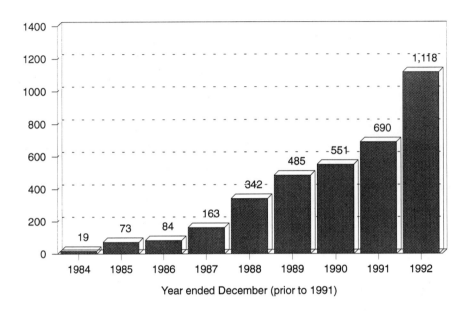

Figure A9.7 Tadpole: estimated totals of CT, IT and NI paid to the Exchequer, 1984–1992 (£000s)

Growth in number of employees

The growth in the average number of Tadpole's employees during each fiscal year is shown in Fig. A9.8. It includes employees entering the group as a result of acquisitions.[20]

Equity financing

The £505,000 of share capital raised in 1984 was sourced from the founding entrepreneurs (especially George Grey, the current chief executive), a number of private individuals and 3i (which took an early investment in the 1984 rights issue and remained a major shareholder until the 1992 flotation). Included in this 1984 equity fundraising was £250,000 provided under the BES. In early 1986 the company also obtained a loan of £75,000 under the Loan Guarantee Scheme, which was repayable in ten equal quarterly install-

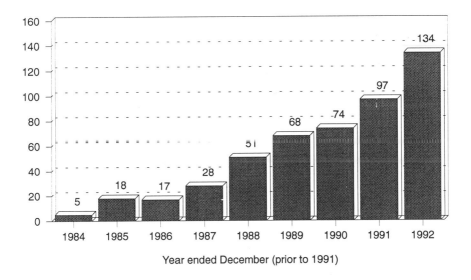

Figure A9.8 Tadpole: average number of employees, 1984–1992

ments commencing in September 1986. These early funds were supplemented via smaller share issues (to both existing and new shareholders) to fund working capital in 1986 and 1987, followed by much heavier (usually) rights issues in 1988, 1989, 1990 and 1992. The funds raised by way of equity issues are as follows. It should be noted, however, that a further £3.6 million was raised at the time of its flotation (December 1992), and loan stock was converted in November 1992.

Year (fiscal)	Amount (£000s)
1984	505
1985	0
1986	63
1987	137
1988	687
1989	1,200
1990	408
1991	18
1992	572

Financing difficulty experienced?

For most of its history, particularly early on, Tadpole experienced conditions of uncertain revenue streams and, as a result, found it difficult to capitalize itself adequately for the markets in which it operated. Operating on limited cash reserves, the company adopted a strategy of raising money in relatively small amounts, as and when trading conditions required. Since its end–1992 flotation, however, the group's balance sheet has greatly improved, thus providing a more financially secure basis for future growth.

Exit

Tadpole went public in December 1992, via a full listing on the UK Stock Exchange. This involved increasing the existing number of shares in the company by 44 per cent, and the placing of 41 per cent of the (thus) enlarged share capital (that is, only a partial exit). The estimated CGT liability resulting from the placing (assuming that all investors were subject to CGT), was £281,000.

Key extracts from P & L and balance sheet (£000s)

Year ended December	1984	1985	1986	1987	1988	1989	1990	1991 (to Sept)	1992 (to Sept)
(a) Total sales	£77	£787	£1 147	£2 565	£4 570	£5 750	£6 659	£9 611	£12 461
Foreign sales	£17	£50	£140	£641	£1 727	£3 810	£4 841	£9 323	£11 713
UK domestic sales	£60	£737	£1 007	£1 924	£2 843	£1 940	£1 818	£288	£748
(b) Staff costs									
wages and salaries	£52	£233	£235	£453	£932	£1 448	£1 625	£1 842	£3 151
social security costs	£5	£13	£24	£47	£104	£99	£129	£176	£312
other pension costs	£0	£0	£0	£0	£53	£119	£78	£89	£94
(c) Employees	5	18	17	28	51	68	74	97	134
UK employees	5	18	17	28	n.a.	n.a.	n.a.	n.a.	n.a.
(d) Issue of shares (before issue costs)	£505	£0	£63	£137	£687	£1 200	£408	£18	572
(e) Pretax profit	(£231)	(£137)	£73	£348	£462	(£935)	(£269)	£684	(£1 690)
(% of sales)	–300%	–17%	6%	14%	10%	–16%	–4%	7%	–14%
Gross staff costs as a % of total sales	74.0%	31.3%	22.6%	19.5%	23.8%	29.0%	27.5%	21.9%	28.5%

Estimate of cash flowing to/(from) Exchequer from taxes and NI (first 9 years) (£000s)

Year ended December	1984	1985	1986	1987	1988	1989	1990	1991 (to Sept)	1992 (to Sept)
(a) CT paid	£0	£0	£0	£0	£0	£16	£7	£44	£2
(b) Employer's NI	£5	£13	£24	£47	£104	£99	£129	£176	£312
(% of gross salary)	9.6%	5.6%	10.2%	10.4%	11.2	6.8%	7.9%	9.6%	9.9%
(c) Employees' NI	£3	£13	£13	£25	£51	£80	£89	£101	£173
(% of gross salary)	5.5%	5.5%	5.5%	5.5%	5.5%	5.5%	5.5%	5.5%	5.5%
(d) Employees' IT	£10	£47	£47	£91	£186	£290	£325	£368	£630
(% of gross salary)	20.0%	20.0%	20.0%	20.0%	20.0%	20.0%	20.0%	20.0%	20.0%
Total tax cashflow	£19	£73	£84	£163	£342	£485	£551	£690	£1 118
as % of sales	24.2%	9.2%	7.3%	6.3%	7.5%	8.4%	8.3%	7.2%	9.0%
Cumulative cashflow	£19	£91	£176	£338	£681	£1 165	£1 716	£2 406	£3 524

Denotes an estimated value

Assumed to equal 'social security costs'

PVs of key parameters as a % of total sales (over period shown):

(1) Corporation tax = 0.15%
(2) National insurance (employer and employee) and income taxes = 7.99%
(3) Gross staff costs = 25.87%
(4) Pretax profit = –3.67%
(5) Equity = 9.01%

Case Study 5: Macro 4

Business profile

The principal activity of Macro 4 is 'the development, production and marketing of computer software for the mainframe sector of the computer market'.[20] The company was formed in February 1968, was the subject of a management buy-out in December of 1983, and went public two years later in January 1986. According to the 1986 'offer for sale' document:

> Macro 4, which is one of the longest established independent software companies in the world, develops and markets systems software for IBM and IBM compatible mainframe computers ... All of Macro 4's products are marketed in a standardised packaged format so that they will interface automatically with the customer's operating system. They can therefore simply be mailed to the customer on a magnetic tape, avoiding the need for expensive marketing, installation and customer support. Macro 4 typically contracts with its customers on the basis of an annual rental contract, with rentals payable monthly in advance ... Macro 4 is committed to the mainframe sector of the computer market; it is not involved in the micro or mini computer markets.

Trading record

Macro 4's trading record since its formation has been obtained from the company's annual reports,[21] and is summarized in Table A9.5.

Table A9.5   Trading record of Macro 4, 1981–1992 (£000s)

	Total sales	Export sales	Domestic sales	Pretax profit	Pretax margin
1981	1,159	657	502	(22)	–
1982	1,424	854	507	(69)	–
1983	2,236	1,430	806	98	4%
1984	3,377	2,490	887	518	15%
1985	5,060	3,835	1,225	1,847	37%
1986	6,778	5,084	1,694	2,766	41%
1987	8,915	6,743	2,172	4,106	46%
1988	10,508	7,829	2,679	5,509	52%
1989	13,131	9,947	3,184	6,501	50%
1990	14,775	11,257	3,518	7,353	50%
1991	18,028	14,119	3,909	7,647	42%
1992	19,016	14,904	4,112	8,750	46%

Estimated cashflow to Exchequer

An estimate of the amount of cashflow paid to the Exchequer (in the form of

CT, IT and NI), as a result of the company's activities during seven of the nine accounting periods since the MBO is given in Fig. A9.9.[22]

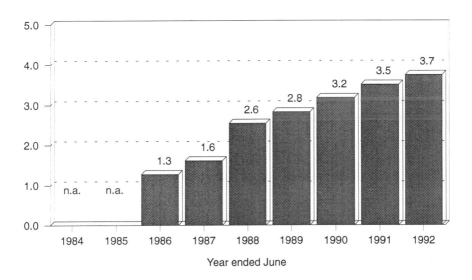

Figure A9.9 Macro 4: estimated totals of CT, IT and NI paid to the Exchequer, 1986–1992 (£m)

Growth in number of employees
The growth in the average number of Macro 4's employees during each fiscal year is shown in Fig. A9.10. It includes employees entering the group as a result of acquisitions.[23]

Equity financing
Since the 'venture capital' transaction in this case study was an MBO, the role of the venture capitalist (Advent) was rather different from that in the other cases, in that it provided MBO finance to the *management* rather than the company. In doing so, it also established an 'arm's length' share price for tax purposes.

The only 'expansion equity' required by Macro 4 since the MBO was issued at the time of its January 1986 flotation, in order to purchase the company's American associate, Macro 4 Inc. All subsequent share issues are related to share option activity. The company's equity history since the MBO is as follows (1986 reflects the US acquisition).

Venture Capital Funding: Recommendations for the UK

Year (fiscal)	Amount (£000s)
1984	1
1985	0
1986	921
1987	6
1988	5
1989	78
1990	15
1991	0
1992	553

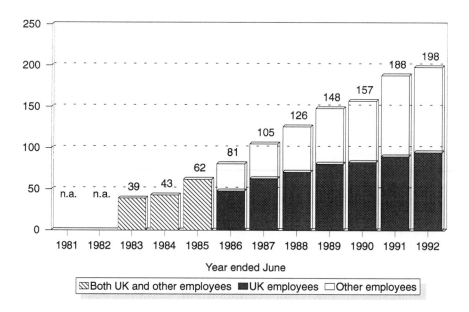

Figure A9.10 Macro 4: average number of employees, 1983–1992

Financing difficulty experienced?
It is understood that the management of Macro 4 did not have any particular difficulties in raising money for the MBO.

Exit
Macro 4 went public in January 1986, by obtaining a full listing on the UK Stock Exchange. This involved increasing the existing number of shares in the company by 17 per cent (issued in consideration for the acquisition of Macro 4, Inc.), and an offer for sale of 25 per cent of the (thus) enlarged share

capital (that is, only a partial exit). No CGT liability resulted from the placing of the shares issued in consideration for the acquisition of Macro 4, Inc. as these were issued to non–UK residents.

Macro 4: more details

Key extracts from P & L and balance sheet (£000s)

Year ended June		1981	1982	1983	1984 (MBO)	1985	1986	1987	1988	1989	1990	1991	1992
(a)	Total sales	£1 159	£1 424	£2 236	£3 377	£5 060	£6 778	£8 915	£10 508	£13 131	£14 775	£18 028	£19 016
	Foreign sales	£657	£854	£1 430	£2 490	£3 835	£5 084	£6 743	£7 829	£9 947	£11 257	£14 119	£14 904
	UK domestic sales	£502	£570	£806	£887	£1 225	£1 694	£2 172	£2 679	£3 184	£3 518	£3 909	£4 112
(b1)	Total staff costs												
	wages and salaries	n.a.	n.a.	n.a.	£1 120	£2 266	£2 482	£2 950	£3 341	£4 078	£4 947	£6 086	£6 548
	social security costs	n.a.	n.a.	n.a.	£37	£85	£187	£345	£390	£505	£620	£744	£305
	other pension costs	n.a.	n.a.	n.a.	£130	£134	£135	£172	£169	£190	£166	£180	£226
(b2)	UK staff costs												
	wages and salaries	n.a.	n.a.	n.a.	n.a.	n.a.	£1 405	£1 722	£1 886	£2 264	£2 616	£2 875	£3 223
	social security costs	n.a.	n.a.	n.a.	n.a.	n.a.	£114	£175	£193	£234	£268	£298	£336
	other pension costs	n.a.	n.a.	n.a.	n.a.	n.a.	£76	£108	£96	£118	£137	£152	£196
(c)	Employees	n.a.	n.a.	n.a.	43	62	81	105	126	148	157	188	198
	UK employees	n.a.	n.a.	n.a.	n.a.	n.a.	48	63	71	81	83	90	95
(d)	Issue of shares (before issue costs)	n.a.	n.a.	n.a.	£1	£0	£921	£6	£5	£78	£15	£0	£553
(e)	Pretax profit	(£22)	(£69)	£98	£518	£1 847	£2 766	£4 106	£5 509	£6 501	£7 353	£7 647	£8 750
	(% of sales)	-2%	-5%	4%	15%	37%	41%	46%	52%	50%	50%	42%	46%
	Gross total staff costs as a % of total sales	n.a.	n.a.	n.a.	38.1%	49.1%	41.4%	38.9%	37.1%	36.3%	38.8%	38.9%	37.2%
	Gross UK staff costs as a % of total sales	n.a.	n.a.	n.a.	n.a.	n.a.	23.5%	22.5%	20.7%	19.9%	20.4%	18.4%	19.7%

Estimate of cash flowing to/(from) Exchequer from taxes and NI (following the MBO) (£000)

Year ended June		1981	1982	1983	1984 (MBO)	1985	1986	1987	1988	1989	1990	1991	1992
(a)	CT paid	n.a.	n.a.	n.a.	n.a.	n.a.	£650	£908	£1 708	£1 934	£2 141	£2 333	£2 304
(b)	Employer's NI	n.a.	n.a.	n.a.	n.a.	n.a.	£114	£175	£193	£234	£268	£298	£336
	(% of gross UK salary)	n.a.	n.a.	n.a.	n.a.	n.a.	8.1%	10.2%	10.2%	10.3%	10.2%	10.4%	10.4%
(c)	Employees' NI	n.a.	n.a.	n.a.	n.a.	n.a.	£26	£55	£79	£89	£100	£111	£156
	(% of gross UK salary)	n.a.	n.a.	n.a.	n.a.	n.a.	1.9%	3.2%	4.2%	3.9%	3.8%	3.9%	4.8%
(d)	Employees' IT	n.a.	n.a.	n.a.	n.a.	n.a.	£486	£477	£571	£572	£673	£767	£948
	(% of gross UK salary)	n.a.	n.a.	n.a.	n.a.	n.a.	34.6%	27.7%	30.3%	25.3%	25.7%	26.7%	29.4%
	Total tax cashflow	n.a.	n.a.	n.a.	n.a.	n.a.	£1 276	£1 616	£2 551	£2 829	£3 182	£3 509	£3 744
	as % of sales	n.a.	n.a.	n.a.	n.a.	n.a.	18.8%	18.1%	24.3%	21.5%	21.5%	19.5%	19.7%
	cumulative cashflow	n.a.	n.a.	n.a.	n.a.	n.a.	£1 276	£2 891	£5 442	£8 271	£11 453	£14 962	£18 706
(e)	Estimated net VAT	n.a.	n.a.	n.a.	n.a.	n.a.	£152	£195	£236	£336	£91	£386	£539

PVs of key parameters as a % of total sales (to date):

(1) Corporation tax = 11.66%
(2) National insurance (employer and employee) and income taxes = 6.62%
(3) Gross total staff costs = 38.90%
(4) Pretax profit = 44.71%
(5) Equity = n.a.

Case Study 6: Datapaq

Business profile
The principal activity of Datapaq is 'the development, manufacture and sale of in–process thermal monitoring systems for use in semi–continuous batch operations'.[24] The company was formed in April 1984, and was sold in its entirety to the Quota Group Ltd nearly eight years later in January 1992.

The company's product range is based around the Datapaq 'Tracker', which is a microprocessor–driven device that can be sent through (say) a paint curing oven along with the component requiring curing. In so doing, the tracker is able to analyse the curing temperature profile of that component through sensors clipped to its surface. Thus the curing process can be optimised.[25] The principal customers for Datapaq products are those involved in the finishing (such as paint curing), food processing, electronics and ceramics industries. Having said this, the company's turnover is understood to be dominated by the finishing industry, which was the first to be served by Datapaq products.

Trading record
Datapaq's trading record since its formation has been obtained from the company's annual reports,[26] and is summarized in Table A9.6.

Table A9.6   Trading record of Datapaq, 1985–1992 (£000s)

	Total sales	Export sales	Domestic sales	Pretax profit	Pretax margin
1985	10	0	10	(145)	–
1986	499	350	149	(128)	–
1987	960	770	190	25	3%
1988	1,781	1,561	220	182	10%
1989	2,637	2,150	487	332	13%
1990	3,199	2,829	370	173	5%
1991	2,924	2,529	395	(122)	–
1992	3,407	2,962	445	233	7%

Estimated cashflow to Exchequer
An estimate of the amount of cashflow paid to the Exchequer (in the form of CT, IT and NI) as a result of the company's activities during the eight accounting periods since its formation is given in Fig. A9.11.[27]

306 Venture Capital Funding: Recommendations for the UK

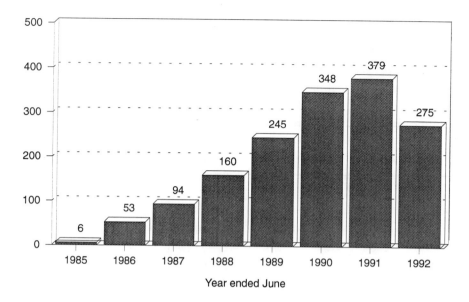

Figure A9.11 Datapaq: estimated totals of CT, IT and NI paid to the Exchequer, 1985–1992 (£000s)

Growth in number of employees

The growth in the average number of Datapaq's employees during each fiscal year is shown in Fig. A9.12. It includes employees entering the group as a result of acquisitions.[28]

Equity financing

Datapaq was started in April 1984, with $10,000 of equity from the four founders (A. J. Bates, J. R. Wells, R. A. Shapiro and R. L. Tenney) in equal amounts (the average exchange rate was £1 = $1.22 at the time). After developing three working prototypes of what was to become the Tracker, and obtaining provisional orders for three machines, it obtained £500,000 of backing from 3i and CIN, composed of half equity and half debt (on 4 June 1985). Despite cutting things fine (the end June 1986 balance sheet showed shareholders' funds of just over £18,000), no further equity capital was raised, except in response to the exercise of options. The company's equity history since formation is as follows.

Year (fiscal)	Amount (£000s)
1985	285
1986	0
1987	0
1988	0
1989	25
1990	0
1991	0
1992	23

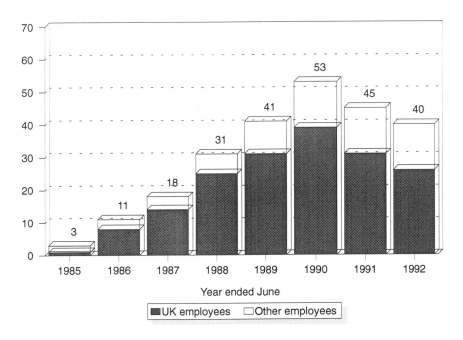

Figure A9.12 Datapaq: average number of employees, 1985–1992

Financing difficulty experienced?
Since two of the four founders were US citizens, the company briefly explored the possibility of a US source of venture capital during the early part of 1984. Unfortunately, the US IPO 'feeding frenzy' of 1983 had left many investors in technology IPOs holding significant losses, with a number of NTBF start–ups having failed spectacularly. Somewhat in contrast to the US, within the UK venture capital community at that time, 'everybody seemed to

be interested in doing start–ups.' As a result, presentation of a draft business plan to five potential UK venture capital investors resulted in one outline offer. On reflection, though, the entrepreneurs decided that the initial amount of equity required by this investor (50 per cent) was too high and the deal left no room for mistakes.

As time passed, however, the company's bargaining position was significantly worsened by its deteriorating cash situation, and it eventually settled on the 3i/CIN deal for an amount (£500,000) that was substantially less than originally asked for ($1 million/£820,000). By providing less than the firm turned out to require, the venture capitalists were put in a strong bargaining position when Datapaq, in due course, got into cashflow difficulties.

Exit

The entire share capital of Datapaq was sold in January 1992 to Quota Group Ltd for an undisclosed sum. It is believed, however, that the likely return to the venture capitalists could have been around 20 per cent or so, while that to the founders might have been in the region of ten times their initial investment. It has not been possible to estimate the CGT liability resulting from the sale of the company in 1992, as insufficient details of the transaction are in the public domain.

Datapaq: more details
Key extracts from P & L and balance sheet (£000s)

Year ended June	1985	1986	1987	1988	1989	1990	1991	1992
(a) Total sales	£10	£499	£960	£1 781	£2 637	£3 199	£2 924	£3 407
Foreign sales	£0	£350	£770	£1 561	£2 150	£2 829	£2 529	£2 962
UK domestic sales	£10	£149	£190	£220	£487	£370	£395	£445
(b) Staff costs								
wages and salaries	£20	£155	£265	£465	£691	£932	£954	£932
social security costs	£1	£13	£25	£41	£69	£85	£85	£84
other pension costs	£0	£0	£0	£0	£0	£26	£40	£27
(c) Employees	3	11	18	31	41	53	45	40
UK employees	1	8	14	25	31	39	31	26
(d) Issue of shares	£285	£0	£0	£0	£25	£0	£0	£23
(e) Pretax profit	(£145)	(£128)	£25	£182	£332	£173	(£122)	£233
(% of sales)	-1450%	-26%	3%	10%	13%	5%	-4%	7%
Gross staff costs as a % of total sales	210.0%	33.7%	30.2%	28.4%	28.8%	32.6%	36.9%	30.6%

Estimate of cash flowing to/(from) Exchequer from taxes and NI (first 8 years) (£000s)

Year ended June	1985	1986	1987	1988	1989	1990	1991	1992
(a) CT paid	£0	£0	£1	£0	£0	£25	£51	(£47)
(b) Employer's NI	£1	£13	£25	£41	£69	£85	£85	£84
(% of gross salary)	5.0%	8.4%	9.4%	8.8%	10.0%	9.1%	8.9%	9.0%
(c) Employees' NI	£1	£9	£15	£26	£38	£51	£52	£51
(% of gross salary)	5.5%	5.5%	5.5%	5.5%	5.5%	5.5%	5.5%	5.5%
(d) Employees' IT	£4	£31	£53	£93	£138	£186	£191	£186
(% of gross salary)	20.0%	20.0%	20.0%	20.0%	20.0%	20.0%	20.0%	20.0%
Total tax cashflow	£6	£53	£94	£160	£245	£348	£379	£275
as % of sales	61.0%	10.5%	9.7%	9.0%	9.3%	10.9%	13.0%	8.1%
Cumulative cashflow	£6	£59	£152	£312	£557	£905	£1 284	£1 559

Denotes an estimated value

Assumed to equal 'social security costs'

PVs of key parameters as a % of total sales (over period shown):

(1) Corporation tax =	0.21%
(2) National insurance (employer and employee) and income taxes =	9.91%
(3) Gross staff costs =	31.78%
(4) Pretax profit =	3.18%
(5) Equity =	2.75%

Case Study 7: British Bio–technology Group (BBTG)

Business profile

The principal activity of BBTG is 'pharmaceutical research and development'.[29] BBTG was formed in 1986 and it became a public company six years later in July 1992, when its shares were offered to UK, US and international investors. The following has been extracted from the UK and international offer document of July 1992.[30]

> British Bio–technology is an emerging pharmaceutical company which is currently pursuing research and development in four medical areas:
>
> (i) inflammation and inflammatory diseases such as asthma and arthritis;
> (ii) cancer, particularly tumour invasion and spread;
> (iii) vascular diseases such as thrombosis and heart attack; and
> (iv) immunotherapy of viral disease, particularly AIDS.
>
> Arising from its research in these fields, British Bio–technology now has two potential pharmaceutical products in clinical trials and one due to commence clinical trials in August 1992 . . . As these and other potential products progress towards the market, British Bio–technology intends to establish and build an international business in ethical pharmaceuticals.
>
> In addition, British Bio-technology has established a business in the manufacture, marketing and distribution of laboratory reagents, fine chemicals and research diagnostic assays in the fields of cell and molecular biology.

Trading record

BBTG's trading record since its formation has been obtained from the company's annual reports,[31] and is summarized in Table A9.7.

Table A9.7 Trading record of BBTG, 1987–1993 (£000s)

	Total sales	Export sales	Domestic sales	Pretax profit
1987	37	0	37	(745)
1988	1,182	1,160	22	(1,492)
1989	3,301	3,058	243	(1,927)
1990	3,751	3,477	274	(1,702)
1991	5,241	4,583	658	(6,126)
1992	5,005	2,979	2,026	(11,612)
1993	n.a.	n.a.	n.a	(13,100)

Estimated cashflow to Exchequer

An estimate of the amount of cashflow paid to the Exchequer (in the form of

CT, IT and NI) as a result of the company's activities during five of the seven accounting periods since its formation is given in Fig. A9.13.[32]

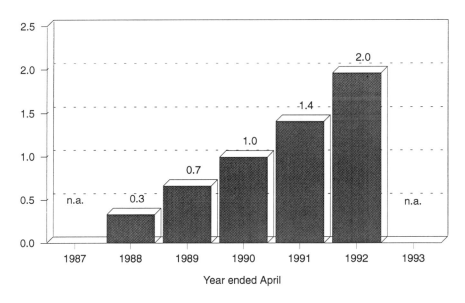

Figure A9.13 BBTG: estimated totals of CT, IT and NI paid to the Exchequer, 1988–1992 (£m)

Growth in number of employees
The growth in the average number of the BBTG's employees during each fiscal year is shown in Fig. A9.14. It includes employees entering the group as a result of acquisitions.[33] The July 1992 figure refers to the number of employees at the time of the company's flotation.

Equity financing
By the end of fiscal 1995, BBTG had undertaken five financing rounds. The initial financing (July 1986) of £2.5 million (Preferred Shares) was raised from four venture capital investors, including a 'corporate venturing' subsidiary of SmithKline Beecham. In the second round of financing (January 1988, £8 million, Preferred), capital was raised from three of the four initial shareholders and nine new venture capital investors (four UK and five US), including a subsidiary of Johnson & Johnson. The third round (May 1989, £22.7 million, Preferred), included a further twelve UK financial institutions and three Japanese investors (JAFCO and two corporates). In the fourth round (July 1991, £40 million), UK and US institutions were added to the shareholder list, which in the fifth round (July 1992, £30 million) was

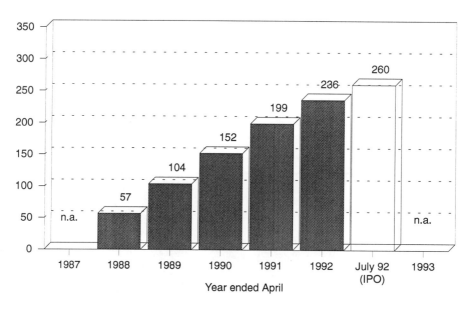

Figure A9.14 BBTG: average number of employees, 1988–1992

expanded further in geographical terms. The aim at each financing round has been to build the breadth and depth of the investor base.

Year (fiscal)	Amount (£,000s)
1987	2,500
1988	7,875
1989	0
1990	21,567
1991	0
1992	38,037
1993	30,000

Financing difficulty experienced?
No financing difficulties are known.

Exit
Although BBTG's shares were offered to the UK and international investment communities in July 1992, the offering consisted entirely of new shares in the company. Since investors did not realize any cash from their investment, no CGT liability arose as a result of the UK and international offering of the company's shares.

British Bio-technology Group: more details
Key extracts from P & L and balance sheet (£000s)

Year ended April	1987	1988	1989	1990	1991	1992	1993
(a) Total sales	£37	£1 182	£3 301	£3 751	£5 241	£5 005	n.a.
Foreign sales	£0	£1 160	£3 058	£3 477	£4 583	£2 979	n.a.
UK domestic sales	£37	£22	£243	£274	£658	£2 026	n.a.
(b) Staff costs							
wages & salaries	n.a.	£920	£1 850	£2 787	£3 909	£5 558	n.a.
social security costs	n.a.	£95	£190	£284	£411	£544	n.a.
other pension costs	n.a.	£15	£68	£167	£233	£331	n.a.
(c) Employees	n.a.	57	104	152	199	236	n.a.
UK employees	n.a.	n.a.	n.a.	n.a.	n.a.	n.a.	n.a.
(d) Issue of shares (before issue costs)	£2 500	£7 875	£0	£21 567	£0	£38 037	£30 000
(e) Pretax profit	(£745)	(£1 492)	(£1 927)	(£1 702)	(£6 126)	(£11 612)	(£13 100)
(% of sales)	−2014%	−126%	−58%	−45%	−117%	−232%	n.a.
Gross staff costs as a % of total sales	n.a.	87.1%	63.9%	86.3%	86.9%	128.5%	n.a.

Estimate of cash flowing to/(from) Exchequer from taxes and NI (first 7 years) (£000s)

Year ended April	1987	1988	1989	1990	1991	1992	1993
(a) CT paid	£0	£0	£0	£0	£0	£0	n.a.
(b) Employer's NI	n.a	£95	£190	£284	£411	£544	n.a.
(%) of gross salary	n.a	10.3%	10.3%	10.2%	10.5%	9.8%	n.a.
(c) Employees' NI	n.a	£51	£102	£153	£215	£306	n.a.
(% of gross salary)	n.a	5.5%	5.5%	5.5.%	5.5%	5.5%	n.a.
(d) Employees' IT	n.a	£184	£370	£557	£782	£1 112	n.a.
(% of gross salary)	n.a	20.0%	20.0%	20.0%	20.0%	20.0%	n.a.
Total tax cashflow	n.a	£330	£662	£995	£1 408	£1 961	n.a.
as % of sales	n.a	27.9%	20.0%	26.5%	26.9%	39.2%	n.a.
cumulative cashfow	n.a	£330	£991	£1 986	£3 394	£5 355	n.a.

Denotes an estimated value

Assumed to equal 'social security costs'

PVs of key parameters as a % of total sales (over period shown):

(1) Corporation tax =	0.00%
(2) National insurance (employer and employee) and income taxes =	28.52%
(3) Gross staff costs =	92.39%
(4) Pretax profit =	−124.42%
(5) Equity =	373.15%

Case Study 8: 'Advanced Chemical Intermediates' (ACI)

Business profile
The principal activities of ACI are the manufacture, marketing and sale of advanced chemical intermediates and related services. (All names in this case study are disguised but the information about the company is genuine. The study was written in and describes the situation as at mid-1993.) The company was formed on 19 December 1991, to exploit the proprietary knowhow of Dr Stewart Drive of First University. For two years or so prior to forming ACI, Stewart had been working with a large multinational corporation, with the aim of developing a subsidiary company to carry out similar activities to those now carried out by ACI. During this period, he had managed to obtain small laboratory facilities on favourable terms in the First area and had commenced trading. Partly due to the high added–value of the products, he was able to start the commercialization process and achieve significant growth. The relationship with the multinational was terminated in October of 1991, however, after failing to agree suitable business terms.

Today, ACI has three key business activities: the manufacture and sale of advanced chemical intermediates from an extensive catalogue; the manufacture and sale of customized advanced chemicals; and a consultancy service for the synthesis of sophisticated chemicals. ACI's products have a wide range of potential applications in the chemical, pharmaceutical and electronics industries.

Trading record
In the eighteen months or so since its formation, ACI's turnover has grown rapidly. While it is not yet required to publish a profit and loss account, its turnover is understood to have climbed to around £500,000 per annum on an annual basis and is continuing to increase monthly. Despite this growth, ACI is believed to be approaching the breakeven level, although its desire to invest for growth (it has also just hired a new managing director) will result in the company remaining 'in the red' in the short/medium term.

Export sales are estimated to represent around 40 per cent of turnover.

Estimated cashflow to Exchequer
It is understood that cumulative gross salaries paid to employees since ACI's formation have been roughly £175,000, and that the total cash paid to the Exchequer so far (in the form of CT, IT and NI) has been roughly £51,000.

Growth in number of employees
The company employs eight people at the present time, all of whom are based

in the UK. This total is expected to roughly double over the next twelve months.

Equity financing
ACI was formed on 19 December 1991 with £100 of share capital, which was subsequently increased to £100,000 on 3 April 1992, via capital provided under the Business Expansion Scheme.[34] (In the six months prior to this infusion, following the termination of the relationship with the multinational, the business was financed through bank loans carrying personal guarantees from Stewart.) This increase in equity capital was principally provided by Stewart and three business angels (Nick Cash, Ian Loan and Tim Capital) who had been introduced to him in January 1992. At the same time as the equity injection, Nick and Ian (who had both become independently wealthy from a previous highly successful business venture in property development) also personally guaranteed a banking facility for the company, which increased their exposure by £500,000. A further equity infusion (once again under the BES) was given to the company a year later on 2 April 1993, following the publication of ACI's balance sheet showing a deficit of just over £23,000 on shareholders' funds. This equity was sourced, on a *pro rata* basis, from the original investors and their spouses.

It should be noted that 90 per cent of the equity provided to ACI was supplied under a BES arrangement. In this regard, Stewart indicated that without the benefit of the BES taxation relief on his first equity investment, he would have been unable to participate fully in the follow-on round of investment and would thus have been likely to suffer dilution. In addition, and probably more importantly, the business angels noted that without the BES provisions for *both* tax relief on their initial investment *and* CGT relief when they ultimately exit, the risks associated with the investment would have far outweighed the potential rewards. As a result, they would *certainly* not have provided *any* capital to the start-up.

In addition to the equity and loan financing outlined above, ACI managed to obtain seed, start-up and early stage funding from two other sources: the multinational, in that it paid an estimated £60,000 to a leading consultancy for an assessment of the potential market for ACI's products (at the seed stage); and a SMART award, of £45,000 in the current year, which will hopefully be followed by a further £60,000 next year.

Financing difficulty experienced?
At around the time that Stewart was in the process of withdrawing from the multinational relationship, he and some of the ex-employees from the multinational approached half a dozen venture capitalists, with a view to raising

finance to start up ACI. It should be noted that, at that stage, Stewart perceived that his only requirement from the venture capitalists would be their capital, as he already believed that he had a complete management team.

Two of those approached, both of whom asked qualified chemists to look at the possible transaction, came back quickly. Unfortunately, Stewart perceived two problems: the venture capitalists wanted to take at least three to six months to be able to evaluate their potential investment; and he saw them as having too short-term a view of the business, in that they were looking to grow the company as fast as possible in order to be able to exit after a period of only three to five years. Stewart felt he was more interested in maximizing the long-term value of the company, which he believed would require investors to think in terms of a seven to ten years investment timescale.

As time progressed into early 1992, his would-be management team took up offers elsewhere, and he was thus left with a need for both money and management. As chance would have it, the business angels could offer both. Tim, who had had a substantial amount of prior experience in the area of high technology businesses, offered to act as ACI's managing director until a suitable candidate could be found. Nick, who was a qualified accountant, offered to act indefinitely as finance director. In addition, both Nick and Ian had been involved with the development of Moneytown Business Park just outside First, and would be able to secure there the much larger laboratory facilities now required by the company on favourable terms.

As regards the financing, the business angels were looking for a long-term, 'hands-on' involvement with ACI, and a seven to ten years timescale was fine by them. Nick and Ian had, in addition, both been to university at First and were very much wanting to 'put something back into the place'.

Exit

Very little thought appears to have been devoted so far to the question of exiting the investment, except to say (as noted above) that the likely time before such an exit will be made, assuming that the company continues to grow successfully, will be of the order of seven to ten years. It is understood, however, that the company has already received interest from would-be corporate purchasers.

Case Study 9: 'Servo Integrated Solutions' (SIS)

Business profile
The principal activity of SIS is the manufacture and sale of automated precision arc-welding equipment. (All names in this case study are disguised but the information about the company is genuine.) The Cambridge-based company was formed on 14 April 1986 in order to exploit the expertise of the founders, all of whom were former Cambridge University engineering graduates. It passed into receivership some three and a half years later.

SIS specialized in automated precision TIG (Titanium Inert Gas) welding equipment, principally used for critical-application stainless steel work. With the SIS equipment, it was possible to produce substantially more accurate (with tolerances of the order of 0.001 inch) and reliable welds than hitherto achieved, at a very cost-effective price (helped by the dramatic reduction in the amount of scrap). The company initially produced a range of standard products which were capable of being adapted to the client's particular operating environment. As the business grew, however, SIS also started to offer clients fully customized products. SIS's principal markets were in the nuclear, aerospace and defence industries, for particular use wherever it was necessary to produce safety-critical welds. Despite passing into receivership, some of the business is still in existence today, having been bought from the receiver by another small company in a related area of activity.

Trading record
Although the company was too small to be required to file profit and loss accounts at Companies House, it is understood that its turnover growth and export sales were in accordance with Table. A9.8.

Table A9.8   Trading record of SIS, 1986–7 to 1988–9 (£000s)

	Total sales	Export sales	Domestic sales	Pretax profit
1986–7	139	7	132	(108)
1987–8	146	7	139	(178)
1988–9	420	116	304	(106)

Estimated cashflow to Exchequer
An estimate of the amount of cashflow paid to the Exchequer (in the form of CT, IT and NI) as a result of the company's activities during the three accounting periods between its formation and its receivership is given in Fig. A9.15.

318 Venture Capital Funding: Recommendations for the UK

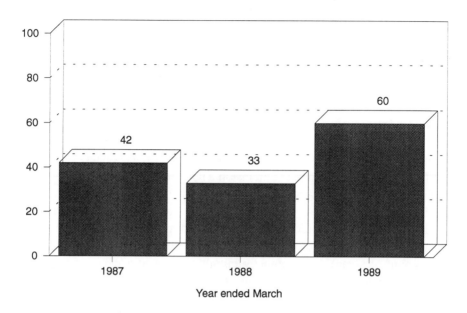

Figure A9.15 SIS: estimated totals of CT, IT and NI paid to the Excehquer, 1987–1989 (£000s)

Growth in number of employees

The average number of SIS's employees rose from five in 1987, to seven in 1988, to ten in 1989. They were all UK based.

Equity financing

The company was formed on 14 April 1986 with £95,500 of issued equity share capital, in the form of 950 × £1 Ordinary Shares.[35] This money was sourced from the four founders (under the BES), Rob Wonder (£25,132), Ken Growth (£18,095), Mark Future (£9,047) and Steve Stock (£8,042), in addition to £35,184 from a recently formed venture capitalist, Grafpitch Ventures. All shares were issued at the same price. Due to the accumulating deficit on shareholders' funds, £200,000 of further finance was raised on 19 July 1988, through the issue of 261 Convertible Preference Shares (for £100,000) and £100,000 of Convertible Unsecured Loan Stock (CULS) to Grafpitch. This was followed by the issue of a further £50,000 of CULS on 8 November 1988. The company's equity history is given in the following table.

Year (fiscal)	Amount (£,000s)
1987	96
1988	0
1989	100

Financing difficulty experienced?

SIS began looking for capital at a time when there was an abundance of money flowing into the venture capital industry. Probably due to the inexperience of the founding entrepreneurs (particularly in financial matters), however, they eventually settled on a small and recent entrant to the venture capital business, Grafpitch Ventures, as their sole source of external finance. Of particular note was that Grafpitch had never invested in a seed and/or start-up situation prior to SIS, and would not be providing any other 'added value' in addition to finance.

At the outset, the entrepreneurs and Grafpitch had agreed that they would fund the first year's seed activities themselves from the initial share capital. During this period SIS would develop its 'on paper' product ideas and commence initial sales of the equipment, thus proving that the business idea was sound. It was then intended that Grafpitch would provide further finance and procure interest from other investors to do likewise. Unfortunately, despite hitting the target for product development and initial sales (estimated at £139,000 in the first year), Grafpitch proved unable to interest other outside investors.

As a result of Grafpitch's inability to deliver the promised new money and investors, the entrepreneurs themselves decided to approach a number of other, more established venture capitalists. Typical of the responses they received were that the venture capitalists were not interested in doing technology start-up deals but, instead, were focusing both their attention and their funding on later stage expansions. Nevertheless, in the end two substantial funds decided to investigate the company's potential more thoroughly; they subsequently dropped out because of changes in funding policy at the top of these organizations (one firm had a new chief executive who put a moratorium on new investments, while the other decided to move away from early stage deals). Quite remarkably, however, one of these funds sent SIS the bill for their due diligence!

Exit

SIS went into liquidation shortly into its fiscal 1990 year. It was bought from the receiver by another small company in a related field soon after.

SIS: more details
Key extracts from P & L and balance sheet (£000s)

Year ended March	1987	1988	1989
(a) Total sales	£139	£146	£420
UK export sales	*£7*	*£7*	*£116*
UK domestic sales	*£132*	*£139*	*£304*
(b) Staff costs			
wages and salaries	£84	£82	£139
social security costs	£9	£8	£14
other pension costs	£0	£0	£0
(c) Employees	5	7	10
UK employees	*5*	*7*	*10*
(d) Issue of shares (before issue costs)	£96	£0	£100
(e) Pretax profit	(£108)	(£178)	(£106)
(% of sales)	*−78%*	*−122%*	*−25%*
Gross staff costs as a % of total sales	**66.7%**	**61.6%**	**36.5%**

Estimate of cash flowing to/(from) Exchequer from taxes and NI (£000s)

Year ended March	1987	1988	1989
(a) CT paid	£0	£0	£0
(b) Employer's NI	£11	£8	£17
(% of gross salary)	*13.1%*	*9.8%*	*12.2%*
(c) Employees' NI	£8	£5	£12
(% of gross salary)	*9.5%*	*6.1%*	*8.6%*
(d) Employees' IT	£23	£20	£31
(% of gross salary)	*27.4%*	*24.5%*	*22.3%*
Total tax cashflow	**£42**	**£33**	**£60**
as % of sales	**30.2%**	**22.6%**	**14.3%**
Cumulative cashflow	**£42**	**£75**	**£135**

PVs of key parameters as a % of total sales (over period shown):

(1) Corporation tax =	0.00%
(2) National insurance (employer and employee) and income taxes =	19.45%
(3) Gross staff costs =	48.30%
(4) Pretax profit =	−56.92%
(5) Equity =	28.36%

Appendix 9.10 PV of 'fixed assets and maintenance' in case study companies

Linx Printing Technologies

Year (£000s)	1987	1988	1989	1990	1991	1992
(a) Year end fixed assets	198	257	792	823	1 599	2 263
(b) Depreciation charge	10	35	72	105	169	235
(a) + (b)	208	292	864	928	1 768	2 498
(c) Assets bought during year	208	94	607	136	945	899
FA&M = (b) + (c)	218	129	679	241	1 114	1 134

Total PV of FA&M using a 6.0% discount rate = 2 713

PV of sales = 17 385   therefore ratio of PVs of FA&M to sales = 15.6%

Domino printing sciences

Year (£000s)	1984	1985	1986	1987	1988	1989	1990	199	1992
(a) Year end fixed assets	1 020	1 414	2 497	4 728	10 578	16 943	17 638	16 11	19 270
(b) Depreciation charge	129	192	326	501	735	1 040	1 414	1 66	1 965
(a) + (b)	1 149	1 606	2 823	5 229	11 313	17 983	19 052	17 78	21 235
(c) Assets bought during year	n.a.	586	1 409	2 732	6 585	7 405	2 109	15	5 116
FA&M = (b) + (c)	n.a.	778	1 735	3 233	7 320	8 445	3 523	1 81	7 081

Total PV of FA&M using a 6.0% discount rate = 25 237

PV of sales = 212 517   therefore ratio of PVs of FA&M to sales = 11.9%

Appendix 9.10 (Continued...)

Psion

Year (£000s)	1981	1982	1983	1984	1985	1986	1987	1988	1989	1990	1991	1992
(a) Year end fixed assets	6	150	663	1 195	1 655	1 946	2 076	2 386	4 432	5 321	5 246	5 795
(b) Depreciation charge	1	9	49	186	186	209	251	307	622	975	988	1 447
(a) + (b)	7	159	712	1 381	1 841	2 155	2 327	2 693	5 054	6 296	6 234	7 242
(c) Assets bought during year	7	153	562	718	646	500	381	617	2 668	1 864	913	1 996
FA&M = (b) + (c)	8	162	611	904	832	709	632	924	3 290	2 839	1 901	3 443

Total PV of FA&M using a 6.0% discount rate = 9 747

PV of sales = 100 715 therefore ratio of PVs of FA&M to sales = 9.7%

Tadpole Technology

Year (£000s)	1984	1985	1986	1987	1988	1989	1990	1991	1992
(a) Year end fixed assets	100	138	163	432	618	648	624	1 496	1 879
(b) Depreciation charge	11	29	35	86	145	227	219	267	617
(a) + (b)	111	167	198	518	763	875	843	1 763	2 496
(c) Assets bought during year	111	67	60	355	331	257	195	1 139	1 000
FA&M = (b) + (c)	122	96	95	441	476	484	414	1 406	1 617

Total PV of FA&M using a 6.0% discount rate = 3 441

PV of sales = 29 071 therefore ratio of PVs of FA&M to sales = 11.8%

UK NTBF Case Studies and Analysis 323

Macro 4

Year (£000s)		1984	1985	1986	1987	1988	1989	1990	1991	1992
(a)	Year end fixed assets	236	2 488	2 653	2 913	3 228	5 316	7 219	7 642	7 805
(b)	Depreciation charge	77	220	282	345	373	493	713	1 015	1 050
	(a) + (b)	313	2 708	2 935	3 258	3 601	5 809	7 932	8 657	8 855
(c)	Assets bought during year	n.a.	2 472	447	605	688	2 581	2 616	1 438	1 213
FA&M = (b) + (c)		n.a.	2 692	729	950	1 061	3 074	3 329	2 453	2 263

Total PV of FA&M using a 6.0% discount rate = 12 522

PV of sales = 70 763   therefore ratio of PVs of FA&M to sales = 17.7%

Datapaq

Year (£000s)		1985	1986	1987	1988	1989	1990	1991	1992
(a)	Year end fixed assets	27	55	84	132	186	293	238	159
(b)	Depreciation charge	6	19	32	36	43	58	81	77
	(a) + (b)	33	74	116	168	229	351	319	236
(c)	Assets bought during year	33	47	61	84	97	165	26	(2)
FA&M = (b) + (c)		39	66	93	120	140	223	107	75

Total PV of FA&M using a 6.0% discount rate = 649

PV of sales = 10 978   therefore ratio of PVs of FA&M to sales = 5.9%

Appendix 9.10 (Continued...)
British Bio-technology Group

Year (£000s)	1987	1988	1989	1990	1991	1992
(a) Year end fixed assets	2 017	4 112	6 349	9 217	13 753	14 595
(b) Depreciation charge	n.a.	238	420	612	927	1 587
(a) + (b)	n.a.	4 350	6 769	9 829	14 680	16 182
(c) Assets bought during year	n.a.	2 333	2 657	3 480	5 463	2 429
FA&M = (b) + (c)	n.a.	2 571	3 077	4 092	6 390	4 016

Total PV of FA&M using a 6.0% discount rate = 16 662

PV of sales = 15 094   therefore ratio of PVs of FA&M to sales = 110.4%

'Servo Integrated Solutions'

Year (£000s)	1985	1986	1987
(a) Year end fixed assets	11	41	72
(b) Depreciation charge	1	4	7
(a) + (b)	12	45	79
(c) Assets bought during year	12	34	38
FA&M = (b) + (c)	13	38	45

Total PV of FA&M using a 6.0% discount rate = 84

PV of sales = 614   therefore ratio of PVs of FA&M to sales = 13.7%

Notes

1. 'Casebook: a venture capital classic', *UK Venture Capital Journal*, Sept. 1992, p. 17.
2. 'Linx Printing Technologies plc: placing document', Morgan Grenfell & Co. Ltd, Oct. 1992, p. 6.
3. Linx's annual reports and accounts were obtained on microfiche from Companies House.
4. From Linx's annual report and accounts.
5. Ibid.; Della Bradshaw, 'The little guys think big', *Financial Times*, 24 June 1993, p. 16.
6. From 'Domino Printing Sciences plc: annual card', Extel Financial Ltd, Mar. 1993.
7. 'Domino Printing Sciences plc', case study, London Business School, 1988.
8. 'Domino's annual reports and accounts were obtained on microfiche from Companies House.
9. From Domino's annual report and accounts, in addition to our own estimates.
10. Ibid.
11. From 'Psion plc: annual card', Extel Financial Ltd, 1992.
12. 'Psion Ltd (A)', case study, London Business School, 1992.
13. Psion's annual reports and accounts were obtained on microfiche from Companies House.
14. From Psion's annual report and accounts, in addition to our own estimates.
15. Ibid.
16. From 'Tadpole plc: annual card', Extel Financial Ltd, Feb. 1993.
17. 'How Tadpole became a big fish', *Financial Times*, 19 Mar. 1993, p. 37.
18. Tadpole's annual reports and accounts were obtained on microfiche from Companies House.
19. From Tadpole's annual reports and accounts, in addition to our own estimates.
20. From 'Macro 4 plc: annual card', Extel Financial Ltd, Sept. 1992.
21. Macro 4's annual reports and accounts were obtained on microfiche from Companies House.
22. From Macro 4's annual report and accounts, in addition to our own estimates.
23. Ibid.
24. From Datapaq's annual report and accounts, the directors' report for the year ended 30 June 1991.
25. From Datapaq Ltd case studies, A and B (condensed) and C, Datapaq Ltd, 1989.
26. Datapaq's annual reports and accounts were obtained on microfiche from Companies House.
27. From Datapaq's annual report and accounts, in addition to our own estimates.
28. Ibid.
29. From BBTG's annual report and accounts, the directors' report for the year ended 30 April 1992.
30. From the UK and international offer document, Kleinwort Benson, July 1992.
31. BBTG's annual reports and accounts were obtained on microfiche from Companies House.
32. From BBTG's annual report and accounts, in addition to our own estimates.
33. Ibid.
34. ACI's annual balance sheets were obtained on microfiche from Companies House; its share capital record was obtained from its annual returns to Companies House.
35. SIS's annual balance sheets were obtained on microfiche from Companies House; its share capital record was obtained from its annual returns to Companies House.

10

SPECIFIC PROPOSALS AND RECOMMENDATIONS

In the previous two chapters we developed and reality tested a reasonably simple, although fairly robust, *a priori* model which sought to establish the magnitude and distribution of returns from UK–based NTBF formation and development. Based on this model's output (and certain other research findings), we concluded that a strong case could be made for providing taxation related incentives to encourage the formation and growth of UK–based NTBFs, although this finding was a generalized result and independent of the particular form that such incentives should take. The aims of this final chapter, therefore, are threefold:

- to touch briefly on some of the *specific* problems faced by UK–based NTBFs which we believe are capable of being solved or significantly eased by taxation-related measures (in doing so, we shall draw on the experiences of both the UK case study companies and of the other contributors to this work);
- to suggest and consider several taxation-related measures which may provide the most cost-effective way of both encouraging NTBF funding within the UK and of 'levelling the playing field' against our strongest competitor nations;
- to consider the impact that the suggested measures might have had on the case study firms and their investors.

OUTLINE OF NTBF PROBLEMS

The principal current and anticipated future problems experienced by NTBFs in their seed, start-up and early stage development phases, for which tax-based solutions are perceived as being likely to be effective, include an increasing aversion to financing such NTBFs by the formal venture capital industry (with the exception of the seed capitalists); the possible loss of a significant amount of equity capital provided by business angels to NTBFs, following the replacement of the BES with the EIS; and the difficulties experienced by entrepreneurs as a consequence of the constraints of the BES (which persist in the EIS) and the inability to attract experienced managers.

Increasing aversion of formal venture capital industry to NTBF investments

We saw in Chapter 5 how the supply of formal risk capital made available by the venture capital industry for financing UK-based NTBFs (particularly in terms of the category's share of all investments) has been steadily deteriorating over the last decade. A number of reasons for this change in emphasis by the industry have been put forward, many of which are related to the reportedly poorer returns generated on such investments relative to other opportunities such as expansion financings and MBOs. It should be noted, however, that investments in early stage NTBFs appear to have been not only less profitable to investors in venture capital funds but also, *and probably much more importantly*, less profitable to the venture capital firms/partners themselves. In this regard, it should be remembered that since it is the venture capitalists who invariably make the investment decisions, they will naturally and rightly seek to make investments which maximize their own profitability (see Chapter 1).

In order to improve the flow of capital to NTBFs from the formal venture capital industry, therefore, it would appear that measures to improve returns to *both* fund investors and venture capitalists would be effective.

The need for BES/EIS type initiatives

During the course of our case study research it was evident how important the existence of the BES had been in facilitating the capital-raising process for a number of firms. For the business angels who provided capital under the BES, the presence of taxation incentives on the invested amount (significantly reduced under the EIS) and on any capital gains was probably *the* factor that persuaded them to invest in the NTBFs. Indeed, according to a business angel who backed one of the case study firms along with his partners, their investment would certainly not have been made without the provisions of the BES:

> None of us [i.e. *including* the entrepreneur] would have invested without the benefit of the BES tax incentives on investment and the provision for tax-free capital gains . . .
>
> We originally looked upon the investment as a bit of a high risk 'punt', after all we were dealing with a new product, in a new market, with an incomplete and untried management team . . .
>
> Based upon my experience, business doesn't come much riskier than that, so we had to believe that, if we got it right, there would be a very substantial upside.

In this case neither the business angels *nor* the entrepreneur (and, indeed, other 'connected/associated' persons) would have invested in the start-up without the presence of the BES, since the rewards were perceived as being insufficient to compensate for the risks involved. Thus, it is likely that the BES also promotes a degree of *additionality* of investment from entrepreneurs and connected/associated persons.

This finding would appear to throw into question what is probably the main component of the underlying rationale behind the BES restrictions on relief (see below), that is, that BES relief cannot be justified for the entrepreneur, his/her associates and other connected persons on the basis of anticipated additionality, since they would have invested in the company anyway.

As a rider to the above, in the three case studies where BES investments are known to have been made, the BES had enabled the founding entrepreneurs to achieve a larger equity stake in the firm by allowing them to invest a larger gross amount. In one case, for example, the tax relief obtained on the first round of equity investment allowed the entrepreneur to participate in the second round and, thus, maintain his share of the enlarged equity.

Difficulties caused by constraints imposed on BES investments

Three recurrent criticisms – from entrepreneurs, business angels, venture capitalists and professional advisers – were evident in almost all conversations relating to the constraints imposed by the BES:

1. the fact that BES relief was not available on investments made by manager/entrepreneurs who drew salaries from the investee company;
2. the fact that BES relief was not available to investments made by 'closely connected' or 'associated' persons (such as employees, family, business partners);
3. the fact that in several instances businesses were known to have suffered because actions that would have been in the best interests of the business

could not be taken because they would have resulted in loss of BES relief to the investors.

The first restriction resulted in at least one of the entrepreneurial investors (among the three case study firms known to have used the BES) choosing not to take a significant and active role in the business, because this would result in the loss of his BES relief. Instead, his attention had to be focused on another source of paid employment in order for him to be able to make a living, and his skills were diverted, to the possible detriment of the business. In this way, having to choose between receiving BES relief and close involvement in the company can have negative effects.

The third criticism was provoked by restrictions on the maximum allowable investment by any one person, on shareholding ceilings and on changes of share ownership during the first five years, and these had acted to the detriment of the firms backed in a number of instances.

For the most part, the criticisms of the first two BES restrictions cited have invariably been based on the principle of 'fair and equivalent' treatment to all investors which, taken alone, is not held by the government as being sufficient cause for granting taxation reliefs. We believe, however, that good anecdotal evidence exists to suggest that a strong case can be made on the grounds of additionality.

In light of all of the foregoing work making the case for taxation incentives for NTBFs, we would suggest that the benefit of the doubt regarding the additionality arising from extending BES relief to cases (1) and (2) above should be granted in favour of these investors, at least in the case of NTBFs. Changes made to certain of these BES restrictions under the EIS, while regarded as a step in the right direction, have been criticized as being unworkable.

Other problems

CGT rollover relief for entrepreneurs, announced in the March 1993 Budget (and since enhanced), was widely welcomed. There was, however, one restriction which appeared to be both unnecessary and based on a false premise; the relief was restricted to gains on the disposal of trading companies and was not to be allowed on gains from, say, investment or property companies. It is understood that the rationale for this restriction was that since the government wishes to encourage trading companies, it would be of greater benefit to have entrepreneurial investors who have relevant experience in trading company activities.

We would suggest that this premise is false, however, and offer by way of example the ACI case study. Here, although the NTBF is very much a trading company, critical skills and resources desperately needed by ACI and provided by its business angel/'serial entrepreneur' investors were finance related (in order to ensure that proper financial systems and controls were in place); and property related (in procuring suitable property on favourable terms for the NTBF's activities). Indeed, it appears that these are precisely the skills that the majority of new companies (especially NTBFs) are most in need of, yet are least likely to be able to obtain at reasonable cost. It would therefore appear to be counterproductive to deny rollover relief to the very types of successful entrepreneur who are likely to have these skills and could most benefit such companies. The November 1993 Budget, however, appears to have dealt with this particular detrimental restriction.

PROPOSED TAXATION MEASURES

The following proposals for tax measures are intended to be restricted to seed, start-up and early stage investments in NTBFs *only*. In defining an NTBF, however, there are several possible approaches (which are not necessarily mutually exclusive). They may be:

- firms whose products have been substantially developed to exploit intellectual property arising as a result of 'scientific research', as defined in Section 508 (3) TA 1988 – with any approvals under this section being given by the Secretary of State in the normal way (Section 508 (1)(a));
- firms whose products have been substantially developed to exploit intellectual property arising as a 'result of science, engineering and technology research';
- firms whose products fall into the 'new' definition of high technology industries, as described in a 1987 paper by the Department of Trade and Industry (or even a subsequent 'new' definition of appropriate categories).[1]

With regard to how 'seed, start-up and early stage' investments should be defined, we believe that it would probably be best to make any definition relate to the period that has elapsed since the company commenced trading. We note that although 'trade' (and hence, the 'commencement of trading') has been defined in Section 832 (1) TA 1988, it may be appropriate to produce special ground rules for specific types of NTBF (in particular biotechnology firms), where the period of R&D required to develop key products is unusually long. Such special rules for the definition of 'trade' for certain types of NTBF would not be inconsistent with other special definitions that were developed for, say, oil industry exploration in the North Sea.

In making these proposals, we have not been too concerned with the precise details of how they stand in relation to the UK taxation system as a whole, and it is almost certain, therefore, that they will need to be reshaped in order to be consistent with other aspects of this system. Nevertheless, it is anticipated that any reshaping of the proposals could be done in such a way as to reproduce the same overall effect.

Finally, before setting out these proposals, we wish to acknowledge and express our gratitude for the informal help and advice given to us by members of both Price Waterhouse and Coopers and Lybrand with respect to our initial thoughts on the subject (and, indeed, on other matters contained elsewhere in the book). We believe that the book has benefited significantly from their expertise but note that the final views and suggestions are those of the authors, who bear sole responsibility for any errors or omissions.

Specific proposals

Six 'new' types of taxation relief are proposed:

1 Equity investment relief (EIR);
2 Capital gains tax relief (CGTR);
3 Portfolio relief (PR);
4 See-through relief (STR);
5 Interest relief (IR);
6 Illiquid company shares relief (ICSR).

While the precise form of these reliefs may have some degree of novelty, we believe that the underlying *principles* are not especially new to the world of taxation. In particular, reliefs (1) and (2) are, in part, designed as a replacement for the BES/EIS initiatives and deal with the issues of initial equity investment and terminal capital gains. Relief (3), on the other hand, involves only a relatively small extension to existing tax law. Reliefs (4) and (5) are more significant extensions of current tax law, and are intended to 'level the playing field' with regard to related schemes in the US (under the sub-S corporation election) and in Germany (the taxation treatment of typical and atypical silent partnerships). Finally, relief (6) is the only one that is not specifically related to NTBFs and seeks to deal with the chronic illiquidity of small company shares in the UK equity markets. This measure is anticipated to benefit not only NTBFs at the time of exit, but small company shares in general.

Equity investment relief

The details of this proposal for relief are as follows.

1 A tax credit *for the benefit of the firm*, known as EIR, will be allowed on seed or start-up capital equity investments in NTBFs. Here, 'seed capital' refers to equity capital provided prior to the company commencing trading, while 'start-up capital' refers to equity capital provided in the first year of the company's trading.
2 Additional EIR tax credits will be allowed, on a reducing scale, for early stage equity capital invested during the following three years.
3 The magnitude of the credit will be expressed as a percentage of the equity investment in each year, being 60 per cent for seed and start-up equity, 45 per cent for second-year equity, 30 per cent for third-year equity and 15 per cent for fourth-year equity.
4 As the NTBF trades, and CT, NI and IT fall due, it will be allowed to retain up to the accumulated (but as yet unutilized) EIR credit at that date, for its own benefit.
5 As the EIR is utilized, the cash saving will be capitalized and new shares will be issued to the investors, *pro rata* to their additional share entitlements (first-year investors will receive up to 60 per cent more shares, fourth-year investors up to 15 per cent more shares). Alternatively, the original shares could be issued in 'partly paid' form and become fully paid as EIR is utilized and included in the (non-distributable) capital account.
6 It will be permissible to carry out secondary transactions in the shares in the normal way, since any increase in value of the original equity investment due to realized EIR will have been *earned* by the company between the time of purchase of the shares and their sale. The buying-back of shares for cancellation by the company will be restricted in value to the original investment plus the utilized proportion of the EIR credit.

There are a number of advantages from the government's point of view in structuring the tax credit/incentive in the proposed way (rather than just allowing, say, an immediate and fixed cash tax credit to the investor as the equity is invested). These include:

- the NTBF has to *earn* the cash to pay for the credit/incentive;
- the scale of relief given to the investors is related to the risk that they are bearing;
- the income foregone by the Exchequer will automatically be scaled down for unsuccessful NTBF investments, as shown in Fig. 10.1 (see also the Appendix for the detailed calculations);

- the Exchequer does not have to pay out cash to those subscribing for equity on an 'up front' basis and, as a result, is always 'in pocket' in cash terms; and perhaps most importantly of all
- since we have seen that the vast majority of tax generated by NTBFs takes the form of *employment taxes* (IT and employers' and employees' NI contributions) then, to some degree, *EIR represents a relief based on the extent of employment creation.*

Figure 10.1 has been generated using the model contained in the Appendix and assuming that an investment of 100 units (in nominal terms) is made in a start-up company, distributed over a four-year period. It exemplifies a typical pattern for the variation of the maximum cumulative cashflow foregone by the Exchequer, due to EIR, as a function of the rate of return (ROR) on the equity invested. The important point to note is that the amount foregone is *automatically* scaled down for poor investments, that is, those generating negative or zero RORs.

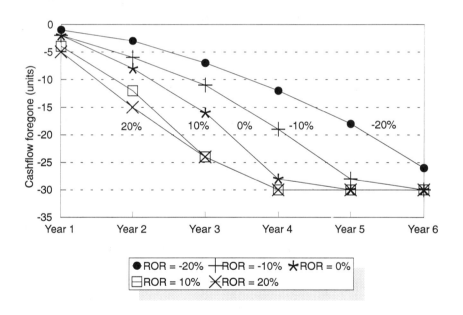

Figure 10.1 The effect of EIR: variations in the maximum cumulative cashflow foregone by the Exchequer according to ROR

Capital gains tax relief

When a sale or partial sale of the company's equity occurs, it is proposed that

CGTR will be given in such a way that the adjusted CGT liability will be calculated as follows:

1. chargeable gain on sale or partial sale = £x;
2. CGT on chargeable gain at an assumed CGT rate of 40 per cent = £0.4x;
3. let the cumulative total of the CT, NI and IT (before taking into account EIR) liabilities at the time of the sale or partial sale = £y;
4. let the cumulative EIR utilized by the company at the time of sale or partial sale = £z;
5. then CGTR = £(y–z) and the adjusted CGT liability on sale or partial sale = £(0.4x–y+z).

There are two advantages from the Exchequer's point of view of structuring CGTR in this way, as opposed to giving a 'fixed amount per entrepreneur' or allowing a reduced rate of CGT.

- The amount of CGTR that exiting shareholders enjoy is *equivalent* to the amount of taxation cash that the Exchequer has received over the course of the company's trading history, up until the date of exit. As a result, the CGTR 'reward' is directly proportional to the benefit that the Exchequer has received from the NTBF's activities and, thus, might be seen as 'fair'.
- There is an incentive for the investors and entrepreneurs to stay with the business for at least long enough to obtain CGTR on their entire shareholding, which can be 'earned' by generating further taxes from trading.

Likely impact of EIR and CGTR on investor IRRs

Using the model outlined in the Appendix to generate theoretical investor IRRs as a function of the ROR on the equity invested demonstrates the likely impact of the combined EIR and CGTR tax measures. They would appear significantly to improve post-tax IRRs on seed, start-up and early stage investments in NTBFs. What can also be seen in Fig. 10.2, however, is that IRRs/gains are enhanced to a greater extent for NTBFs producing only modest RORs on the invested money (say, 0–10 per cent) than for higher RORs. For example, with an ROR of 10 per cent, the investors' post-tax IRR calculated by the model is almost tripled from 6.4 per cent to 17.4 per cent. For an ROR of 50 per cent, on the other hand, the investors' post-tax IRR increases by just under two-thirds, that is, from 37.2 per cent to 60.8 per cent, according to the model. The net impact of this effect is likely to be that entrepreneurs and investors will perceive the returns to be much more reasonable (relative to the risks assumed and the effort required) in the event that the NTBF does not become the next Apple Computer or Genentech (as will almost always be the case).

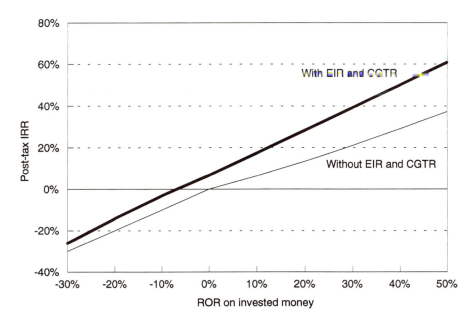

Figure 10.2 Impact of EIR and CGTR on investors' post-tax IRRs (a theoretical example)

In this regard, many economists and decision scientists would agree that this is precisely the point of the risk/reward curve that is most likely to affect the entrepreneur's/investor's decisions to go ahead and start a business. In plain language, when faced with a risky situation, research shows that most people tend to place more importance on evaluating whether the outcome of their decision is likely to be a modest loss or a modest profit than they do of whether the outcome will be a large profit or an extremely large one.

Portfolio relief

Simply put, PR allows capital losses incurred as a result of investment in one or more NTBFs to be offset against capital gains generated in one or more other NTBF investments. The main difference between the existing taxation relief of losses and the proposed PR is that, under PR, capital losses from

NTBF investments can be offset against capital gains from NTBF investments in prior years, or carried forward against future NTBF investment profits, *indefinitely*.

See-through relief

The provisions of STR are in many ways similar to those already allowed under the S corporation election in the US and via silent partnership formation in Germany. In brief, the proposal is that NTBF equity investors be allowed to benefit from the immediate 'pass through' of the NTBF's net operating losses to their own individual returns, subject to similar 'at risk', 'basis' and 'passive loss' conditions to those imposed on S corporations in the US.[2] This allowance would be of great benefit to NTBFs which invariably experience a period of operating losses following start-up, often due to high R&D costs relative to the initial level of sales (for an extreme example, see the British Bio-technology case study). As noted earlier, this is the first of two proposed measures intended to 'level the playing field' relative to the US and Germany.

Interest relief

At present, an entrepreneur who borrows money to buy shares in his or her new company is allowed to offset the interest charged on those funds against his or her income (earned or passive), provided that the company is either 'close' or 'employee controlled'. The second 'field levelling' proposal is to extend this existing provision for NTBFs in the following two respects: to allow *all equity* investors to enjoy this relief; to allow interest paid to *all* providers of *fixed-rate medium/long-term loans* (of three years duration and over) to the NTBF to be received on a 'tax free' basis for the first five years after the NTBF's formation, that is, interest received by the loan provider will not be subject to taxation.

In this way, many of the benefits enjoyed by German investors who invest by way of the silent partnerships will become available to UK investors. In addition, the relief on fixed-rate medium-term/long-term loans will promote the supply of this form of debt and discourage the UK propensity towards variable-rate and short-term overdraft financing, which can be recalled at short notice and increases the financial vulnerability of the NTBF.[3] These measures, in combination, should considerably lower the cost of capital to NTBFs by increasing capital availability and permitting increased gearing via stable fixed-rate, long-term debt.

Illiquid company shares relief

A great deal of debate has been generated regarding the poor quality of the UK and other European equity markets for small company shares which, as we saw in Chapter 6, are orders of magnitude smaller and less liquid than their US counterparts. This lack of scale and liquidity has caused serious concern among not only Stock Exchange authorities, quoted companies and investors, but also among venture capitalists who feel that the lack of venture-backed IPO activity in the UK acts to the detriment of venture capital financing of all companies, especially NTBFs.

To improve the liquidity of small company shares within the UK (and Europe), several solutions have been suggested, including the formation of a pan-European stock market for small companies[4] and various other structural and taxation related measures.[5] We believe that trying to establish a pan-European stock market for smaller companies from scratch, however, is fraught with difficulties (logistics, settlement systems, anticipated lack of investors in such a market, political factors, etc.) and, in brief, is unlikely to happen within the foreseeable future. While we see merit in several of the various other structural and taxation measures, we would like to suggest a potential (and much simpler) solution which is capable of being enacted more or less immediately; our combined experience as a stock market practitioner, on the one hand, and from a further detailed study, on the other, make us think it likely to be effective.

The proposal is that capital gains from trading illiquid company shares (ICSs) be reduced, initially, to zero. The conditions that a company's shares must meet for qualification as ICSs would be set by reference to the 'total' and 'free' market capitalization of the company's equity; and the average daily trading volume, by value, over the preceding year (as is normally reported to and measured by the Stock Exchange). A list of company shares qualifying as ICSs would be provided by the Stock Exchange/Inland Revenue at the start of each calendar year, with the period of qualification being one year and qualification being renewable indefinitely.

After an initial period of perhaps one or two years, to allow investors and their advisers to become accustomed to the changes that ICS status will bring about, the scheme will be reviewed. If successful, the applicable rate of capital gains tax for ICS qualifying shares could be raised to (say) 5–10 per cent on a permanent basis. If the rise in liquidity is anything like that anticipated, the Exchequer is likely to receive more CGT than at present on the trading of qualifying shares. (It is intended that the ICS designation could be granted to both USM and listed securities.)

These measures are thought to offer a number of advantages over other suggested solutions to the problem.

- The initial change can be enacted rapidly, and the CGT rate can be fine tuned after a year or two, so as to maximize revenue to the Exchequer while achieving the initial objective of boosting liquidity in ICS designated shares.
- It is conceivable that the ICS designation and enhanced liquidity could attract other European small companies to be quoted on the London market, so that London becomes the *de facto* pan-European stock market for small companies. In this regard, a key factor encouraging small non-US companies to be quoted in the US is the far superior liquidity of the US markets. The proposed ICSR could thus be seen as a competitively aggressive move designed to steal the initiative for the UK, strengthening the London market's position as *the* European securities trading centre.
- It is likely that the main beneficiaries of the proposed relief will be UK private clients, who account for roughly three-quarters of all equity transactions taking place on the London Stock Exchange and are all exposed to CGT (unlike many of the institutional investors, such as pension funds, who are able to avoid CGT). For these investors, the ability to deal in shares which are exempt from CGT (or are subject to a significantly reduced rate of CGT) is likely to prove an attractive proposition. This, in turn, may also have the politically desirable side effect of increasing popular share ownership in much the same way as the PEPs.

We noted in Chapter 4 that Japanese individuals were not subject to taxes on capital gains from share trading prior to April 1989. This fact is commonly regarded as having been a significant contributory factor in channelling Japanese personal savings into the stock market and may also have been an underlying explanation for the resilience of the Japanese stock market in the face of the global market crash of late 1987. Indeed, the Japanese market 'crashed' at the end of 1989 *after* the imposition of gains tax on share trading for private individuals.

Likely impact of combined reliefs on investor IRRs

While it is difficult to assess the potential impact of either PR or ICSR, because of the nature of these reliefs, we have attempted to assess the impact of the remaining four reliefs, once again using the model outlined in the Appendix to generate theoretical investor IRRs as a function of the ROR on the equity invested. The results obtained are shown in Fig. 10.3. As can be seen, the addition of STR and IR to the other two reliefs (EIR and CGTR) modelled earlier, results in a further enhancement of investor IRRs. It should be noted that the upward curvature in the 'all reliefs' line at higher RORs is solely due to the fact that the model assumes initial losses to be greater for companies with higher growth potential. Thus STR increases in significance the higher the ROR of the NTBF. In the event that the extent of initial losses is more or less independent of the rate of growth, then no such upward curvature will be observed.

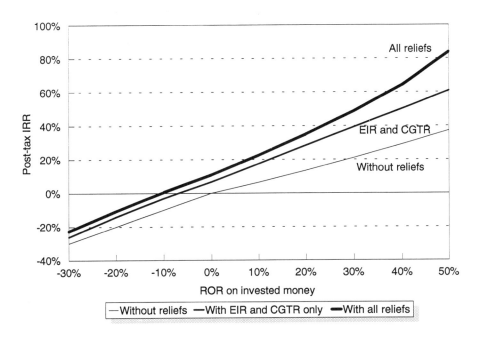

Figure 10.3 Impact of EIR, CGTR, STR and IR on investors' post-tax IRRs (a theoretical example)

ESTIMATED IMPACT ON UK NTBF CASE STUDY

We shall now consider the likely impact that the measures, modelled in Fig. 10.3, may have had on one of the case study companies, had they been in force at the appropriate time. While it is clearly not possible to judge *ex post* the exact extent of any impact that the proposed tax incentives might have had on items such as the firm's capital structure, its development and the behaviour of the management, we can use the case study data to estimate what the impact might have been, *if all else had remained constant*.

Linx Printing Technologies

We have modelled the impact of the four reliefs on the historic data relating to Linx Printing Technologies in the Appendix. In the absence of any of the proposed reliefs, we estimate that the pretax IRR (ROR) on the equity invested in Linx, based on the flotation price of the equity sold, was 59 per cent per annum. If investors would have been subject to CGT at a rate of 40 per cent, the post-tax IRR on their investment would have been around 46 per cent per annum.

If all the reliefs had been in place throughout the investment, however, then the partial sale of Linx's equity at flotation would not have been subject to *any* CGT (since the CGT liability would have been more than covered by the accumulated CGTR). Principally as a result of this, the investor IRR would have soared to almost 92 per cent per annum, although this would have been on the basis of a significantly smaller amount of *net* investor equity invested in the company (£355,000 versus £1.1 million). The extent of the increase in the IRR on investment – from 46 per cent to 92 per cent – is entirely consistent with Fig. 10.3 showing the theoretical impact of the reliefs on post-tax IRRs. The actual amount received by the selling investors would have increased by 60 per cent, from £1.7 million to £2.7 million. Despite a marked increase in investor returns, due to lower equity exposure and no CGT liability, the Exchequer would still have received cumulatively a net £2.2 million (Fig. 10.4). Furthermore, from June 1993 onwards, the Exchequer is expected to receive over £1 million in taxes *every year*, at Linx's current rate of progress!

As a rider to the above, two final points are worth noting: under the proposed taxation reliefs, the investors would be able to avoid paying capital gains tax on any of their shareholding, although it is likely that this would take at least another four years to achieve; and, Linx has created 175 quality jobs in a leading-edge technology area since its formation. In addition, it has passed through the £10 million turnover barrier, more than 70 per cent of which is exported.

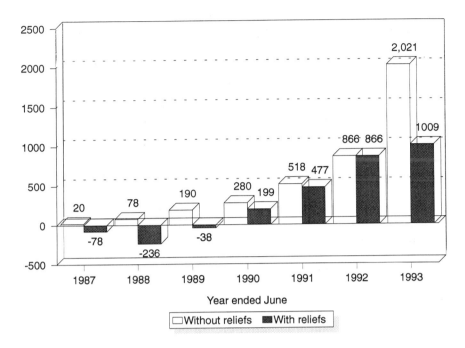

Figure 10.4 Application of the proposals to the case of Linx: reduction in initial cashflows to the Exchequer (£000s)

SUMMARY

In this final chapter we have suggested several specific taxation measures which we anticipate would improve substantially the situation vis-à-vis the financing of NTBFs, and would encourage a greater number of entrepreneurs to start up such companies. In particular, the measures and other suggestions were designed to address a number of problems summarized here.

- The increasing aversion of the formal venture capital industry to fund NTBF investments – by improving the returns on such investments to both the fund investors and the venture capitalists themselves.
- Difficulties with the BES/EIS – by providing cost-effective alternative measures with several desirable cashflow and other characteristics (EIR, CGTR and PR). Since the benefits of these measures can also be enjoyed by entrepreneurs and connected/associated persons, unlike those of the BES/EIS, they are likely to be of help in attracting experienced managers to run the NTBFs by improving the risk/reward ratio for such persons. In

addition, because of the way that EIR and CGTR are structured, there is no need for most of the constraints imposed by the BES/EIS in order to curb abuse.
- The significantly higher cost of capital to UK-based NTBFs relative to their counterparts in (in particular) Germany – by allowing investors to offset the NTBF's initial losses against their personal tax charge (STR) and by allowing relief of (possibly nominal) interest on the funds invested (IR).
- The poor liquidity of small company shares on the London Stock Exchange (and, indeed, elsewhere within Europe), by providing relief from capital gains on small and illiquid company shares (ICSR). One beneficial side-effect of such a measure is that it could lead to the London Stock Exchange becoming the *de facto* pan-European stock market for small companies.

Finally, while the precise form of the proposed measures may have certain novel features, the underlying principles are not new to the world of taxation and, indeed, in most cases similar schemes operating elsewhere in the world are available for study.

To conclude, we believe that implementation of these or similar taxation measures proceed with all haste. If that happens, entrepreneurs, venture capitalists, business angels and all others involved in NTBF formation and growth will receive the clearest possible signal that *now* is the time to start the long process of 'realizing our potential' (in the words of the White Paper) in science, engineering and technology. Indeed, the message must be unequivocal: *today* is the day for the UK to start investing for the future.

APPENDICES

Estimated impact of the proposed taxation reliefs

We have built a quantitative model to assess the likely impact on investor cashflows and IRRs of four of the proposed reliefs, EIR, CGTR, STR and IR. The model assumes:

1 a situation in which an NTBF is started up, with equity provided over the first four years in steadily increasing amounts (of 10, 20, 30 and 40 units, respectively);
2 that the sales growth of the NTBF is linear, although losses are made in the first two years, with breakeven being obtained in the third year; and
3 that the amount of taxes generated from the NTBF's activities are broadly in agreement with the model developed in Chapter 8, although it must be stressed that the 'units' quoted in the spreadsheets are stated in *nominal* not PV terms.

The results of the base case are sensitized to the overall ROR on invested cash (including the EIR tax credits utilized).

Proposed Taxation Reliefs: Base Case Assumptions

(a) **'Equity investment relief' (EIR) rates**
EIR rate on equity investment in seed or start-up company = | 60.0%
(Also allowed on additional start-up equity investments in the first year.)
EIR on equity investment in an early-stage company:
    In 2nd year after start-up = | 45.0%
    In 3rd year after start-up = | 30.0%
    In 4th year after start-up = | 15.0%
As CT, NI and IT fall due to be paid, the comany can retain up to the accumulated but unutilised EIR at that date, for its own benefit.

(b) **'Capital gains tax relief' (CGTR)**
The adjusted CGT liability arising upon the sale or partial sale of shares benefiting from EIR is calculated as follows:
  (i) Chargeable gain upon sale or partial sale = £x.
  (ii) CGT on chargable gain @ 40% = £$0.4x$
  (iii) Let the cumulative total of CT, NI & IT (before taking into account EIR) at the time of the sale or partial sale = £y.
  (iv) Let the cumulative EIR utilized by the company at the time of sale or partial sale = £z.
  (v) Then CGTR = £$(y-z)$ and the adjusted CGT liability upon sale or partial sale = £$(0.4x - y + z)$.

(c) **'See – through relief' (STR)**
Assumed marginal tax rate of investor = | 40.0%

(d) **'Interest relief'**
Assumed pretax interest rate = | 10.0%

Estimated Impact Of Reliefs

Assuming that, for a start-up company 'NEWCO':
  (i) Equity investments in NEWCO are made as:

10	units at start of year 1 (16 after utilising EIR)
20	units at start of year 2 (29 after utilising EIR)
30	units at start of year 3 (39 after utilising EIR)
40	units at start of year 4 (46 after utilising EIR)
0	units at start of year 5 (0 after utilising EIR)
0	units at start of year 6 (0 after utilising EIR)

  (ii)
ROR on year 1 investment =	30.0%
ROR on year 2 investment =	30.0%
ROR on year 3 investment =	30.0%
ROR on year 4 investment =	30.0%
ROR on year 5 investment =	30.0%
ROR on year 6 investment =	30.0%

Therefore, with EIR:
If NEWCO is sold at end of year 6, implied sales proceeds =   397 units.
Chargeable gain (based upon investor's pre-EIR equity) =   297 units.

But, without EIR:
If NEWCO is sold at end of year 6, implied sales proceeds =   397 units.
Chargeable gain (if investors make up for EIR absence) =   267 units.

Specific Proposals and Recommendations 345

Equity investment relief

On year 1 investment =	<u>6</u> units.	Cumulative EIR =	<u>6</u> units.
On year 2 investment =	<u>9</u> units.	Cumulative EIR =	<u>15</u> units.
On year 3 investment =	<u>9</u> units.	Cumulative EIR =	<u>24</u> units.
On year 4 investment =	<u>6</u> units.	Cumulative EIR =	<u>30</u> units.

Tax paid on NEWCO's trading activities with EIR (during first 6 years)

If NEWCO is sold on 15 times year 6 earnings, which in turn represent 7.5% of its sales (10% pretax margin – 25% tax), then year 6 sales =   <u>353</u> units.

If sales growth is linear, gross salary costs represent 36% of sales, IT & NI amount to 36% of gross salary, CT rate = 25% of pretax profit (after carry-forward of losses) and margins are –20% (year 1), –10% (year 2), 0% (year 3), 5% (year 4), 8% (year 5) & 10% (year 6), then:

Year (Units)	1	2	3	4	5	6
Sales	59	118	117	235	294	353
Gross salary	21	42	64	85	106	127
IT + NI on salary	8	15	23	31	38	46
Pretax profit	–12	–12	0	12	24	35
CT on profit	0	0	0	0	0	3
Total tax & NI due	**8**	**15**	**23**	**31**	**38**	**49**
Cumulative tax & NI due (before EIR) =		<u>163</u> units.				
EIR brought forward	0	0	0	0	0	0
EIR for period	6	9	9	6	0	0
EIR utilised in period	–6	–9	–9	–6	0	0
EIR carried forward	0	0	0	0	0	0
Total tax & NI paid (after utilisation of EIR)	**2**	**6**	**14**	**25**	**38**	**49**
Cumulative tax & NI paid (after EIR) =		<u>133</u> units.				

The above analysis: ignores incremental taxes paid by suppliers and their employees; assumes that IT & NI is paid in the year in which it falls due; assumes that CT is paid in the year following that in which it falls due.

Adjusted CGT liability on sale

With proposed EIR & CGTR:	
Chargeable gain on sale =	297 units.
CGT @ 40% =	119 units.
Less: cumulative tax paid after EIR (= CGTR) =	–133 units.
Therefore, adjusted CGT liability on sale =	<u>0</u> units.
But, without proposed EIR & CGTR:	
Chargeable gain on sale =	<u>267</u> units.
CGT @ 40% =	<u>107</u> units.

Impact of EIR & CGTR on investor cashflows & IRR

(1) Without proposed EIR & CGTR

Year	1	2	3	4	5	6
Equity invested	−16	−29	−39	−46	0	0
Sale value						397
IRR on equity =		30.0%				
@ which point NPV =		0.0				
Post-tax IRR on equity =		21.0%				
@ which point NPV =		0.0				

(2) With proposed EIR & CGTR

Year	1	2	3	4	5	6
Net equity invested	−10	−20	−30	−40	0	0
Sale value						397
IRR on equity =		39.2%				
@ which point NPV =		0.0				
Post-tax IRR on equity =		39.2%				
@ which point NPV =		0.0				

Additional impact of STR & IR on investor cashflows & IRR

Year	1	2	3	4	5	6
STR						
Pretax losses	−12	−12				
Marginal tax rate =	40%	40%				
Benefit to investor	5	5				
IR						
Total equity investment	10	30	60	100	100	
Interest rate	10%	10%	10%	10%	10%	
Marginal tax rate	40%	40%	40%	40%	40%	
Benefit to investor	0	1	2	4	4	
Net investor benefit	5	6	2	4	4	0

(3) With all proposed reliefs (i.e. EIR, CGTR, STR & IR)

Year	1	2	3	4	5	6
Net equity invested	−5	−14	−28	−36	4	0
Sale value						397
IRR on equity =		48.5%				
@ which point NPV =		0.0				
Post-tax IRR on equity =		48.5%				
@ which point NPV =		0.0				

Estimated impact of the proposed reliefs on Linx Printing Technologies

We have tried to estimate the impact of four of the proposed tax incentives (EIR, CGTR, STR and IR) on investor IRRs, Exchequer cashflows, etc., in the case of Linx Printing Technologies. It is, of course, impossible in reality to know what the impact of the proposed incentives would have been had they been in force at the time of Linx's formation and during the period of its pre-IPO growth. We note, therefore, that the results of the following analysis are based on an assumption of 'all else being equal'.

Estimated impact of EIR

Year ended June	1987 (6 months)	1988	1989	1990	1991	1992	1993
Adjusted equity investment	£302 344	£324 138	£6 210	£5 353			
EIR rate (as % of equity)	60%	45%	30%	15%			
Brought forward	£0	£161 799	£230 093	£42 082			
Relief for period	£181 407	£145 862	£1 863	£803			
Utilized in period	(£19 608)	(£77 568)	(£189 874)	(£42 885)			
Carried forward	£161 799	£230 093	£42 082	NIL			
Adjusted total cashflow	£0	£0	£0	£237 559	£518 401	£865 855	£1 009 260
Cumulative total cashflow (available for 'CGTR')	£0	£0	£0	£237 559	£755 960	£1 621 815	£2 631 075
Cumulative saving	£19 608	£97 175	£287 049	£329 935	£329 935	£329 935	£329 935
As % of equity	4.1%	10.2%	29.8%	34.1%	32.4%	29.5%	29.5%

Estimated impact of CGTR

Year ended June	1987 (6 months)	1988	1989	1990	1991	1992	1993
IPO proceeds (Oct. 92)						£2 710 184	
Esimated CGT liability						£1 012 155	
Less: 'CGTR'						(£1 012 155)	
CGTR carried forward						£1 618 920	

Estimated impact of STR

Year ended June	1987 (6 months)	1988	1989	1990	1991	1992	1993
Pretax losses	(£150 000)	(£496 000)					
Benefit to 40% tax payer	£60 000	£198 400					

Estimated impact of IR

Year ended June	1987 (6 months)	1988	1989	1990	1991	1992	1993
Total adjusted equity investment	£302 344	£626 482	£632 692	£638 045	£687 355		
Assumed interest rate	10%	10%	10%	10%	10%		
Benefit to 40% tax payer	£18 141	£37 589	£37 962	£38 283	£41 241		

Estimated combined impact of EIR, CGTR, STR & IR on investor cashflow

Year ended June	1987 (6 months)	1988	1989	1990	1991	1992	1993
Actual equity invested	£483 751	£470 000	£8 073	£6 156	£49 310	£99 275	(£1 698 029)
Less: EIR credits	(£181 407)	(£145 862)	(£1 863)	(£803)			
STR	(£60 000)	(£198 400)					
IR	(£18 141)	(£37 589)	(£37 962)	(£38 283)	(£41 241)		
CGTR							(£1 012 155)
Net equity invested	£224 204	£88 149	(£31 752)	(£32 930)	£8 069	£99 275	(£2 710 184)

Estimate of investor pre- & post-tax IRRs without proposed reliefs

Year ended June	1987 (6 months)	1988	1989	1990	1991	1992	1993
Pre-tax IRRs							
Total equity invested	(£483 751)	(£470 000)	(£8 073)	(£6 156)	(£49 310)	(£99 275)	
Company valuation @ IPO							£12 946 672
Valuation of equity sold @ IPO							£2 710 184
Pro-rata equity invested	(£101 266)	(£98 387)	(£1 690)	(£1 289)	(£10 322)	(£20 782)	
IRR (pre-tax)		59.0%					
To give an NPV of		£0					
Post-tax IRRs							
Theoretical CGT liability upon sale of equity (@ 40%)							(£1 012 155)
Estimated post-tax valuation							£1 698 029
IRR (post-tax, on equity sold)		46.0%					
To give an NPV of		£0					

The above calculation: ignores the (small) dividend paid in 1992; assumes that shareholders will be subject to CGT @ 40%, which isn't true if (say) pension funds are the ultimate investors in the venture capital funds holding the shares. Nevertheless, the calculated IRRs are accurate for shareholders who are subject to 40% CGT., in particular the entrepreneurs; assumes that the equity investments were made at the start of the fiscal year, while the 'valuation of equity sold @ IPO' figure is taken as being at 30 June 1992

Estimate of investor pre- & post-tax IRRs without proposed reliefs

Year ended June	1987 (6 months)	1988	1989	1990	1991	1992	1993
Pre-tax IRRs							
Total adjusted equity invested	(£224 204)	(£88 149)	£31 752	£32 930	(£8 069)	(£99 275)	
Company valuation @ IPO							£12 946 672
Valuation of equity sold @ IPO							£2 710 184
Pro-rata equity invested	(£46 934)	(£18 453)	£6 647	£6 893	(£1 689)	(£20 782)	
IRR (pre-tax)		91.6%					
To give an NPV of		£0					
Post-tax IRRs							
Adjusted theoretical CGT liability upon sale of equity							£0
Estimated post-tax valuation							£2 710 184
IRR (post-tax, on equity sold)		91.6%					
To give an NPV of		£0					

Reduction in initial cashflows to the Exchequer

Year ended June	1987 6 months	1988	1989	1990	1991	1992	1993
Without measures	£19 608	£77 568	£189 874	£280 444	£518 401	£865 855	£2 021 415
Less: EIR utilised	(£19 608)	(£77 568)	(£189 874)	(£42 885)			
STR	(£60 000)	(£198 400)					
IR	(£18 141)	(£37 589)	(£37 962)	(£38 283)	(£41 241)		
CGTR							(£1 012 155)
Total	(£97 748)	(£313 557)	(£227 835)	(£81 168)	(£41 241)	£0	(£1 012 155)
With measures	(£78 141)	(£235 989)	(£37 962)	£199 276	£447 160	£865 855	£1 009 260

Notes

1. R. L. Butchart, 'A new UK definition of the high technology industries', Department of Trade and Industry, Economic Trends 400, Feb. 1987, pp. 82–8.
2. 'S corporations and small business stock', Tax information planning series, no. 34, Price Waterhouse, revised May 1992.
3. Presentation at the London Business School Enterprise Network meeting by David McMeekin, Corporate Finance Director, Midland Bank plc, 28 Sept. 1993.
4. William Bygrave, Michael Hay and Jos Peeters (eds), *Realising Investment Value* (Pitman/Financial Times, London, 1994).
5. 'Finance for growth: meeting the financing needs of small and medium enterprises', a report of the CBI Smaller Firms Council, Aug. 1993.

INDEX

academic institutions 165
acquisitions, as an exit route 57-60
'Advanced Chemical Intermediates' 272, 314-16
Advanced Micro Devices 8
Advent 84
American Research & Development (ARD) 5-6, 10
American Totalizer 10
Anderson, Harlan 10
Apax 84
Apollo 13
Apple 11, 12
ARD (American Research & Development) 5-6, 10
Atlas 84

banks
  role in markets
    Germany 80, 81-4, 202
    Japan 116, 129-30, 202
    United Kingdom 165, 202
    United States 18, 52, 55, 202
  target return on funds 137, 183
Beckman, Arnold 8
BES see Business Expansion Scheme
biotechnology industry 13-14, 51, 122
Birch, David 6
BJTU (Beteiligungskapital für junge Technologieunternehmen) 94, 96-9, 102
  and cost of capital 223, 226, 227
BMFT (Federal Ministry for Research and Technology) 95, 96
British Bio–technology Group (BBTG) 271, 272, 274, 276, 310-12
BSS (see Business Start–up Scheme)
business angels 3, 89, 187, 327
Business Expansion Scheme (BES) 27, 152-3, 168, 169, 183, 184-6
  constraints on 328-9
  and cost of capital 223, 227
  need for 327-8
Business Start–up Scheme (BSS) 152
Byers, Brook 56
Bygrave, Bill 66

capital, costs of 215, 218-20

capital gains tax (CGT) 65-6, 100-1, 140, 183
  and cost of capital 223, 227
  proposals for 331, 333-5, 339
  rollover relief 329-30
capital investment companies 87
capital sources
  comparison between countries 18-19, 202, 203-5
  Germany 81-9
  governments 26-7
  Japan 125-31
  United Kingdom 168-75
  United States 44, 53-5
  see also finance
case studies
  D Electron & Electric Wire Ltd 144
  'Advanced Chemical Intermediates' 272, 314-16
  British Bio–technology Group (BBTG) 271, 272, 274, 276, 310-12
  data summary 272
  Datapaq 272, 276, 305-8
  DBG (Deutsche Beteiligungsgesellschaften) 108
  Domino Printing Sciences 272, 285-8
  Linx Printing Technologies 272, 277, 278, 280-3, 340, 347
  Macro 4 271, 272, 276-7, 277-8, 300-303
  Morphosys GmbH 107-8
  Psion 271, 272, 290-3
  Seed Capital Fund GmbH 106
  'Servo Integrated Solutions' (SIS) 272, 276, 317-19
  Tadpole Technology 272, 274, 295-8
cashflow, present value of components 254-7
Citicorp Venture Capital 85
classic venture capital
  and biotechnology industry 13-14
  compared to development capital 21-5
  and computer industry 10-13
  funds applied to UK technology–based firms 16
  incentive structure 23
  need for 6-7
  originations 5-6, 115-16
  role of helping young companies 26-8
  and semiconductor industry 8-9

see also development capital; venture capital
computer industry 10–13, 50–1
Control Data Corporation (CDC) 11
Coopers & Lybrand survey 6–7
corporate financial funds 44, 53, 55
corporate industrial funds 44, 53, 54–5
corporation tax 131, 235, 238, 241
costs
    capital 215, 218–20
    debt 215–16, 220
    employment 255
    equity 215, 216–17, 221
    financing 222–6
        and taxation 223, 226–7
    fixed assets 255
    funds 215, 217–18, 222
    raw materials 255
    venture capital 220–2
Cray, Seymour 11

D Electron & Electric Wire Ltd, case study 144
Datapaq 272, 276, 305–8
DBG (Deutsche Beteiligungsgesellschaften) 83, 91
    case study 108
debt, costs of 215–16, 220
DEC (Digital Equipment Corporation) 6, 10
Deutsche Ausgleichsbank 103
Deutsche Bank 83
Deutsche Wagnisfinanzierung GmbH 95
development capital 21–5
    incentive structure 23
    see also classic venture capital; venture capital
Diamond Capital Corporation 126
Digital Equipment Corporation (DEC) 6, 10
disbursements
    by industry sector 49–51, 75–8, 122–3, 158–61, 200
    trends by funding stage 46, 47–9, 74–5, 121–2, 155–8, 199
    see also investments
divestments
    in German venture capital industry 90–3
    in United Kingdom venture capital industry 176–7
    see also harvesting investments
Domino Printing Sciences 272, 285–8
Doriot, General Georges 5
Dresdner Bank 83

early growth finance 5, 47–9, 74, 122, 199
    cost of funds 222
Eckert–Maulchy Corporation 10
economic growth
    rates of 28–30
    and small firms 6–7
economic models
    and case studies 270–6
    on Exchequer support costs 265

parameters 269–70, 276–8
present value concept 234, 253–4
for wealth distribution 231, 234–6, 257–8
Economic Recovery Tax Act (1981) 64
EIR (*see* Equity Investment Relief)
EIS (*see* Enterprise Investment Scheme)
electrical technology industry 122
electronic technology industry 122
employees
    benefits from sales of new technology firms 233, 241, 244, 257–8
    national insurance 235, 238–9, 241, 277
employer national insurance 235, 238–9, 241
employment
    cost of 255
    in Japan 113–14
    taxation impact of creation of 242
    see also job creation
Employment Retirement Income Security Act (ERISA) 64, 223
endowments 52
Enterprise Boards 187–8, 223, 226
Enterprise Investment Scheme (EIS) 185–6, 327–9
entrepreneurs
    benefits from sales of new technology firms 233, 241, 244, 257–8
    provision of taxation and related incentives to 232
    relationship with venture capitalists 55–6, 90–91, 132–3
    social attitudes towards 114
environmental technology industry 122
equity, costs of 215, 216–17, 221
Equity Investment Relief (EIR) 331, 332–3, 334–5, 339
ERISA (*see* Employment Retirement Income Security Act)
ESCFN (*see* European Seed Capital Fund Network)
Europe, venture capital industry in 17–19
European Recovery Program 85
European Seed Capital Fund Network 100–1, 222
Euroventures 84
Exchequer
    accrued benefits from sales of new technology firms 233–43, 257–8
    returns on support costs to 244–9, 265–6
expansion finance 5, 74–5
exports, and venture capital backed companies 6, 236

factory automation industry 122
Fairchild Semiconductor 8
Fairchild, Sherman 8, 9
family trusts 164–5
fees, of venture capital funds 21
finance
    costs of 222–6, 223, 226–7

debt versus equity 131
disbursement trends by finance stage 46, 47–9, 74–5, 121–2, 204
economic model for wealth distribution 231, 234–6, 257–8
national differences in types of 204
stage definitions of 4–5
see also capital sources
fixed assets, cost of 255
Flanders, Ralph 5
flotations 91–2, 111, 113
see also initial public offerings (IPO)
formal venture capital 3, 9
aversion to new technology investments 327
foundations 52
France, trade balance 32
Fraunhofer–Institut 88, 98, 102, 103, 105, 211
Freiverkehr 109
fund management groups 165, 166
funds, costs of 215, 217–18, 222

gatekeepers 40, 42
GDP (Gross Domestic Product) (see GDP)
growth rates 28–30
and taxation 241, 242
Gen–Probe 14
Genentech 13–14, 59
Geregelter Markt 208
Germany
attitude to venture capital 68–70
case studies 106–8
characteristics of investors 80–1
costs of capital 214–22
and government initiatives 222–6
and taxation 226–7
disbursement trends by funding stage 74–5, 199
entrepreneurs and venture capitalist relationships 89–90
funding sources 81–9, 202, 203–5
government initiatives 95–100, 222–6
growth and performance of new technology firms 102–5
harvesting investments 26, 90–3, 205–10
industry sectors attracting investment 75–8, 200
investment size 78–9, 201
machine tool industry 69
market size and growth 70–4, 198–9
returns on investment 93–4, 210–12
economic and social 101–2
stock markets 108–9, 208
taxation 83, 99–100, 100–1, 226–7
government receipts of 249
trade balance 32
Glass–Steagall Act 18, 112, 202
governments
benefits from sales of new technology firms 233–43, 257–8
cost of funds and initiatives by 222–6

expenditure on science and technology 232
initiatives
Germany 95–100
Japan 139–40, 222–6
United Kingdom 165, 166, 168, 184–8, 222–6
United States 63–5
policy on support for new technology firms 232–3
returns from expenditure of 16
returns on support costs 244–9, 265–6
role in encouraging manufacturing industry 30
as a source of capital 26–7
Gross Domestic Product (see GDP)
Grove, Andrew 9

harvesting investments 5, 25–6, 205–10
in Germany 90–3
in Japan 121, 133–6
in United Kingdom 176–82
in United States 56–61
healthcare industry 51, 122
Hoff, Ted 8
Hybritech 14

IBM 10, 12, 13
illiquid company shares relief 331, 337–8
income tax 235, 238–9, 241, 279
independent private funds 44, 53–4
Indivers 20
informal venture capital 3–4, 9
initial public offerings (IPO) 5, 26, 206–9
Japan 121, 133, 134–6
United Kingdom 178–81
United States 40–1, 56–61
see also flotations
insurance companies 202
Germany 80, 81–3
United Kingdom 164, 166
United States 52
Intel 8, 9, 11, 13
interest relief 331, 336, 339
International Venture Capital Managers 84–5
Investment Enterprise Partnerships (IEPs) 113, 116
investments
holding periods 56–7, 91, 134, 177, 206–7
returns on 19–21, 45, 61–3, 93–4, 136–8, 182–4, 210–12
economic and social 101–2, 141, 189–91, 251–2
size of 51–2, 78–9, 123, 158, 161–4, 201
valuation 59–60, 92–3, 136, 180–2, 209–10
see also disbursements
investors, characteristics of 52–3, 80–1, 123–5, 164–8
IPO (see initial public offerings)
JAFCO 120, 123, 125–6, 132–3, 134
Japan

case study 144
characteristics of investors 123–5
characteristics of leading firms 145–6
costs of capital 214–22
  and government initiatives 222–6
  and taxation 226–7
definition of venture enterprise 111–13
disbursement trends by funding stage 121–2, 199
employment in 33, 113–14
entrepreneurs and venture capitalist relationships 132–3
funding sources 125–31, 202, 203–5
government initiatives 139–40, 222–6
growth and performance of new technology firms 141–3
harvesting investments 133–6, 205–10
history of venture capital 115–16
industry sectors attracting investment 122–3, 200
investment size 123, 201
joint stock companies 141
manufacturing industries 141, 142
market size and growth 117–20, 198–9
obstacles to venture enterprise 113–15
R&D support in 147
returns on investment 136–8, 210–12
  economic and social 141
Small Business Investment Companies (SBICs) 115, 127–8, 139, 141, 223, 226, 227
stock markets 115, 135
taxation 131, 140, 226–7
trade balance 32
venture capital industry 17–19, 116–17
Japan Associated Finance Company (JAFCO) 116
Japan Small Business Corporation 139
job creation 32–4
  and taxation 242
  and venture capital backed companies 6–7
Jobs, Steven 11

KBGs (Kapitalbeiteligungsgesellschaften) 81–4, 88–9, 90, 203
keiretsu 114, 141
KfW (Kreditanstalt für Wiederaufbau) 98–9
Kohlberg, Kravis, Roberts and Co. 198
Kyocera 115

Länderfonds 81, 85–6
legislation 39, 40, 63–4
  anti-trust laws 121, 115, 130
  Economic Recovery Tax Act (1981) 64
  Employment Retirement Income Security Act (ERISA) 64
  Glass–Steagall Act 18, 112, 202
  Japanese Small Business Investment Law (1963) 127
  Revenue Act (1978) 64
  Small Business Equity Enhancement Act (1992) 64
  UBG (Unternehmensbeteiligungsgesellschaften Gesetze) law 99–100

Leveraged Buy Outs (LBO) 49, 51, 198
life sciences industry 122
life–cycles of new technology firms 4–5, 250
Linx Printing Technologies 272, 277, 278, 280–3, 340, 347
loan guarantee scheme 27, 126, 129, 183, 186
  and cost of capital 223, 226, 227
local authorities 165, 166, 168
Lotus 13

McCauley, Robert N. 214–15
Macro 4 271, 272, 276–7, 277–8, 300–303
management, shortage of experienced managers 250–1
management buy outs (MBOs) 21, 26, 74, 117, 157, 164, 210
management buy–backs (MBBs) 91–2, 207, 209, 210
manufacturing industries 30–2
  Japan 141, 142
Markkula, Mike 11
Massachusetts Institute of Technology (MIT) 5, 15
MBGs (Mittelständische Beteiligungsgesellschaften) 81, 86–7, 88, 89, 91, 203
MBOs (*see* Management Buy Outs)
merchant capital, (*see* development capital)
Microsoft 13
MIT (Massachusetts Institute of Technology) 5, 15
Mitsubishi Bank 126
models, see economic models
Moore, Gordon 8
Morphosys GmbH, case study 107–8

NASDAQ 208
National Finance Corporation 139, 223, 227
National Insurance 235, 238–9, 241, 277
  analysis 259–64
National Semiconductor 8
Nikkei Venture Capital Survey 120, 122, 129
Norris, William 11
Noyce, Robert 8

Olsen, Ken 10
OTC markets 208

Partnership Funds 113, 124
partnerships
  limited 40
  silent 87–9, 93, 223, 227
pension funds 18, 202, 225
  Germany 81

Japan 124
United Kingdom 164, 166, 167
United States 52
Perkins, Kleiner 12, 13
portfolio relief 331, 335–6
present value 234, 253–4
private independent funds 44, 53–4, 202
Psion 271, 272, 290–3

rates of return
  banks' required 137, 183
  comparison between countries 210–12
  Germany 93–4
  impact of tax proposals on 334–5, 338–9
  industry performance 19–21
  Japan 136–8
  United Kingdom 182–4
  United States 45, 61–3
raw materials, cost of 255
Remington Rand 10
Revenue Act (1978) 64
Rock, Arthur 8, 9

Sapienza, H.J. 55
SBICs (see Small Business Investment Companies)
securities houses
  as a source of capital 129–30, 202
  target return on funds by 137, 138
see–through relief 331, 336, 339
Seed Capital Fund GmbH, case study 106
seed capital funds 87, 174–5
seed finance 4, 13, 47–9, 74–5
  and tax credits 249
semiconductor industry 8–9
'Servo Integrated Solutions' (SIS) 272, 276, 317–19
shareholders, benefits from sales of new technology firms 233, 241, 244, 257–8
Shockley, William 8
Shoko Chukin Bank 139
silent partnerships 87–9, 93, 223, 227
Small Business Credit Insurance Corporation 139
Small Business Equity Enhancement Act (1992) 64
Small Business Finance Corporation 139, 223, 227
Small Business Investment Companies (SBICs)
  in Japan 115, 127–8, 139, 141, 223, 226, 227
  in the United States 39–40, 55, 63–4, 226, 227
Small Business Investment Incentive Act (1980) 64
Small and Medium Enterprise Agency 139
  survey 135, 141
SMART awards 27, 187, 190, 211, 212
  and cost of capital 223, 226, 227
  DTI analysis of 248

social returns, of venture capital investments 101–2, 141, 189–91, 251–2
Stanford 15
start–up finance 5, 47–9, 74–5
  and tax credits 249
stock markets
  comparison 208
  Germany 108–9
  Japan 115, 135
  secondary 179, 208
  United Kingdom 179–80
Sun Microsystems 13
suppliers 233, 241, 244, 257–8
  taxes generated by 239–40
Swanson, Robert 13
Tadpole Technology 272, 274, 295–8
Tandem Computer 12–13
tax credits 244–7, 267
  optimal use of 249–51
taxation
  capital gains tax (CGT) 65–6, 100–1, 140, 183
    and cost of capital 223, 227
    proposals for 331, 333–5, 339
    rollover relief 329–30
  corporation tax 131, 235, 238, 241
    and cost of funds 223, 226–7
  and employment creation 242
  and GDP 241, 242
  in Germany 83, 99–100, 100–2, 249
  income tax 235, 238–9, 241, 279
  incremental taxes 259–64
  in Japan 131, 140
  National Insurance 235, 238–9, 241, 259–64, 277
  proposals for 330–8
  returns to the Exchequer 244–7
  and silent partnerships 87, 89, 93
  suppliers and 239–40
  United Kingdom environment 188–9
  in the United States 65–6
  Value Added Tax (VAT) 235, 236–8, 241
  see also Business Expansion Scheme; Enterprise Investment Scheme
TBG (Technologie Beteiligungsgesellschaft) 96–7, 98
Technologieholding GmbH 85
technology clusters 15, 16
Textron 6
Third Market 179
Timmons, J.A. 55
TOU (Technologie Unternehmensgründungen) scheme 96, 103–6, 211, 248, 249
  and cost of capital 223, 226, 227
Toushi Jigyo Kumiai funds 116
trade balances 31–2
trade sales, as an exit route 57–60, 91, 92, 207, 209
Training and Enterprise Councils (TECs) 187, 223, 225, 226

Treybig, James 12–13
TVM 84

UBGs (Unternehmensbeteiligungsgesellschaft) 95, 99–100, 223, 227
United Kingdom
  categories of venture capital firms 149
  characteristics of investors 164–8
  costs of capital 214–22
    and government initiatives 222–6
    and taxation 226–7
  disbursement trends by funding stage 155–8, 199
  funding sources 168–75, 202, 203–5
  GDP growth rates 28–30
  government initiatives 165, 166, 168, 184–8, 222–6
  growth and performance of new technology firms 191–2
  harvesting investments 176–82, 205–10
  industry sectors attracting investment 158–61, 200
  investment size 161–4, 201
  manufacturing industry 30–2
  market size and growth 150–4, 198–9
  need for new technology driven economic regeneration 28–34
  provision of venture capital 15–16, 17, 171–4
  returns on investment 182–4, 210–12
    economic and social 189–91
  stock markets 179–80, 208
  taxation environment 188–9, 226–7
  technology–based industries 15–16
United States
  advantages of new technology firms 14–16
  characteristics of investors 52–3
  costs of capital 214–22
    and government initiatives 222–6
    and taxation 226–7
  disbursement trends by funding stage 46, 47–9, 199
  entrepreneurs and venture capitalist relationships 55–6
  funding sources 17–9, 53–5, 202, 203–5
  government initiatives 63–5, 222–6
  harvesting investments 56–61, 205–10
  industry sectors attracting investment 49–51, 200
  investment size 51–2, 201
  job creation in 7, 32–4
  market size and growth 17–9, 40–7, 198–9
  originations of classic venture capital 5–6
  returns on investment 61–3, 210–12
  Small Business Investment Companies (SBICs) 39–40, 55, 63–4, 226, 227
  taxation environment 65–6, 226–7
UNIVAC 10, 12
Unlisted Securities Market (USM) 179–80, 208

valuation, of investments 59–60, 92–3, 136, 180–2, 209–10
Value Added Tax (VAT) 235, 236–8, 241
venture capital
  changing emphasis of 21–7
  cost of 220–2
  formal 3, 9
    aversion to new technology investments 327
  fund fees 21
  informal 3–4, 9
  market size and growth 17–8, 40–7, 70–4, 117–20, 150–4, 198–9
  returns on 19–21, 45, 61–3, 93–4, 136–8, 182–4, 210–12
    economic and social 101–2, 141, 189–91, 251–2
  sources of see capital sources
  UK provision of 15–16, 17, 171–4
  see also development capital; classic venture capital
venture capital groups 84–5
Venture Economics
  rates of return database 19, 20–1
  survey 6–7
Venture Enterprise Centre 111, 112, 115, 122, 127, 129, 141
  loan guarantee scheme 126, 129

Westdeutsche Landesbank 83
WFG (Wagnisfinanzierungs Gesellschaft) 85
Wozniak, Stephan 11

Xerox 44

Zimmer, Steven A. 214–15